Operations Management

Second Edition

Howard Barnett

MACMILLAN
Business

First edition 1992
Reprinted 1993, 1994
Second edition 1996

Published by
MACMILLAN PRESS LTD
Houndmills, Basingstoke, Hampshire RG21 6XS
and London
Companies and representatives
throughout the world

ISBN 0–333–66210–5

A catalogue record for this book is available
from the British Library

10   9   8   7   6   5   4   3   2
06   05   04   03   02   01   00   99   98

Printed and bound in Great Britain by
Antony Rowe Ltd, Chippenham, Wiltshire

*Dedicated to my wife, Elizabeth,
and my parents, Lilian and Jack*

Contents

Preface to the First Edition

I wrote this book to meet the needs of several different groups of people. First, some may be students who are learning about Operations Management as part of their course of study. They may have enrolled on a Higher National Diploma in Engineering, or are studying Operations Management on a BA in Business Studies degree course. They will not have any first-hand knowledge of Operations Management as they have hardly started on their working career.

Second, some may be taking a Diploma in Management Studies as part of their post-graduate/post-experience qualification, and therefore have some years of industry or commerce behind them. These people are often experienced in their own fields such as accounting, marketing or personnel, but have no real experience in Operations Management. Other professional courses such as those related to the Management Charter Initiative also have Operations Management content. Many non-management courses also require some management input, which generally includes Operations Management.

Some people may work closely with those in Operations Management yet find it difficult to appreciate the rationale for decisions made; they therefore need to increase their knowledge of the subject. Some readers may have just begun to work in Operations Management and need to gain a rapid insight into it. Finally some people will read the book just for interest and personal development. For all these reasons, this book covers a wide range of topics.

Just what **is** Operations Management? Briefly – making the most **efficient use** of whatever **resources** an organisation has, so as to provide the goods or services their customers need, in a timely and cost-effective manner.

Operations Management is therefore relevant to every organisation, whether in industry, commerce, services or public sector; whether engaged in profit-making or in a 'not for profit' enterprise. Operations Managers are found not only in large manufacturing companies, but increasingly in organisations like mail-order houses, hotel and theatre chains, airports and docks. Sometimes they will not have 'Operations Manager' as their job title. They may be functional managers such as Departmental managers,

Marketing managers, Sales managers and so on. There is every reason to expect to see them fulfilling a key role in hospitals, sports and leisure complexes, and financial organisations as well as in traditional manufacturing industries. Currently it is not so likely that small companies will have an Operations Manager as such, but that kind of work still has to be done by someone regardless of company size.

Because of this wide readership, several chapters have been written using a particular case study as a vehicle for presenting the key aspects of each topic. This serves two purposes. The first is that those who have no experience of industry or commerce can immediately see a problem or situation which is relevant to that topic. The second is that a case study helps to provide some consistency throughout the chapter and not give the feeling of jumping from one disconnected example to another. Each chapter states its **Learning Objectives**, and contains **Activities** for the reader to carry out. At the end of each chapter are **Review Questions** covering important concepts in that chapter. Brief answers to these questions are given at the end of the book.

The subject-matter is divided up into chapters for convenience of presentation. However, no-one should be under any illusion that real life in any organisation comes in neatly defined parcels labelled 'finance', 'productivity', 'quality' or 'stock control'. Real life is a (never-ending) series of difficult, ill-defined situations requiring prompt solutions, many of them needing a quick fix to keep things ticking over while more lasting and effective solutions are found. For this reason, the student is cautioned against thinking 'If I ever meet this next time I'll know what to do'. You will not meet exactly 'this' next time: all you will meet is a situation which is not precisely the same as you have met before.

What I hope is, that with the insight of knowledge gained and a constant internal reminder that there are no watertight compartments in management, you will be able to pick and choose from what you have learned, and begin to form a unique solution of your own to the problem in hand.

I have included the word 'management' in the title, so I must say what I think it means. Management involves taking the **initiative** in a situation, so as to affect its **outcome** in a positive and useful manner. It therefore includes several essential activities such as planning and co-ordination, leadership and delegation, follow up and control. It is an art, not a science. Good managers are right far more often than they are wrong, which is why they are good. They do the right things, and they do them right. Whatever extra help they can get by using appropriate management techniques, so much the better.

I have already mentioned the wide range of topics covered in this book. These topics do not, however, build one upon the other in a fixed sequence such as in mathematics. The emphasis in the book is on ways to solve different problems of how work is done. Less emphasis is therefore placed on problems associated with people (e.g. those of leadership, motivation, pay, succession, training, promotion, personal and interpersonal skills). This does not mean they are less important. It means that you as the student must not think that because you can solve an operational problem, that is the end of it. That is the probably just the beginning, as now it has to be **implemented** successfully.

The topics in this book can be thought of as being similar to those in a carpenter's toolbox. The right one must be selected for the task in hand. If not, the result may be unsuccessful. The tool will not be at fault: it is the ability of the carpenter in selecting the tools for the task, coupled with his or her skill and experience, which produces a fine piece of furniture. Similarly with Operations Management – the topics are the tools, but they must be coupled with the manager's personal skills to be successful. This book is your tool for learning. Write in it if you want to, and wear it out through constant use!

Using the Book

For each chapter, make sure you read the Learning Objectives first, and check afterwards that you have *achieved* them. Try to do at least some of the Activities suggested, and answer the Chapter Review Questions.

If you are not very familiar with basic statistical methods, you may need to read Chapter 14 on managing numbers before you read Chapter 3 on reliability, Chapter 15 on statistical process control or Chapter 16 on forecasting.

The book does not have to be read strictly in the sequence it is written, but you should read **Chapter 1 first**. Here is one possibility, grouping the chapters around the key resources in every organisation – People, Equipment, Material, Money, and Time. Within each grouping, read the chapters in the sequence shown.

Introduction
1

Managing and controlling the product 2, 3, 4	Managing materials 5, 6	Managing money 7
Managing process and performance 8, 9, 10, 11	Managing time 12	Managing plant 13
Managing numbers 14,[1] 15	Managing the future: Forecasting 16	Managing complexity: Operational Research 17

[1] *Read this section prior to Chapters 3, 15 and 16 if necessary.*

To make sure you have understood any Computational Methods, Activity Questions marked * have answers printed on pp. 432–42.

Some of the book is based on articles I wrote for *Purchasing and Supply Management*, the journal of the Chartered Institute of Purchasing and Supply and are used with their permission. Several of these included computer programs for readers to experiment with the topic discussed. A list of these articles is included in the Bibliography.

While this book is a distillation of my knowledge and experience accumulated over the years, I would like to thank my students at the University's Business School who have used many of the activities and cases described, and who have therefore helped to refine them. My thanks also to Professor Bill Gage, who stimulated and developed my interest in Operations Management when he was my Head of Department at the (then) Polytechnic of Central London's School of Management Studies.

Every effort has been made to acknowledge sources. I welcome your comments on this book for its future enhancement. All errors and omissions are mine. I hope you find it useful and enjoyable. Good reading, good revision, good luck and good results.

HOWARD BARNETT

Preface to the Second Edition

I am grateful for feedback from students and colleagues since the first edition was published. This has resulted in my enlarging Chapter 1 to include content on Business Strategy, Research and Development, and Design; and a new Chapter 17 which extends linear programming to include transportation and assignment methods. There is additional content in Chapter 5 and Chapter 11. The text as a whole includes revisions and many more activities than previously. Thank you all for your suggestions.

HOWARD BARNETT

Acknowledgements

The author and publishers wish to thank the following for permission to reproduce copyright material:

The Volvo Car Corporation, for Figures 13.7, 13.8 and 13.10, from their publicity information on the Kalmar plant in Sweden (1984).

The Controller of Her Majesty's Stationery Office for figures from *CAS Occasional Paper No. 9: Clerical Work Measurement and Materials Handling – Selecting the Equipment* (1977).

PCL, for data in the Warehouse Elevator case study in Chapter 9.

Heinemann, for Figure 10.1, from D. Whitmore, *Work Measurement* (1987).

MTM Association Ltd, for Figure 10.2, from their MTM-X manual 1983 and MOMET manual 1975.

Harold Whitehead & Partners, for data in the Kleen-a-Glow case study in Chapter 11.

The British Petroleum Company plc for data from *BP Statistical Review of World Energy* (1990).

BSI Standards for extracts from BS 5701: 1993.

Every effort has been made to trace all copyright-holders, but if any have been inadvertently overlooked the publishers will be pleased to make the necessary arrangement at the first opportunity.

1   Introduction

Learning Objectives

By the end of this chapter you should:

1 know what **Operations Management** is, and what it does
2 be able to identify the key **resources** available to any organisation
3 be familiar with examples of the **input–output function**
4 know what **other functions do** in a manufacturing organisation, including Research and Development, and Design.

1.1   What is Operations Management?

Just what **is** Operations Management? Primarily, it is concerned with making the most **efficient use** of whatever **resources** an organisation has, so as to provide the goods or services their customers need, in a timely and cost-effective manner. This description can apply to virtually any kind of organisation, whether it operates in industry or commerce, services or the public sector. Every organisation must be concerned with efficiency whether or not it exists to make a profit, because it still needs to give as much value for money as possible to its customers. But like every other activity in a company, Operations Management operates via the organisational structure which currently exists. Because of this, it is important to note that Operations Management also includes the examination, assessment, analysis and re-design of a new structure with subsequent review of its suitability to ensure it is able to achieve what is supposed to, i.e. its main objective stated above. In many cases the most important criteria will be that of the productivity and effectiveness of its resources in serving the markets.

This in turn leads us to ask if Operations Management has any role to play in helping to achieve the company's objectives, and if so how can it be done. A company achieves its **objectives** via its **overall strategy**. Its objectives

1

are designed to meet in the longer term its **mission statement**. A mission statement is a statement which relatively briefly states what the company would like to do or be. For example – British Telecom's mission statement (Annual Report 1995) is 'to provide world class telecommunications and information products and services and to develop and exploit their networks at home and overseas, so that they can: meet their customers' requirements, sustain growth in the earnings of the group on behalf of shareholders and make a fitting contribution to the community in which they conduct their business'. Abbey National plc (Annual Report 1994) states its **corporate purpose** 'is to achieve above average growth in shareholder value over the long term. This can only be done if we meet the needs of our customers, our staff and all of the other stakeholders in our business.' The mission statement of a large hospital is stated as 'being committed to providing quality health care, enhanced by research, training and development, to meet the needs of our patients and staff'. Mission statements tend to be couched in somewhat general terms, but they give the public a good idea of their *raison d'être*, and provide a focus for the company. They state 'what' the company wants to do and/or be.

The **aims/objectives/goals** (we will use the terms interchangeably) of a company are several statements of a rather more specific nature and are designed to support the achievement of the mission statement. These aims generally have a time horizon. They will say where a company will be and what it wants to achieve in the nearer term, say one to five years. Such aims/ objectives state the specific 'what' is to be achieved and 'when' it is to be achieved in support of the mission statement. They are the result of careful planning at top level in the company, but must incorporate inputs as needed from all areas and levels in the company. Abbey National plc (Annual Report for 1994) states 'our corporate objectives are to strengthen Abbey National's market position in UK personal financial services; to win and hold competitive advantage through superior customer service; to continue to diversify profit streams away from our traditional mortgage and savings activities; to remain a low cost operator; to maintain strong management of risks; to promote brand strength, and to develop synergies between the three main mutually supporting businesses'.

A company's overall strategy or strategies state how it proposes to meet its aims. There will be different strategies at different levels of the organisation, just as there will be different aims at different levels and for different departments/functions. What is important is that each set of aims and strategies for each department must form a hierarchy, designed to achieve the overall aims of the company via its overall strategy. A particular example of an overall strategy may therefore be BT's statement 'to develop its opportunities vigorously in its traditional home market, and at the same time, establish itself in new markets for advanced services both in the UK and overseas' (1995 Annual Report). These strategies answer the 'how' the company is going to achieve its aims. Such overall strategy requires a hierarchy of strategies below it, designed to support its achievement. So for example, Research and Development will have its own aims and strategies.

Supporting each set of strategies are a set of **policies**, for each function in the company. These policies are operational rules designed to help ensure that strategies remain consistent in their application. For example, a company whose aim is 'to be the biggest successful mortgage provider in the UK', may have as one of its strategies 'to be willing to lend to the widest range of prospective borrowers possible'. One of its policies may be 'we do not lend to people with a poor credit rating'. Why? – because without that as an operating rule, while they want to lend to a wide range of people, lending to high risk clients will adversely affect in the longer term their objective of 'being... successful... providers'. Examples of other policies may be 'we will not normally lend more than two and one half times a person's annual basic salary' or 'all loans must be secured against real property'.

Finally, there are **plans** and **procedures** which are what you intend to do in the short term. These function at the operational level. There are a myriad of them and they should dovetail together to support the departmental and functional strategies already laid down.

Operations Management along with other functions in a company must therefore make a positive contribution to the company in helping to meet its overall aims. It is not sufficient for Operations Management to be a passive reactive function, i.e. 'tell us what needs doing and we will do it'. What **it must do** is to be positive and proactive, so that it not only achieves its short-term aims on a daily, weekly and monthly basis, but is capable of making contributions as to how best it can help the company meet its customers' needs. It can only do this (a) if it knows precisely the kind of market it operates in, or will be operating in, (b) if it can identify actual or potential demand patterns for that market, and (c) if it can identify what kind of response the company is intending for this particular market. Every company operates within the overall economy, and then its own market. Within that, it may often operate in a particular segment. To do this effectively requires a **Business Plan**. Such a plan may well be the result of a formal Strengths, Weaknesses, Opportunities and Threats (SWOT) analysis of the company. The strengths and weaknesses analysis are factors internal to the company. The opportunities and threats are factors external to the company. A careful evaluation of these four factors will help determine the aims/objectives, and the Business Plan will be tailored to suit them.

The company's Business Plan will be made up of separate but related plans in each of the key functional areas, e.g. Operations, Finance, Human Resources and Marketing, etc. Each of these functions will include plans/policies pertaining to that function, but determined in collaboration with all department heads, so that there is a melding effect as each separate target is achieved. For this to be so, Operations Management, for example, will include factors such as purchase requirements, inventory levels, work force sizes, equipment needs, service levels, production rates, etc. It cannot do this effectively if it is not clear what market it is in, what products must be offered and what kind of service will be provided to satisfy that market. For example, if a company wants to extend its mail order catalogue service for all gardening needs, throughout the UK, then among other factors, service level parameters need to be clearly established, in terms of responding to customers when they place their orders, and delivery and after-sales service level standards afterwards. Operations Management needs therefore to examine closely how well the current internal structure serves the new purpose; and if it has shortcomings, they must then be at the forefront of instigating re-examination and re-design.

Similarly, we can expect Finance to have plans relating to cash inflows and outflows, capital needs, salary levels, credit needs, etc. Human Resources will have plans relating to overall work force needs, training needs, recruitment needs and information systems. Marketing will have plans relating to promotion, product ranges, new products, new geographical areas, sales, and product mix factors (see later).

All the above plans will be aggregated as they work upwards towards the overall aims set by senior management. At each stage, adjustment may be necessary during the formulation process if it is apparent that there are clashes of sub-aims in different departments. When general agreement has been reached, the plans will be worked to and monitored on a regular and short-term basis, so that corrective action can be taken to correct any shortfall in actuality. The ideal result will then be (you hope) that with each functional area using its relevant and carefully structured plans and policies, the department/function aims will be achieved and by the end of the year, that year's aims for the company will have been achieved.

Of all the topics embracing Operations Management that you will see in this book, if we were to highlight the crucial ones of prime concern to the Operations Manager, we should certainly include:

Quality – no company can hope to keep its customers if the product or service it provides is less than perfect all the time.

Inventory – its proper management and control save money for the company and improves service to the customers.

Productivity – constantly striving to increase output per unit input helps lower unit costs and improve profitability.

Planning – careful management of time and capacity are essential for helping to meet schedules and matching resources to requirements.

Activity

As a small group, select the annual reports of some major companies in manufacturing, service and utilities organisations. Find their mission statements and corporate objectives. Does there seem to be a common factor among companies in the same sector; and between sectors despite their different emphases? Do they have an overall set of strategies? How do they state their operational standards for the customer and do they state how well they have achieved them?

Activity

In a small group, imagine you are going to start up a business of your own.

(a) decide on the business itself
(b) prepare your mission statement
(c) prepare your overall aim, and secondary aims
(d) develop a business plan resulting from a SWOT analysis
(e) develop a strategy/strategies to achieve the above

1.2 **What are an Organisation's Resources?**

All organisations have only five different kinds of resources to work with. These are:

* People *

* Equipment *

* Material *

* Money *

* Time *

(a) People

The most important asset and resource of any company is its people. However much a truism this may be, it is apparent that not all companies in the past recognised this. This was particularly the case at times when labour was plentiful. As is usual, however, enlightened companies such as ICI & Marks and Spencer have long treated their employees as the important asset they are and have realised the rewards associated with that philosophy. People should be treated as a major long-term investment in order that the company realises their full potential, and in such a way that employees feel themselves treated with respect and dignity: taking people for granted is a sure way to make them feel unappreciated. The ideal result will be that everyone is working towards a common goal: that of serving their customers. People are not only a resource, they are often the **interface between the customer and the company**: in the customers' eyes, those people **are** the company. As such, it is important that there is no discrepancy between what the customer perceives and what the company intends. One way to avoid this is by appropriate **training**, and the development of a high degree of **motivation**.

Until the beginning of the Second World War most organisations, particularly manufacturing organisations, employed large numbers of people. Since that time, and because of increasing efficiency and the increasing use of automation, fewer people have produced the same or an increasing amount of their good or service. This has had the effect of reducing the unit cost of production, although it seems as if the UK tends to be a more expensive producer than many of its overseas competitors. This is perhaps because laying off people has always been considered by some as an easy option in order to achieve quick reductions in unit costs, so that people have traditionally been thought of as more a commodity than a key resource. To some extent, this has become a self-defeating solution as in many instances labour costs now no longer make up the very large percentage of total unit costs they once did.

Until recently, the proportion of labour cost in a product was very high (as much as 50% or more), and although the cost per hour was not very large, the total labour cost as a proportion was sufficiently large so as to make it a dominating factor. It therefore loomed large as the key factor to be improved. As the proportion of labour content has been reduced over the years (to perhaps as little as 15–20%) by improved design and more sophisticated equipment this pressure has to some extent been reduced. Properly trained labour has become more scarce and more expensive both to hire and keep. Nevertheless, the productive use of time by people is by nature somewhat less easy to control than machine time, and so management still needs to know exactly **how** a job should be done, and **how long** it should take. This theme of productivity is one we shall refer to again in Chapters 9, 10 and 11.

(b) Equipment

The start of the Industrial Revolution, about the middle of the 18th century, heralded the beginning of the machine age and this development continues today with the development and manufacture of robots and the increasing use of computers in all areas of enterprise. Work which for thousands of years had been done only manually, and often by hundreds of people at a time (e.g. working on construction sites), is now done by relatively few including those who attend and service the machines. Bulldozers and cranes can now work many orders of magnitude faster than the thousands of people who were employed as navvies to build our railways and canals.

An example of this is weaving. Before the advent of the loom, weaving was a cottage industry, with highly individualistic, variable and low output. Since that time, thousands of jobs have disappeared, but it has brought the product to millions of people at a price they can afford. Paradoxically, it is this very situation of vast, cheap and standardised product which has enabled some people to move back into knitting to produce successfully goods of high quality, design and price.

This process of mechanisation continues apace even today, but 'people-less' factories are still very rare. Such complexity, while reducing the unit cost of the good or service, represents a major **investment in equipment** by the organisation. It is therefore of paramount importance to utilise that equipment efficiently and to ensure its long life by proper planned **maintenance**.

(c) Material

Particularly in manufacturing, but also in the areas of commerce and public service, materials play a key role in the overall conversion process. The supply of suitable raw materials, in terms of both quality and price, for the process in hand is of vital importance if processing is to proceed smoothly. Much thought has therefore to be given to the correct **specification, source, control** and **delivery** of material to the appropriate work station in good time. Without this forethought and planning, there will be extra cost and delays, often accompanied by a lower than acceptable initial quality level, none of which can be tolerated but which can also rarely be recovered by an increase in price. The management of materials from supplier through processor to customer via wholesalers and retailers if necessary, is often called **logistics.** This term was originally taken from the military, where it denotes the management of the supply of personnel and material to the battle front. Of prime importance to management, it expresses their concern for the productive and effective movement and storage of goods, and use of associated information; from suppliers through manufacturing or other processing, wholesalers and retailers to the customer. In other words, logistics is concerned with all the activities in the Supply Chain.

(d) Money

This is the most **liquid resource** any company has. It is used to buy a blend, in proper proportions, of all the other resources. We often talk of 'buying time', but this is a mere colloquialism; we can postpone something, but this is just exchanging one problem for another which at that particular moment is considered to be more important. The only occasion a company will have money as its sole resource is when it has just been capitalised. From then on, although money is important, and a proportion of any company's total assets must be in cash, the company needs to acquire other resources so as to be able to perform its prime objective.

(e) Time

This is the only resource which **cannot be accumulated for subsequent use**. It follows therefore that time must not be wasted; there can be no buffers of time in the sense that we talk about a stock of material. The efficient use of time, the efficient use of equipment through careful matching of requirement and availability together with preventive maintenance: all help to reap dividends for a company by helping to produce its good or service at the lowest cost. Much effort is put into producing efficient schedules, which do not allow excessive wasted time. We shall look in some detail at scheduling in Chapter 12.

1.3 The Input–Output Concept

The basic idea of resource conversion can be conveniently expressed as: **INPUT** > > > > **CONVERSION** > > > > **OUTPUT**. This principle is completely general, and so applicable to any organisation. It can be applied at several levels within an organisation: at the highest level it will represent a statement of the **overall objectives** of a company, and at departmental level it will represent the **work of that department**. If it is assembling a radio, then inputs will be material and labour; the process assembling separate parts using people and equipment, and the output the completed radio. I shall refer to this basic conversion process again, when talking about control in Chapter 4 and when referring to computer integrated manufacture in Chapter 8. Let us now have a look at some examples of different conversion processes.

(a) Manufacturing

Manufacturing goods such as cars, washing machines, vacuum cleaners, television sets and desk top computers represent examples at one end of the resource conversion spectrum: that end where the output is a **product**. There is a clear input of labour and materials at the beginning of the process, and by using equipment of various kinds during the process, the material is converted into a clearly recognisable end product. It is also fairly easy to judge in many cases how well the conversion process has taken place. Quite often, these end products are the results of inputs from many different companies, who have themselves made those parts. The conversion process is thus carried out at many levels. Final assembly of cars is an example of a conversion process which is easily recognised by most people. It also is a fascinating operation to watch, and companies like Ford and General Motors allow people to visit their plants and see them at work.

(b) A fast-food restaurant

At first glance you may think that a restaurant would have little in common with our theme of resource conversion, and certainly not comparable with our earlier example. But some thought will indicate that they certainly use **equipment** in the form of ovens, fryers, toasters, and mixers. They also have

stocks of raw material in the form of potatoes, buns, fish, hamburgers and sauces. They have **storerooms** in the guise of cold stores. They have **people** doing the preparation, the cooking and the clearing away. And they have a **management structure** as well. You will agree they also have a well-defined **end product**.

Interestingly, therefore, fast-food outlets do have a lot in common with the kind of manufacturing described above. This is because, in many instances, both organisations produce their goods in large quantities and limited variety. The menu of a fast-food outlet can often be put on one side of a sheet of paper. That is what they produce and they can hardly vary the product range at all. To do so is more of a major marketing exercise, with a new product being hailed as a major breakthrough for the company in recognising and satisfying a new customer's new need. Fast-food chains are also exceedingly preoccupied with quality and efficiency, topics we will be referring to in Chapters 2, 9, 10 and 11.

(c) A garage

The inputs here are **labour** in the form of a mechanic, an electrician, a panel beater (getting rarer and rarer these days) and a sprayer. **Equipment** such as hoists, jacks and test gear are used, and after expenditure on replacement parts, the **output** is a vehicle performing (we hope) to the original specification. In this case there is not such a clearly defined output as before, and in fact part of the input was the outputted item. Outputs are much more irregular than earlier examples, partly because of the less easily defined input conditions and process formulation. It takes some degree of skill to decide what the remedy is when a car owner brings a car in and says 'can you do something, it rattles as I go round corners, and sometimes the lights come on too'. Nevertheless, all garages are very clearly concerned with efficiency and those associated with a manufacturer have predetermined time standards against which to work, at least for the more usual work they carry out.

It is now a little less easy readily to associate the end product or service received with the amount spent to obtain it. This means it is a little more difficult to tell if you are getting value for money.

(d) A hospital

This is remarkably similar in principle to the example of the garage above. The hospital provides a service, but the people are more highly trained, the equipment is more expensive, the diagnoses often more difficult and the outcome somewhat more uncertain. Because of these factors, hospitals are very concerned with the **efficient use** of all their resources – so much so that it is very common in the USA for them to employ an Industrial Engineer to ensure that the hospital's efficient functioning is closely monitored. It will not be too surprising if that becomes the norm in the UK, particularly as hospitals are becoming more commercial. The main result is that all processes are examined to see if they can be improved. The **output is a repaired human being**. Although I have suggested that a hospital is rather closer to a service orientated organisation, it is quite possible to visualise certain parts as a production line (e.g. hip replacements, cataract operations and a maternity unit). In the latter example, there is already much comment about the scheduling of births on some occasions when the medical prognosis might not seem to indicate it (i.e. for caesarean sections).

(e) Estate agents

What exactly do estate agents do? They are service orientated organisations but the 'end product' is not always obvious – perhaps it is when the sale or exchange of a property is completed to the full satisfaction of the parties involved. Agents certainly employ people in administration and selling and perhaps surveying capacities. They use a limited range of equipment that we probably would not call 'machinery' – for example, word processors, duplicating and franking machines. Does this mean that they would not be interested in running their businesses efficiently? Of course not, because providing a service efficiently and at high quality means that a formal review of systems used cannot help but be useful. One could argue that when a service is provided, it is even more important to operate efficiently so that it is clear to all exactly **what is being provided for the fee involved**.

(f) Local government

Local government is probably the biggest employer in the UK. It provides services, and in this case, more than many others, we are concerned to receive value for money because we pay so much for what is provided. For many years local government has used all the management techniques available in the quest for improvement. Management Services departments have been established, and spent much on training programmes. As local government makes more and more use of direct services, and operates more closely on commercial lines, **quality** is playing an ever more important role in its activities in areas where a few years ago it might have seemed strange. Examples are the provision of social services and mental health.

(g) Other organisations

We have seen in the examples above that a gradation of organisations exists, from those that manufacture a product to those who are entirely service orientated. We have also seen that the basic definition of Operations Management we have used, really does apply just as well to all organisations.

Activity

For the organisations listed below, see if you can recognise what resources are used and how the unit of output can be defined.

(a) a hotel in the Bahamas
(b) a mail order catalogue business
(c) a one-man window-cleaning business
(d) a builder
(e) a major international airport
(f) any of the big five Clearing Banks
(g) a comprehensive school
(h) a university
(i) a building society
(j) a water authority
(k) a museum
(l) a major airline
(m) an arts complex
(n) a large theatre

1.4 Operations Management and Other Functions

Operations Management involves working closely with other departments in a company. It is a staff function, but needs to be able to ensure that it has the ability to meet targets set, both in **monetary** and in **product** terms. To see why this is so look at Figure 1.1.

You can see the conversion process for a manufactured product as shown vertically down the centre of Figure 1.1. The raw materials, component parts already made and other items bought in from the outside are converted to the end product as labour and equipment work on them, adding value as the process proceeds.

(a) Work in progress

Work in progress is the partly finished product which is passing through that process. Prior to the start there are raw materials and component parts, and at the end of the process there are finished goods. It is essential to keep work in progress as low as possible, not only because it represents money tied up (as does all stock), but because it is the area where little (if any) money can be received should it be urgently needed. Who would pay for (say) 500 partly assembled overhead projectors which do not have any optics or electric motors and wiring?

Work in progress also takes up **space** and requires **handling** to move it. The more there is, the more effort goes into its scheduling and control. We must try to eliminate it completely, converting the raw materials to the end

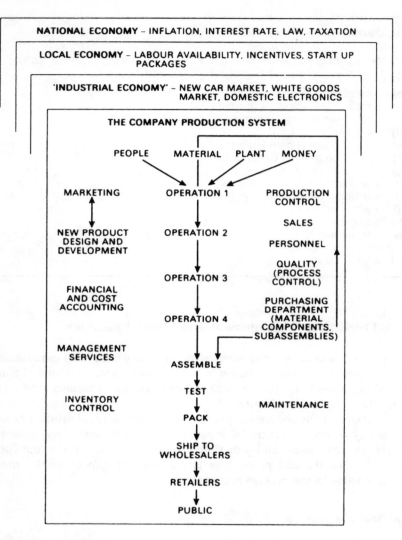

Fig 1.1   The conversion process

product without interruption and in quantities which match current requirements. The **Just in Time** scheduling method helps to, do this, and we will meet it in Chapter 6. If this approach is not used we find that about one-third of inventory costs are made up of work-in-progress costs, the other two-thirds being raw materials and finished goods costs. It is this rationale that dictates that you sometimes have to wait for your 'fishburger' at the fast-food takeaway, because it is not as popular as a hamburger: a fishburger which has stood for some time as finished goods would not be too appetising. In fact many such establishments have a policy of disposing of any cooked product not sold within a specified period of time.

Work in progress may be damaged as it is repeatedly handled, and this may be referred to an industrial engineer for an examination, perhaps, of current materials handling procedures.

(b) Functional areas within the company

As mentioned earlier, operations management needs to liaise with other functional areas in a company, and this applies to any organisation. If we continue the theme in our example of manufacturing, we can see what some of these areas are.

- Problems of **maintaining** and **improving quality** will occur and will require solving. Apart from their importance in their own right, such problems may affect the scheduling of jobs and will therefore be of concern to the operations manager. Any rejected work which is generated will require decisions to be made by the appropriate authority, in this example by manufacturing or production engineers.
- Pay and conditions are always important, and particularly so if people are working on some form of incentive scheme. There will have to be some form of **work checking** and **logging**, coupled with calculations of **performance**, so that final wages can be determined which will be usually a combination of basic rates and an extra amount related to performance. Any queries regarding wages will need to be solved in conjunction with the records held of the amount of work completed. Problems associated with standard times (see Chapter 10) will have to be resolved with the Management Services department, some of whose people will be responsible for setting the appropriate time standards.
- **Industrial relations** problems may occur from time to time, perhaps in connection with a proposed change in working practices, changes in rates for overtime working or where work is currently being conducted in an unsafe working environment. These will affect the smooth running of the departments concerned with the direct work, and will have to be solved with the help of the unions and personnel department.
- The operations performed to produce the final product incur costs because of the labour and materials expended upon them. They will also incur a proportion of the company's **overheads** which have to be recovered. For each operation these actual costs will be compared with corresponding standard costs in the costing department, and an analysis of the differences made for later action. An attempt is made to explain all **variances from standard**, so that adverse causes of excess labour or material input, or low output, can be avoided next time. Such cost data is then used to update **future standard costs**, so that they are as realistic as

possible. Inputs regarding quantities and dates as work progresses will also be required by the sales people, via the production control department.

- Ideas for improving the product processes naturally arise, often from those working on the various operations required. **Quality Circles** are widely used for these and other purposes. Such ideas for improvements are then fed back to the Management Services department, for example, so that a careful evaluation can be made of the ideas with a view to subsequent implementation.

- New product development should liaise closely not only with marketing to ensure that what is being developed closely matches customers' perceived needs, but also with the manufacturing and industrial engineers to help ensure that the product can be made in the most economical way. Wherever possible, these activities should be **concurrent** with each other, in order to reduce the time for new products to reach the market. As an illustration of the first point, Sir Clive Sinclair's electric three-wheel car (the C5) was an interesting concept, but appeared not to meet the public's perception of a safe, viable means of personal transport. In April 1989, Tulip Computers, a Dutch firm, was reported as saying that it already had a Multi Channel Architecture computer which it could put into production, but it claimed that its research had shown little demand in Europe, possibly excepting the UK, for such a machine (*PC User*, 18 April 1989).

We shall now look at the key activities of other functional departments in a manufacturing company.

(i) Marketing
Marketing is the management process responsible for identifying, anticipating and satisfying customer requirements profitably (chartered institute of marketing). To that extent, marketing operates primarily **externally** to the company. Its key area of operation to achieve this is known as the **marketing mix**, and consists of at least four elements:

- **Price**
- **Product**
- **Promotion**
- **Place**.

- **Price:** This factor has to take into account the overall costs of developing and producing the product, which means that decisions have to be made regarding the **expected life** of the product.

    Products have a life cycle which generally include a development phase, followed by launch, growth, maturation and, finally, decline stages. Figure 1.2 illustrates this cycle. Such an estimate of product life is important, as is the anticipated volume that will occur in each year of the

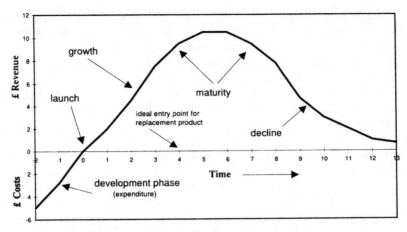

Fig 1.2   The product life cycle

life cycle. The price has to be such that it will produce sufficient surplus revenue to enable the company to remain in business and to expend sufficient funds into new research and development and design for new products for the company's future. The price level must be such that it takes into account specific policies regarding the extent to which the company aims to recover much of its initial costs from its initial sales (e.g. a 'creaming' policy), so that later on it can reduce its price.

The price a company sets also has to be competitive with respect to other companies' prices, as well as fitting comfortably into its own price structure for complementary products.

The price itself is therefore hardly ever the simple sum of the cost elements plus a margin for profit. By careful consideration of the factors mentioned, price becomes a powerful tool which can be used to stimulate or damp down demand, in much the same way as rail services charge a premium for peak time travel, and lower their prices for less busy periods, as well offering special discounted prices for particular periods or events.

- **Product:** It is recognised that customers buy the **benefits** or **services** a good provides, and rarely buy it for its own sake. The Sales department must therefore ensure that it concentrates on what the product has to offer. Such selling activity often concentrates on a product's **unique attributes** – i.e. what it is that distinguishes it from its competitors. An example of product differentiation is the way Japanese car makers equip their vehicles to a high level, by making items as standard equipment that British car makers used to consider as extras. The result has been that the customer's level of expectation has been raised, and customers now regard such erstwhile extras as quite normal. It is not unusual now to see promotional material which not only praises the company's own product, but criticises their competitors'. There are, however, ethical questions involved here.

Packaging often forms an important part of a product's image besides being a protective shell, and can be used to enhance the image, the apparent value or the apparent amount of the product. An example of such a product is perfume. The same thinking applies to the materials used, the colour and the style of packaging.

To a lesser extent, but sometimes important, is the kind of transport used – for example, home delivery in an antique vehicle by a major London store.

- **Place:** This is concerned with how the company **gets the goods to the customer**. We can distinguish the strategy of distribution from the physical routes of distribution. Such a strategy might be for the company to distribute only to wholesalers, their rationale being that this is a relatively well-defined operation in terms of numbers and locations, as well as eliminating the job of transporting many orders of small quantities over a very large geographical area. Some companies may sell direct to the public, because they rate highly the formation of a close link in the public's mind between the company and the product. Other companies sell door to door, like the Fuller Brush company and the Kleenezee company. Companies like Amway UK, Tupperware and Avon Cosmetics all value highly the social nature of selling and their distribution methods reflect this. It is quite common for some companies to sell mainly by catalogue, like Argos or GUS. Other possibilities which affect distribution methods are cash-and-carry and help yourself from semi-broken-down 'wholesale loads'.

- **Promotion:** This is how a company brings the product **to the attention of the customer**, whether they are wholesalers, public or original user. The company can do this by advertising in the trade press, on radio, on television or in popular journals. Competitions where holidays are given as prizes, or where slogans are thought up extolling the product's virtues bring heightened product awareness, albeit for a relatively short time. Promotional deals are useful on those occasions where a product can usefully be coupled with another complimentary product – for example, a cleaning mop can be coupled with a bottle of floor cleaner. Price discounts for certain quantity purchases, or coupon offers for indirect discounts, are very popular with soap and detergent products.

(ii) Personnel

Human Resources is the term becoming more commonly used, hopefully recognising the importance of a company's prime resource. The Personnel or Human Resources department has responsibility for everything that affects a **person at work**, and some employers also ensure they become involved in the wider concept of the employee's general well-being and welfare. An example of this thinking was the work of Rowntree and Cadbury in the Midlands in the 19th century. Many employers try to play an active role in the employee's social well-being as well.

The Personnel department, like others mentioned here, has a staff role and it can implement only what has been agreed between unions and management, although Personnel staff may play a key role in that process. In many cases, where policy is not clear or has not yet been established, they can suggest a line of action, which may or may not later be approved.

Personnel will be concerned with, at least:

- the development, formulation and execution of a company's **policies** at different levels, so as to help it achieve its overall objectives via clearly stated, hierarchical and cohesive statements of purpose and action;
- negotiating and administrating current **pay policy**, and updating such policies so as to ensure the company remains competitive in its salary structure, yet flexible enough to attract people of the correct calibre even when shortages exist;
- the development and execution of policies regarding **recruitment** and **training**, coupled with exercises designed to forecast shortages or surpluses of people at different levels in the company as well as to anticipate future needs in areas not currently applicable; they will often work closely with local Polytechnics and Universities as well as local employment agencies;
- compliance with statutory requirements regarding Health and Safety at Work, minimum wages, etc.

(iii) **Production control**

This is a staff function found mainly in manufacturing companies. It is the department responsible for the successful management and completion of all the activities necessary to **produce the product on time**. It therefore liaises very closely with virtually every other department in the company, because anything which may jeopardise the on time completion of work to target is its legitimate concern. It is not directly concerned with the actual technology of production, but where, for example, there has been a change from one method to another, such a change will be of legitimate concern, because it may affect subsequent timely completion of the product.

Production Control determines and issues (manufacturing) plans, it collects and analyses appropriate data, and it disseminates relevant information so as to control (manufacturing) activity according to those plans. You can see that while this description applies to manufacturing, it still makes sense even when 'manufacturing' is omitted. It can then apply to many other situations which are unconnected to manufacturing. This is because such control will apply principally to the management of activities, rather than to the technology of the activities themselves.

Production control has three primary functions:

- **Planning:** dividing the total task into smaller segments called operations, often on a hierarchical basis, so that it becomes easier to handle. For planning purposes, it is also necessary to have ensured that the work methods involved are as good as possible under the current situation, and that it is known how long it should take to perform these operations. We examine the methods for achieving this in Chapters 9, 10 and 11.

- **Scheduling:** Schedules are needed to show when each operation should **start** and **finish**. It is also necessary to know which operations go to make a part of the finished product, which parts go to make parts of a higher level, and when the final operations to assemble the parts at the highest level should start and finish, so producing the end product. We look at this aspect of production in more detail when we examine materials requirements planning in Chapter 6, and this is shown diagrammatically in Figure 6.2. The schedules so prepared must be issued to all concerned so that they know what has to be done, and when it should start and finish.

   Even though all plans have been properly made well in advance of the required dates, not much will happen at the first work centre, nor subsequently, if the raw material is not there in good time, together with the correct jigs and fixtures and current drawings, and the correct inspection equipment is not available. This activity is often called 'kitting out'.

- **Monitoring and progress chasing:** It is not enough merely to plan and issue instructions for what has to be done. For a variety of reasons the planned activities may not occur – for example, because of absences of staff, machine breakdowns, missing or defective materials, failure by suppliers to deliver, or essential items being rejected during the course of their own manufacture. All operations have to be **monitored** on a regular basis – often daily – so that it can promptly be seen if certain operations have not been started or are falling behind schedule.

   On a shorter timescale – often several times a day – the activity of monitoring is known as **progress chasing**. To some degree this is a less formal activity (often directed to problem areas, and conducted on a more personal basis) than regular monitoring, which may be carried out by the use of data collection centres. Because Production Control is intimately connected with the management of production, it must work closely with the Purchasing Department and Inventory Control Departments as it is not possible to make realistic plans for planning without knowing when material is **due** and what the **levels of stock** are in hand.

We will have a closer look at some of the work of production control in Chapters 4 and 12.

(iv) **Purchasing**

Purchasing is responsible for the procurement of all materials and services that a company requires in order to produce its products. Non-manufacturing organisations also require a purchasing department for items used in the ordinary course of their business – for example, stationery, furniture, office equipment, computers, furnishings, and so on.

In many manufacturing companies, the purchasing department is concerned chiefly with materials purchases. The department may be **centralised** – i.e. just one purchasing department located centrally may handle the entire purchasing for the five divisions of the company which may be located in five different locations in the UK. The advantages of such a strategy are savings in manpower, a convenient way to concentrate buying power, a way to exert some influence over selected suppliers because of that purchasing power, and an opportunity to standardise procedures because there is only one key department. You may think that the removal of the purchasing officer from the scene of the requirement, a lack of local divisional sensitivity, and a possible increase in the overall delivery times to the end user, are possible disadvantages.

An alternative strategy may be for the purchasing function to be **localised**. Each division has a small unit responsible for all its purchases. The advantages of this method counter, to some extent, the disadvantages of the centralised purchasing, and vice versa. Sometimes a combination of both these ideas results in a small head office purchasing function with responsibility for purchases over a fixed amount, and for capital purchases, while local purchasing departments buy less expensive items from local suppliers.

Purchasing are responsible for buying materials at the right **price**, at the right **time**, at the right **quality** and in the correct **volume** and **proportions**.

- Buying at the right price can only be the result of careful sourcing to discover competitive prices and careful negotiations to safeguard them in the light of future needs, possible world shortages and competitive bids. Sometimes orders will be negotiated into the future with call-offs at a predetermined time. There is a fine line between prudent purchasing as a hedge against possible near term price increases, and a tendency to speculate with a company's money so as to make a profit on the deal. Several years ago, buyers of cocoa for a chocolate manufacturer speculated in that market, as did the buyers of silver used in the photographic industry. Both came to grief.
- 'In time' means having the material when the various schedules say you are going to **need** it. It is therefore important to know different suppliers who are reliable, even though they may have different lead times for the same item. It is still common to have at least two suppliers for key items, to avoid problems if one fails to deliver as promised but there is a growing tendency for some companies to deal with only one supplier in an effort to foster a close relationship, with the advantages that brings in terms of price, loyalty, quality and control. What happens in cases of prolonged strikes is not so clear: it would then appear that the company was very vulnerable.
- Having confidence in your supplier's quality is of utmost importance to ensure the continued satisfaction of the customer with your own product. This can be done only in conjunction with your (potential) suppliers by

working closely with them so that they know what you want, and you are satisfied that they have the systems to **control their quality** once established. A large company will often do this by developing **vendor rating schemes**, which assign points to each factor selected as being important by the company.

In essence these schemes quantify the most important factors that a company requires from its suppliers, and then rates the supplier and compares the total score achieved with its pass level requirement. Typical factors may be technical know-how, cleanliness, price, capacity and delivery, and lead time and quality. Carefully written specifications, close collaboration, appropriate control of quality throughout manufacture to agreed standards are likely to produce satisfactory results for both company and supplier.

- Knowing **how much** to order and **when** is a problem to which there is no precise answer. High volume low unit cost parts are not handled the same way as low volume high unit cost items. The precise quantities will be decided in ways similar to those we will look at in Chapter 5. Those quantities may or may not be delivered all at one time, they may be called in at agreed intervals of a blanket order, designed to reduce administrative effort. Factors which affect the volume delivered will be space available, likelihood of spoilage or deterioration, availability of special storage facilities such as refrigerated stores, humidity controlled areas, secure areas for chemicals or precious metals and the actual scheduled requirement.

1.5 Company Organisation

Figure 1.3 suggests how departments in a company might be organised. The exact configuration of an organisation chart will depend on management's experience of what works satisfactorily for them: there is no definitive answer. Figure 1.3 illustrates a conventional pyramidal structure. In a manufacturing company, it would indicate a line and staff organisation. These terms are borrowed from the military. 'Line' refers to those having **executive** authority and 'staff' refers to those who act in an **advisory** capacity. Management Services, Personnel and Marketing are staff, while Production are line.

There is a growing trend for companies to reduce the number of management layers in their organisation, and Figure 1.3 reflects this. This helps to make communication between different levels easier and quicker: it reduces the **inertia** inherent in an organisation with many layers. The Royal Mail (£4 billion annual turnover and 175,000 employees) announced that by 1992 they expected to have eliminated three layers from their nine-layer management structure. This would reduce duplication of work, and improve profitability and customer service. By 1995, Ford will have reduced its

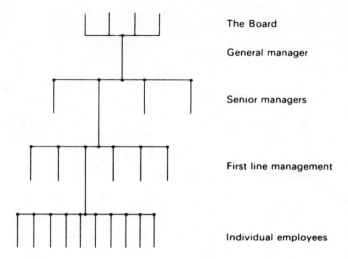

The Board

General manager

Senior managers

First line management

Individual employees

Fig 1.3   A conventional organisation chart

average number of layers within its organisation, from fourteen to seven. This is part of its programme to merge its North American and European operations into one structure.

(a) Matrix format

An organisation, or part of it, may be structured in a matrix format. This is common in **project management**, where different people are responsible for different projects. A matrix is simply shown by a chart with a horizontal and a vertical axis; the vertical axis will show the names of the people in that department, and the horizontal axis will show all the projects the department is working on or knows about, both current and proposed (see Figure 1.4). The intersections on the chart show who is responsible for what project.

Figure 1.4 is an example of a pharmaceutical company whose organisation is a combination of a conventional and matrix design. The conventional structure exists for each geographic division, and the matrix structure ties each of the various product groups to a Product Manager in the appropriate division. This aspect is overseen by a Marketing Manager who reports to the Managing Director. In each division, and for each product in a product group, specific people in each function are responsible for each product.

The Ford restructuring above will also include a change to matrix management from conventional pyramidal structure for most managers. This means that they will report to a manager from one of the vehicle

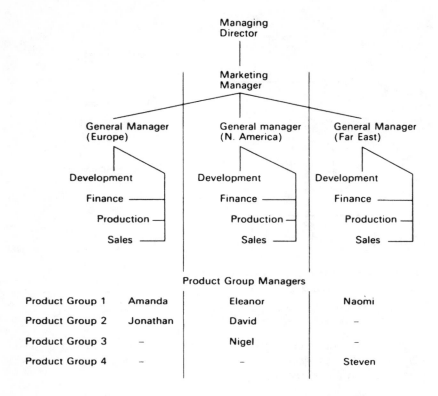

Fig 1.4   Organisation chart: combined conventional and matrix form

centres **and** to a functional manager, e.g. in manufacturing or marketing; that is, they will have more than one boss.

(b) Centralisation and decentralisation

Problems involving centralisation or decentralisation are always difficult to resolve, and over a period of years each may be tried and tested for effectiveness and suitability for the company's needs. If a company has a chief administrator, then all administrative staff report directly to that person. On a daily basis, however, they are working for, and are, *de facto* responsible to the person to whom they have been assigned. They really have two bosses: something which is difficult to reconcile. This is the result of decentralisation.

It is not unusual for companies to change their organisational structure to respond to **external circumstances** – e.g. to create a new division to respond to competition.

Activity

1 At your college or place of work, find or develop the organisation structure. Is it a conventional hierarchical tree as in Figure 1.3? Talk to some of the people concerned. Does it seem to work well? How many layers are there? What is a 'good' structure?

2 Is the structure a matrix (where you may have in a college, for example, courses on one axis and subject groups on the other, or where in a company you may have product groups on one axis and people on the other)? Is this better than a hierarchical structure?

3 Can you envisage a wheel structure with a hub and a rim? Who would be the hub and who the rim? What might the spokes represent?

4 Visit a doctor's surgery, a fast-food takeaway and a supermarket. Note and list examples at each location of their key resources. Determine similarities and differences between each organisation, indicating where opportunities exist for measurements of and improvements in efficiency; how productivity could be measured, and what service standards might be set as related to customer satisfaction.

1.6 Research and Development

A company with a vibrant research and development activity, with a well-managed design operation, and which fosters an innovative atmosphere, tends to be better placed to take on its competitors than those who are deficient in one or more of these features. Many of the major companies will not only have mission statements for the company as a whole, but will have them for the key functions as well. These will be designed to support the company's overall mission statement. For example, the Research and Development mission statement for a major glass manufacturer is "to conduct high quality research in science and engineering, with a five to ten-year horizon'. The accompanying overall objective is 'to develop vital technology which will enhance the company to progress its developmental products better, quicker and cheaper than the competition'.

We can identify three types of research activity. **Basic 'blue sky' research**, i.e. pure research, is undertaken by those companies who are searching for a fuller and more complete understanding of basic physical laws and material properties. At this level of research, they recognise that specific payoffs may be difficult to identify in terms of timing, financial amount and the area in which they may finally occur. When indeed a breakthrough is made, it sometimes appears that there is now a solution waiting for a problem. Such results may include new knowledge, new principles, new theories and new ideas. For example, the mathematical research resulting in fractals, while initially extremely interesting and a breakthrough in relevant theory, has now found application as a means to greatly compress data prior to storing. To the uninformed however, there seems little connection between the fascinating pictures with unending detail that one can produce quite simply from fractal software, and subsequently being able to store data efficiently on disk.

Applied research is research with emphasis on the practical application of existing knowledge. To this extent, the results of such research tend to have application to current problems, recognised as warranting such activity in the first place. Such research is conducted by a larger number of companies than pure research, because it tends to have more practical results, the associated benefits are somewhat easier to estimate, the risks are lower and the associated costs are lower than for more fundamental research. The results of such research may be seen in new materials or their uses, and new processes; e.g. the use of carbon fibre in car body design and kevlar in high impact protection situations.

Development is the design and practical application of the results of applied research to prototype products, and as such needs to be thought of as part of the overall innovative approach so important to a company, embracing creativity, receptiveness to new ideas, well-trained and motivated people and an organisation structure which fosters rapid feedback of ideas, together with the design function described below. Here we might expect to see the results of such endeavours as improved products in terms of versatility in use, higher quality, greater reliability, improved safety, reduced maintenance, simplicity of design and use, lower production cost ideally affecting selling price (but not always), environmental friendliness in terms of use and final disposal, and longer useful life. It is the development phase, more than the other two, which needs to be in close contact with design and marketing; also coupled with good communication and rapid feedback combined with internal flexibility and good communication.

We can visualise the Research and Development activity as consisting of inputs, a process and outputs. As well as inputting the usual resources available to any organisation, we also see the key use of knowledge, time, effort and creativity as key factors. However, by its nature, and more so with fundamental research, Research and Development is time consuming, costly and uncertain in terms of results. Some major companies combine with others with certain aspects of Research and Development.

Motorola, Apple and IBM worked together on the design of the Power PC microprocessor chip. Intel collaborates with Hewlett Packard on the development for a new chip; such development costs being in the order of several hundred million dollars.

It is difficult to manage effectively; for example, how much pressure for results can be applied to such work, and how well can interim progress be judged? Just as important, how is an effective Research and Development team developed and nurtured? How is success measured? It is well recognised that Research and Development should be a continuing activity; not one to be started, stopped and restarted, if the chances for success are not to be lowered unnecessarily. If we imagine that basic Research and Development, applied research, prototyping and regular production all lie in sequence, then the ease with which conventional management techniques can be applied to each, becomes easier as we move from basic Research and Development to production.

However difficult it is to manage, an organised approach is to be recommended. Some key aspects to be considered are:

(a) Define the scope and objective of the particular Research and Development programme under consideration.

(b) Produce clear documentation as a proper reference for the future, when monitoring the activity.

(c) Have a clear rationale as to how the Research and Development team will be established in terms of its size, skills, sub-section membership, leadership, responsibility (both for people and expenditure) and the nature of the authority of the team leader.

(d) Establish how and when progress will be monitored. By definition, it will be difficult to establish this, but in order to avoid problems later it should be established at an early stage.

(e) If a project is funded from outside the company, then it will be necessary to say precisely who has authority for expenditure, what the rationale will be for such expenditure, to whom the team leader is truly responsible, to whom and in what proportions do any benefits from the research accrue and who has authority to cancel the project and under what circumstances.

(f) What is the relation of a particular research project to other current projects in terms of priority, cash allocation and assignment of resources.

(g) The use of formal project control techniques should be used to assist in the management of progress, so as to be able clearly to highlight problems, ideally before they endanger the project.

Research and Development in a company may be organised as:

(a) A centralised Research and Development department which has reporting to it a number of projects, one or more of which may be grouped by particular types of Research and Development activity. This centralised Research and Development department will have a person at Director level responsible for the entire activity, and will choose areas for research, assign personnel and money accordingly.

(b) A decentralised Research and Development activity, where there is a small central co-ordinating role and the main activity is undertaken by divisional or group Research and Development sections. Such sections will be responsible for nearly all the research activity, merely reporting back to the central section.

A matrix of projects with team leaders is not unusual and works well providing roles and responsibilities have been clearly established.

Because not all companies can or are willing to conduct research, we can identify four categories of company. This assumes that all companies at least recognise the long-term importance of research, to a greater or lesser degree.

(a) Those who do very little if any research. Their products use well-established materials, equipment and processes. The technology involved changes very slowly. They have long runs and few model variations.

(b) The company who manufactures using processes, materials or equipment obtained via licence. The costs of this option are far more determinable than the next two options; although the costs may still be high. The risks are greatly reduced, because the company is buying proven results.

(c) This company notes what the leading companies are doing in a particular field. If it looks promising, they decide to step in with a project team and hope not to be too far behind. The risks are somewhat greater than **(b)** above but less than **(d)** below.

(d) This kind of company is noted for its Research and Development activity. It has projects of great variety always in existence and is willing to fund them extensively for considerable periods of time. For successful outcomes, the rewards are great, not only in enhanced earnings, share price rises and leading edge products, but by also being able to attract and keep the most able researchers. The risks are also great but such a company is willing to take them.

The table below shows the top ranking Research and Development (R and D) spending companies worldwide (source: 1993 UK R and D Scoreboard by Company Reporting Ltd).

Rank	Company		R and D spend in £000s	R and D spend per employee in £000s	R and D as a % of sales
1	General Motors USA		3,908,120	5.21	4.47
2	Daimler Benz Germany		3,796,941	10.09	9.45
3	Siemans	Germany	3,418,960	8.28	10.68
4	IBM	USA	3,357,331	11.13	7.88
5	FORD	USA	2,861,294	8.80	4.33
6	Hitachi	Japan	2,748,809	8.48	6.69
7	Toyota	Japan	2,365,079	21.86	4.40
8	Matsushita	Japan	2,212,015	9.13	5.61
9	Fujitsu	Japan	2,073,465	13.31	11.39
10	A T and T	USA	1,922,721	6.15	4.78
*	*		*	*	*
46	BCE	Canada	650,116	5.24	6.05
47	ICI	UK	647,000	5.51	5.36
48	PSA	France	627,734	4.00	3.28
49	NT	Canada	614,597	10.61	11.07
50	Eli Lilly	USA	610,303	18.61	14.98
51	Xerox	USA	608,982	6.13	5.41

Rank	Company		R and D spend in £000s	R and D spend per employee in £000s	R and D as a % of sales
52	Glaxo	UK	595,000	16.05	14.53
53	Nippondenso	Jpn	585,714	10.33	7.26
54	Pfizer	USA	570,145	14.01	11.94
55	Procter & Gamble USA		568,692	5.37	2.93
*	*		*	*	*
61	Smithkline Beecham	UK	478,000	8.90	9.16
62	Unilever	UK	461,000	1.61	1.87
63	Sanyo	Japan	450,264	8.02	5.54
64	Shell	UK	435,000	3.43	0.60
65	Monsanto	USA	429,986	12.72	8.39
66	GEC	UK	417,000	3.97	7.22

Activity

In small groups, survey local industries and determine: **(a)** Do they conduct any R and D? If so, would they be willing to tell you it as a percentage of sales? **(b)** Do they classify it according to basic, applied or development categories? If no; classify them according to the four types of non R and D categories. In both situations, try to ascertain **why** they do what they do, *vis-à-vis* their strategy.

Activity

In the table above, and from other financial sources, can you detect a connection between R and D spend and profitability? Profitability data need not be for same year.

1.7 Design

The concept of design is assuming greater importance than ever before. It has become an integral part of product development and as such demands a close examination to see the part it has to play in eventual customer satisfaction.

What **is** design, and how can we apply the concept? Does it only refer to physical products, like toasters, cars, TVs and washing machines? A definition of design that we can find in a dictionary is: a plan or scheme conceived in the mind; a preliminary sketch from which an item can be made; the action or art of planning or creating in accordance with aesthetic and functional criteria (*New Shorter Oxford English Dictionary*, 1993). Clearly, this definition seems to be product orientated, but increasingly the concept of design is also used to embrace services. In service industries where the product is intangible the design of the system used to provide that service is very important. A poorly designed system will hinder the efficient and effective provision of the service being provided. We can also embrace design to include the design of management information systems. The concept of design can include job design, i.e. trying to make a task more efficient, reliable and quality orientated, as well as more satisfying and interesting for people to do. You will notice that we seem to be using the term 'design' as a verb, i.e. a doing action. In all these cases, design implies examination, evaluation, development, implementation and review.

But if we consider design pertaining to physical products, design is not, and must not be, merely the aesthetic features of the physical product. Unfortunately, design is often used in this context alone, but is misleading, for while good aesthetic design is important, so are the other factors mentioned below.

Before we examine design further, why might a company engage in design and development, and what factors might it consider? It is, after all, time-consuming, expensive and somewhat uncertain. Some suggested questions, to which answers need to be found, are:

(a) At what stages in their life cycles are the company's key products at present? Is the product range ageing when compared to other companies' products?
(b) What is the remaining potential demand likely to be for these products over the next few years?
(c) What is the state of the competition in relation to these products and which of the company's products, if any, have a 'unique' position in the market?
(d) How does these products' profitability rank with their revenue, i.e. do the products that sell the best also have the most profit margin?
(e) Does the company need to increase its market penetration in certain product areas?
(f) What is the company's overall profitability?

Once the company has some answers to the above, it may need to consider other factors, before and during design and development, including:

(a) How cash rich is the company at present and what major commitments does it have which may deplete this, other than the design and development programme being considered?
(b) Does it have the in-house skills for a design programme or will it need to buy this in?
(c) What existing product or products might be replaced?
(d) Are complementary products needed to strengthen a product range?

Early on in the stages described below answers would also be needed to questions such as:

(a) How well does the new product respond to customer feedback from earlier similar products?

(b) Can it be made cost-effectively and to the appropriate quality and reliability standards?

(c) Can it be priced competitively and still be profitable according to forecasted demand?

(d) Will the projected development time fit in with the age profile of product it is intended to replace?

(e) Are there any current or potential health and safety problems, environmental issues or legal aspects to consider?

So how does management become involved in design and, initially at least, what is involved in designing a product? What is meant by a 'good' design, for example? Management becomes involved because it is vital that the final product or service – i.e. what the consumer will finally use – will be able not only to satisfy customers' needs, but also be able to be produced economically and efficiently, be a quality product, be simple, safe and reliable to use, have good ergonomic features, be environmentally friendly both when in use and in disposal (if we are referring to a physical product) and be economic and simple to maintain. This cannot be done if the only factor which is considered is – 'does it look good'?

If design is to make a proper impact in the areas referred to above, then it is vital that those responsible for design be brought in at the earliest possible stage. It does not fundamentally matter whether they are members of the company itself or whether the company buys in a design service from outside; the key point is that design is not a bolted-on consideration or last-minute thought. The concept of design for manufacture (also see Chapter 2) cannot be considered to be effective unless Design liaises with other departments/functions such as marketing, engineering, production, purchasing and accounts at the very least. Design for production means that at this stage, factors which will affect the ease and cost of manufacture, the time and cost of assembly, the cost of maintenance and repair, will be carefully considered so as to ensure these costs will be as low as possible.

Design as a function is part of the innovative process itself and to that extent designers must be totally familiar with the market they are designing for and the image the company wishes to present to its customers. While there is a strong tendency currently for companies to satisfy global markets, there are nevertheless strong national differences which can make the difference between a successful and superlative product.

(a) **The stages of design**

(i) **Organisation**

Design is more effectively carried out by a team, rather than by a single person. The reason is that with increasing complexity of technology, customers' requirements, material specification coupled with speed of development and mandatory reduction in time to market, the possibility of one person having sufficient expertise to cover all aspects is negligible. Moreover, a multidisciplinary team which is concerned with a product or range right from the start through to the launch, is more likely to do a superior job compared with a team which is involved only at the start. With such teams in place, formal progress meetings can be implemented regarding costs and specifications. Individuals can be assigned to monitor not only internal progress but external results relating to customer feedback during the entire design phase.

The management of design also requires regular progress reviews by management. Is there, for example, a person at senior management level on the board, who has responsibility for design? Some companies, but necessarily only small ones, may use an outside design house as consultants, with responsibility for developing and maintaining a design style for their products, and who by familiarisation with their client, can call upon sufficient expertise to solve problems as they arise. Design is often better accomplished by organising it in project matrix form, i.e. the vertical side of the matrix identifies a number of different projects, many of them perhaps running at the same time. The horizontal side of the matrix identifies a number of different departments, e.g. design, engineering, production, marketing, purchasing, accounting. For each project there is a designated project leader. In each key department, there will be a person or persons designated to a particular project. Thus the project leader will lead a team of people having specific responsibility for a project reporting to him or her, but who will still report to their own supervisor in the normal way.

Procedures for efficient design need to be carefully and formally established so that information both on the design itself and on progress made can flow unhindered, progress and problems be recorded, and best use be made of for example computer aided design where appropriate, together with necessary cost information. At all stages close liaison is imperative between all interested parties. Bottlenecks, once identified, need to be removed, just as those in a production environment. The ability for feedback to occur is essential as design is largely an iterative process, and not something with a definitive answer at any particular stage.

(ii) **Objectives**

Regardless of whether the design team is internal or external to the company, it is essential for the design team to have a **design brief.** This will probably be most effectively done as a result of a market survey. It should contain the key overall specification for the product. If we consider a home electric generator for emergency use, this might be (a) not too heavy to be moved by one person, (b) not too expensive, (c) not too noisy when running, (d) able to power several lights, (e) be reliable and maintenance free and (f) sell at a specific price. These parameters must then be answered in more detail as a result of a market survey. From this, a working document, the brief would be prepared and this, with regular updates, would guide the team throughout the project.

(iii) **Conception**
This takes the brief one stage further, and establishes what has to be done to try to fulfil the brief. For example, a model or full-size example may be built which has the look and feel in general, but not necessarily all the details, of what such a generator might finally be. It may then be found to be able to achieve the power requirements, but not within the size and weight brief. Furthermore, current generators may not be as maintenance free as the brief requires for the price constraint. Therefore, some features in the model may be a simulation or non-working example. But nevertheless, it would be clear, in a general way, what the new generator would look like.

(iv) **Embodiment**
This phase must clearly establish how the product will work and what is required for it to do so. If the key features of the brief cannot yet be met, then this is where they must be re-examined for feasibility and change if necessary. All physical requirements must be met and problems overcome before the next phase. This includes the overall appearance of the product, and is where the stylist makes a contribution. No longer is it sufficient for something merely to work properly. It must also look right This aspect of design is important, and many successful companies are able to produce products with a consistent theme, such that they look right as well as work properly. The next stage, of detail design, must not be attempted if this stage is not well done.

(v) **Detailing**
In this phase, the precise details in terms of shape, size, materials, tolerances, source, cost and conformance to appropriate quality standards are decided for every single item in the product. The success at this stage depends greatly on how well each of the preceding stages have been completed, particularly with respect to information feedback to the design team on results of tests both internal and external, customer reaction, and the findings of other departments concerned, e.g. costing, production, engineering, purchasing.

(v) **Pre-production batch**
A pre-production batch needs to be successfully made which meets all quality and cost criteria, and includes any feedback from the market. This information must be formally evaluated and adjustments made prior to full and normal production. There is no doubt that effort put into the design and development phase, each stage of which is often managed concurrently with earlier and subsequent stages, will amply repay that effort many times over, with a successful final product. For example, it is quite common for new

major software to be issued to key users, in a 'beta' version prior to design finalisation. The feedback received helps to ensure that major bugs are very unlikely to be passed on in the final version to customers.

(vii) Customer feedback

We cannot consider the design phase for a product to be fully complete however, until the finalised version has been in general use for some time, and the feedback from customers carefully analysed and fed back to the appropriate areas in the firm. This information will come from warranty data while under guarantee and from failure and repair data in the field. It can be quite difficult to collect this data via field service personnel, but it must be done if the best possible product is to be given to the customer. When analysis shows that performance shortcomings are not, or no longer, design related, one can consider this final phase complete. There is no substitute for a completely satisfied customer.

Activity

1 Find six examples of domestic products which you consider to be well designed, and identify the features/characteristics of each, which caused you to make your choice. Conversely, find some poorly designed products and identify their shortcomings. Try to establish where in the design sequence failure to recognise these shortcomings might have occurred.

2 Why are countries like Italy, France and Germany so often thought of as being able to produce products of style and so aesthetically pleasing?

3 What features make a well-designed house? In your team, let two people be prospective buyers for a custom-designed house. The other team members are to draw up the design brief based on the purchaser's requirements/wishes.

4 What are the symptoms of a poorly designed system? What are the characteristics, necessary and desirable, of a well-designed system:
  (a) for a multi-doctor clinic in an inner-city location
  (b) for a motor rescue organisation operating nation-wide
  (c) for a theatre ticket agency in a major city
  (d) for a mail-order catalogue company?

5 What do you consider are the key design features for a well-designed pair of climbing boots, a two-person tent, a pair of skis, a tennis racket?

Chapter Review Questions

1 What are the key resources applicable to any organisation?

2 In what ways is a fast-food takeaway similar to a factory?

3 With what areas is Operations Management primarily concerned?

4 Why should Research and new product Development liaise with Marketing?

5 Why should work in progress be kept as low as possible, or eliminated wherever possible?

6 What main factors affect the marketing mix?

7 Name four key activities in the Personnel department.

8 'Production Control controls the machines finished goods are packed in': True or False?

9 Name three key areas in Production Control.

10 What information do you need to know in order to schedule work in a department?

11 Why progress chase when you will find out what happened at the end of the week?

12 What are the advantages of a centralised Purchasing Department?

13 How might a company attempt to assess a potential supplier's reliability?

14 How are aims/objectives/goals, mission statements, plans/procedures, policies, and strategies all related to each other in business?

15 What factors might a company have considered prior to developing its Business Plan?

16 A Business Plan is likely to be made up from separate ...

17 What is the purpose of R and D for a company?

18 Identify three types of R and D activity options which a company may consider.

19 R and D programmes are difficult to manage. How might a manager attempt to reduce this problem?

20 Design is largely a problem of aesthetics: True or False?

21 What has been found to be an effective way to organise Design activity?

22 What are the key stages in Design development?

2   Managing the Product

Chapter 2 is concerned with what has to be done so that products or services **meet customers' needs**. We have already said that customers buy the benefits provided rather than the product or service for its own sake; those benefits must therefore meet their needs precisely. It is also important to ensure that a product is no more complicated than necessary – that is, it should perform as required but not more than that. We shall be discussing value analysis/ value engineering and quality in this chapter.

Learning Objectives

By the end of this chapter you should:

1 know the difference between **value analysis** and **value engineering**, and be able to identify different categories of value
2 know what constitutes **quality** in a good or service, and how it fits under the umbrella of Total Quality Management
3 be able to identify the main **components** of quality and their associated **costs**
4 become familiar with a range of techniques useful for **quality control**
5 know what an **acceptance sampling plan** is and what it does, and be able to develop a simple but practical version of such a scheme.

Case Study: Jack's DIY – Episode 1

Andrew Jack, Managing Director of Jack's DIY, a company making small tools for the DIY market, had been seriously worried about costs for some time. A year ago he had told everybody to cut costs, 'for your own good as well as that of the company' he had said somewhat forcefully. The Works Manager, with Andrew Jack's backing, had sent out a directive that he needed a 10% cut in costs across the board in the next six months, and that he would check once a month to see the results.

Everyone including the salesmen were involved, and they were in a good position to see what went on in other companies. 'They might get some good ideas?,' he'd said. It didn't happen; the momentum soon dropped off the cost reduction campaign. The Works Manager was at his wits' end, for he knew Andrew Jack meant what he said. He thought he would have a go himself.

The 'camm-o-loc' was a quick-acting device for holding two or more pieces of material together while they were being worked on. It was made with machined metal parts and assembled with proprietary bought-in fasteners such as washers, nuts and bolts. It was quite a good seller but the Works Manager had chosen it because he had noticed that sales to date were somewhat below the corresponding period last year, and even last year's sales were down on previously record sales. If he could make savings here it would obviously be worthwhile, and coupled maybe with a revised price structure, sales could be on the increase. They sold 20,000 last year at £7.75 each excluding VAT. A camm-o-loc consisted of 35 separate items and bought-in item value was 25% of the material cost. Total product cost was £6.00, of which £2 was material, £1 was labour and overheads were 150% on material.

Now where should he start?

2.1 Value Analysis (VA)

'Value Analysis' was a term coined by Lawrence Miles of the General Electric Co. in the USA, about 1947. He was conducting traditional cost-reduction exercises on a number of the company's products, and these led him to consider the actual nature of **value**. He developed a series of questions which he then used to help establish the value of the part or product under review. This technique seems to have been introduced into the UK in about the mid-1950s. Miles has said that about 25% of manufacturing cost is unnecessary; these unnecessary costs are there because of past practices, constrained thinking, unoriginal thinking, difficulties in creative thinking and an attitude of 'why change something that seems to be satisfactory?'.

(a) The value analysis procedure

Value analysis is thus the name given to a procedure consisting of the **systematic examination** of the components of a product to see if the company is getting value for its money. Like all simple techniques, much of its strength comes from its **organised approach** to the problem, in order that there will be a very low probability of missing any conceivable idea which, if it had been considered, might have made a contribution to the search for better value for money.

When value analysis is carried out on a product at the design stage (i.e. before the product ever goes into production), it is often referred to as **value engineering**, where the term 'engineering' is used in the sense of arranging for something to include certain features.

Cost-cutting exercises were much more popular in the 1950s and 1960s than they are now, and as you can see in Jack's DIY, it did not succeed, especially on a continuing basis. One of the reasons is that it is difficult to maintain momentum in what is essentially a fragmented and individually attempted exercise. The constant call for reduced costs, while good in itself left people not knowing what to do next in order to 'come up with something'. In other words, pressure can be kept on only for a limited time.

The value analysis exercise when completed must by definition not have affected adversely the quality or function of the product. At the very least, the quality and functionality must remain as it was before the exercise was conducted. Value analysis looks at the basic design of a product:

- to identify its **function(s)**
- to examine all other possible ways of **achieving them**
- to choose, on a rational basis, **the best way:** this best way relates to current circumstances, and will include lowest cost, most convenient manufacturing methods, and shortest implementation time being considered.

It is quite possible that some of these factors will conflict with each other, and it is usual to translate them all into **cost data**, and simply choose on the basis of lowest cost.

(b) The 'value' referred to in value analysis

A dictionary definition of value, is '**the intrinsic worth or goodness of a thing; that property which renders it useful or estimable**'.

A product can have several different values at the same time. Initially you can equate the value to the **price**. The camm-o-loc is priced at £7.75, but if it is not worth that then eventually no one will buy it. We can divide the overall value into two parts

- its value in **use**
- its value in **esteem**.

So we can say that

$$\text{Exchange value} = \text{Use value} + \text{Esteem value}$$

The 'exchange value' is a combination of market factors which influence the extent to which the product is held to be both useful and estimable. If you run short of drinking water in the Sahara, then you must expect to pay a lot for water: its exchange value will be enormous. If you feel you must have a Porsche, then its exchange value to you will be great, and most of that will be made up of esteem value.

Notice also that

$$\text{Esteem value} = \text{Exchange value} - \text{Use value}$$

and this ties in quite nicely with what we mean when we say that someone has paid 'over the odds': they have paid more than the current exchange value, and it has been for either the esteem or use of the product (or both). In the case of the camm-o-loc people might be prepared to pay over the odds for the use factor, but not for the esteem factor.

Figure 2.1 shows the relationship between use and esteem, for various items. It should be clear that the nail is 100% useful with zero esteem, but the painting is 100% estimable.

See if you can think of some other products which you can slot into place on Figure 2.1, which are not quite as readily defined as my four examples. You are going to try to identify products with both use and esteem values, but in different and probably not so pronounced proportions as mine. Where, for example, might you locate a Rolls Royce, a Morris Minor, a CD player, an Edison phonograph, a paint brush, Gucci shoes, Chanel No. 5 and an outfit for Ladies' Day at Ascot?

The cost of a product we will define as the **sum of all the costs incurred** in producing the product. Therefore,

$$\text{Exchange value} = \text{Cost} + \text{Profit}$$

and for most situations a company tries to increase its profit, which it can do by reducing the cost, or by increasing the normal exchange value, or by doing some of each. In many competitive situations it is not practical to increase the exchange value, so it is the **cost** which has to be decreased.

(c) General applicability of value analysis

The formal investigative procedures of value analysis, like those of work study (Chapters 9 and 10), are applicable in many non-manufacturing situations. The reason is that just as we question the underlying functions

---

Fig 2.1   Relationship between use and esteem

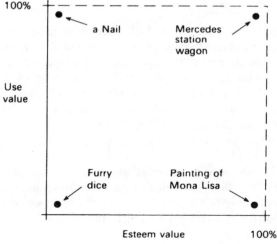

of a product, we can question fundamentally what a department in a company does, and how it does it. We search for the **essential activities** that have to be performed, and then concisely describe them. Having built up a list of the fundamental activities, we can then **rate** them according to importance and how well they are being done. By comparing the overall score against the cost of performing each of those activities, we can see more easily if we are getting value for money. Where there seems to be some doubt, that is where further investigations of the type described below will need to be conducted.

Case Study: Jack's DIY – Episode 2

We left Jack's Works Manager wondering how to begin, and we will assume that we are going to act as a value analysis consultant to the company. If we had a choice as to what product to choose for initial analysis, we could have suggested choosing a product made up of many parts, on the basis that there would be more scope for savings to be made than in a rather simpler one. We could have said 'Let us choose from a product whose sales are beginning to fall, so that if improvements can be made coupled with reduction in cost, it may have an augmented life.' If a product is running on very small profit margins, or is up against severe pressure from the competition, then it may also be a candidate.

In this case, the product has been chosen. Basic costs of the product have already been obtained, but at a later date detailed costs for all the parts will have to be ascertained. The Cost Accounting section will be able to help here. If not, then the Purchasing department will at least be able to supply the bought-in items' costs, and estimates will have to be made of the manufacturing costs for the remaining items.

(d) The value analysis team

Instead of the individual attempts by Jack's personnel in cutting costs, value analysis is better conducted by a team of people drawn from the key functions within the company. It should be a small team of about four or five people, and who can co-opt others for specific tasks as and when required. The team ought not to be permanent, but rather have a life determined by its current brief, in this case the camm-o-loc. Team members must be drawn from among such key functions as design, engineering, production, quality, sales, marketing, purchasing, accounting, work study and production control.

If the team is too large it becomes unwieldy, difficult to control and unable to arrive at decisions, as well as sometimes becoming politically split into factions to preserve self-interests. One of the team needs to act as co-ordinator but not try to exert his authority other than as it relates to the exercise in hand.

(i) Recording the facts

All the costs of the individual component parts must be recorded. This means that a list must also be made of every part, together with where else it is used apart from in the product being examined. A record of every function of the product must also be made. Many products will perform more than one function, so the **primary function** must be identified. The more succinctly these descriptions can be made, the better. Too long a description obscures the clarity with which we really want to operate: ambiguity is the curse of clear thinking. You will also have to establish a **ranking system** for the importance of a multi-functional product, and you will do this by putting yourself in the place of the consumer. Determine the quantities involved both for the product and its components, currently and in the future.

Activity

What do you think is the primary function, and what are the other functions, of the camm-o-loc?

(ii) How to achieve the primary function

This is where the strength of the value analysis team lies, and this is why a team is really necessary. You are trying to obtain any and all ideas relating to the primary function, without inhibiting the free flow of ideas. Such ideas are obtained during '**brainstorming**' sessions. This requires an informal atmosphere, no criticism and a desire by all to participate in a positive manner. The team leader has the job of stimulating the creative process. In particular, value judgements must be avoided on any ideas produced during these sessions.

It is very helpful at this stage to keep in mind three key techniques that also apply to the 'examine' phase of method study which we will look at in Chapter 9. These are:

- Eliminate
- Simplify
- Combine

and they should be considered in the sequence given. If a part can be eliminated (without of course degrading the function or quality of the product), costs and problems are also eliminated along with it. If that is not possible, then it is useful to see if a part can be simplified; if not, can it be combined with another part to perform a dual function?

(iii) Assigning costs

Costs must be assigned by estimating or using appropriate past data if applicable. This should be done after any creative thinking sessions such as those described above. Then select the best two or three other possibilities, and examine them carefully, using the skills of all the team members, so as to establish the feasibility and performance potential of each.

(iv) Pick the best idea

Analyse the selected choices above and determine which is the best – i.e. which should be developed further. The new choice may not have all the functions which the current product has; it will then be necessary to decide those which need to be incorporated into the new proposal. Remember that all this development must take place without any degradation of the benefits held by the original product.

(v) Sell the idea

Jack's value analysis team is an advisory one. Because the composition of the team is wide-ranging and representative, it likely that by the time a final recommendation has been made there may be little resistance to the proposed changes. However, such is human nature that we all seem to be built with a certain amount of resistance to change, so it may be necessary to sell the ideas to all the key personnel concerned, who in fact may well be the heads of the functions represented on the value analysis team. It is not unknown for a designer of the original product to be somewhat affronted when 'his' product is chosen for subsequent analysis. He may feel, 'it's worked well for so long it can't be that bad, can it?' He may not have to *say* these words, but if they are felt they will certainly contribute to a failure to achieve the freely flowing ideas session described above.

It may be necessary to produce a **model** of the proposal, so that everyone can get their hands on it. Quantifying the anticipated savings and expenditure involved, together with the improvements in benefits and a proper plan for the implementation of the proposal, will go a long way towards acceptance by all.

(e) Summary of the key steps involved

- Select a product on a rational basis
- Choose the value analysis team
- Record all parts, functions and costs
- Brainstorm for new ideas, but don't judge them yet
- Pick the best idea, double-check and cost it
- Sell that idea to the decision-makers
- Implement and bring to fruition; then monitor.

Figure 2.2 shows just where the major cost components are located.

Between them, work study and value analysis seek to ensure that a product meets the customer's requirements and no more, and that there is no unnecessary work content contributing to the total product cost.

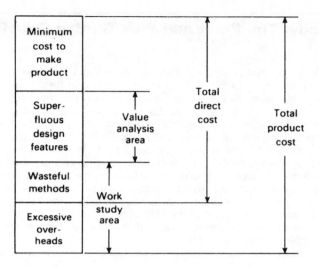

Fig 2.2   The components of cost

Activity

Work as a small group of not more than four people. Analyse a digital watch using as many of the steps above as you can.

2.2 Design for Manufacturing

Design for manufacturing is a computerised innovation, developed by Professor Boothroyd of the University of Rhode Island, which is reported to reduce the number of parts and suppliers for a new product by as much as 85%. The overall result is stated to be increased productivity and lower costs. A suite of computer software translates computer screen design to the end product without any intervening prototypes. Purchasing officers can work effectively with their own engineers, customer, representatives and suppliers, to ensure maximum co-operation regarding the end product.

IBM was able to produce a printer with 65% fewer parts and 75% less assembly time than a similar Japanese printer they had been examining. NCR Corporation built a cash register with no screws or bolts and an assembly time of less than two minutes. There are similar impressive claims made for IBM's new point of sale terminal.

Breaking down the traditional barriers between design and manufacturing, plus the team approach, is the key feature for success.

Case Study: The Plant and Pick Garden Co. (PPG) – Episode 1

PPG is a small but growing company, making and selling a wide variety of garden tools for the enthusiastic gardener. They incurred last year total quality costs of £60,000 on a turnover of £300,000. Ruthanna Lewise, the MD, tells you 'everything here gets 100% inspected, there's no way we would cut corners. Nothing gets through to the customer that shouldn't, and if it does, we replace it.'

Replying to one of your questions Daisy, the chief inspector, says that one typical item, a mower spindle, is causing problems. These spindles are bought-in items and are received in batches of 1500. 100 are sampled from the batch, and the batch is rejected if six or more spindles are found to be defective in the sample of 100. They have always used an Acceptable Quality Level (AQL) of 2%, but recent experience has shown incoming batches to be more like 8% defective. Daisy wonders what to do to get at the root of the problem. It costs them 5p to inspect a spindle at goods-inwards inspection, but it costs £5 if a reject spindle gets through into a subsequent assembly.

2.3 Total Quality Management (TQM)

(a) 'Quality'

Let us first define the term 'quality'. A short and reasonable definition is:

A quality product or service is one that is fit for its intended purpose, and is produced at an acceptable cost

By this, we mean that if all the product's features are such that the benefits conferred satisfactorily meet the customers' needs, then they have received a quality product or service. It is worth noting that **overspecifying** the product to produce features or refinements that are not wanted does not improve the quality. A window cleaner's gold-plated bucket is not of higher quality than an ordinary galvanised one, but a plastic bucket which soon splits near the handle connections after use is an inferior product. If a ladder that the window cleaner uses is so flexible that it is rather dangerous to use at first-floor levels or higher, then it is a poor quality product. A plastic carrier bag is not, however, inherently a low quality product when compared with a leather briefcase.

Similar thinking provides examples in the service sector. If you have to wait 20 minutes to get served in a fast-food establishment, then you are getting poor service. If every time you have a query at the bank you get passed from one person to the next, none of whom seems to know what to do, then the service you are getting is probably not adequate. A repair which is not done correctly the first time is poor service for the person who wanted a good job done.

It is becoming more and more common for companies to make overt statements to the public, about their policy on quality. IBM's 1990 *Annual Report* stated that the foundation of their strategy in the future was **market driven quality**. They intended to identify and meet customer and market needs with defect-free products and services, developed and delivered on a timely competitive basis. They would continually examine and improve business processes, and measure and assess the progress. Their goal was total customer satisfaction.

British Telecom's *Annual Review* for 1995 included statements on service level. More than 99.5% of UK inland call attempts were successful first time. 96% of their 120,000 public pay phones were operational at any one time. In 1992, 94.8% of service calls to directory assistance were answered within 15 seconds. Network faults per line per annum were 0.15.

In the National Provident Institution's (a mutual insurance company) 1991 *Report* to its members, they stated that they were determined to provide the highest levels of service. Their policy on quality was a commitment to meet the requirements of their customers, both internal and external, for all products all of the time. Every member of staff has received training in quality designed to improve their service to customers.

The New Zealand Family Medicine Training Programme incorporates the '**Quality in General Practice Project**'. A quality assurance package has been developed which includes comments from patients, registrars and regional directors. Peer review and visits to other practices are also part of the package. Early test results suggest that the time spent is producing considerable benefits.

Nor does it follow that only manufacturing companies have posts associated with quality.

Scope (formerly The Spastics Society) has as one of its five directors a head of Quality Assurance, whose job it is to evaluate the quality of the society's work. Teams including people with disabilities monitor the effectiveness of Scope's services.

The Leicestershire (East Midlands UK) Health Service advertised in 1991 to appoint a Director of Contracts and Quality Assurance. Part of the job is to ensure that quality assurance advice is provided and included within all service contracts negotiated.

(b) Total quality management

This is a term which embodies the very ethos of giving customers what they want. It is far more than having effective procedures for control, or suitable sampling schemes, although we will examine them later. Rather it is the **spirit of quality** which is imbued in every employee from top management down, every one of whom is devoted to doing the best in their own particular job. Because of the motivation everyone has, there is the highest probability that customers will get precisely what they need.

The company must have a single aim of providing what the customer needs, on the basis that only by satisfying customers can a company expect in the long term to stay in business. This aim is becoming more widespread, and it is not unusual, as we have just seen, for advertisements to be based on this theme. What is noticeable is that not all companies who advertise like this manage to put it into practice. It is, however, a step in the right direction.

I have suggested that the concept of Total Quality Management requires singularity of purpose in this area. This necessarily applies to all those in the company, and as such requires considerable efforts of motivation. One way to achieve this is for all people in the company to undergo some form of **training** which makes clear to them the importance of their own job in relation to the end product(s) and the customer. Hiring people with appropriate levels of education is a start. Such people will already have the ability to grasp the importance of new ideas, be more able to learn and be better at their job as well. In the UK the education of workers at all levels seems to be somewhat lower than our European, USA, or Japanese counterparts, and this is at last being recognised by UK management.

All new staff should have a short **induction period** in which they are able to learn more about the company – and, more important, how their own job contributes to the final product or service. Every person and department should see themselves united in the effort to satisfy the customer. They must recognise that they are an **internal customer and supplier**. This is more likely to be achieved if supervisory and higher levels of management do not see themselves engaged in a guerrilla war of personal and departmental survival. Short training courses in TQM may be very useful.

The Personnel department, in conjunction with each person's own supervisor, should plan a programme of training for them amounting to perhaps the equivalent of four or five days each year. Such training should be directed to helping the employee do their job better. It has never been a satisfactory situation that when a person joins a company they are seated next to a long-serving employee to pick up 'the essentials'. All that ever gets picked up is that employee's idea of what the job does and does not entail, plus a lifetime's accumulation of their prejudices.

Mutual solving of current problems in a department plays an important part in forming a departmental team with a common interest. Solutions found by people who actually have to implement them are as useful as those found by professional problem solvers (e.g. those in Management Services). Anyone who has to solve a problem will do well to listen to those who do the work. Much publicity has been accorded to **Quality Circles** as a means of achieving results, and no doubt they help. The important thing is not the title, but the fact that an opportunity has been found for people to come together with a common purpose, the good of the company. You can therefore have any type of circle you wish – an Inventory Circle, for example.

Suggestion schemes where employees reap some of the total benefit accruing to the company when a good suggestion is implemented are a favourite with many companies. They are quite good motivators and tend to enhance an individual's standing in the peer group. Some difficulties may occur in determining the size of the payout, and whether to pay for an idea which is good in principle but may be expensive to implement. Such schemes require careful management but can give good results, provided they are always kept viable. Once suggestion schemes have been relegated to one or two grubby boxes, and no one is certain if are being used or not, their effectiveness is minimal.

For many years, **quality scoreboards** have been used to inform everyone in a company as to what the current levels of quality costs are. They may inform by section, department, division and company. Such information may relate to total costs or costs within categories, which we will look at later. They may include information regarding absolute costs, costs as a percentage of revenue or profit, or as quantities of items lost, or as percentages of defects generated. In all cases, such information must be used in a competitive but positive manner, designed yet again to enhance the spirit of total quality management. It must not be used to score points at the expense of other sections. Such information must indicate **trends** to be useful, and a nominal prize may be given for 'this month's best department.

Activity

What parameters could be measured to provide an indication of service and quality, in:

(a) a garage, **(b)** an airport, **(c)** a hospital, **(d)** a college, **(e)** a restaurant, **(f)** a hotel or motel, **(g)** a bank, **(h)** an estate agent, **(i)** a supermarket, **(j)** a bus service, **(k)** a railway station, **(l)** a theatre, **(m)** a sports complex?

2.4 Quality Assurance (QA)

TQM is the overall quality ethos that should pervade any company which purports to be interested in quality. But that in itself is not enough. Under that whole umbrella and embraced by it is the concept of 'quality assurance'. QA is concerned with all the procedural aspects of what it takes to **assure the quality** of the product. It is therefore concerned with ensuring that **systems** are designed so that it can be seen by customers that a company so organised is exerting effective control over its quality on a continuing basis: in other words, that the company has installed a proper quality system.

(a) **The quality system**

The prime standard to be followed in this case is British Standard 5750: 1993 (ISO 9000: 1993). This provides for the assurance of quality at three basic levels:

- specifying the quality system when the requirements of material or service have been quoted in terms of required performance rather than for the design itself;
- similar to above but when the design has been established; and
- when conformance to specifications can be established by inspection and tests on finished material and services.

   This standard therefore enables a company to establish, document and maintain an effective and economical quality system. The implementation of such a system is a major exercise, and one person must be given the responsibility for co-ordinating it. Similarly, once all the key functions affecting quality have been identified, one person must be solely responsible for managing (i.e. **monitoring** and **controlling** the system). From time to time, the working of the system must be assessed, and improved where found deficient.

   Typically, the system must include aspects such as design and development, manufacturing or subcontracting, clear specifications and work drawings, calibration and test records of equipment, prompt and effective corrective action, control of reliability, and the use of feedback of defective item data and final inspection and test, including sampling. There are organisations who will confirm (or otherwise) that a particular company has a quality control system which conforms to BS 5750. This may be used by potential customers in their evaluation of how well that company is likely to perform as a supplier.

(b) **The three key factors of quality**

Above, I mentioned 'conformance', an unusual term outside a quality environment. Before defining it, let us look more closely at what the three key factors of quality are:

- quality of **design**
- quality of **conformance**
- **reliability**.

'Reliability' is how well the product performs to specification over a given period of time. It is a function of design and conformance, and is covered in Chapter 3.

(i) Quality of design

By 'quality of design' we mean that the design itself is the result of close collaboration between the **provider** of the product and the **end user**. We are confident that the design (on paper or in the computer) meets, as closely as possible, the needs of the customer. If it does, all is well so far. For example, BR brought out its Pacer trains in 1983; four years later there were serious problems with failing gearboxes, cracked wheels, leaky roofs and uncertain door operation. Subsequently, it was felt the problems stemmed from the basic design which provided for reduced costs for lightly loaded routes. The carriages had two axles instead of four; this feature also caused wheel wear. Balancing holes in the wheels began to result in cracking, when the balancing was really intended to have improved the ride.

(ii) Quality of conformance

Quality of conformance is the closeness with which the specifications of the designs are put into practice. If the design is good and the quality of conformance is high then all should be well. On the other hand, however well you conform to a poor specification you are not going to be able to satisfy the customer. For BR, no matter how closely manufacture conformed to the specification, the customer did not get a quality product and service.

(iii) Reliability

As reliability is a function of both the inherent quality of design and the actual quality of design, the trains referred to provided an unreliable service – 'reliability' being defined as trouble-free, on-time service for the customer.

Case Study: The Plant and Pick Garden Co. (PPG) – Episode 2

Ms Lewise must have a fundamental think about TQM before going any further. She must decide how she will communicate the fundamental change in attitude from apparently an inspection orientated company to one with a TQM philosophy. Having instigated such a change, she will begin to see what is involved in a quality assurance approach. Among other factors to be considered will be those of costs. She will need to know the **extent** and **source** of costs associated with poor quality. Once obtained, these can be analysed period by period by department, by person, by machine, or by supplier. **Trends** can therefore be established and monitored so that the results of **corrective action** can be seen.

Upon further questioning, the £60,000 of quality costs were made up of scrapped parts or product. PPG being a reputable company, it always honoured its warranties; if there was any doubt whether a product was still under warranty or not, PPG erred on the side of the customer.

2.5 **The Costs of Quality**

Some quality costs are associated only with **inadequate** quality. If a part is produced right the first time, these costs vanish. Such costs, if not subject to close control, can be a substantial percentage of turnover (easily as much as 15%). If they are reduced or eliminated, then the money saved goes straight to increase profits. Sensibly, then, we can say to everyone regardless of their job, that **'Do it right first time'** should be your motto. We can differentiate four areas of such costs:

(a) **Internal costs**

These are costs associated with quality failures **inside the company**. They will include the costs of scrap and rework during production. If a batch of 50 items is to be produced but 52 sets have to be issued initially, then there is a 3.8% scrap rate. If, however, during production of 25 lawnmowers, two body shells need to have the dents removed from them because they were dropped during the process, then the cost of repairing them is known as rework and will include the cost of labour and materials to achieve this.

Rework costs must be recorded separately from, but be ultimately relatable to, the cost of **normal production** of the batch in question. In this way the analysis of such rework and subsequent corrective action will, it is hoped, lead to an elimination of that cost. Before rework begins, a decision about the rejected material must be made by an engineer, so that such rework follows an authorised sequence. A different **account number** from that assigned to the normal batch must be opened to collect all rework charges.

PPG had good records of scrap costs, because they had to hand over a material request note to stores before they could get a replacement part. The note then went to accounts to be costed. No records were available for rework time. One or two of the more skilled production people worked the repair backlog off as and when they could, during their regular production work.

(b) **External costs**

These are the costs of the product failing **after it has been shipped** to the customer. It is vital to try to eliminate them because they worsen the profit picture and damage the company's reputation. When a product fails in service, it also causes some expense to the customer in terms of down time, loss of continuity of work flow and possible rescheduling of other work.

Careful records of such failures in service must be kept so that when analysis of that data is made a picture of **likely cause** can be built up and corrective action be taken. Perhaps the product reached the customer in an unsatisfactory condition; perhaps it was received damaged. In that case, are there any clues as to why? The means of **transportation** should be examined. Where was the product **stored** before shipment and upon arrival? Was the outer and/or inner **packaging damaged?** Did the product appear to have been correctly **packed?**

If the product has been **used**, then it will be important to discover if the product was being used for the purpose intended, how old the product was, did the customer receive any training in its use, and did they know how to carry out simple maintenance? Did the product fail while actually being used, or did it not start as it was supposed to? Was the product being overloaded at the time it failed? Did the performance seem to deteriorate and then fail, or did it work properly and fail suddenly? Is the product still under warranty?

When repairs are made, whether permanent or temporary, a record should be made of the parts which appear to be faulty and these must be returned to the factory for subsequent examination by engineers and quality staff. The **time spent** and **replacement part details** must also be recorded so that these costs can form part of the overall costs of external failure and become the target for elimination.

(c) Appraisal costs

These are the costs incurred through the **measuring, evaluation** and **auditing** of raw materials, work in progress and finished goods, as well as the checking and calibration of all the tools and instruments associated with manufacture. Such costs will be incurred in the goods-inwards inspection section, inspection prior to the start of a process and during the process, and inspection at the final stages of production. In some instances, companies have been able to reduce significantly, or even eliminate, costs associated with incoming inspection. They have done this by placing the onus for producing good work clearly on their **suppliers** along with the responsibility for any inspection required. In such cases, material received goes into the company's stores after identification and without any inspection by them. Such an arrangement clearly needs the close co-operation of the supplier. It may not be possible for PPG to achieve this, but a review of their sampling scheme seems necessary, and we will look at what is involved later in this chapter.

(d) Prevention costs

Prevention costs are those incurred in analysing the requirements of designing, installing and maintaining **a total quality system** which meets the company's needs.

A company which spends very little on prevention or has no real quality system, may spend a lot on the costs detailed in sections (a), (b) and (c) above. However, it is not possible to inspect quality into a product. In any case, the product itself is likely to have received some rework during the course of its manufacture. It is better therefore to spend more on a **planned prevention programme** so that the benefits will gradually show themselves as lower costs incurred on internal and external failures and appraisal. Additionally, the products will be produced right the first time. By spending more in the area of prevention, we expect the **total costs** of quality to fall appreciably, and this is one of the features we monitor regularly.

The costs of increasing the ability of a company to meet customers' needs, or provide an increasing level of service offered, or trying to approach closer to perfection, are often shown as increasing very steeply. On this basis, one would never try to upgrade the service level. However, there is no substitute for the completely satisfied customer, and any increasing costs incurred will be more than repaid by increased sales and lower poor-quality costs. There is every reason therefore to continue to chip away at the causes of such costs, remembering that **zero defects** is a worthwhile and reasonable aim.

2.6 Quality Control Techniques

There are nine key techniques available to help control quality during and after production:

(a) Data gathering

Some techniques involve data gathering (i.e. counting OK items and defectives, and measuring dimensions of particular importance).

(b) Histograms

We can use histograms for obtaining a picture based on individual data obtained; histograms show frequency of occurrence against a particular parameter of interest.

(c) Scatter diagrams

We can use scatter diagrams which show data as a series of dots on graph paper, to give us a visual picture prior to deciding how to model the data for subsequent analysis.

(d) Graphs

We can use graphs showing trends in costs, defectives or percentages; these techniques are covered in more detail in Chapter 14.

(e) **Pareto analysis**

In Pareto analysis we get a visual picture of the kind which illustrates that (for example) most of our problems come from a few of our suppliers. In Chapter 5 there is an example of Pareto analysis in stock control. Similar logic can be applied in many other areas of business, such as in quality control here.

(f) **Statistical process control**

This uses data from measurements taken on an important process. From this data, estimates of its **variability** are made and statistically derived limits are established. Therefore, if subsequent data is plotted which fails outside those limits, it has a known probability of doing so. The limits are chosen to allow this to happen on suitably rare occasions (e.g. 1 in 25 or 1 in 100). As the process continues, and more plots are made, it becomes possible to determine whether the process is becoming more variable, or whether the fluctuations are occurring by chance and so may be ignored for the time being. We examine how this is done in more detail in Chapter 15. Statistical process control is not confined to manufacturing, and can be successfully applied in service industries.

Fig 2.3   A cause–effect chart (fishbone diagram)

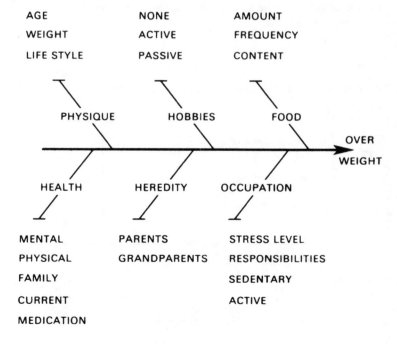

(g) Cause and effect diagrams

The cause and effect diagram is also known as an **Ishikawa diagram**, after the person who popularised its use. It is a pictorial method of showing, in a logical sequence, the possible causes of various effects relating to different aspects of processes in making a product. Figure 2.3 shows the arrangement of some causes of being overweight. The outcome is the right hand side of the diagram, and the 'fishbones' lead in at various points. They are the key factors. At the end of each fishbone are other variables, each of which may contribute to a particular factor.

Such a diagram is merely an orderly representation of all the processes involved, in much the same way that a flow process chart shows pictorially the operations involved, when carrying out a method study analysis (see Chapter 9). Such a chart does not imply true cause-and-effect relationships by itself: rather, it indicates **possible inputs** and **associated effects**. True cause and effects will have to be established by careful experimentation.

(h) Multi-vari charts

A multi-vari chart is a convenient way to show graphically the variation **within** and **between samples taken of a process** while it is being done. The samples are taken at intervals during production, and the range of the measurements of a particular activity is shown as a vertical line on the chart. Figure 2.4 shows that the process is inherently too variable at present to produce a product with the key dimension inside required limits, no matter how the process is adjusted.

Fig 2.4   A process with too much inherent variation

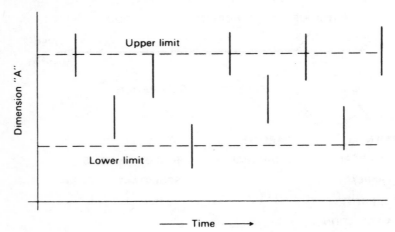

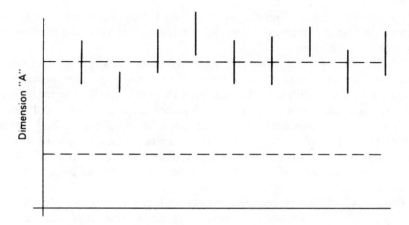

Fig 2.5   A process set too high

Figure 2.5 shows that the inherent variability of the process is such that the process will not produce rejects provided the process is adjusted to produce an **average dimension** closer to the nominal dimension on the drawing.

Both the charts in Figures 2.4 and 2.5 show the range of measurements when taking samples of five rods at a time every 15 minutes, and measuring a key dimension, e.g. the length. The specification may state that it should be 25.00 mm ± 0.01 mm. Sometimes the average of each sample is marked as a dot on the vertical line for that sample.

(i) Taguchi methods

Genichi Taguchi was an engineer with the Nippon Telephone and Telegraph company in the 1950s. He developed numerical methods to approach quality engineering problems which concerned off line quality control in areas of planning, research and development, design research and production engineering.

(i) The definition of quality

Taguchi defined quality in an unusual way. He saw quality as the losses caused after shipment of a product by the variability of function, and by harmful side effects excluding any losses caused by the product's intrinsic function. For example, harmful side effects often existed when using powerful medicine; similarly, the exhaust gases of car engine combustion were known to be noxious. An example of variability of function of a cross-channel hovercraft service, would be that service was often suspended when the sea was rough, not something that happens to normal cross-channel ferries. Taguchi said he used this definition of quality because he wanted to avoid the subjective concept of value inherent in the more usual definition.

Quality control is not, however, about reducing the loss a product might inflict on society through its inherent functions (e.g. non-intoxicating alcohol would be a different product, even though drunks cause accidents); similarly, a cricket ball must be hard by specification and not soft, even though batsmen sometimes get injured when hit by a cricket ball. Better quality means providing the same utility to the consumer, with less loss (e.g. ensuring that clothes do not wrinkle badly when worn and that their colours do not run when washed). People buy a product when the price is less or equal to its utility – i.e. what it can provide.

Taguchi distinguishes between **variety** and **quality** (e.g. service life is a quality problem, but colour range is variety). The flavour of an unusual food may be variety, but the taste of half-cooked potatoes is a quality problem.

(ii) Quantitative methods
Taguchi developed quantitative methods designed to decide on standard sizes (of shirts, for example) which produced manufacturing savings, but balanced them against the deviation from optimum size for any specific customer, so that the loss due to the failure to get the exact size was small. This is a problem of **size tolerance**, and Taguchi determined at what deviation from true size a customer would refuse to buy the product because he could find a shirt with a good fit.

Such methods involve including costs in the optimal setting of tolerances by design departments, such tolerances then being passed to the production department as specifications. The processes involved must be capable of producing material to these specifications. This design process includes system design where the appropriate process is chosen; parameter design where optimum working conditions are decided including materials and parts to buy; and tolerance design where tolerances of the process conditions and sources of variability are set so as to reduce quality variation by eliminating its cause.

2.7 Acceptance Sampling Schemes

An acceptance sampling scheme uses statistical techniques to make decisions about a batch of 'goods', based on information obtained from a sample taken from that batch.

(a) Use of sampling schemes

The most common kind of decision in sampling schemes is to decide whether or not to accept a batch, based on results from a **sample**. Sampling schemes are used because they save time; it is not necessary to inspect every item in a batch to make a decision. However, you cannot get something for nothing. Sometimes you will accept the batch when it should have been rejected, and sometimes you will reject the batch when it should have been accepted. You are **taking a risk** when you sample, and you must know what the risk is. We will develop a simple sampling scheme to illustrate the key principles involved, but first we must look at some definitions of terms used in sampling.

(b) Terms used in sampling

Sampling schemes such as these tend to concentrate on sorting the good from the bad. They deal with **what has already happened**. They can make a useful contribution to quality improvement when the resultant information is fed back to the supplier and appropriate corrective action is taken. Acceptance sampling schemes do not operate in real time, as do the statistical process control methods discussed in Chapter 15.

- The **consumer's risk** is the risk you take that inadvertently you have accepted a batch which should have been rejected. This was because you drew an optimistic sample.
- The **supplier's risk** is the risk a supplier takes that a good batch will be rejected by the results of a pessimistic sample.
- **Acceptable quality level (AQL)** is the highest percentage of defectives which you consider as being acceptable.

Fig 2.6   An operating characteristic

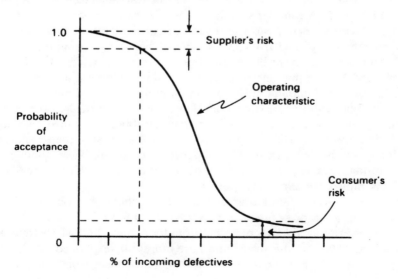

- The **lot tolerance percentage of defectives (LTPD)** is that level at which you want a very low probability of acceptance, as this percentage of defectives is unacceptably high. Although we need this definition, it rather conflicts with an overall policy of continual improvement: it suggests that there is a level of rejects we can live with.
- The **operating characteristic** of a sampling scheme is the curve from which you can read the probability of acceptance for various incoming percentages of defectives.

Figure 2.6 shows all these terms on a graph which includes the operating characteristic for a scheme. Note that it can never be vertical and completely discriminate between percentages of defects above and below the AQL. By varying the sample size and the number of defectives upon which we base our decision, we can, however, alter its slope.

Before we develop a simple scheme, let us describe the scheme the PPG company uses on their spindles.

PPG's Sampling Scheme

Take a random sample of 100 items from the batch. Inspect each item in the sample and decide whether it is acceptable or a reject. If there are 5 or fewer rejects, accept the entire batch. If there are 6 or more rejects, reject the entire batch.

(c) Discrimination in the scheme

What we need to know is how well the scheme **discriminates** between good and bad batches. A random sample means that every spindle has an equal chance of being chosen. Note also that the decision about the batch is made with information gained from the sample. Other things being equal, it is more economical to have bigger batches than smaller batches for a given sample size, but we must never intentionally interfere with batches merely for convenience. Sampling must be very carefully done, so that the results are truly representative of the batch. Sampling may be **random** (i.e. taken from anywhere in the batch) or it may be **stratified**. Stratified sampling involves choosing particular portions of the batch and then sampling randomly within those areas. This is particularly useful where goods may settle during travel (e.g. flour or grain delivered in bulk). Office work is also readily sampled, for similar purposes.

To develop the operating characteristic of the scheme, we use the Poisson distribution, a graph of which is shown in Figure 2.7. The Poisson distribution is applicable where we have random events, and where we **count** rejects. The details of this distribution are more fully explained in Chapter 14. When using the Poisson distribution we do not take into account the size

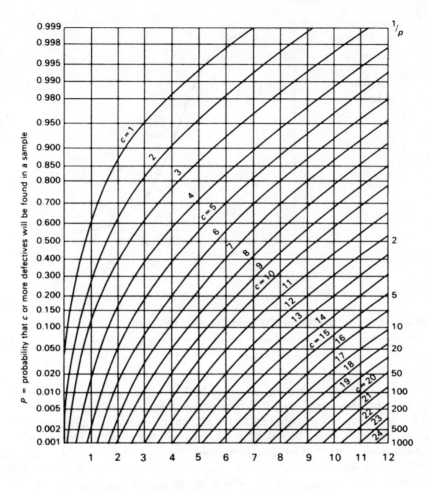

Fig 2.7 Poisson chart

of the batch, but where this is big compared to the sample size, no practical problem occurs.

The horizontal axis of the graph shows the average number a' of occurrences expected – in this case, rejects expected. The curved lines show values $c = 1$ reject, $c = 2$ rejects, $c = 3$ rejects, etc. The left-hand vertical axis shows the probability of getting $c = 1$, $c = 2$ rejects, etc. We can use this information to develop the operating characteristic.

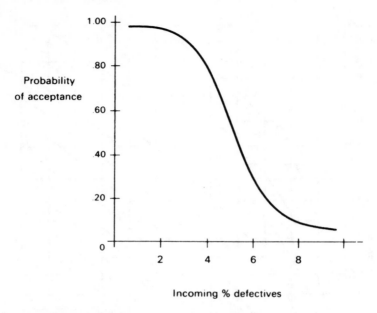

Incoming % defectives

Fig 2.8   Precise operating characteristic for PPG Co.

To develop the operating characteristic, we will assume that spindles arrive in batches containing different percentages of defectives.

Suppose batches of spindles arrive with a 1.5% level of defectives. We would expect to find $100 \times 0.015 = 1.5$ defective spindles on average in our sample. Using the Poisson graph we look vertically up from the x axis at $a = 1.5$, and see where the curved line $c = 6$ crosses it. $c = 6$ corresponds to the 6 or more criterion at which we reject the batch based on our sample results. At that point, we read off the probability of that occurrence, from the left-hand vertical scale. This is the probability of rejecting in the long term batches which arrive with 1.5% defectives. From the graph, this probability is 0.003. The probability of acceptance $= 1.0 - 0.003 = 0.997$.

We can apply the same logic to incoming batches with 2% defectives. The probability of acceptance is now 0.98. Remember that the expected number of defectives in the sample will be $100 \times 0.02 = 2$.

Similarly, we can find the probability of acceptance for incoming percentage defective rates of 3%, 4%, 5%, 6%, 7% and 8%. For practical reasons we have not considered incoming defective rates above 8%, although we could if we wished. These probabilities are 0.90, 0.78, 0.60, 0.43, 0.29 and 0.18. Figure 2.8 shows the exact operating characteristic for this scheme. From looking at this scheme we can see that about 18% of incoming batches, i.e. 1 in 5 or 6, will be accepted by this scheme, although it is very good when incoming defectives are at a low level. No wonder PPG have problems.

As we have said, we cannot get something for nothing when sampling; intuition may suggest that if we increase our sample size that may help.

Activity

Repeat the calculations above, but use new sample sizes of 150 and 200 items instead of 100. Also use acceptance numbers of 2, 4 and 7. Draw each of the curves and see the difference between them. Would this be more suitable for PPG's current problem?

Activity

Draw the operating characteristic for the following sampling scheme. Sample size = 50 units. Reject the batch if 4 or more rejects are found in the sample. How does this compare with the same scheme but if you reject the batch if 2 or more rejects are found in the sample? Graph your results for a range of incoming percentage rejects of zero to 20%. Interpret the results in terms of their effectiveness if incoming reject percentage is actually (a) 2%, and (b) 8%.

2.8 Average Outgoing Quality Level (AOQL)

It is important to know how the level of rejects in the stores may vary as a result of the acceptances and rejections of incoming batches according to a particular sampling scheme. Assume that if any batches are rejected, they are inspected 100% and all rejects are replaced with good items, and they are accepted into the stores. We assume here that 100% inspection is 100% effective, which it really is not. We also assume that any items rejected in the sample taken are replaced with good items.

The level of rejects in your stores will be made up of a combination of batches which got through because they were accepted by the sample, and batches which were rejected by the sample and received 100% screening before acceptance. Such batches are virtually reject free. We will also assume that the batch is very big compared to the sample – say, at least 10 times bigger. Hence we can say that the percentage of rejects in your stores of items subject to acceptance sampling will be:

The probability of acceptance of a batch × the level of rejects in that batch (all rejected batches will he virtually error free by definition) = Potential level of rejects in your stores for that item

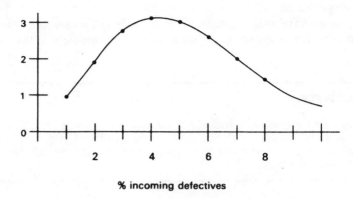

Fig 2.9   Average outgoing quality level

In PPG's original scheme we have:

% rejects incoming	Probability of acceptance	% rejects outgoing
1.5	0.997	1.50
2	0.98	1.96
3	0.90	2.70
4	0.78	3.12
5	0.60	3.00
6	0.43	2.58
7	0.29	2.03
8	0.18	1.44

Figure 2.9 shows the average outgoing level curve, which you can see peaks at 3.12%, which is more than 1% point more than PPG's AQL.

Activity

Each person in the class counts how often the letter E (upper or lower case) occurs on two pages of this book. They do this once only and write the result on a piece of paper without telling anyone their count. The lecturer then writes the counts from the class on the board. Was 100% inspection 100% effective? If not, why not? What is the true count? How variable were the results? Were any two the same? What have you learned?

2.9 The Relative Costs of Inspection

We can identify three different cost situations:

1 when **no inspection** is done at all
2 when **every item** in each batch is inspected **100%**
3 when sampling is conducted **as each batch arrives**

Let us summarise the costs and quantities in the PPG case.

N $= 1500$ $=$ size of the incoming batches
n $= 100$ $=$ size of the sample taken
A $= £5.00$ $=$ cost if a defective spindle slips through onto an assembly
I $= £0.05$ $=$ cost when sampling to inspect one spindle
p $= 8\%$ $=$ percentage defectives in incoming batches
$p(acc) = 0.18$ $=$ probability of accepting a batch as bad as this
         (as calculated above for the operating characteristic).

1 Costs if **no inspection** carried out are simply the cost of a defective spindle finding its way into an assembly × the number of such spindles

$$= A \times N \times p$$
$$= £5.00 \times 1500 \times 0.08 = £600.00$$

2 Costs if every item in a batch is inspected are the cost of inspecting one spindle × the number of defective spindles there are:

$$= N \times £I$$
$$= 1500 \times £.05$$
$$= £75$$

3 Costs when sampling as each batch arrives are a combination of costs when defectives get through to an assembly, because a batch was accepted by its sample, plus the costs of inspecting some of the batches 100% because the sampling scheme rejected them:

$= (n \times I)$ $+$ $\{p(acc) \times (N - n) \times p \times A\}$ $+$ $\{(1 - p(acc)) \times (N - n) \times £I\}$
$= (100 \times £0.05) + \{0.18 \times (1500 - 100) \times 0.08 \times £5\} + \{(1 - 0.18) \times 1500 - 100) \times £0.05)\}$
$= £5$ $+$ £100.80 $+$ £57.4
$= £163.20$

Activity

Calculate the long-term costs of sampling if the incoming batches are 2% defective. (*Hint*: note that the operating characteristic for the current scheme gives a probability of acceptance of 0.98.)

Chapter Review Questions

1 What is value analysis called if conducted at the design stage?
2 What must not be affected by value analysis in the quest for better value?
3 Identify three different values of a product.
4 What is the exchange value of a product?
5 How should value analysis be implemented?
6 What is 'brainstorming' and when is it used?
7 'Total quality management implies total product control': True or False?
8 Define the term 'quality' and its two key components.
9 What are the six main costs of quality?
10 Which area of cost is usually increased in a quality programme?
11 What is an Ishikawa diagram?
12 'A multi-vari chart usually monitors rework costs': True or False?
13 How does Taguchi define quality?
14 What is meant by the producer's risk and the consumer's risk?
15 'The operating characteristic shows the probability of accepting batches of differing incoming percentage defectives': True or False?
16 What does 'average outgoing quality' refer to?
17 'It always costs more to sample than to do no inspection at all': True or False?

3 Reliability

In Chapter 2 we examined quality and its characteristics, and noted two key components: quality of design and quality of conformance. Inextricably bound up with both of them is a third component, that of **reliability**. Reliability is the ability of the product to perform to the required standard of **performance** under the specified **conditions**, for the required period of **time**. If either the degree of design or conformance falls below what is really required, a products reliability will be jeopardised.

In Chapter 3 we look at the need for reliability, different models of failure, and how to increase levels of reliability in simple systems.

Learning Objectives

By the end of this chapter you should:
1 be able to recognise different types of **failure modes**
2 be able to calculate the **mean time to failure** for a grouped set of data.
3 be able to **analyse a set of grouped data** for a product exhibiting wear characteristics
4 be able to calculate **system reliability** for simple systems comprising series and/or parallel connected elements.

3.1 What is 'Reliability'?

Every customer needs the product to be reliable so as to satisfy completely the purpose for which that product was bought. A good-looking and economical car is unsatisfactory if it does not start consistently. An inexpensive copier is no bargain if sometimes it produces dark copies and sometimes light ones for no apparent reason. A train or bus service which does not run to time, or suffers from irregular or reduced levels of service, is unreliable. It follows that assuring the reliability of a product is very important: without doubt, sales will be adversely affected if reliability is below a customer's expectations.

63

Reliability may be partially assessed in products which are not yet in full production, and this can be useful if the phase of maturity is clearly stated (e.g. the product is a design prototype, preproduction, or ready for field tests). The length of the test period must also be stated, and in this context the units of the length of test can be replaced by distance, cycles, revolutions or other appropriate units indicating duration.

Case Study: Key Systems Ltd

Larry Lomax runs a small but thriving business as a subcontractor designing and making electronic assemblies for MegaCorp International, a Ministry of Defence major supplier. Some of his products include a complex sensor system which enables a preprogrammed set of actions to be initiated if there are any significant changes to preset levels in the environment relating to movement, pressure, temperature or ambient light. Another successful product is a programmable rotary switch. A virtually unlimited sequence of preset contacts can be made to initiate action in any piece of equipment that is designed to respond to a signal voltage of a very low level. A bread-and-butter line are relays which actuate timers. These come in many different sizes and load-carrying versions, and new ones are always being developed.

3.2 Failure

'Failure' can be classified conveniently into the **cause**, the **mode** and the actual **mechanism** of the failure itself. Failure can be sudden, gradual, partial, intermittent or complete.

- A sudden failure occurs when a camshaft belt breaks or a big end breaks on a car. The driver is in no doubt that a sudden failure of something has occurred.
- A gradual failure may occur when the wear on the steering wheel is sufficiently great so that it is virtually impossible to steer without many compensating turns as the car veers to one side or the other.
- There may be a partial failure of the braking system if one hydraulic line springs a leak, so that braking is limited to the opposite diagonal wheels. When a precision machine tool begins to wear out, so that it becomes increasingly difficult to maintain the expected tolerances on work, then we would suggest gradual or partial failure.
- An intermittent failure in the electric system of a car may show itself as lights which go on and off every time the car goes over a bump in the road.
- Complete failure occurs when so many functions of the product cease to work that the product is useless. When a car doing 30 mph has brake failure, a seized-up engine and four flat tyres, everyone would call such a failure catastrophic.

Different failure rates (and it is important to notice the word 'rates') may also be detected over three fairly recognisable stages of a product's life:

- the very early life period showing **decreasing** failure rates
- the mid-life period showing a somewhat **constant** failure rate
- the end of a product's life showing a **rising** failure rate.

Such periods are often shown conceptually for the whole life of a system, as in Figure 3.1.

The 'bathtub curve' shape does not necessarily apply to all electronic products, and is not in itself a mathematical model. The test results shown in the examples which follow are snapshots of the performance of the product at a particular point in its life.

The very early life period indicates a decreasing failure rate as design faults are corrected and components are replaced. A feature of such systems is that items commonly either fail early or have a full life; they are less likely to have an intermediate life.

Fig 3.1   A bathtub curve

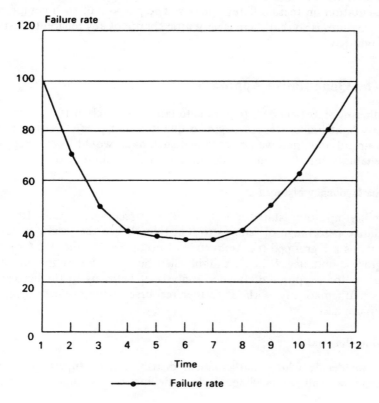

Time

Failure rate

The mid-life period suggests that in maintained systems after the ages of renewable corrupt parts have become randomised, irrespective of time to failure of individual components, the system will have a nearly constant rate of failure. This will apply if failures are independent of each other.

The end of a product's life suggests that long life components are wearing out and not being maintained, or that non-maintainable components begin to fail.

A **reliability programme** will help to ensure (as a measure of quality) that adequate effective effort is brought to bear on reliability throughout the entire life of an item from pre-design definition through to the end of its working life. This will extend from design through development, production, installation, commissioning, functioning and maintenance. No analysis can be performed without meticulous data gathering, and it is essential that all the details of performance and environment be recorded.

Even more important is the careful specification for reliability that is required for an item being designed. Such specifications may sometimes be a simple statement of such requirements. Often a more comprehensive document is required for each stage in the item's development, from target specification, function, product and materials specification, through to installation, use and maintenance. BS 5760: 1: 1993 has comprehensive documentation on these different phases. The purpose of such comprehensive procedures is so that there is very little chance of key reliability features being omitted.

3.3 **The Quantitative Approach**

By gathering statistical data (e.g. time to failure for each of 100 special high intensity light bulbs) we can begin to quantify and predict certain results which up till now, had we not obtained such data, would have meant that our reliability specifications would have been unsubstantiated.

(a) **The frequency histogram**

Reliability up to a stated duration as a percentage, equals 100 − the cumulative percentage of failures to that time. When the results of testing those items are grouped (i.e. frequency of occurrence vs time), a **frequency histogram** is obtained. When a suitable distribution is superimposed on the histogram for purposes of further analysis, it helps us to predict certain results mathematically, without further recourse to the original histogram (see Figure 3.2).

(b) **Modelling data**

When we decide which mathematical distribution to superimpose on a histogram we call it **modelling**. Such modelling is very important because

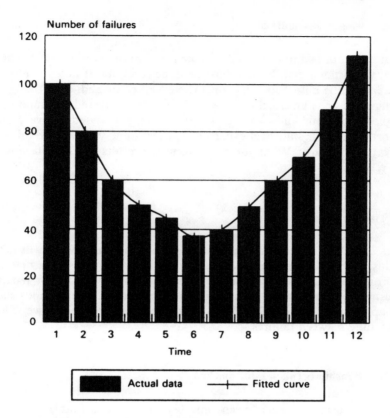

Fig 3.2   Fitting a curve to a histogram

we can calculate results relatively simply, and predict what such results will be if we change certain parameters of the model. A model is a concise way to handle data, and when a lifelike model is chosen, the numerical results will be meaningful. Experimentation becomes much easier.

The area under a distribution is always made equal to **unity**. This ensures that the sum of all the probabilities involved will also equal unity: this is an essential feature of probability. There are convenient measures for the parameters of these distributions which identify their important characteristics. The most common such parameters are the **mean** and **standard deviation**. The mean is the arithmetic average, and the standard deviation indicates the spread of the data about the mean. The standard deviation has several convenient properties which relate how much of the data we can expect to find within multiples of the standard deviation about the mean.

(c) **Choosing a distribution**

What must not be forgotten is that there are a lot of distributions to choose from. Choosing a distribution must be done carefully. If not, the resulting answers will be unrealistic and conclusions will be invalid, even though the calculations are numerically correct. Your judgement and common sense, coupled with your knowledge of the items being analysed, is every bit as important as your statistical expertise. The last thing you want to do is just to play with figures. What you really want are results and conclusions you can rely on.

(d) **Time to failure**

Time to failure is a useful measure when the items under test will not be readily accessible for maintenance, or may be used in a severe operating environment, but if the equipment is fairly readily available for repair or adjustment, time between failures is more appropriate. The methods shown can apply to either situation. In the simplified situation below, we will use mean time between failures.

(e) **Relationship between mtbf and fr**

The relationship between **mean time between failures (mtbf)** and **failure rate (fr)** is that $fr = 1/mtbf$ and $mtbf = 1/fr$. A dot matrix printer might have a stated mtbf of 5,000,000 lines. The corresponding failure rate is therefore 1/5,000,000. A computer disc drive may have a stated mtbf of 20,000 hours, in which case the failure rate is 0.00005 disc drives per hour.

To illustrate the relationship between **mtbf** and **fr**, let us consider the following simplified situation. It is worth noting that numerically there is no difference between testing 10 units for 100 hours, and testing 1000 units for 1 hour. In real life, however, there is a great deal of difference. In the first situation, 10 units may not be a very big sample, but the length of the test may well be adequate. In the second situation, 1000 units is a very large sample, but the length of the test is probably unrealistic regarding the length of time we should expect the units to last. Careful testing, with due regard for sample size and test duration, will result in customers ultimately getting products which closely match their expectations and needs.

Ten items are put on test for a maximum of 100 hours, at which point the test is terminated. The results are shown below, and the items failed at the hours stated.

Hours on test	Quantity at start of period	Results at end of period	Failure rate in units per hour
20	10	1 fails	$1/(10 \times 20)$ $= 0.0050$
40	9	1 fails	$1/(9 \times 40)$ $= 0.0028$
70	8	1 fails	$1/(8 \times 70)$ $= 0.0018$
90	7	1 fails	$1/(7 \times 90)$ $= 0.0016$
100	6	0 fail	0

- **Calculating the failure rate (fr) first:**
  The overall failure rate is

The number of units failed divided by [(the sum of each failure multiplied by the hours at which it failed) plus (the number of units which survived multiplied by the maximum length of the test)].

We therefore have:

$$4/[(l \times 20 + 1 \times 40 + 1 \times 70 + 1 \times 90 + (6 \times 100)]$$

$$= 4/820$$

$$= 0.0049 \text{ units per hour}$$

Mean time between failures is therefore $820/4 = 205$ hours.

- **Calculating the mean time between failures (mtbf) first:**

The mtbf is the total hours of the survivors divided by the number of units which failed.

We therefore have:

$$[10 \times (20 - 0) + 9 \times (40 - 20) + 8 \times (70 - 40) + 7 \times (90 - 70) + 6$$
$$\times (100 - 90)]/4 = 820/4$$

$$= 205 \text{ hours mtbf.}$$

Failure rate is therefore

$$4/820 = 0.0049 \text{ units per hour.}$$

In the context of reliability, the term **hazard** is defined as the ratio of failures during a period divided by the survivors at the start of that period. The **hazard rate** is the instantaneous failure $z(t)$, and is the hazard per unit time. In our examples we have made all the time periods one unit wide, so the failure rates in Figures 3.4 and 3.9 are assumed to be the same as $z(t)$.

Example 1

A quality control analyst put 200 Key Systems' sensor systems on to test for a maximum of 100 hours. He then recorded the time to failure for each one. The results have been summarised and given to you for analysis. Notice that you do not have the precise time at which each sensor failed, but only the results as shown in the table that follows.

Hours on test/10	Quantity at start	Quantity failed	Quantity at end	Quantity removed from test
1	200	20	180	–
2	180	18	162	–
3	162	16	146	–
4	146	15	131	–
5	131	13	118	–
6	118	12	106	–
7	106	11	95	–
8	95	10	85	–
9	85	9	76	–
10	76	8	68	68

Calculate the **mean** (i.e. the average) and the **standard deviation** for the above data, using the tabulated method below. If you are not sure what is meant by the mean or standard deviation, read Chapter 14 first. The next table shows the method for doing this.

$x = hrs/10$	$f = Quantity$ failed	$f \times x$	x^2	$f \times x^2$
1	20	20	1	20
2	18	36	4	72
3	16	48	9	144
4	15	60	16	240
5	13	65	25	325
6	12	72	36	432
7	11	77	49	539
8	10	80	64	640
9	9	81	81	729
10	8	80	100	800
	$\sum f =$ 132	$\sum f \times x =$ 619		$\sum f \times x^2 =$ 3941

The mean $\sum fx / \sum f = 619/132 = 4.69$, but as we worked with hours/10, we must now multiply back by 10, which gives us mean time to failure = 46.9 hours.

Note that this result refers only to the original tabulated failure data. If the test had been open-ended and this pattern had continued, the mean would have more closely matched the theoretical value of the mean time to failure (mttf): see below:

$$\textbf{Standard deviation} = \sqrt{\left[\frac{(\sum (f \times x^2))}{\sum f} - \text{mean}^2\right]}$$

$$= \sqrt{[(3941/132) - 4.69^2]}$$

$$= 2.81$$

But as we worked with hours/10, we must now multiply back by 10, which gives us 28.1 hours. For a complete open-ended test where this existing pattern continued, the standard deviation would match the mean more nearly.

Mean time to failure (mttf) for all items $= \sum (f \times x)$ for all items/quantity that failed. $(f \times x)$ now equals $619 + (68$ items that did not fail $\times 10) -$ i.e. those 68 were still good when taken off test, and this data should not be excluded from this calculation.

$$\text{Mttf for all items} = ((619 + 680)/132) = 9.84$$

$$= 9.84 \times 10 = 98.4 \text{ hours}$$

The **median value** in our tabulated failure rates is that of the middle item when arranged in sequence, and has a value of approximately $3.9 \times 10 = 39$ hours.

The failure histogram is shown in Figure 3.3, and the failure rate per period histogram is shown in Figure 3.4.

From the failure rate histogram in Figure 3.4, we estimate the failure rate at 10% (i.e. 0.1). In reliability jargon, the failure rate $= \lambda = 0.1$, and the mttf $= \Theta = 10$.

Fig 3.3 Failures over time

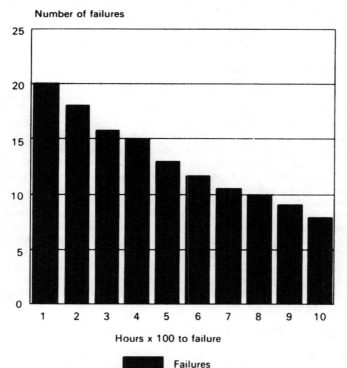

Number of failures

Hours x 100 to failure

■ Failures

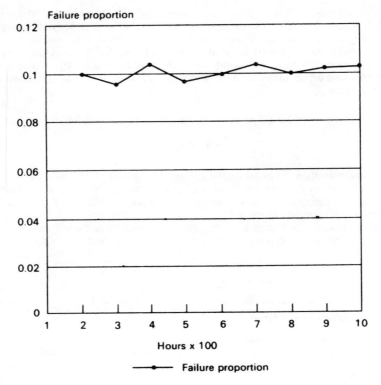

Fig 3.4   **Failures vs survivors**

Now what would the most suitable distribution be, given what we know? Looking at the histogram of failures per period, we notice that the number of failures is high at first, and then gradually decreases. The failure rate per period is fairly constant, although it does rise a little towards the end of the test. This suggests that the negative exponential curve may be appropriate. Our own knowledge of the sensor tells us that failures can be caused by any of the many different components in it. From all this, we feel fairly confident that the negative exponential curve may not only be numerically appropriate, but also realistically so. For this curve, the **standard deviation equals the mean**. In our analysis above, this was not the case, but our histogram is fairly heavily truncated at the right-hand end, as 68 sensors did not fail.

Figure 3.5 shows the relative frequency of the failure histogram, which was obtained by dividing each periods failure by the number in the sample = $n = 200$.

The negative exponential probability density function **pdf** (the area under a specified portion of the curve) is:

$$\textbf{pdf} = \lambda \times \textbf{e}^{-(\lambda \times t)}, \quad \textbf{where e} = \textbf{2.71828}$$

The value of t is the time you are interested in. By using this formula and substituting values for t in tens of hours, you can calculate the probability of

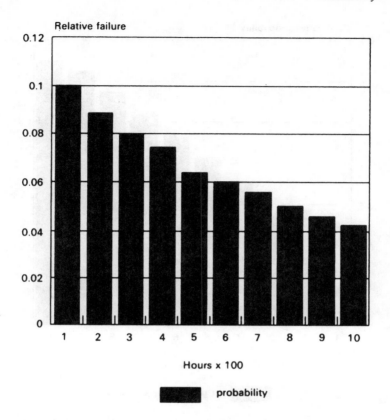

Fig 3.5   Relative failure (= failures/200)

failure in any particular period. Every scientific calculator has an exponential button, and when doing any calculations always remember the basic rules of arithmetic.

Using the formula above, with $\lambda = 0.1$ and $t = 1$, we have:

probability of failure = $0.1 \times e^{[-(0.1 \times 1)]} = 0.091$.

Use the same formula to make sure you obtain the results below, and use other t values.

The probability of failure in the first hour = 0.091; in the second hour, 0.082; in the third hour, 0.074; in the sixth hour, 0.055; in the 10th hour, 0.037. If you compare these theoretical probabilities with those in Figure 3.5, the match appears quite good.

But what about **reliability prediction**? If you draw the cumulative relative failure histogram it looks like Figure 3.6, and the survival histogram is shown in Figure 3.7. Figure 3.6 cumulates the probabilities in Figure 3.5, and Figure 3.7 is 1 − the probabilities in Figure 3.6.

Figure 3.7 shows, for example, that the probability of a sensor surviving to the end of period 5 is 0.59.

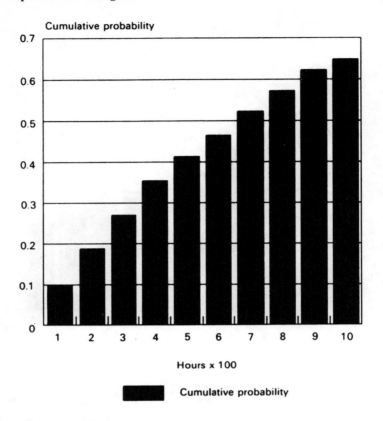

Fig 3.6   Cumulative relative failure

Reliability = probability of survival to the stated number of hours

$$\textbf{Reliability} = \textbf{e}^{-(\lambda \times t)}$$

Using the formula above with $\lambda = 0.1$ and $t = 1$. we have:

$$\text{Reliability} = e^{[-(0.1 \times 1)]} = 0.905$$

Use other values of λ and t to ensure that you can obtain the results below.
Using various values of t in tens in the formula above, we obtain the following results:

Survival to the end of the first hour $= 0.905$
third hour $= 0.740$
fifth hour $= 0.607$
seventh hour $= 0.497$
ninth hour $= 0.407$.

You can see that the theoretical results are fairly close to those in Figure 3.7.

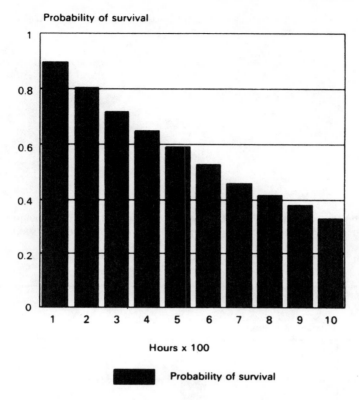

Probability of survival

Hours x 100

■ Probability of survival

Fig 3.7   Reliability (survival)

So using the negative exponential curve, and without referring to your original data because this model incorporates it, you can make various predictions, test them, modify, retest, repredict and so on.

Activity

A hard disk has a mean time between failure of 35,000 hours and a five-year guarantee. It runs 50 hours a week for 52 weeks per year. What is the probability of it surviving to five years?

Example 2

You have put 50 of Key Systems' high-speed programmable rotary switches on to life test. You know from past experience that if anything does go wrong, it is quite likely to be due to wear on the central spindle which then tends to allow unprogrammed switch sequences to occur, thus failing the switch. The summary results are now shown:

Hours on test/100	Quantity at start	Quantity failed	Quantity at end	Quantity removed from test
0–1	50	0	50	–
1–2	50	1	49	–
2–3	49	3	46	–
3–4	46	7	39	–
4–5	39	12	27	–
5–6	27	9	18	–
6–7	18	6	12	–
7–8	12	4	8	–
8–9	8	3	5	–
9–10	5	2	3	3

Omitting the tabulations for calculating the mean and standard deviation (but using the same method and using the mid-points of each interval), we have:

$$\sum f = 47, \qquad \sum f \times x = 205.5, \qquad \sum f \times x^2 = 1497.75.$$

Fig 3.8   A failure histogram

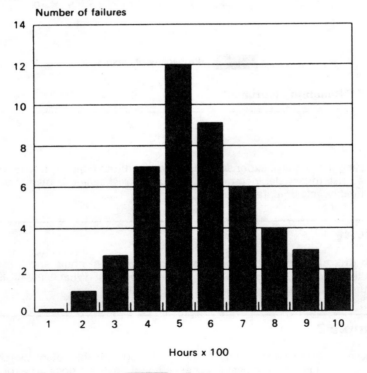

Hours x 100

███ Number failed

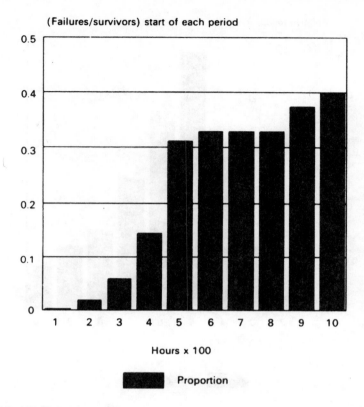

(Failures/survivors) start of each period

Hours x 100

■ Proportion

Fig 3.9   Failure proportion

The mean = 533 hours, the standard deviation = 186 hours, mttf = [250.5 + (3 × 10)] × 100/47 = 597 hours, and the median value = 511 hours.

Figure 3.8 and Figure 3.9 show the failure histogram and failure rate per period histogram respectively.

What model might be the most suitable for what we know about this situation? The failure rate per period certainly is not constant in this set-up, and the failure histogram is fairly symmetrical. The mttf of 597 is not too close to the median value of 511, but our experience of this product means that we know wear is a key cause of failure. From this information we will use the normal distribution as our model for further analysis, even though Figure 3.8 shows that our distribution is not completely symmetrical. We will not expect a very close match between our actual data and our theoretical calculations.

The relative frequency of failure histogram is shown in Figure 3.10.

Because the probability density function for this curve is complicated, we use the values of a standardised form of the normal curve (see Chapter 14) to find the theoretical value for the probability of failures between any two time periods.

What percentage of failures will occur between 300 and 600 hours on test? Our time intervals are of width one time period, and we will use the mid-point

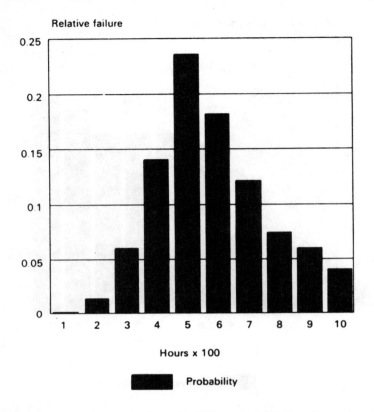

Fig 3.10   Relative failure (= failures/50)

values in our calculations. In this case they are 250 and 650. Let us call each of them *x*.

The standardised value (*sv*) for a given *x*, is:
sv = (*x*-mean)/standard deviation

sv for $250 = (250 - 533)/186 = -1.52$

sv for $650 = (650 - 533)/186 = 0.63$

Using the statistical tables available for the probability density function of the standardised normal curve, the area under the curve between these two points is 0.67 (i.e. 67% will fail in theory as compared with the 56% on our histogram). We have found the shaded area of the curve in Figure 3.11. The same methodology will find you the probability between any other two values in which you are interested.

What about predicting the **reliability at various times**? The cumulative relative failure histogram and the survival histogram are shown in Figures 3.12 and 3.13 respectively.

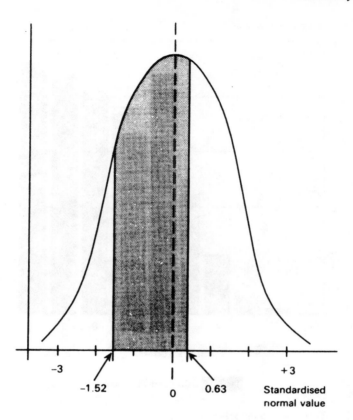

Fig 3.11 A normal curve

Figure 3.13 shows, for example, that:

(a) the probability of a switch surviving 400 hours on test is 0.78 (78% will survive), and

(b) the probability of a switch surviving 800 hours on test is 0.16 (16% of switches will survive; the theoretical probability of survival is given by the area under the curve from the hour in question, up to infinity).

Reliability = probability of survival
= integral of the function from time *t* to infinity

Infinity is at the extreme right-hand side of the curve, and has a standardised value of 3.5 approximately.

For example **(a)**, we use the mid-point 350.

sv for $350 = (350 - 533)/186 = -0.984$. The other *sv* is 3.5. From statistical tables we find the area under the curve to be 0.83 compared with 0.78 in our histogram.

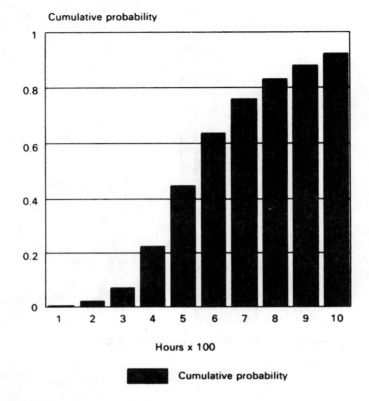

Cumulative probability

Hours x 100

■ Cumulative probability

Fig 3.12   Cumulative relative failure

For example **(b)**, we use the mid-point 850.

sv for $850 = (850 - 533)/186 = 1.704$. The other *sv* is 3.5. From the normal table we find the area under the curve to be 0.044 compared with 0.16 in our histogram. As in Example 1 we can proceed with further similar analysis using the normal curve as above. The more symmetrical the distribution of the actual data is, the better the calculated values will fit the data.

3.4 System Reliability

(a) Elements of the overall system

In many cases, a system consists of several individual elements or subsystems. Each element will have a reliability value of its own which contributes to the **overall system reliability**. As well as the individual

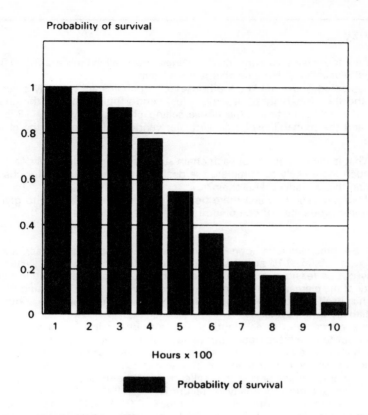

Probability of survival

Hours x 100

■ Probability of survival

Fig 3.13   Reliability (survival)

---

reliability of each element, the system reliability will be affected by the way those elements are connected together. They may be connected:

(a) in series (i.e. one after the other, so that the failure of any one piece, means the failure of the system);

(b) in parallel (i.e. side by side);

(c) a combination of **(a)** or **(b)**, which is quite common.

By 'reliability' we mean the probability of functioning when required. So a system which has a reliability of 0.95 will operate 95 times out of 100, in the long term. If there are five individual elements connected in series, with each element having a reliability of 0.99, the overall system reliability would have been 0.99^5 which $= 0.95099$ or 95.1%. If there were 10 such elements so connected, the overall reliability would have been 0.99^{10} which $= 0.90438$ or 90.4%.

Activity

1 There are four elements connected in series. Their reliabilities are 0.9, 0.8, 0.7 and 0.6 respectively. How reliable is the system?

2 In a depressed house market, the house-selling chains are typically 5 vendors long and the probability of any individual vendor pulling out of the chain is about 0.2. In better times, the house-selling chains are typically 13 parties long, and the probability of any particular vendor pulling out of the chain is 0.05.

   (a) What is the probability of each chain successfully completing a deal? How much more likely to complete the deal will the more successful chain be than the less successful chain?

   (b) How few vendors need there be in the less successful chain to give it a similar probability of completion to the more successful chain?

There are three elements connected in series. The probability of each element not working is 0.05, 0.10 and 0.15 respectively. How reliable is the system?

It may not be feasible, practical or economic to try to increase the individual reliability of the elements to extraordinarily high levels in order to ensure that the system has itself an acceptably high reliability. How can we achieve sufficiently high reliability in the system?

Assume we connect three identical elements in parallel (i.e. a single 'wire' branches out to give a separate input to each of the three elements). The output from each element then combines to form a single 'wire' as output. The reliability of this set-up will be higher than that of any of the individual identical elements.

As an example, let us connect in parallel three elements each of reliability 0.99. For each element the probability of failure is $(1 - 0.99) = 0.01$. For three such elements, the probability of failure of all three is $0.01^3 = 0.001$. The reliability of the system is therefore $(1 - 0.001) = 0.999$. The system is therefore more reliable than any of its individual elements, and will operate 999 times out of 1000 in the long term.

As another example, four elements are connected in parallel. The reliability of each element is 0.8, 0.85, 0.9 and 0.95. What is the system's reliability? Using the method above, we can calculate it as:

$$1 - [(1 - 0.8) \times (1 - 0.85) \times (1 - 0.9) \times (1 - 0.95)] = 0.99985$$

or 99.99% reliable, a very big improvement.

Activity

Two elements of 0.95 and 0.90 reliability respectively, are connected in parallel. How reliable is the overall system?

A system consists of three parts, A B and C which are connected to each other in series. Part A consists of two elements of 0.97 and 0.95 reliability, connected in parallel. Part B consists of three elements of 0.98, 0.96 and 0.94 reliability, connected in parallel. Part C is a single element of reliability 0.93. How reliable is the system?

Why are parallel set-ups of the same elements not used whenever very high reliability is required? Sometimes they are when conditions of extreme safety are essential. More units may be installed in parallel than are actually needed to operate the system – i.e. redundancy. But, more often, considerations of cost, space and weight preclude the general use of parallel identical elements.

(b) Active parallel redundancy

Further analysis of systems may be made by asking: what is the lowest reliability of such a system which will still function correctly when (say) two of its five identical elements are still working (i.e. as many as three fail)?

Let the number of surviving elements $= m$, and the number of identical parallel elements $= n = 5$. Let the reliability of each element $= a = 0.8$. We will therefore be worried if there are only zero or one survivors, as then our system, by definition, will not work. The **probability of $(n - m)$** failures is calculated as:

$$\frac{n!}{(n - m)! \times m!} \times (a^m) \times (1 - a)^{(n-m)}$$

where for example $3! = 3 \times 2 \times 1 = 6$, or $5! 5 \times 4 \times 3 \times 2 \times 1 = 120$. By definition $0! = 1$. The calculations are now shown.

	Number of ways to occur	×	Reliability (a^m)	×	Failure $(1 - a)^{(n - m)}$	=	Probability
$m = 5$; $p(n - m) =$ prob 0 fail	$5!/(0! \times 5!)$		0.8^5		0.2^0		0.32768
$m = 4$; $p(n - m) =$ prob 1 fails	$5!/(1! \times 4!)$		0.8^4		0.2^1		0.40960
$m = 3$; $p(n - m) =$ prob 2 fail	$5!/(2! \times 3!)$		0.8^3		0.2^2		0.2048
$m = 2$; $p(n - m) =$ prob 3 fail	$5!/(3! \times 2!)$		0.8^2		0.2^3		0.0512
$m = 1$; $p(n - m) =$ prob 4 fail	$5!/(4! \times 1!)$		0.8^1		0.2^4		0.0064
$m = 0$; $p(n - m) =$ prob 5 fail	$5!/(5! \times 0!)$		0.8^0		0.2^5		0.00032
							1.00000

From this table, we can see that the probability of four or five failures is $(0.0064 + 0.00032) = 0.00672$. This gives a reliability for the system of $(1 - 0.000672) = 0.99328$ or 99.33%. The analysis above assumes that each of the constituent five elements is always available – i.e. active.

Chapter Review Questions

1 What is a suitable definition of 'reliability'?
2 Identify the three key categories of failure.
3 What is the difference between 'failures' and 'failure rates'?
4 What is meant by the terms 'hazard', and 'hazard rate'?
5 How are mtbf and failure rate related?
6 In a negative exponential distribution, what is the standard deviation equal to?
7 If wear is suspected as a failure cause, what might be a suitable distribution?
8 What is meant by 'series' and by 'parallel' connections?
9 It is not possible to get higher reliability from a system than those of its elements: True or false?
10 How many ways can you choose three from six?
11 What is meant by active parallel redundancy?

4 Planning and Control

Chapter 4 is concerned with the arrangements that have to be made by a company so that its plans materialise into **actions** and produce **results** at the required time. It is not concerned directly with the technology of production, but rather with the **organisational effort** required to achieve those results. Because such activities are most commonly concerned with production, planning and control is known as Production Control when used in manufacturing organisations, but we will see below that the principles can apply to most kinds of organisations.

Learning Objectives

By the end of this chapter you should:

1 know the **purpose** of planning and control and what it involves in general
2 know the key components required to exert effective **control**
3 be able to ascertain whether or not an **existing system** meets the essential criteria for effective control
4 be able to estimate a department's **workload** and compare it with its nominal **capacity**
5 be able to suggest how a service organisation may attempt to balance its **demand** against its **capacity**, together with the **implications.**

Case Study: The Rolling Mill – The Existing System for Planning and Control

The Platter Rolling Mill at Thinsem Down takes steel ingots and cold rolls them to a specified size and finish, finally heat-treating them. Rush work and frequent specification changes are a regular part of its service. The company often juggles its production plans to help customers in an emergency.

The plant has modern equipment and employs 300 people. Its systems have tended not to keep pace with its equipment and other modern facilities.

When received, a sales order is sent to the Works Manager from the sales office, then to the credit department and finally to the production office. An **acceptance note** is then sent from the production office to the customer. This contains a delivery promise, or verification of a salesman's promise already made.

A **production order** is made out in quadruplicate and two copies are retained by the production office. One of them is filed by production order number and the other is filed by customer name. The third copy goes to the sales office and the fourth copy goes to the shipping room. A **shop order** is made out in triplicate. Two copies go to the shop office, one for use in progress chasing and one for use by the booking clerk. The third is cardboard backed and goes to the pickle room foreman (pickling is an acid treatment to clean metal) and is kept with the work and shows the operations required.

The pickle room foreman is in charge of the raw material stockroom. He is also in charge of descaling. These are the initial steps of all orders. He looks daily at all orders and decides how much of what material to start. He tries to ensure no one will run out of work. If necessary he liaises with the progress chaser, shop supervisor, production office or even the Works Manager.

After the two initial stages, the material moves to the next department if the pickle room foreman has stopped the first available fork lift truck driver and told him to move it, or the foreman of the next department has come looking for his next job, or the progress chaser notices or is told by either foreman that a job is ready. The progress chaser then moves it. Information on the **progress** of each job is recorded only on the progress chaser's copy of the shop order.

Work proceeds like this through the various operations until the material reaches the **shipping room**. Here, a notice of partial or total completion is made on several copies, which go to the shop office, production office, billing department and shipping room file. Any variation in the material on an order is recorded by the production office on a **change notice form** from which the information is transferred to all copies of the production order and shop order that have been filed throughout the plant. Examples of changes might be in quantity or delivery date.

Upon receipt of a change notice, the progress chaser tries to meet the new requirements of that order. This often involves shuffling a number of other orders which themselves get pushed back.

Customers often enquire about their orders, and a production office clerk follows this sequence:

1 Ascertain customer order number and item required
2 Obtain production order number from customer file
3 Check production order copy in sales folder, for any shipments
4 Check with production office for any completion notices or if any shipping slips have yet to be posted
5 Check progress chaser's mill folder for schedule
6 Make best estimate of delivery
7 Advise customer, and then follow up.

4.1 Activities in Production Control

These can be conveniently divided into four key areas:

(a) Determining **manufacturing plans** for a number of periods ahead of the time when planning is being conducted. These plans are often made on a **rolling basis**

(b) Ensuring the timely **implementation** of those plans, so that work starts on schedule

(c) Collecting and recording data, and disseminating information relating to the progress of those plans in a timely manner, so that management will be able effectively to monitor progress and take corrective action

(d) Control can be exerted to ensure that output will coincide with the corresponding plan at the appropriate time.

We will now look at these four activities in more detail. They are still relevant even if a company does not manufacture: virtually every organisation needs to make plans, to monitor them, to inform people about progress and, if necessary, to take corrective action. The way an organisation operates regarding these aspects of its business will have a strong bearing on how close to schedule it meets its customers' requirements and the level of service it provides.

(a) Making plans

We need first to suggest why plans are necessary. Well-made plans will at least contribute to:

- **reducing production costs** by avoiding expensive bottlenecks and hence overloading and underloading
- reducing the need for **undue storage space** owing to work produced which is not yet required
- a **lower level of stock investment** as measured by raw material, work in progress and finished stock
- a better control of **cash flow**, both out for expenditure on material, and in from finished goods shipments.

As well as the above, planning will help to increase:

- the **utilisation** of labour and equipment
- **customer satisfaction**, by having work completed to schedules already agreed by the customer
- **operator morale**, because work arrives in the quantities and at the time expected, and operators are not provided with an unscheduled work overload on some occasions, and a dearth of work on others.

(i) To plan or not to plan?

Planning is a management activity and must be done well ahead of the actual implementation date. This is the ideal situation: in reality, it is often the case that planning horizons are less than ideal in terms of time available, but this should not preclude planning.

There are at least two ways to look at planning. The first suggests that planning is a fruitless exercise because plans have to be changed almost as soon as they have been made, so why plan at all? The second says that with planning you have a better chance of meeting targets than without it.

Like many simplifications which try to make a point, the truth lies in between, but it is generally better to plan and to modify than not to plan at all.

Activity

What activities would you include in your plans to:

(a) go camping in the south of France
(b) set up a roadside mobile coffee stall
(c) look for a new job
(d) buy some stocks and shares
(e) study for a higher degree via distance learning
(f) build an extension to your home
(g) plant an acre of vines and make your own wine?

(ii) Who should do the planning?

Plans must be **realistic** and **achievable** if they are to be of any use to management. These plans will form part of the company's strategy which will enable it to meet its overall objectives – of profit, production, growth and market share, for example. The plans will form a hierarchy in themselves, and as far as production is concerned, there will be daily, weekly, monthly and quarterly plans designed to make the company's annual targets achievable.

(iii) Team approach to planning

Because of the complex and interactive nature of planning, it is essential that planning be a team approach. The team may consist of one representative from each of production control, marketing, sales, inventory, purchasing, accounts and production. In this way decisions as to **what** to produce, and **how much**, can be made with the appropriate inputs from each key department. Once the plans have been made, that information must be transmitted to all concerned well before the start of the production period.

(b) Timely implementation

All planning, however well done, will be of little use if there is no clear effort made to ensure that production begins when it should, and that everything necessary is readily available. This is often called 'kitting out'. People in production control must ensure that the **physical parts** for each job are at the first work centre before the job is scheduled to start. All **drawings** and **planning sheets** which describe in detail how each part is to be made must be with the parts, and those documents must be up to date. Any **jigs**, **tools** and

fixtures must be available as required and must have been checked prior to use, to ensure that they are fit for use and are the current version. After use everything relating to completed jobs must be returned to its own area for subsequent checking and safe storage until next time.

(c) **Progress**
(i) **Data collection**
Progress cannot be monitored unless there is a regular supply of **timely information** available to management. They will then know the actual state of play as time passes for each of the many jobs which are currently being worked upon. There is a need, therefore, for a system of **data collection** at various key points in the plant, so that data regarding operator, time started, time finished, job and operation number, quantity good and quantity rejected, etc. can always be gathered. Such data may be collected at each of the main work centres by using computerised data collection terminals at several strategic points. Key features of such terminals are that they should be simple and convenient to use, that they should be flexible enough to collect different data as needs change, and that the system of which they are a part really does provide the information that management needs.

(ii) **Control documentation**
There is an essential core of information which is required to be able safely to move work about the various departments without confusion. This particularly applies to work being processed in batches (see Chapter 8). Often, such planning for production is based upon Materials Requirements Planning, and consequently the work is batch oriented. This contrasts strongly with work produced by a cell whose workforce owns all responsibility for that production. In this case work is conducted within that cell and control documentation is minimal. Batch sizes may vary from one unit upwards (see Chapter 6).

1 **The planning layout:** this contains every instruction to make each part of the order. This document is produced by the production engineering department, and copies will be required by the costing section, the production control office and the progress chaser.
2 **A job card:** this is needed for each part and is attached to the order authorising manufacture of that part. The job card will contain details of the raw material needed for the part, how much raw material is needed for this batch quantity, the detailed operations in sequence for manufacturing the part, at what stages the part needs inspecting and the quantity required. There will also be space for recording the quantity of parts passing inspection.
3 **A route card:** this shows the route which the part must follow (e.g. starting with the raw material and finishing with a store).

4 A move ticket: this, when authorised by inspection, enables a batch of parts to be moved from its current work station (e.g. the drilling section) to the next work station (e.g. threading section). The move ticket ensures that only **fit work** is moved on, and ensures that faulty work is clearly identified and separated from good work. Items (2), (3) and (4) are often combined for simplicity.

(d) Monitoring and progress

If you are working to a weekly plan, it is not good enough to wait until Friday to discover whether or not jobs scheduled for completion that week have or have not been completed. If not, there is now no time available for taking any corrective action which could ensure completion on schedule. It is necessary therefore to make frequent checks on the status of all jobs so that if there is a problem which might jeopardise the on time completion of a job, then there will be a good chance of solving that particular problem and meeting the original target date.

(i) Action on scheduling problems

Progress chasers meet many problems, and these are often best solved when there is a good rapport between them and the people in the department where **action needs to be taken**. Production Control is a staff function, and its personnel do not have any executive authority to issue orders for a particular course of action to solve the problem in hand. If severely formal relations exist, then it is necessary for requests to be sent vertically up the organisation tree until they meet a person who has responsibility for both production control and the department for whom action is being requested.

When authorisation has been given, it travels down to the progress chaser who will then take action. This is time-consuming, and is better handled by informal requests to the relevant supervisor. This can be done only when good relationships exist. Progressing is often not regarded as being very skilled, but in practice such work makes an enormous difference to how well targets are met.

(ii) Scheduling delays

There are many kinds of problems which may cause delays in a schedule and which must be solved. Some examples are:

1 Suppliers fail to meet promised **delivery dates** for material bought in. This is particularly serious where a company is operating with minimal inventory, such as a Just in Time system (see Chapter 6).
2 Other departments within the company fail to meet their **own delivery dates**.
3 **Absenteeism** above the level allowed for occurs in departments within the factory.

4 Work takes longer than anticipated because schedules were not **realistic** when initially formulated.
5 **Equipment** unexpectedly breaks down, causing delays to jobs requiring processing on those machines.
6 Changes are made to the order by the **customer** at a stage when the jobs relating to that order have been distributed to the various departments for manufacture. This happens when the customer is buying a customised rather than a standard product.
7 **Drawing errors** are detected which delay processing.
8 Parts from **outside suppliers** contain errors which cause rejection at incoming inspection (see Chapter 2), or are discovered to be faulty during subsequent processing.
9 Errors in **processing** are made during manufacture which lead to rejection at initial or in process inspection.

Can all these problems be solved? Probably not, as in many cases it may not be within the power of the company to affect the situation. But all problems that cannot be solved promptly by direct action must be brought to the attention of more senior management for action. If the problem cannot be solved in time, then changes of plan must be recommended which at least will minimise disturbance to the original schedules. Progress chasing is an active job, and it is not unusual in larger companies for chasers to concentrate their activities in specific departments. This enables them to develop a deeper knowledge of how those departments operate and consequently a better knowledge of how to solve some of the problems.

4.2 The Essence of Control

There are certain principles which need to be observed in the design of a system which purports to be able to control an activity of some kind. It does not matter whether the activity is to be controlled by people or automatically.

(a) Control mechanisms in the mechanical environment

Figure 4.1 shows a governor of the type which could be used to control the speed of a steam driven mechanism, or to control the turntable speed of an old phonograph.

The linkage assembly with the two weights in Figure 4.1a, revolved as the mechanism performed its function. The collar B was able to slide up and down the vertical spindle, and at the same time was always connected to the steam control valve. Centrifugal force caused the weights to fly outwards and upwards. The faster the linkage spun, the higher the sleeve B rose (see Figure 4.1b). The higher the sleeve rose, the more the sleeve connection began to close off the supply of steam. The speed slackened, the weights fell, and the supply of steam began to increase again. The speed was therefore

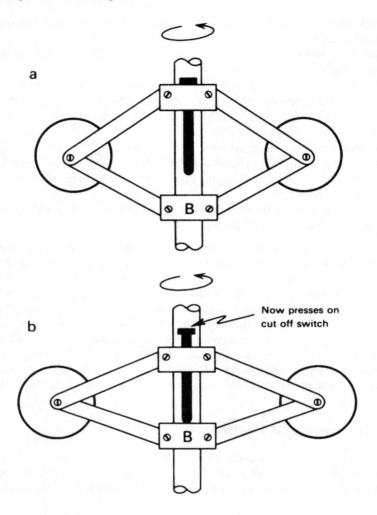

Fig 4.1 A governor
a   At low speed, weights push collar B down
b   At high speed, weights fly out and collar B rises

being controlled by the action of the mechanism itself, and was **self-regulating**.

A modern example is the thermostat used to control the temperature in a room. Upper and lower temperature settings are made on the thermostat, and as the upper or lower limit is reached, the boiler is either switched off or switched on. The more precise and sensitive the system, the closer are the limits within which the temperature can be controlled.

(b) Control mechanisms in the company

Figure 4.2 shows a more realistic representation of the essentials of a management control system.

The **input** in Figure 4.2 is any job or jobs which are scheduled for the period being considered. **Execute** refers to carrying out the set of operations required to complete those jobs. When that is done, the data collection system described above records output achieved, compares it with the relevant plan and produces a **variance report**. This variance report may be in terms of units of output, money, or both. This is distributed to management in a timely manner and decisions then need to be made by them as to how to respond to such variances.

Output in that period may have exceeded target, in which case management may be satisfied, or they may wish to set a higher target for

Fig 4.2   The control function in essence

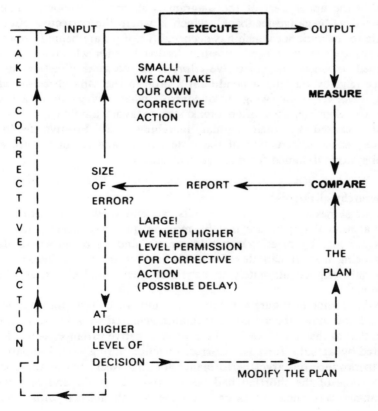

the next period so as to get ahead of schedule for the monthly or quarterly targets. If output has not met current targets, management will have to make a decision regarding how they will make up the shortfall. It may be by overtime, by extra manpower or by equipment being brought to bear on the task or, perhaps in a more extreme situation, by subcontracting out some of the work involved. The last possibility will not always be practical owing to the nature of the work, the difficulty of finding a suitable supplier with capacity at that time or one who is able to do it at the right price and quality.

Figure 4.2 shows that some of the corrective action decisions may be made by the managers concerned in conjunction with production control, if the error is small. Other options such as subcontracting will require a higher level of decision-making capability, such as the Works Manager, or the Manufacturing Manager in conjunction with the Sales Manager and other senior people, if the size of the error is too great.

(i) Negative feedback

A feature of the control mechanism in Figure 4.2 is that the direction of the arrows in the upper part of the diagram is shown as **clockwise**. This is interpreted as 'negative feedback', which is where the corrective effort is opposite to the variance which has occurred (i.e. if we are behind target we take steps to achieve target). Positive feedback, with which we are not concerned, is where the corrective effort is in the same direction as the variance (e.g. by pushing a pendulum a little in the same direction as it swings, it will very soon swing out of control): when soldiers march across a bridge, for example, they often break step to avoid amplification of the vibration caused by their regular marching beat. Positive feedback ultimately causes destruction of the system itself, and is not a feature of control systems designed for management purposes.

(ii) Hierarchy of targets

Figure 4.3 shows a target and the results, week by week. It is important to note that annual targets are met by meeting quarterly targets, quarterly targets are met by meeting monthly targets, and so on down to daily targets being met. It can therefore be seen that there is a hierarchy of targets, all designed ultimately to help meet the **overall objectives** of the company.

The dotted line in Figure 4.3 shows the cumulative target for each week. The solid line shows the actual performance achieved week by week. It can be seen that at the end of week 1 there was a negative variance, as would be measured by 'actual − forecast'. Corrective action during week 1 apparently failed to produce on-target performance for that week, but at the end of week 2 some of the shortfall had been corrected. By the end of week 3 performance was ahead of target, and the month finished with a small

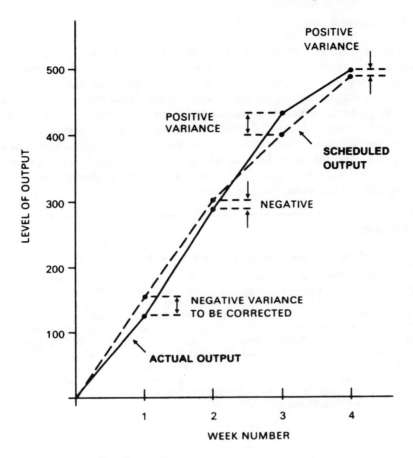

Fig 4.3 Cumulative schedule

positive variance. It is a matter of skill and judgement to set a realistic target, and to determine how it should be split up week by week. It will depend on available **resources**, as well as what management thinks is possible. Unrealistic targets are unhelpful, motivate no one and do not enable a company to realise its potential in that area of activity.

4.3 Information for Production Control

Production Control needs to originate different kinds of information so that it is always in a position to know how the various department loads compare with predicted requirements, and therefore how schedules may be affected.

(a) Departmental load

Production Control will need to estimate on a rolling weekly basis, for example, the load in each of the key departments of work based upon orders received. This may be achieved as follows. As orders are received by the Sales department, they are passed to and broken down by the Production Engineering department into a realistic set of operations for every part in the order, and the appropriate department is set against each operation. From past records where similar jobs have been done before, or by making a new estimate for new jobs (via the Management Services department), the time required for each operation and for setting up is determined. This information is then passed to production control.

Example

Power Saw section: new work required: week 23

Set-up time is the time required to ensure that a new job can be started on the appropriate equipment, and that after the batch has been processed the equipment is cleared of anything connected with that batch. Setting-up time is not related to the size of the batch to be processed and management tries to keep this time as low as possible. This reduction of set-up times is vital when producing low quantities, otherwise the set-up costs are too large a proportion of the total time to make a small batch. Impressive reductions in set-up times have been made by Japanese manufacturers; in many cases they have reduced set-up times from hours to minutes. This objective is often termed 'single minute exchange of die' (a die is a tool often used in a press). Set-up times in the power-saw section are listed below.

a	b	c	d	e = (b × c) + d
		Standard	Set-up	
New parts codes	Batch quantity	time per piece	standard time/batch	Total time for batch
104863	50	0.5	15	40.0
211318	250	0.75	20	207.5
709255	1100	0.4	10	450.0
651890	300	0.6	25	205.0
432787	1500	0.3	30	480.0
				1382.5 mins.

Or 23.04 hours of new load.

The load in the power-saw section for the current and subsequent four weeks is shown below. There is one person in this section who helps in the stores if he is not fully occupied in the saw section. He works a nominal 40-hour week, and is available for productive work for 36 hours per week. Records show he works at about 80% efficiency on measured work (see Chapters 9, 10 and 11).

Week no	Load in standard hours
20	35 (current week)
21	43
22	31
23	23
24	10

Figure 4.4a shows this data in histogram form.

Because he works at 80% efficiency, it will actually take the man 35 hours/ 0.8 = 44 actual hours to do the work in week 20. (The standards set by the Production Engineering department or Management Services are all based on **standard performance**). The same logic will produce actual hours likely to be taken for the work scheduled to be done in weeks 21 to 24.

The new picture looks like this:

Week no.	Load in actual hours taken	
20	44	8 hours overtime required
21	54	8 hours overtime required
22	39 ·	8 hours overtime required
23	29	
24	13	

Figure 4.4b shows this data in histogram format.

If all materials are available for all jobs then it may be possible to work 8 extra hours in week 20, 21 and 22. This will incur extra costs and cause an adverse labour variance, and such overtime must therefore be approved prior to being worked.

Figure 4.4c shows the picture if overtime is allowed.

(b) Load and resources match

There is no automatic solution as to how to obtain the best match between **load** and **resources**, as we shall see below. In the long term, everything is variable. In the short term, one tries to match load to resources by juggling with some or all of the following:

1 Improving the **methods** so that jobs can be produced quicker and with fewer resources (see Chapters 9, 10 and 11).
2 Introducing or extending the use of **overtime** if possible. This is a popular option and hence one which is rather too readily used. A little overtime may be a worthwhile option; too much overtime results in people relying on it as a regular part of their wage, and productivity falls off as the amount of overtime increases. It also becomes a simple panacea for problems which should really be **solved**.
3 Hiring more labour, either temporary or permanent. Temporary labour may sometimes be obtained from other departments, or from agencies. Permanent new hiring is a much more involved decision depending in part as to how permanent the extra load of work is likely to be. Semi-permanent labour hired for the duration of a major project is not an unusual step.
4 Increasing the **plant** available, either by hiring some or subcontracting to someone with capacity available.
5 If all else fails, **adjusting the programme**, but as I have indicated in Figure 4.2 this is often a decision which should not be taken by the Production Control department alone.

Fig 4.4   Load in power-saw section

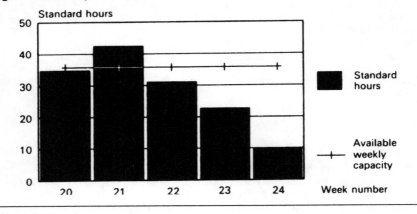

b   Actual hours (= standard hours/0.8)

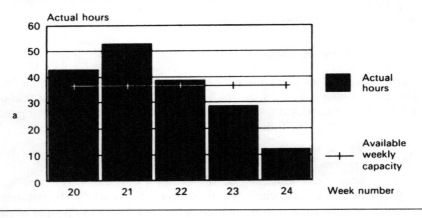

c   Using overtime

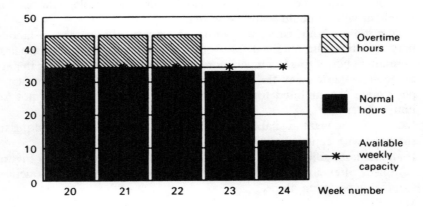

6 Smoothing out fluctuating demand. If we consider firms making fireworks: ahead of Fireworks night on 5 November demand is so large for a relatively short period of time that production must continue at a level higher than the intermediate demand throughout the year, so that by the time October is reached there are sufficient stocks available. A similar situation exists for poppies produced for Remembrance Sunday. This kind of logic can be applied to demand for other seasonal products such as hot cross buns or ice cream. In some of the examples above, a well thought-out marketing policy will help to smooth out fluctuating demand, as well as raise it.

(c) Rejection and scrap rates

The Production Control department will also need to know rejection rates and scrap rates so that they can anticipate any losses along the way. Such losses whether permanent (scrap) or temporary (repair) will have an adverse affect on schedules and the targets originally set. In the worst-case scenario, scheduled quantities may have to be higher than required, and started earlier, so that the final quantity is that required and the completion date meets the overall schedule. This is a bad position to be in, and is not recommended. Causes must be sought and solutions found.

(d) Learning curve time

Learning curves for new operatives (see Chapter 16) or for new jobs must also be allowed for when planning, because work will take longer than standard to complete, although each week will see a reduction in the time taken.

(e) Projected data required

Reports must go to the supervisors of each department giving the status of current jobs, and showing projected load against capacity week by week. Production control must also work very closely with the Stock Control and Purchasing departments, as no plan will be realistic if parts are not readily available when required.

Case Study: The Rolling Mill – Does the Existing System Offer Control?

We have considered in some detail what production control entails. In a case like the Platter Rolling Mill there will not be a definitive answer, but much will be gained by re-reading the case, and in a critical manner beginning by asking questions about the current set-up. For these questions, answers need to be found and, where judged unsatisfactory, new routines developed, tested and implemented.

Activity

1 Why is the sales order sent to the Works Manager?

2 What is the essential difference between a production order and a shop order?

3 Why are there so many copies made and are all (or any) of them needed?

4 What are the exact criteria for laying out new work – e.g. how late is an order, how much is the order for, how much work is already in the department?

5 Why is there no mention of labour loading techniques? Could they be used here?

6 Why does the pickle room foreman confer with so many different people? How much of what he currently does is outside the usual remit of a foreman?

7 There seems to be no formal system for job movement from shop to shop. Should there be?

8 The progress of jobs is not recorded by a timekeeper. Is there/should there be a system for this?

9 What priority should be given to customer change to an order?

10 Is there a system, and if not should there be one, for a progress chaser to meet new change requirements for a customer's existing order?

11 Where should the liaison point be when customers contact the company regarding their order? How should the chain of enquiry from the initial enquiry run?

12 There seem to be unfilled orders all over the place. What should really occur?

Other questions will no doubt occur to you, and you will then consider whether the responses you develop seem reasonable or not. Where you feel they are not, you will begin to develop routines and systems, together with appropriate paperwork. Any systems you propose should conform to the principles of control, and be appropriate for the **size** and **kind** of business operated. Your system should be easy to understand and use. It should be cheap to run and easy to adapt as circumstances change in the company over a period of time. In real life you would develop your ideas in conjunction with those who work there. In this case example, you will develop your ideas and compare them with the key principles outlined. You would also need to get your proposals approved by the company management, and then work closely with those who are the **future users** to ensure that any bugs are removed during the test period. You would not consider the task of designing and implementing a new system to be complete until the new system runs as planned or with required modifications, and has the agreement of management that the system has produced the advantages you claimed it would have when you gave your proposal presentation.

4.4 **The Tools of Production Control**

Production Control uses many different tools for planning and scheduling.

(a) Charting (see Chapter 16)

1 Z charts are charts which display on the same sheet, current production, cumulative production and a moving total.

2 Bar charts are charts which display on a horizontal timescale all the jobs which are to be done at a specific work centre or department.

3 Histograms are graphs which relate load or frequency on a vertical scale, with time or size on the horizontal scale.

(b) Forecasting (see Chapter 16)

1 Moving averages are averages which are calculated by adding the most recent data and removing the oldest data on a regular basis. They are less sensitive to individual changes.

2 Exponential smoothing is a technique which attaches less weight to old data than to new data. It is used to forecast one period ahead at a time.

(c) Scheduling (see Chapter 12)

1 Sequential scheduling involves scheduling different batches of work, each of which has to pass through a fixed sequence of operations.

2 Project scheduling involves scheduling a one-off job with a clear set of tasks to be done, where those tasks involve concurrent and serial working.

3 Line of balance is a technique which is useful for scheduling an important order which requires more than usual management control.

(d) Linear programming (see Chapter 17)

Linear programming is a mathematical technique which optimises a result when conflicting conditions or constraining conditions occur.

In the chapters noted above you will find a fuller description and examples of the use of these techniques, gathered together in a separate chapter for convenience: real problems do not come neatly labelled.

4.5 Production Control and Production Method

The production control described in this chapter relates primarily to work produced in batches. As you will see in Chapter 8, there are other production methods available, namely job and flow production. In job production, where a job is completed from start to finish before the next job is started, control is simple because of the lack of complexity in the system being used. Flow production is used for very large quantities but in practice these can often be considered as very large batches, and many of the principles of batch control will apply. There are some processes (such as refining oil) which are flow production in the usual sense of the term, and apart from consideration of set-up and priority of product, are rather specialised. By far the most common form of production is batch production, to which most of this chapter applies.

4.6 Capacity Planning

Earlier we saw how necessary it is to know how to match departmental **load** and **capacity**. This also raises the question of how to manage an organisation's capacity in general, and what scope there may be for improving overall the match between customer demand and capacity available. Such problems need addressing whether or not the company makes a product or offers a service.

(a) Costs of too much capacity

If there is too much capacity available for a given level of demand, then while the customers will receive prompt service, the costs incurred by the company in offering such a service will be excessively high and eventually result in these costs being passed on to the customer. The net result may be a reduction in the service offered, higher prices and reduced demand. In such cases it would not be unreasonable to find other companies wanting to step in to try to be more competitive.

It is therefore the matching of the short to medium demand and capacity that we are discussing. In the long run everything is adjustable and some problems may then be solved only by company or division closure.

(b) Need for immediate capacity

The problem is somewhat more difficult when organisations providing services rather than products are being considered because it is not possible to store a service. By definition, a service also has the feature of immediacy and direct contact between the provider and recipient. When a road accident occurs, there are considerable repercussions if the accident department in the nearest hospital is closed, or full up, or lacks specific facilities: coming back in two days is not a good alternative.

(c) Measures of capacity

Whereas we can often measure or estimate work content in standard hours (see Chapter 10), for some organisations we need other and perhaps more general measures.

- A restaurant may need to establish its capacity in meals per day, as well as knowing the pattern and level of demand.
- Garages may need to know their capacity in repairs of various kinds per day.
- Doctors' surgeries have a capacity of a certain number of appointments per day.
- Airlines will have a capacity for a certain number of flights per day or week, or passenger miles per month.

Activity

What measures of capacity can be used for: **(a)** a hotel, **(b)** a bank, **(c)** a leisure centre, **(d)** a hospital, **(e)** a theatre or cinema?

(d) Flexible capacity

What often tends to compound the problem is that demand may be erratic yet the overall nominal capacity is fairly stable. The problem is how to reconcile the two. The most common means are those which offer some flexibility without longer-term commitment. Some possibilities are:

1 Vary the **mix of people**, having both full and part-time personnel, yet have contracts which allow flexible working hours. You may need to hire some temporary full and/or part-time employees to cope with an upsurge in demand.
2 Be in a position to work **overtime**, so that extra capacity is available using existing staff who already have the appropriate skills. This means that working overtime should not be, as is often the case, simply custom and practice, a way to augment low wages. If this is so, the extra output will be gained only at the expense of very poor productivity.
3 **Subcontract** out some of the extra work to other companies or divisions. This does not help if offering a service, except that (for example) a hotel which is full may make a working agreement to have some of its guests stay at alternative hotels. Customers are sensitive to changes such as these, and such a solution can have unforeseen ramifications such as subsequently losing customers to the competition.
4 **Use price** as a demand-altering tool. This is used by British Rail and London Underground, as well as hotels, theatres and cinemas. If this is coupled with restrictions as to availability of such concessions, it is quite a useful means of demand manipulation.
5 Considering whether to **buy** an item as well as to produce it. This is of limited use to the very short-term problem as it is not easy to find the right alternative product precisely when required. It also provides revenue for your competition, and places you at a modest disadvantage.

6 Allow some **queuing** in the system, by the customer, to act as a buffer between the supply and demand. This is a two-edged weapon, because although it can be reasonably effective, customers may not like the delay unless it is very short. If it is a very short queue, then it is unlikely to be providing the buffer you actually need.

7 Get the **customer** to perform part of the service you are offering. This will have the effect not only of reducing the cost, but will lower the load imposed on the organisation. Examples of this technique are self-service filling stations, serve-yourself restaurants, and many general department stores. It is reasonably effective, but opens the way for niche marketing organisations to try to provide the service you are no longer providing.

Activity

Lampeter Lighting Ltd

Lampeter Lighting make a wide range of domestic light fittings, to be sold via retail stores and mail order. One of their new table lamps recently introduced is highly successful. One of their key customers, Clifford Enterprises, phoned in this morning to check the status of their outstanding order for 2100 of these lamps.

Upon checking, it is found that owing to a clerical error, the order has not been scheduled into the factory programme for manufacture and assembly. If Lampeter's cannot deliver on time, their cash flow and sales targets will be missed and they will also run the risk of losing Clifford's as a valuable customer. This is not a viable option.

Having checked the stock status, it is found that all parts are available except four special parts which are P, Q, R and S. The following operation layouts refer to the manufacture of the four parts and the final assembly of the lamps themselves. The operation number denotes the sequence in which the operations must be done.

Operation layout	Operation number	Set-up time in hours	Production rate in units per hour	Department
Part P	1	10	50	A
	2	20	100	C
	3	10	70	B
	4	15	210	D
Part Q	1	10	50	E
	2	20	210	D
	3	10	100	C
Part R	1	10	210	A
	2	5	70	C
	3	10	70	B
	4	15	210	D
	5	10	70	E
Part S	1	10	100	D
	2	15	100	A
Final assembly	1	15	200	Assembly department

Note the following:

(a) The normal working week is 5 days of 8 hours each. Because of the urgent situation, two hours overtime is authorised per day if required.
(b) A department can only work on any one part at a time.
(c) Moves between departments require a nominal eight hours per occasion.

Required
Prepare a Gantt chart of the situation, trying to complete Clifford's order in as short an overall time as possible, i.e. from the start of the first part in the schedule to the end of the assembly batch

Chapter Review Questions

1 'Production Control is concerned mainly with production techniques': True or False?
2 What are the six key activities in Production Control?
3 'For increased accuracy, planning is better left as close to the actual event to be planned as possible': True or False?
4 'Plans can themselves be in the form of a hierarchy': True or False?
5 What is meant by dispatching or kitting out?
6 What are the essential documents required for processing work in batches?
7 Why is progress chasing a necessary part of production control?
8 What are the essentials of a good progress chaser?
9 Identify five possible causes of jobs failing to be completed to schedule.
10 What is the function of a governor in a control system?
11 (a) What is 'feedback', and (b) what kinds of feedback are there?
12 What can sometimes occur in a system with positive feedback?
13 When actual and target performances are not the same, what is the difference called?
14 'When targets cannot be met, altering the target is always a viable option': True or False?
15 How can you try to ensure annual targets are met?
16 Why should new workload be calculated on a regular basis?
17 How can load and capacity be reconciled?
18 Why do scrap and rework affect schedules?
19 What is a 'learning curve', and why can it affect schedules?

5 Managing Independent Inventory

The careful management of **inventory**, a key capital investment, will be repaid by a reduction in the number of line items held, a realistic stock turnover rate, and stock-holding levels which are compatible with demand. Better service levels to the customer as well as lower stock-holding cost often result. Chapter 5 is concerned with inventory whose demand is independent of other items, and includes retail inventory applications such as supermarkets and shops, and some industrial applications such as maintenance stores. The theme of this chapter is not completely applicable to manufacturing inventory for the reasons given in Chapter 6, dealing with demand-dependent inventory.

Learning Objectives

By the end of this chapter you should:

1 know the difference between **independent** and **dependent demand**
2 understand the reasons for **holding stock**
3 be able to identity **sources of stock** in a company
4 be able to identify the **stock-holding cost components**, and estimate an annual overall figure
5 know what is meant by order-processing cost, stock-holding cost and total variable cost and their **relationship** for a given ordering strategy
6 be able to calculate a **re-order level** (ROL) and a **re-order quantity** (ROQ) for a given item's past usage
7 be able to calculate an **economic order quantity** (EOQ), and to know its limitations
8 know how to **analyse price discounts**
9 appreciate the effect of **staged deliveries** of an order quantity
10 know how to use **Pareto analysis** to analyse stock according to ABC categories.

Case Study: Harry Stokes Hardware Ltd

Harry Stokes owns a small but profitable business. He has one of those shops you see in the High Street which sells spares of all sorts for washing machines, dryers. vacuum cleaners, lawnmowers as well as a selection of DIY spares like hinges, locks, lengths of wood, paints and varnishes, etc. He has been in business for five years and makes a reasonable profit.

(a) **Cost of stock**

The high cost of his stock has always concerned him, and now it is accentuated by current high interest rates. A key reason for this is the wide variety of lines he holds upon which he has built his reputation. He suspects it is costing him more than it should, but he cannot quite decide how and where to begin to attack the problem.

(b) **A typical line item**

Consider an 8 mm brass hinge sold in pairs, and typically used on front doors of houses. Harry orders them in pairs usually about twice a year, when the representative of the wholesaler comes in. He sells about 1200 pairs a year, and they cost him £3 a pair. He always has a plentiful supply and although they are popular he has never run out. This provides good service, but he has doubts about the overall picture, because that situation applies to most of his lines, of which he has about 750. He has often wondered if could reduce the level of his stock, and maybe even the variety, without affecting the level of his business or the service he provides his customers.

(c) **Initial analysis**

How can we try to analyse Harry's problem, and make some suggestions? Remember that managers make decisions which are not based only on numerical information. That means even if we can present numerically convincing arguments for something, if Harry has some other good reason for not doing it, then he shouldn't. This does not devalue our analysis but shows there are other reasons for action or non-action besides purely quantitative ones. However, Harry will at least be making a more informed judgement, and relying less on intuition. In this case, he may decide to go against our recommendations because of what his competition is doing and because his current set-up is convenient.

5.1 **Why Keep Stock?**

Why does a shop owner like Harry keep stock in the first place?

- He wants to be able to show his customers a good **range**. That will give them some ideas and he can satisfy their demand immediately.
- If he holds some stock, he will be able to cope with increased **demand**.
- He might buy more than he wants because he is getting a **price discount** for buying above a certain quantity at a time.
- If he has some stock on hand, that will soften the impact of **price increases** for a little while, as he will have some older stock to sell.

Note that if we *were* considering a manufacturing situation, holding stock would be useful to separate successive stages in the manufacturing process. If it were not possible to proceed directly from one operation to the next in the sequence of operations required to make a component, there would always be other stock from which to formulate different plans from those originally envisaged. It is not suggested that this is desirable, but merely a possible course of action. Indeed, as you will see in Chapter 6 on dependent demand, the holding of stock for such purposes is to be avoided.

Activity

What reasons can you think of which might make it disadvantageous to hold stock for the reason given above?

5.2 **Where is Stock Held in an Organisation?**

Just before we explore further, does every organisation have stock? Where can you find it? Consider service industries.

- In Harry's shop, not only is there his saleable stock, but of course there are his fixtures and fittings.
- In a bank, there will be all the fixtures and a vast variety of stationery and data processing equipment.
- A garage will have its range of spares and tools.
- Organisations such as the AA, British Gas or British Telecom will have very large amounts of stock out in the field, ready for use as spares, in order to provide a good service.
- Vineyards have wine laid down which will not be mature for many years. Whisky distillers often keep whisky for seven years or more before it is ready for sale. Abattoirs may keep carcasses for some weeks to allow them to mature on the bone.

Now consider a manufacturer. It is very likely that a manufacturer will have stock classified under one or more of the following headings.

(a) Raw material (i.e. material used to make products) which is purchased from suppliers in its unprocessed or unmachined form (e.g. rods of brass or sheets of aluminium).
(b) Work in progress (i.e. partly finished product which has absorbed a portion of labour and overheads, as well as some raw-material costs).
(c) Finished goods (i.e. the completed product already packed and waiting shipment from the factory).

(d) Items bought in from outside suppliers; these will be separately identified, even if in some instances the company also makes that item. Examples of bought-in items are light bulbs, electric switches, wire and small fasteners. These items require rather specialised equipment to make, are relatively cheap to buy and have wide application in many products.

(e) Scrap is a valuable source of money in many cases, even though we try not to produce it in the first place.

(f) Items awaiting rework are still stock, but because they do not conform in some way to the required specification, they need separate handling and cost control procedures while the repairs are being made. All manufacturers will try to avoid the need for scrap and rework completely.

(g) Material held on consignment at the manufacturer's location, which has been supplied free by the customer for inclusion in the product being made specifically for that customer.

Occasionally, a company may ship their product to a customer or agent before it has received payment. Such goods in transit will still be classified as stock, as the product still belongs to the company.

Activity

In your own organisation: **(a)** identify and classify the different kinds of stock held; **(b)** estimate its average value over the year; **(c)** estimate the number of times the average stock value can be divided into the current annual value of sales.

5.3 Controlling Stock

Why should stocks be carefully controlled? Harry knows intuitively that he has got to do something. Here are four good reasons.

- The **costs** associated with holding stock may be reduced with careful control.
- If Harry controls his stock carefully, he is less likely to run out, or to hold **excessive** amounts.
- Careful stock control will help keep stock within the **space** available. This is particularly important if dealing with valuable materials or perishable goods.
- Although not in Harry's case, stock may have to be kept in the correct **proportions**. For example, every car during assembly needs five wheels, two headlamps and (at least) two doors.

5.4 The Cost of Holding Stock

One of the reasons for controlling stock is that it costs money. How much does it cost?

There are seven key costs associated with holding stock:

- **Tied-up capital:** the cost associated with Harry having put his money into stock and not, shall we say, into a Building Society. He is therefore losing what he could be getting as interest. He might also be borrowing the money to buy his stock, and so he will be paying the current rate of interest on the loan.
- It costs him money to **handle** his stock, both in terms of **people** and **equipment**.
- Some of the stock may become **obsolete**, particularly in high-technology businesses, or in the fashion trade.
- Some stock may **spoil** because it is perishable, especially if it is food or chemicals: for example, blood stocks must normally be used within 5 weeks.
- **Insurance** costs money too, as he will want to protect his investment.
- Stock takes up **space** and there are very definite costs associated with that in the form of **rent** or **lease**.
- Stock also needs to be **counted** and **audited** from time to time.

The annual cost of each of these elements is estimated and then totalled. An estimate of the average value of stock held is also made – the year-end stock value may be used. The totalled value of cost elements is then divided by the average value of stock held, and for convenience expressed usually as a percentage. It is this percentage value which is referred to as the **holding cost factor (hcf)**.

In the absence of an actual estimate of the factors described above, a reasonable figure to use for the hcf is 25% per annum, or a little over two pence in the £ per month, for every pound sterling of stock you have. If your product is one where obsolescence or perishability is important, then 35% to 40% is not unreasonable. As an example, if Harry values his stock at £250,000, then it will cost him about (£250,000 × 25/100) = £62,500 per year to finance. This is why he is so concerned about stock-holding costs.

Activity

Try to determine the estimated annual percentage holding cost factor for your organisation or division. Is this information known by anyone in Inventory Control or in the Purchasing department?

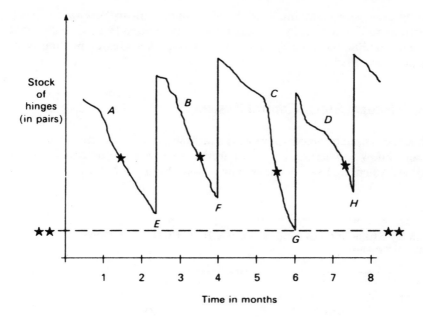

Fig 5.1   Harry's stock usage

5.5 A Graph of Stock Usage

To be able to analyse the process of ordering his hinges, Harry has to know what **stock movement** looks like as time passes. Figure 5.1 shows a simplified plot of the stock level of hinges.

The sloping lines *A* to *D* in Figure 5.1 show how the stock of hinges fails as the demand is satisfied. The slope of these lines is not constant, as the demand for the hinges is not constant. The vertical lines *E* to *H* show that orders for hinges previously placed at * have come in (the whole order at one time (no partial deliveries).

For practical purposes this means that the orders were placed some time earlier, and this is called the **lead time**. The lead time is the time between Harry noticing he needs some more hinges and the time when he has some more in stock and readily available for use. It is not just his supplier's delivery time. The interval between re-orders is currently about six months, with a lead time which varies somewhat but is about one month. The lead time is indicated by the distance from * to its respective vertical line on its right.

Notice that the stock of hinges below the horizontal line ** − **, is never used. This is his safety stock and is an **idle part** of his investment which is costing money to maintain. It is therefore important to be aware of such situations so that action can be taken. Here, the unused level of stock could be reduced, but the accompanying risk is one of a greater possibility of running out of stock.

5.6 A Simple Stock Control System

While the system outlined above works satisfactorily in practice, what Harry doesn't know is whether it is cost **effective** – i.e. whether he could operate another system and save some money as well. Figure 5.2 shows the essence

---

Fig 5.2   Stock level of hinges: a basic ROL–ROQ 2-bin stock control system

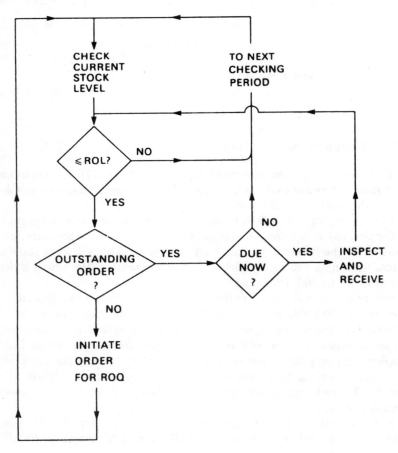

of a simple two-parameter stock re-ordering system, which consists of knowing:

- **how much** to order
- **when to place** the order.

(a) The 2-bin system

This system is also often referred to as the '2-bin system'. There do not really have to be only two bins; if we assume there are, then the stock in the second bin corresponds to the re-order level, so that a new order is initiated when the stock in this bin is first used. Actual bins are not necessary; the stock identified as being the re-order level stock merely has to be identified as such.

(b) The order processing cost

You will notice that we haven't yet discussed the **order processing cost (opc)**. This is the cost of doing everything necessary to process the order and to receive the parts when they come in, and put them on the shelves. The cost of doing this is often an intelligent 'guesstimate', but if you wanted to do it more formally, you could use some of the appropriate method study techniques indicated in Chapter 9.

If you process an order for several different line items, you could estimate an average cost for processing an order by dividing the actual cost by the number of different lines on a representative order. Therefore, if Harry's best estimate is that it costs him £40 to process an average of four items on a common order, then the typical cost for the opc in this case will be £40/4 = £10.00 per item.

5.7 The Re-order Quantity (ROQ)

(a) Harry's options

Let us look at what options Harry has with the re-order quantity (ROQ). This is the quantity he will use whenever (within reason) he needs to replenish his stock. We will ignore any stock on hand.

- He could order the **entire year's supply in one go**. In this case he would spend only £10.00 on the ordering cost, but incur a heavy stock-holding cost which will be made up as follows:

Average stock held	×	Item unit cost	×	Holding cost factor
1200/2	×	£3.00	×	25/100

$$= £450$$

So his total variable costs are:

$$£10 + £450$$
$$= £460$$

- On the other hand he could re-order **once per week**, and the corresponding costs would be:
  Ordering costs

$$= 52 \times £10 = £520$$

Stock-holding costs

$$= (1200/52)/2 \times £3.00 \times 25/100$$
$$= £8.65$$

In this case his total variable cost is:

$$£520.00 + £8.65$$
$$= £528.65$$

- He could adopt a combination of both these policies.

(b) **Minimum total variable cost**

Consider the following table of orders placed, calculated on an annualised basis, where different amounts are ordered to achieve our annual requirements.

1 No. of orders	2 Quantity ordered	3 Order cost £	4 Average stock	5 Holding cost £	6 Total variable cost = cols 3 + 5 £
1	1200	10.00	600	$600 \times 3 \times 0.25$	460.00
2	600	20.00	300	$300 \times 3 \times 0.25$	245.00
3	400	30.00	200	$200 \times 3 \times 0.25$	180.00
4	300	40.00	150	$150 \times 3 \times 0.25$	152.50
6	200	60.00	100	$100 \times 3 \times 0.25$	135.00
8	150	80.00	75	$75 \times 3 \times 0.25$	136.25
10	120	100.00	60	$60 \times 3 \times 0.25$	145.00
12	100	120.00	50	$50 \times 3 \times 0.25$	157.50

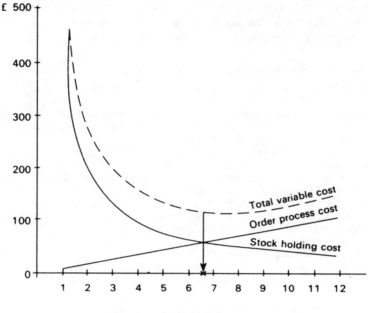

Fig 5.3 Economic order frequency

We have taken only a few different values for the orders placed per year, but it can be seen that the **minimum total variable cost** (which excludes the cost of buying the hinges themselves) is about £135.00. This means that the corresponding number of times we should order per year for this item is about six. At the moment, Harry is ordering about twice per year and it is costing him about £245.

The graph in Figure 5.3 shows the figures in our table in graphical form. The minimum total variable cost is where the two separate variable costs cross each other. This is because at this point the sum of the two cost elements is *less* than the corresponding sum of the two elements at any other point along the horizontal axis, either to the left or to the right of the crossover point.

5.8 **The Economic Order Quantity (EOQ)**

We used our table of orders placed to show the relationship between order-processing cost and holding cost. When we drew the graph, we could see the point where both costs were equal. On the *x* axis, this point corresponded to the **economic order frequency (EOF)**. The economic order quantity is therefore the annual demand in units divided by the EOF.

Activity

1 Using the same data as above, complete the blank tabulation that follows for a range of order quantities varying from 50 units per order occasion to 400 units in steps of 50 units.
2 Draw a new graph of the order-processing, holding and total variable costs. The *y* axis will be money as before, and the *x* axis will be quantity ordered. Ensure that you can see that where the two costs are equal the corresponding point on the *x* axis is the economic order quantity.
3 Compare both graphs. Why is the order-processing cost linear in the first graph, but non-linear in the graph you have just drawn? In the same way, explain the difference for the holding cost.

No. of orders	Order quantity	Order cost £	Average stock	Holding cost £	Total variable cost £
24	50	240	25	18.75	258.75
12	100	120			
8	150				
	200				
	250				
	300				
	350				
	400				

(a) The EOQ formula

We can derive a formula to work out exactly where the two variable costs cross each other (i.e. where the ordering variable cost intersects the holding variable cost), without calculating tables like those above. The solution gives the economic order quantity directly, and it is quick and convenient.

To do this let us identify the factors shown below:

EOQ = economic order quantity

C = cost to process an order through the system

A = annual demand in units

V = cost of one unit

i = the holding cost factor (hcf) as a decimal

Q = a given order quantity

For a given value of Q,

$$\text{the ordering cost} = (A \times C)/Q$$

and

$$\text{the average holding cost} = (Q/2) \times V \times i$$

Where $Q = EOQ$, we see that:

$$(A \times C)/Q = (Q/2) \times V \times i$$

Therefore,

$$Q^2 \times V \times i = 2 \times A \times C$$

$$EOQ = \sqrt{((2 \times A \times C)/(V \times i))}$$

We now have a formula that Harry can use to calculate the EOQ algebraically, instead of by tabulation:

$$EOQ = \sqrt{\left[\frac{2 \times \text{Annual demand} \times \text{Order procurement cost}}{\text{Unit Value} \times \text{Hold cost factor}}\right]}$$

$$= \sqrt{\left[\frac{2 \times 1200 \times £10}{£3 \times 25/100}\right]}$$

$$= 178.9 \text{ pairs, say 179 pairs.}$$

If you work out the stock-holding cost and the order-processing cost separately, you will find they are equal to each other at about £67.08 (i.e. the two separate costs intersect at about 6.7 orders per year which equals an order quantity of 1200/6.7 or 179 pairs of hinges).

(b) Using the EOQ formula

You will also notice that it is not a practical proposition to order 179 pairs at a time, despite our calculations. Does it matter? Not very much, because if you look closely at the graph in Figure 5.3, you will see that the total variable cost curve is steep at the left-hand side, and much flatter on the right-hand side. So within quite a wide range of order frequencies (here, six to ten orders per year) there is not going to be very much of an increase in variable costs above the theoretical ones, and here it seems that ordering every two months might be convenient, with an order quantity of 200 pairs. This is the simplest re-order system, but does not have a trigger for re-ordering based on current stock level.

The total **variable** cost of the annual programme of buying hinges (in this case the EOQ of 179 at a time) is:

$$\text{Total variable cost} = (A \times c)/\text{EOQ} + ((\text{EOQ}/2) \times V \times i)$$
$$= (1200 \times 10)/179 + ((179/2) \times 3 \times 0.25)$$
$$= 67.04 + 67.13$$
$$= £134.7$$

Notice that the two variable costs are not quite identical, as we have used the rounded EOQ value of 179 pairs.

The formula for the **total variable cost** at the EOQ can be found as follows:

$$\text{No. of orders placed} = A/\sqrt{[(2AC)/(Vi)]}$$
$$\text{Cost of processing these orders} = AC/\sqrt{[(2AC)/(Vi)]}$$

We know that at the EOQ the holding cost = the order processing cost, therefore:

$$\text{Total variable cost} = 2AC/\sqrt{[(2AC)/(Vi)]}$$
$$= \sqrt{[2ACVi]}$$

Activity

1 Calculate the EOQ and total variable costs for each of the following situations: if **(a)** the demand has increased from 1200 to 2400 pairs, **(b)** then if the order-processing cost increases to £20, **(c)** then if the unit value is £5. In your company, what do the Purchasing department estimate their order processing costs to be?

2 What is the difference in total variable cost between the EOQ of 179 units and the EOQ of 200 units we chose?

5.9 Limitations of the EOQ

The EOQ is a convenient indication of how much to order if you can believe the estimates of the values you are putting into the formula. The formula assumes that the demand is **constant**: this is because you can put only one value for the demand into the formula. The formula also assumes there are no price discounts for buying in bigger quantities. The EOQ formula is not very useful, as we shall see in Chapter 6, if the item being considered is not independent of other items. However, the EOQ is simple to calculate and as the total variable cost curve has quite an extensive flat portion, the true

EOQ can be departed from without greatly increasing the total variable cost compared with the theoretical minimum total. The examples and formula below will illustrate this.

The following formula allows us to calculate the percentage increase in total variable costs **(tvc)** from the minimum, if we use an order quantity greater or lesser than the economic order quantity.

$$\text{%ge increase in tvc} = (50\,f^2)/(1+f)$$

where f is the **fractional** amount by which we have increased the EOQ.

As an example:

Using the data from 'Harry Stokes' we see the EOQ is 179 units and the minimum total variable cost is £134.16.

(a) Suppose we order 1.676 times the EOQ. The OQ is now 300 units for a total variable cost of £152.50, i.e. 13.7% greater than the minimum. Using the formula we have: **f = 0.676**.
Therefore the %ge increase in total variable cost from the minimum is:

$$(50 \times 0.672^2)/(1 + 0.676) = 13.6\%$$

(b) Suppose we order a new amount which is the EOQ/1.79. The OQ is now 100 units for a total variable cost of £157.50, i.e. 17.4% greater than the minimum.
Using the formula we have: **f = 0.79**.
Therefore the %ge increase in total variable cost from the minimum is:

$$(50 \times 0.79^2)/(1 + 0.79) = 17.4\%$$

Note carefully in the above calculations how only the fractional part is used for **f**, and that whether you increase the EOQ or decrease it, the total variable cost **increases**. If, for example, you were to order twice the EOQ you would be increasing the EOQ by 100%, so **f** would equal 1, and the increase in total variable cost would be 25%. If you ordered half the EOQ, **f** would equal 0.5, and the increase in total variable cost would be 8.3%.

Activity

1 Try other fractions of the EOQ and verify that the formula results match the basic calculation results.

2 Draw the one time graph for general usage of the formula. Let the Y axis be **%age increase in total variable cost**, and the X axis be **%age variation from the EOQ**; with a scale of zero to 100%. Verify the general nature of the graph by taking different examples of variation from the EOQ, calculating the percentage cost increases, and then read those results from the graph which should confirm your work.

5.10 **The Re-order Level (ROL)**

(a) **Re-order level and stock control**

If we calculate a re-order level for Harry, he could use that as the basis for a simple 2-bin system of stock control. This will not be quite the same as simply ordering every two months, but it will be a system that responds more closely to the way his stock of hinges diminishes.

This system will operate as follows. When the stock of hinges fails to or below the re-order level, Harry will place an order for the re-order quantity, provided there is no outstanding order for these items.

The re-order level can be calculated from the following formula:

ROL = Average usage in the lead time + Safety stock

= (average usage per period × no. of lead time periods)

+ (k × standard deviation of demand × $\sqrt{\text{(Average lead time)}}$)

The factor called 'safety stock' is an extra amount which allows for occasions when demand is greater than the average, while waiting for an outstanding order to arrive.

(b) **Service level protection**

k has a value of 2 if we want to provide a theoretical protection of 97.5% service level, or 3 if we want to consider 99.87% service level. These k values are taken from a table of normal distribution ('normal' in this context means symmetrical – i.e. there are about as many demands lower than the average as there are demands above the average). We examine the normal distribution in Chapter 14.

'Service' levels refer to the percentage of non-stockout occasions over a long period of time, during periods when an order is outstanding. These levels are commonly chosen because they represent reasonably realistic levels of service to the customer, and are conveniently represented by simple whole numbers, 2 or 3 respectively.

Suppose a retailer orders a certain product 5 times a year, and has set a service level of 97.5%. This means that theoretically he would experience a stockout situation (i.e. he runs out of stock while waiting for an outstanding order to arrive) about once in every 40 re-order situations. However, if he were ordering once a month using the same service level, he would expect to experience a stockout about once in 40 months (i.e. 3 years 4 months).

This is not the only measure of service level, three others are common:

(Quantity supplied upon request × 100)/(Quantity asked for)

Percentage of orders filled within 24 hours of receipt

Value of orders filled compared with value of orders received for the same period

You may wonder why we do not suggest that Harry caters for a service level of 100%. Some thought will suggest that in order to do this he would have to be able to supply upon request whatever quantity is asked for, and this is not a practical proposition.

Figure 5.4 shows how steeply costs tend to rise when trying to reach a level of 'perfection' – in this case a service level of 100%. In practice, service levels must not fall short of about 98%, because if they did, customers would not receive service at a level which was compatible with their needs.

There are always other business people who will spot such a gap in the market, and attempt to fill it.

(c) Standard deviation of demand

We also have to calculate, or at least estimate, the **standard deviation** of demand. The standard deviation is a measure of the variability of the demand around the average: the greater the standard deviation, the more

---

Fig 5.4 Cost vs service level

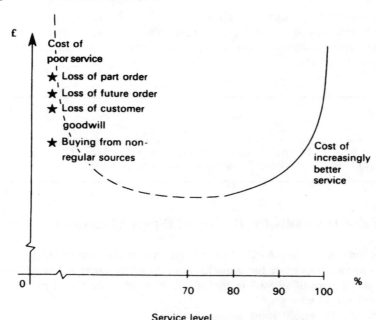

Service level

variable is the demand around the average. We can assume here that demand is normally distributed (Chapter 14), but if we have good reason to suppose otherwise, we can assume that it is distributed according to one of several other common distributions. The principle of analysis remains similar. You can see that safety stock is an allowance which is added on to the usage during the lead time, so that the re-order level is somewhat higher than it would be without it. The safety stock provides added protection when the actual demand is higher than the average.

(d) Calculating the re-order level

A numerical example will help illustrate the calculation of the re-order level.

Assume the average weekly demand to be 25 pairs of hinges. The lead time on average is about four weeks, and we seek about 97.5% protection – i.e. $k = 2$.

The standard deviation of demand has been assumed to be 5.0 pairs.

$$ROL = (25 \times 4) + (2 \times 5 \times \sqrt{(4)})$$
$$= 100 + 20$$
$$= 120 \text{ pairs}$$

So the simple system we have established is that when stock falls to or below the ROL, and there is no order outstanding, a new order for 200 pairs is placed.

This system will mean that theoretically in only one out of about 20 replenishment situations will Harry run out of stock. As he would be ordering about six times a year he would expect to run out of stock about once every three years.

Activity

Calculate the re-order level for each of the following situations: if **(a)** the weekly demand is now for 100 pairs; **(b)** then the lead time increases to an average of 6 weeks; **(c)** then the standard deviation increases to 15 pairs.

5.11 Price Discounts for Buying in Bigger Quantities

The last time the salesman called in at Harry's shop, he said to Harry, 'I can let you have a better price for those hinges if you buy them in lots of 1000; I can do you a price of £2.80 – in fact if you buy 2000 at a time I can let you have them for £2.60 a pair.'

Harry said he would think about it.

(a) Buying quantity and buying frequency

What have we now got to do to analyse this problem for Harry? The problem is similar to that which we have been looking at, but this time we have to include the cost of actually **buying the hinges** in our analysis, as this factor is now a variable too. Let us therefore make an analysis in tabular form of the two suggested possibilities, together with the situation where he buys twice a year and where he buys six times a year. We will do this on an annualised basis as before. We will also assume a continuing demand for the product, and that there is no mixed stock of old and new prices, so that we can make direct arithmetic comparisons.

Policy	Order cost £	Holding cost £	Buying cost £	Total cost £
600 @ 2 occasions/yr	2 × £10	300 × £3 × 0.25	1200 × £3	£3845.00
200 @ 6 occasions/yr	6 × £10	100 × £3 × 0.25	1200 × £3	£3735.00
1000/occasion	1200 × £10/1000	500 × £2.8 × 0.25	1200 × £2.8	£3722.00
2000/occasion	1200 × £10/2000	1000 × £2.6 × 0.25	1200 × £2.6	£3776.00

By looking at the results in this table, we can see that the cheapest possibility is to order 1000 pairs per occasion. Is this the ordering action that Harry should switch to? Perhaps yes, maybe not. Why is this so?

(b) Impact on Harry's business

It should be remembered that data in the table can only show numerical results. But Harry has other things to consider. If he buys larger quantities, he is going to need more **space**. **Payment terms** may not be the same, and that may affect his cash flow. Larger quantities mean that if **demand changes**, he is locked into a large existing stock of items which he may not be able to shift. Hinges may not deteriorate, but other items might, and larger quantities may need special conditions for storage.

Because more money is spent at a time on buying, he may not be able to buy other things he needs which are necessary for his business. So, once again, numerical results on their own cannot give the answer to a management problem, but they are useful in the decision-making process.

All things considered, Harry would not go very far wrong if he used the ROL–ROQ system where he ordered 200 at a time when his stock fell to or below 120, and there was no order outstanding. He could still see the salesman when he came in, but his ordering would be done more closely on the basis of its relation to demand.

Figure 5.5 shows how stock movements will look over several re-order situations.

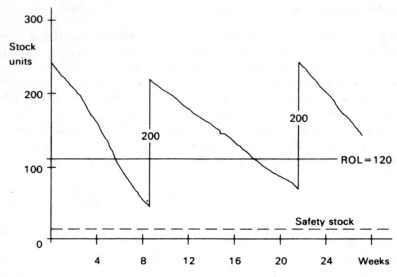

Fig 5.5   Stock movement over time

Activity

What will be the total cost of ordering in the above situation, for a batch quantity of 1500 per occasion for £2.70 per pair? Will it make a difference in any price discount situation if there is not a continuing demand for the item in question?

Activity

Records from stock and purchasing about part JSP123 below, show the following information. Currently, orders are placed with the sales representative every two months. You can assume continuing demand for this part.

Average monthly demand is 50 units with a standard deviation of 5 units. Average lead is 2 months. Cost of one part is £3 if purchased in batches of 300 units, otherwise £3.50 per part if purchased in smaller quantities. Order processing cost is £15 and annual stockholding cost is 25% of average inventory value. A special low price is available at £2.90 per part for batches of 1000 parts.

Analyse the information above and calculate the most appropriate ordering quantity. Suggest any non-financial factors which management also ought to consider.

Activity

A particular high-intensity lamp bulb costs £5.00 and currently 1000 are ordered twice a year to cover the annual usage of 2000. Order processing is estimated to be £40 per occasion, but this can be apportioned among four different items of which this is one. Holding costs are 25% per year. You can obtain a 7.5% discount for buying in batches of 1500; and 12.5% discount for buying in batches of 5000. What is the cheapest ordering quantity strategy? You may assume continuing demand for this item.

Activity

Consider the price data in the Widget make-or-buy situation at the end of this chapter. Compare the total buying costs for these different policies:

(a) buying in lots of 250 at £14.00 each
(b) buying at the EOQ at £14.00 each
(c) buying in lots of 500 at £13.00 each
(d) buying in lots of 1000 at £12.75 each.

Assume a continuing demand at the annual usage level of 1000 units per year, holding cost of 25% per annum and an order processing cost of £10 per occasion.

5.12   The Effect of Staged Deliveries on the EOQ

While many orders may be delivered at one time (no partial deliveries), there are many situations where partial deliveries occur because of **phased requirements** by the customer. In such a case, the vertical line representing instantaneous delivery of the entire order quantity will now slope to the right, representing the effect of stock being used up while subsequent partial deliveries are made.

Figure 5.6 shows this effect.

Let R = the rate of delivery (e.g. 60/week for 3 weeks)
i.e. the EOQ is delivered in 3 partials
Let D = the rate of usage (e.g. 25/week)

$$\textbf{The revised EOQ} = \textbf{REOQ} = \textbf{EOQ} \times \sqrt{(R/(R - D))}$$
$$\text{REOQ} = 179 \times (60/(60 - 25))$$
$$= 179 \times 1.31$$
$$= 234 \text{ units}$$

Notice that in this arrangement Harry would build up his stock at the rate of $(60 - 25)$ units per week. Therefore in three weeks he will have $3 \times 35 = 105$ units more than he has used, so that in the next four weeks he will use 4×25 units and be back where he started.

This example uses the EOQ quantity of 180 units corresponding to an order interval of $52/6.7 = 7.8$ weeks. As drawn there would be a slight

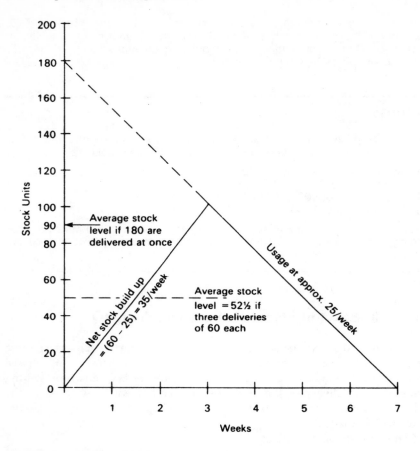

Fig 5.6   Single vs multiple deliveries
Comparing a single delivery of 180 units and 3 partials of 60 units each

discrepancy if the graph was extended to the full 52-week year, because these figures do not give whole multiples of weeks and weekly usage.

The average stock level held $= (EOQ/2)(1 - (D/R))$

Average stock $= 90 \times (1 - (25/60)) = 52.5$ units, a substantial reduction from the average level of stock held if the 180 units are delivered at one time. In this case, the average stock held would have been $180/2 = 90$ units. There has been a $(90 - 52.5) \times 100/90 = 41.7\%$ reduction in average stock held. That is well worth having, but remember that it depends on having **reliable deliveries** and a **demand** not more variable than you estimated, because you do not now have the big initial buffer of 180 units delivered all at once. All the **purchase costs** would have to stay the same also.

Activity

In the auto trade, for high volume items such as the one below, company manufacturing policy dictates that unit production costs must be less than 1% of sum of unit labour plus material plus overhead costs. Currently, six batches of these are made per year (250 working days).

(a) What is the current unit production cost and is it within the target cost?
(b) What is the unit production cost at the EOQ and is it within the target cost?
(c) What percentage more expensive is the costlier option than the cheaper production option?
(d) What will the effects be if (i) usage doubles? (ii) usage halves?

Production rate is 1500 per day. Usage rate is 500 per day. Set-up cost is £100. Stockholding cost is 25% per annum. Unit labour, material and overhead costs are £0.5, £1.50 and £3.00 respectively.

5.13 Top-Up Stock Control System, with Regular Review

(a) Rules for a TUL system

In some cases, it is very important that stock does not exceed a given upper limit, called the **top-up level (TUL)**. This is particularly so if the product is perishable and needs refrigeration, or perhaps the product is a chemical and is poisonous or corrosive. Or maybe the product has to be kept in a bonded area which has limited capacity. If this is the case, then a top-up stock system is useful. It is often used in conjunction with regular review of the stock, and not continuous review as was implied with the ROL–ROQ system, as this is impractical.

Figure 5.7 shows the system in action.

The rule which operates this system is:

**Make a regular review of the stock, and initiate
an order for a quantity OQ such that:**

OQ = (TUL − Inventory held − (Outstanding order))

This system therefore uses a **variable order quantity**, and the unit cost of the product may not be constant.

The economic number of reviews to make on an annual basis

$$= \sqrt{((A \times V \times i)/(2 \times C))}$$
$$= \sqrt{((1200 \times 3 \times 0.25)/(2 \times 10))}$$
$$= 6.7 \text{ reviews per year,}$$

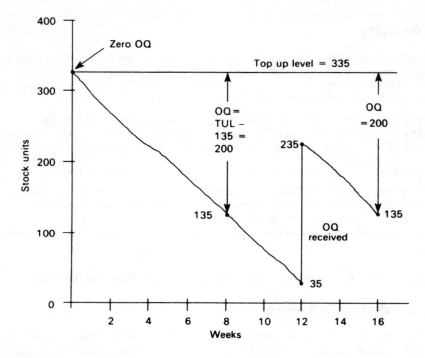

Fig 5.7   Top-up system

---

or an order interval of about 7.8 weeks, which gives an OQ result of 179, the same as our earlier EOQ result. This new review frequency assumes that we order on each review.

(b) Calculating TUL

The top-up level (TUL) can be calculated using our original formula for the ROL, except that now the lead time L consists of the actual lead time which is four weeks on average, plus the interval between reviews which is eight weeks, making a total of twelve weeks in all.

$$\text{TUL} = (D \times L) + (k \times \text{standard deviation demand} \times \sqrt{L})$$

$$= (25 \times 12) = (2 \times 5 \times \sqrt{12})$$

$$= 300 + 34.6$$

$$= 334.6, \text{ say } 335 \text{ units.}$$

5.14 The S–s Stock System, with Regular Review

This is a convenient method which combines the ROL (now the s) of the ROL–ROQ system, with the top-up level (now the S) system.

This system operates as follows.

> **Review the stock regularly. If the stock on hand is equal to or less than s, place an order. The size of the order is $(S-s)$. If the stock on hand is greater than s, then do not order**

Figure 5.8 shows the system in operation.

Because this stock control system has three parameters (S, s and the review interval), it responds rather more to experimentation than the other two. It is a relatively simple system to simulate and fine-tune to specific requirements. As before, the order quantity is variable and so is the order interval (it is the **review interval** which is regular). It is therefore reasonable to assume somewhat more work in the ordering activity, and once again the cost per item may or may not be constant because of the varying order sizes.

Fig 5.8 The top-up/reorder system

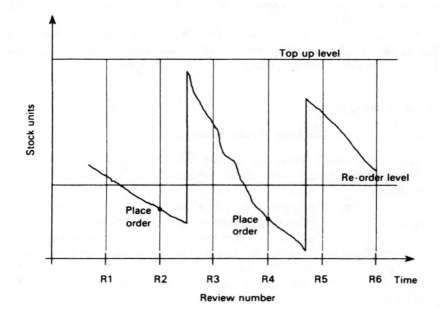

5.15 ABC Analysis

Harry's shop has about 750 lines, and while it is relatively easy to analyse one or two lines in detail, it is not so easy to do the same for several hundred or several thousand, as a supermarket or DIY warehouse may have. It is also important to know which are the items he holds the **most of** in stock, or which items are the **most profitable,** or which have the **greatest turnover.**

Turnover is the ratio of:
Annualised sales value to value (measured
in like manner) of average inventory held

A turnover of four times a year therefore means that the stock held is completely rotated once every three months. A turnover of 0.5 means that the stock is rotated only once every two years. If Harry was running a greengrocer's shop, he would expect to turn his stock over at least 50 times a year.

(a) Pareto analysis

To analyse such variety we use a simple technique first noted by the Italian economist Vilfredo Pareto in the 19th century. He noticed in his study of wealth, that about 1% or 2% of the population had about 95% of the wealth. Subsequently it was found that similar relationships existed in many other diverse areas.

This relationship is often called the 80–20 rule, but note that these two figures do not have to add up to 100. When drawn, the vertical and horizontal scales of the graph are both percentage scales.

(b) A, B and C items

Other examples of this kind of relationship are:

- Most of the orders come from a few customers.
- Only a few suppliers seem to be responsible for most of the quality problems.
- Most of the profit is made from only a few product lines.
- Most of the stock value comes from relatively few key items.
- Most of the questions in a meeting come from one or two people.
- Out of 400 potato varieties, two-thirds of production centres around only four.
- Only a few of a company's employees contribute to most of the absenteeism.

- Most of the rework costs seem to centre around very few parts (or processes) (or people).
- Most of the sales come from a few product lines.

We can use this relationship to analyse and control our stock, by considering it as being in one of three groups:

- **A items:** These will be the low volume usage items probably of relatively high cost. Because of this, we will treat them on an **individual basis** as far as control goes. In an analysis of stock, probably 5 to 10% of line items will fall in this category.
- **B items:** These form about 40 to 50% of line items and can probably be controlled most effectively by the methods described using the ROL–ROQ system or a variation.
- **C items:** These are the high-volume low-priced items where close control is not so important, and they can be controlled by **bulk issue methods** in many cases. Any errors in the control process will not be too disastrous, because they will in total only contribute about 10% of the value, even though they will consist of about 40–55% of all line items.

Because we know this pattern exists in a range of stock items, we can conduct (via a sample, if necessary) an analysis of the stock and begin to categorise line items into these classifications. Then we have a good means of obtaining the best results for our management effort. If we know that by careful effort we can save 15% on the items which contribute 90% of the result, that is going to be much more effective than saving 30% on items which contribute only, say, 25% of the results.

(c) **Pareto analysis ranking**

Three different parameters are shown below: stock quantity in units, unit price and stock value held, for each item.

Item number	Part number	Stock units	Unit price £	Stock value £
1	1032	123	41.5	5,104.5
2	2118	405	9.9	4,009.5
3	8096	611	4.6	2,810.6
4	4001	2202	8.6	18,937.2
5	1235	433	6.7	2,901.1
6	6181	890	24.3	21,627.0
7	5049	910	4.1	3,731.0
8	3116	6206	3.2	19,859.2
9	7091	300	5.1	1,530.0
10	2046	311	2.1	653.1
11	1111	209	1.2	250.8
12	7098	8307	3.3	27,413.1

Three separate Pareto analyses are required in this case, to see how the rankings for the items compare when analysed by units held, unit price and stock value held. The rankings will not necessarily be the same. You can decide if they need to be, or indeed what is the desired ranking. It will then be a matter of policy as to how you set about achieving it. It must not be forgotten that service to the customer is of prime importance.

Start by rearranging the items in order, putting the item with the **greatest quantity held in stock**, at the top of the list, and the item with the next largest quantity beneath that, and so on finishing with the item of which there is the **least in stock**. Finally find the total number of units **held in stock**. This means that in any real analysis of units held all items must be stockable in the same unit of measure. This is not of concern when analysing by value.

Create a new column and express the number of units held, starting at the top, cumulating as you go down the list. Create a third column and translate the second column into cumulative percentages. You can now see, for example, that the top three items account for 80% of the total stock units held.

Fig 5.9   A Pareto curve

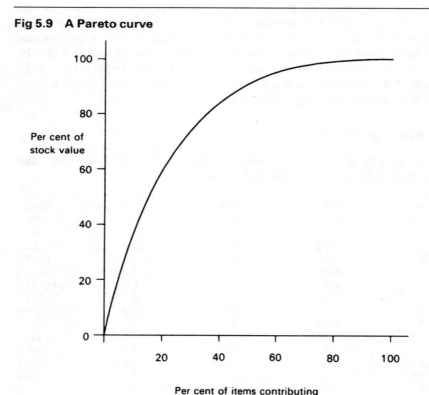

A table ranked by stock value is shown below:

Item number	Part number	Stock value £	Cumul. value £	Cumul. %
12	7098	27,413.1	27,413.1	25.0
6	6181	21,627.0	49,040.1	45.0
8	3116	19,859.2	68,899.3	63.0
4	4001	18,937.2	87,836.5	80.7
1	1032	5,104.5	92,941.0	85.4
2	2118	4,009.5	96,950.5	89.1
7	5049	3,731.0	100,681.5	92.5
5	1235	2,901.1	103,582.6	95.2
3	8096	2,810.6	106,393.2	97.8
9	7091	1,530.0	107,923.2	99.2
10	2046	653.1	108,576.3	99.8
11	1111	250.8	108,827.1	100.0
		£108,827.1		

Figure 5.9 shows what a Pareto analysis looks like graphically for the ranking of items by stock value.

Activity

1 Resequence our sample data for the other parameters, to see if the same part numbers are always at the top of the list. If they are not, should management take any action?

2 If you are employed, obtain (after being given permission) information about a sample of 25 items held in a stores. Analyse the data such as units held, value held, average usage, to see if Pareto's relationship is valid in your situation.

3 In your class over a few weeks, can you ascertain if it is:

(a) the same few students who ask most of the questions
(b) the same few students who always seem to arrive late or be absent
(c) the same few lecturers who start their lectures late (or overrun their time).

4 In your locality, find out how many different line items are held by the following shops. Before you do so, make your own estimate, and later compare it with the quoted figure. How many estimates were within plus or minus 10% of the actual?

(a) chemist or pharmacy, **(b)** furniture showroom, **(c)** DIY, **(d)** food supermarket, **(e)** corner grocers, **(f)** auto spares, **(g)** shoes, **(h)** newsagent/books, **(i)** petshop, **(j)** jewellery, **(k)** fast print franchise, **(l)**toys, **(m)** clothing department/store, **(n)** wine and spirits, **(o)** video rentals, **(p)** electrical goods, **(q)** records, cassettes and discs, **(r)** fast-fit auto centre.

5.16 The Make or Buy Decision

The **make or buy** decision is a common management problem. This is the decision a company makes if it wants to compare the costs of buying a part from an outside supplier with the cost of making that part itself. The final decision may not be made only on the quantitative results, but such information will greatly facilitate the decision-making process. As mentioned earlier, managers make decisions, numerical information merely helps.

(a) Why buy?

(a) Buying in from an outside supplier may make the acquisition process for that item less complex. The problems, for example, of internal scheduling the manufacture of the part through your own plant will no longer exist.
(b) It may be less expensive to buy in the part than to make it yourself. The part in question may be routine for your supplier, but for you it may offer certain problems.
(c) If you are not suitably equipped in your own plant, it may not be worthwhile becoming so, if rather specialised equipment is involved.
(d) The item involved may be a specialised item as far as you are concerned – for example, you would not be likely to make your own light bulbs or electrical wiring unless there were overwhelming reasons for doing so.
(e) By buying an item you may be able to give yourself a buffer against uncertainty in supply if you also are able to make the part yourself.

(b) Why make?

(a) You may find it impossible to buy the item at the appropriate price, quality, quantity or delivery date.
(b) You may want to make the part so that you can keep your own plant operating at the required capacity in certain areas.
(c) If you make your own parts, you are less likely to be held to ransom because of circumstances beyond your control (e.g. strikes by your suppliers or the carriers they use).
(d) By making your own parts you maintain a certain degree of independence, and control over your own destiny.

Activity

Widgets – should we make them or buy them? (a widget is an imaginary item)
   You currently buy complete widgets for £14.00 per unit in batches of 250, and use 1000 per year.
   To make them, you estimate that:

1 Demand will continue at the same rate for at least five years.
2 You will need equipment costing £10,000; it has an estimated life of 5 years and a scrap value of £1,000.

3 It will need a part-time operator at £5,000 per year
4 Your overheads are 200% on your material costs
5 The material will cost £2.00 per unit.

First: **annualise all anticipated costs:**

Equipment	(£10,000 – £1,000)/5 =	1,800
Labour		=	5,000
Material	1,000 × £2.00	=	2,000
Overheads	£2,000 × 200%	=	4,000
Total		=	£12,800

which equals £12.80 per unit to make. Financially, you would make widgets.

- Think of circumstances where, in spite of the lower price, you might decide not to make them in house.

Assume each of the following variations builds on the previous ones.

(a) More automated equipment costs £30,000 and has a scrap value of £3000 over the same life. It does not need an operator. What is the new unit cost to make?*
(b) If material costs were to rise by 10% at the start of the make programme, what is the unit cost to make now?*
(c) If a 20% profit margin were to be incorporated into your make programme, what would be the unit cost to make?
(d) Your accountant tells you it costs 25% per year to hold stock and £10 per occasion to process an order through the system. What is the adjusted 'buying in' cost per widget because you are not buying the 'economic order quantity'?
(e) Productivity improvements have resulted in overhead allocation being 150% on material rather than 200%. What is the new cost to make?
(f) If you were faced with such a make-or-buy decision, what non-quantitative factors might you consider as well as the financial calculations? In reality, all the quantitative data are only estimates. How does this affect your calculations and what should you do about it?

Activity

In groups of two, find out the cost of two or three varieties of sandwich in your college cafeteria or nearby sandwich bar. Now assume you are going to set up in business to sell sandwiches. Determine the factors that will contribute to the cost of making those sandwiches at home and compare your cost with the commercial cost.

Should you make them, or buy in (at commercial rates) and resell?

Chapter Review Questions

1 What is meant by 'independent inventory'?
2 Why does a shop keep stock? Do manufacturing organisations keep stock for the same reasons?
3 Identify four areas where stock can be found in a company.
4 If you did not control your stock, what might you expect to happen?
5 Does it cost money to hold stock, and if so, why?

6 What is meant by the 'hcf' and the 'opc'?

7 What are the two key parameters of the simple 2-bin stock system?

8 The economic order quantity is the quantity which results when what relationship holds between order processing and holding costs?

9 'The EOQ formula copes with variable demand as well as constant demand': True or False?

10 'The re-order level includes an amount for safety stock': True or False?

11 Why do we include the cost of buying the item itself in a quantity discount comparison, but exclude it in an EOQ calculation?

12 Do partial deliveries increase or decrease the average stock held?

13 In what situations might the top-up level stock system be useful?

14 What are the features of the *S–s* stock control system?

15 'The 80–20 rule can mean that 20% of sales come from 80% of the customers'. True or False?

16 What contribution might the make or buy situation make to capacity management?

6 Managing Dependent Demand

Chapter 6 deals with two different kinds of 'planning for build' activity. The first method for planning how much and when to build is called **Material Requirements Planning (MRP1)**. It is a planning activity which is based on working back from the date when you require finished goods in stock, towards the present time, when you should begin the manufacturing processes.

The second method is the **'Just in Time' Technique**, which is based on pulling through the manufacturing system only that amount which corresponds to **current demand**. It relies on close and long-term relationships with suppliers, short set-up times and low quantities. Effective quality assurance and striving to achieve continual improvement are also required. Stock levels throughout the system are kept very low or virtually eliminated.

Learning Objectives

By the end of the chapter you should:

1 understand the **shortcomings** of the economic order quantity as a basis for planning manufacture
2 know what **materials requirements planning** and **manufacturing resource planning** involves, and the difference between the two
3 know how **Just in Time** manufacture operates and how it differs from materials requirements and manufacturing resource planning.

6.1 Dependent Demand

The approach used in Chapter 5 is not very appropriate when planning to build a product. This is because the parts requirements for a product are related to the quantity of the particular product to be built. They may be needed in sets (e.g. five wheels, two headlamps, four doors and a set of windows for a car). In Chapter 5, demand was identified as being independent of any other item or product (e.g. a person went into a pet shop and asked for a packet of budgie seed; the next person wanted a goldfish bowl). This is not the problem we have here as demand is clearly not independent and Chapter 6 will describe appropriate methods for this situation.

Case Study: Karta-Load Products

Karta-Load, among their wide range of products for the garden and horticulture business, make a range of popular-sized wheelbarrows of which the one in Figure 6.1, the PSW3, sells extremely well. What has been causing them concern for some time now is that despite the best efforts of management they never seem to be able to assemble the quantities they thought they would be able to, despite prior planning. This causes problems of meeting demand on time and in the quantities anticipated.

They have the usual operations layouts which detail the manufacturing steps involved in making each part. The parts stores is a little old and not too well organised, but Harry who has been there 15 years can find anything required very quickly. The Production Manager and the Sales Manager meet weekly to firm up next week's production. Late jobs are chased through the plant by an assistant to the Sales Manager.

They do not have a management services section, although one of the draughtsmen has had some experience of this with a previous company. Their plant is certainly not new and is situated on the edge of town in an old post-war industrial estate. The finished products are quite good as far as quality goes, although they pride themselves on catching any finished product problems

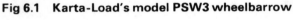

Fig 6.1   Karta-Load's model PSW3 wheelbarrow

('fipps' as they are called) before they leave the factory. They do most of their business with about 15 suppliers, whom they have known over the years. A few give them problems regarding delivery commitments, but management believe it is far better to use someone they have always dealt with.

There is a current demand for model PSW3 of 1200 per year. They currently estimate the cost of borrowing at about 20% per annum, and that it costs £10 to process an order through the plant. The cost of a wheel assembly is £2, the cost of one leg £1, the cost of one handle £1.50, and the cost of one body £5. On the occasions that the barrow is subcontracted out, the bought-in cost is £25 complete. They calculate the economic order quantities for each of the components, and round off the answers and then initiate production for those quantities. They do the same when they order subcontracted wheelbarrows from outside, typically about 200 units per annum.

Item		EOQ	Ordering action
Wheel Assembly	1000	223	200 every 10 weeks
Legs (2 off)	2000	447	500 every 3 months
Handle (2 off)	2000	365	400 five times/year
Body	1000	141	125 every 6 weeks
Bought-in assembly complete	200	28	25 every 6 weeks

What concerns Karta-Load is that although the quantities processed at any one time seem to be correct over a period of several months, even if nothing unexpected happens, they can almost never get the right quantities of everything they need to make a reasonable batch for final assembly. The quantity of 25 bought in complete assemblies causes no problem. The question they need answering is what other approach will enable them to co-ordinate batches of parts for final assembly in appropriate batch sizes?

After talking to their sales, production and production control people, the following information emerged (it is July 19X1 now):

Quantity of finished product to be available for sale next year 19X2 in:

Jan	Feb	Mar	Apr	May	Jun	Jul	Aug	Sep	Oct	Nov	Dec
	300		400					200		100	

It takes a month to assemble batches of the sizes being considered here, and so the batches need to enter final assembly in the months shown below:

					19X2						
Jan	Feb	Mar	Apr	May	Jun	Jul	Aug	Sep	Oct	Nov	Dec
300		400					200		100		

The lead times for the different subassemblies are based on past history:

	Months
Wheel assemblies	2
Legs	1
Handles	1
Bodies	2

and the schedule for entry into the appropriate departments for manufacture is therefore:

This year 19X1		Next year 19X2									
Nov	Dec	Jan	Feb	Mar	Apr	May	Jun	Jul	Aug	Sep	Oct
Handles											
	600		800					400		200	
Body											
300		400					200	100			
Wheel assembly											
300		400					200	100			
Legs											
	600		800					400		200	

The handles require rubber grips which are bought in, and have a lead time of 1 month. The wheels themselves are also bought in with a lead time of 2 months. The orders or call off for the grips and wheels must thus be initiated as follows:

This year 19X1				Next year 19X2							
Sep	Oct	Nov	Dec	Jan	Feb	Mar	Apr	May	Jun	Jul	Aug
		Grips									
		600		800					400		200
Wheels											
300		400					200	100			

Activity

Draw out on a bar chart the timing and quantities for the information above.

6.2 The Explosion

You can see from the individual schedules that the planning process initially identified times in the future when batches of the finished product in certain quantities were required to be available for sale. It then worked backwards towards the present time and calculated the quantities of each of the component parts, and used the lead time information to position the required quantities in the schedule. This process is called the **explosion** because the planning process 'explodes' the required quantities of the finished product into its component parts. The quantities calculated in the example above could also have included allowances for scrap incurred in the processes and spares requirements, and the lead times could also have been varied to suit other specific conditions such as very variable batch sizes.

The explosion is made more complicated in practice because account must also be taken of work in progress, parts in store and already on order, parts already committed to other products but not yet issued and parts which are common to other products, some of which may not be planned for at the time. The use of a computer aids this planning process because of

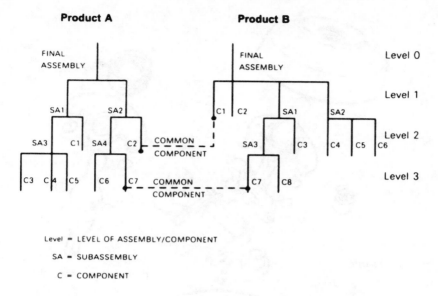

Fig 6.2   The product hierarchy

its ability to handle large quantities of information. In practice, the explosion may cover a very large range of products.

The relationship of a final product to its subassemblies and component parts, together with any common parts, is shown in Figure 6.2.

Just how complex the explosion can become can be seen from an exploded drawing (Figure 6.3) of an old fashioned domestic light switch. Notice the large number of parts required. Some of the parts make up subassemblies and items such as washers and screws are required as sets of four. The springs are needed in sets of two. The rest of the switch is made up of individual items, and some of them may be common to other switches.

6.3 **Materials Requirements Planning (MRP1)**

We have seen the basic planning process in action; now we need to describe the key features of **Material Requirements Planning** (sometimes known as MRP1).

1 MRP is a planning process for products which consist of **assemblies** and **subassemblies**, and it is not used for individual parts whose demand is unrelated to any other part: MRP is not a statistical procedure like the evaluation of re-order levels and quantities.

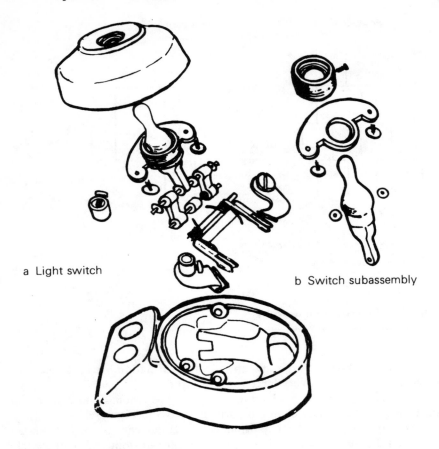

a Light switch   b Switch subassembly

Fig 6.3   The explosion

---

2 The planning process is done on a **regular basis** (e.g. monthly) and is best carried out by a team of people from the key areas of the company. They will be from sales, accounting, production, production control, purchasing and stock control. The reason for the team approach is that there will be sufficient expertise available to be able to take into account as many as possible of the variables in the situation. Some of these will include delivery problems, quality problems, current stock situation, firm and tentative orders for the product, overtime ability, availability of key equipment and the status of work in progress.

3 MRP involves decisions such as **what** key products to make, **how many**, and **when** they should be in stock. For each key product this is decided (on a rolling basis at each meeting). This initial document is known as the **master schedule**, because this is used as the basis for the explosion of each

product. At subsequent meetings, the master schedule is updated according to the latest information available.

4 Working back from the 'final product in stock' date, the quantities and dates are determined for each subassembly and component part using current knowledge of lead times. Start dates and quantities are determined for everything required to make the product. On some occasions, there may be sufficient stock available so that ordering or manufacture of certain parts may not be necessary. This process is the 'explosion' referred to earlier. Where the demand for a product is very low, so that it becomes unrealistic to talk of producing even a small batch of that product, the planning team may decide to have a policy of, say, when one is sold, build another one. Such a policy will result in **extended lead times**, but this will not matter too much if demand is low. It will still be a definite policy and not just a policy left to be operated by formulae. These key products are, after all, class A items and probably represent 80–90% of total revenue.

5 The **accuracy of reports** is vital. If this is not the case, then no matter how good the planning is the actual result will be poor because of the discrepancies between actual and reported stock. The key reports which are used in this situation are **(a)** Bill of Materials, **(b)** Where Used listing, **(c)** Stock report, **(d)** Purchasing records, **(e)** Work in Progress and **(f)** Scrap and Rework reports.

(a)   The **Bill of Materials** is a document which lists for each product every item which goes into that product, down to the last washer and nut. The information will include part number, description, quantity per product, whether made or bought, and where stocked.

(b)   The **Where Used listing** is a report containing the same information as in **(a)** above, but it lists every stockable item and shows which products it is used on. In practice, the same item may be used on several different products, as well as being used for spares. In a well-organised database, this listing may not be required, if any specific part or subassembly for a particular Bill of Materials can be quizzed directly to provide this information.

(c)   **Stock reports** show for every item the quantity in stock, quantity allocated, quantity free for future use, work in progress quantity and quantity on order and quantity at receiving department, and quantity at inspection department.

(d)   **Purchasing records** show for each purchased item its part number, where supplied from, supplier's own part or catalogue number, lead times, orders outstanding, price breaks, order quantities, re-order levels and current status of outstanding orders.

(e)   **Work in Progress reports** show on a regular basis the status of every batch of work throughout the factory. Such reports will show the batch account number, the batch quantity, part number, current work centre, operation number, store destination and appropriate planned due date.

(f) Scrap and Rework reports show the status of all work found to be **non-conforming** during manufacture. The information contained will include its batch account number, assigned repair account number, part number, quantity non-conforming, reason, cause, decision made and any new material required.

Activity

The Planar Widget

	Jan	Feb	Mar	Apr	May	Jun	Jul	Aug	Sep	Oct	Nov	Dec
Sales Forecast	160	140	100	80	60	60	60	80	100	120	140	150
Planned starting stock	0	35	25	20	15	15	15	20	25	30	35	40

A widget consists of 3 main subassemblies, A, B and C. Each widget needs 3 of A, 2 of B and 1 of C. Spare parts needed as a percentage of forecasted demand are: 5% for A, 3% for B and 1% for C. Current problems mean a scrap allowance of 1% for A and 0.5% for B. Lead times in weeks per batch are: 4 weeks for A, 2 weeks for B and 6 weeks for C. You can assume lead times do not vary with batch size.

Required
1 Ideally, when should production start?
2 How many should be assembled each month?
3 Draw the product tree hierarchy.
4 Explode the data and draw a Gantt chart.

Case Study: Marple Electronics

One of Marple's key products is the DCD-1, a portable electronic decoder for satellite transmissions. It consists essentially of three subassemblies A, B and C. Each of these subassemblies consists of various printed circuit boards (pcbs). While each subassembly's pcbs differ considerably in design, for any particular subassembly, the pcbs differ only in the electrical value of the various components.

	Subassembly
A consists of 4 pcbs,	pcb/a/1–4
B consists of 3 pcbs,	pcb/b/1–3
C consists of 2 pcbs,	pcb/c/1–2

Other components for the DCD-1 such as cabling, switches and casing are readily available, and therefore do not form part of the planning problem.

Costs:

pcb/a/1–4 for subassembly A	£1 each
pcb/b/1–3 for subassembly B	£2 each
pcb/c/1–2 for subassembly C	£3 each

	£
Subassembly A complete	8.00
Subassembly B complete	12.00
Subassembly C complete	12.00

DCD-1 fully assembled, tested and packed £55.00

It is now towards the end of 19X3, and Sales and Marketing have produced the following sales forecast for the DCD-1 for 19X4:

					19X4						
Jan	*Feb*	*Mar*	*Apr*	*May*	*Jun*	*Jul*	*Aug*	*Sep*	*Oct*	*Nov*	*Dec*
140	120	100	80	60	60	60	80	100	120	140	140

They also require that the following quantities of the product be in stock at the start of each month:

19X4												*19X5*
Jan	*Feb*	*Mar*	*Apr*	*May*	*Jun*	*Jul*	*Aug*	*Sep*	*Oct*	*Nov*	*Dec*	*(Jan)*
30	25	20	15	10	10	15	15	20	20	30	30	40

Production Control suggests the following lead times per batch which we will assume do not vary with batch sizes:

	Weeks
Make pcb/a/1–4	6
Make pcb/b/1–3	6
Make pcb/c/1–2	8

	Weeks
Assemble subassembly A	4
Assemble subassembly B	2
Assemble subassembly C	6

Final Assembly of DCD-1, test and pack: 2 weeks

Production records suggest 1% scrap for pcb/a/1–4, 3% scrap for pcb/b/1–3 and 2% scrap for pcb/c/1–2. No scrap is produced at the subassembly or final assembly stages.

The service department suggests the spares requirements to be: pcb/a/1–4 3%; pcb/b/1–3 4%; pcb/c/1–2 5%

Activity

1 Does Marples Electronics' position describe a push or a pull situation? Why?
2 Draw a tree to show the different levels of assembly involved. Remember level 0 is the final product itself.
3 Calculate the quantities needed for each stage of production. This must include pcbs, subassemblies and the final product. You will need to remember the relationship: Opening stock + Production − Sales = Closing stock, in order to find out how many DCD-1s to produce each month. The closing stock for one month is the opening stock for the following month. You will then need to consider subassemblies, pcbs, spare part and scrap rates to obtain the appropriate quantities at each stage for each month.
4 Draw a bar chart with a horizontal time scale (no vertical scale needed) to show graphically the lead times and quantities you just calculated. *Note:* the graph of lead times will be the same for each month, but the quantities at each stage will differ.
5 Calculate the economic order quantity (EOQ) for:
   (a) the finished decoder DCD-1 (as if you were buying it in complete from an outside supplier for £55 each); assume the order processing cost is £30 per occasion, and the annual holding cost is 25%

(b) each of the three subassemblies at their own price per subassembly

(c) the individual pcbs for each subassembly. You may assume that as far as this calculation is concerned, the pcbs for a subassembly are sufficiently alike so that (for example) their requirement is 4 times the demand for subassembly A, and so on.

6 Do the EOQs seem to bear any relation to the quantities you calculated in **3** above? Why or why not?

6.4 A Spreadsheet Planning Model

This shows how a spreadsheet can be used as a planning aid to model part of an MRP programme. It caters for only one finished product over a period of 9 months and incorporates some cost data as an example of what could be built into it, to make it more realistic. You can simulate changes in the forecasted demand for this product, as well as some changes to stock levels. It will then indicate the levels of production required and the costs resulting from holding, stockouts and set-ups. The cumulative cost to date and the average cost to date are calculated, as well as the average production required, the average actual closing stock and the average planned closing stock.

(a) Relationships in the model

The two principal relationships upon which the model is based are shown below. All the others are formulae linking the months together or setting the fixed relationships of some of the cells:

1	**Planned production required**	=	**Planned closing stock**	−	**Planned opening stock**	+	**Planned demand**

so that

2	**Actual opening**	+	**Production received**	−	**Actual demand**	=	**Actual stock remaining**

(b) Planned and actual opening and closing quantities

The key relationships of planned and actual opening and closing quantities are shown in Figure 6.4. The lead time for production is set at one month.

(c) The spreadsheet model display

We now look at the key lines of the display shown in Figure 6.5.

	Jan	Feb	Mar	Apr
Planned Opening Stock	200	150	300	250
Actual Opening Stock	200	100	150	0
Planned Closing Stock	150	300	250	200
Production Requirements	350	450	550	450
Production Received	300	350	450	550
Actual Closing Stock	100	150	0	50

Fig 6.4   Input–output relationships

Line 3 is the 'fudge factor' by which you can alter your planned demand. A value of 1.0 leaves the planned demand unaltered. The fudge factor is multiplied by the planned demand to give the actual demand as on line 5.
Line 4 is your estimate of the forecasted demand, and you enter this for months 1 to 6.
Line 6 The planned opening stock is set at 25% of the actual demand.
Line 7 For the first month the actual opening stock is set at 25% of that month's opening planned demand, otherwise it is the previous month's closing actual stock.
Line 9 Each month's planned closing stock is the following month's opening planned stock.
Line 10 Planned production is calculated from relationship **1** above.
Lines 11 and 12 show by how much required production exceeds (if it does) a capacity of 400 units. In line 13, you enter an arbitrary value for January's production received, and subsequent months' production received are the previous month's production scheduled (i.e. one month lead time).
Lines 15, 16 and 17 show the actual stock position, for which there is a factory warehouse, and a public warehouse if stock is greater than 100 units in a month.
Lines 20 and 21 give stock holding costs at a cost of £0.2/item if held in-house or £0.3/item if held in the public warehouse.
Lines 22 and 23 give the cost of running out of stock at £0.5/item; and for producing a batch size less than 300 units a charge of £15 is made per occasion.

Fig 6.5 A spreadsheet model

	A Month	B Jan	C Feb	D Mar	E Apr	F May	G June	H July	I Aug	J Sept
1										
2										
3	Fudge factor: (YOU ENTER)	1.00								
4	Planned dem'd (YOU ENTER)	600	500	400	300	350	450			
5	Actual Demand (3 × 4)	600	500	400	300	350	450			
6	Planned Opening Stock	150	125	100	75	87	112	112		
7	Actual Opening Stock	150	150	50	50	150	200	150		
8										
9	Planned closing stock	125	100	75	87	112	112			
10	Planned Production	575	475	375	312	375	450			
11	Cum prodreq > prod. capacity by	175	250	225	137	112	162	0	0	0
12	Prodn sched < = 400	400	400	400	400	400	400	162	0	0
13	Prod Rcvd (YOU ENTER Jan)	600	400	400	400	400	400	400	162	0
14										
15	Actual Cl Stk (or owing)	150	50	50	150	200	150			
16	Stk in facty (100 max)	100	50	50	100	100	100			
17	XS stk in Public whse	50	0	0	50	100	50			
18										
19	Costs									
20	Facty Holding:£ 2/item	20	10	10	20	20	20			
21	Whse hldng:£ 3/item	15	0	0	15	30	15			
22	Stk out penalty: £.5/item	0	0	0	0	0	0			
23	Ineff prodn line (<300)	0	0	0	0	0	0			
24										
25	Total cost this period	35	10	10	35	50	35			
26	Cumul cost to date	35	45	55	90	140	175			
27	AVGE COST/PERIOD to date	35	22.50	18.33	22.50	28	29.17			
28										
29	Average Prodn reqd	150					427			
30	Average actl closing stk	125	100	83.33	100	120	125			
31	Average planned clsg stk	125	112.50	100	96.75	99.80	101.83			

The summary cost data is given in lines 25 to 27, but for decision-making purposes, other things being equal, you might decide that you would produce the quantities shown up to the month where the average monthly cost (line 27) was a minimum. In the case of Figure 6.5, this would mean initiating manufacturing in January, February and March for an average monthly cost of £18.33.

All the built-in relationships can be altered by you if desired, but initial experimentation will show you how the various parameters move when changes are made, and which appear to be the most sensitive to these changes.

6.5 Manufacturing Resource Planning (MRP2)

Manufacturing Resource Planning integrates information available (or requires that it be made available) on product requirements, procurement, accounting, capacity, and inventory, as well as on engineering, design, distribution, sales and marketing, so that plans can be produced which take into account the **whole capability and limitations** of the entire plant. MRP2 is a 'system' in the true sense of the word, and it is vital that when it is being developed the requirements of the company are known precisely – and, even better, that as much of the system has already been run manually. If this is not possible, then it is essential to retain the existing system for some time after the computerised system is implemented, so that the running-in period is as painless and safe as possible.

In many situations, information required may not be available, or it may not be compatible with computer formats. There is always a huge amount of data to be entered. All this should be done after a careful evaluation and review of the company's present and future needs. It is a matter for management's judgement whether or not a custom or proprietary system is used. The advantage of a custom-designed system is that it should match the exact needs of the company. It will necessarily cost more than a proprietary package. However, if it suits most of a company's needs, and is readily available, simpler to install and to learn, and cheaper, then it may represent good value. It is certain that if a company has not determined fully what its requirements are no system, whether custom or proprietary, will do what the company expects it to.

6.6 Just in Time (JIT) Manufacture

As we saw above, MRP is a system which relies on accurate forecasts of how much, and when, particular finished product is needed. The explosion then works back from the future date towards the present time, calculating the quantity of all parts required and when required. The process itself, while inherently relatively simple, is extremely arduous in reality unless computers are used to handle the vast amount of inter-related data. Work in progress stores tend to proliferate to provide a buffer when things go wrong (e.g. when material does not arrive on time, or forecasts are wrong or work takes longer than estimated). MRP is sometimes known as 'just in case' – i.e. let us have a bit more 'in case...'.

(a) The principle of JIT

The principle of JIT is that parts must arrive from suppliers, whether internal or external, just in time to be used at the appropriate work station. The demand for these parts is triggered by the **user** of that part, and the quantity is usually kept very low. It is kept low because the end user knows that a new part can always be supplied upon request. This is similar to a person who buys one pint of milk at a time from the supermarket: there is no need to buy larger amounts, as there is always milk available.

Such a system naturally requires great co-operation between the company and its suppliers, and the suppliers are required to adhere very closely to agreed schedules and levels of quality. There is also a tendency to reduce the number of suppliers a company deals with, but to foster a much closer and long-term association with them. JIT is really a philosophy of **manufacture**, as it cannot be implemented successfully unless there is clear agreement by all those concerned and this includes suppliers.

(b) Value of JIT

There are many claims made for JIT, such as reductions of work in progress and operating costs. **Lead times** are often reduced by a more efficient layout of machinery into groups and reductions in set-up times. Customer service improves because lead times are reduced, and because of the close attention to quality. Frequency of deliveries increases as quantities being delivered are smaller – often several times a day straight on to the shop floor. **Space** is saved, as central storage of raw materials can be replaced by such material being kept at the point of usage, often the JIT cell. **Manpower** is consequently saved because people whose prime job used to be store-keepers or parts-collectors prior to manufacture are no longer necessary. Such people may be retrained to new jobs as part of the overall job restructuring programme.

(c) 'Right first time' work

Because cells now manufacture well-defined groups of products or parts, better housekeeping results from the greater pride people begin to take in their jobs. Consequently, there is often a higher percentage of **'right first time'** work. Because of better training, the workforce in a cell will be more flexible regarding the number of different jobs they can do. They may not even have a fixed work bench assigned to them. There is a great need for

discipline in operation when JIT is installed, and such a change over is a major exercise in itself.

(d) JIT and suppliers

There is some evidence that the much vaunted reductions in inventory may be achieved by ensuring that it is the **supplier** who holds sufficient stock to be able to deliver as frequently as required. Some successful practitioners of JIT often share their expertise with their key suppliers, so that they themselves can become users of JIT, and so the JIT philosophy becomes extended down through the supply chain. Many small companies find it difficult to implement JIT because they cannot influence their suppliers sufficiently to change their current practice. Price alone must not be the key factor: consistent and appropriate quality, assured delivery and a continuing closeness with the customer are also essential.

(e) JIT and plant layout

As well as close liaison with suppliers, a company needs an efficient and appropriate **plant layout** which avoids circuitous routes and backtracking together with good access for suppliers to deliver right on to or very close to the **point of use** of the parts being delivered.

Group technology (see Chapter 8) and cell manufacture often form part of this overall improvement in manufacturing process. Because of low quantities being demanded at any one time, set-up or change-over times must be reduced to the minimum possible, and this requires constant attention. Often to achieve this, set-ups are taken off line. It can be seen from an examination of the economic order frequency diagram (Figure 5.3) that as the order process cost (equivalent to the set-up cost) is reduced, the slope becomes less steep; the crossover point moves to the right. This means that the frequency of ordering is increased and therefore the economic order quantity is smaller.

The company must also have a system which is able to respond to changes in **demand**, quickly enough so that the response is well within the lead time demanded by changed circumstances.

6.7 JIT Development and Use

(a) The withdrawal, production and manufacture card

JIT began in the 1960s at Toyota in Japan, and is sometimes referred to as the **Kanban** system. 'Kanban' is the Japanese word for a card, and a card is used as authorisation for:

(**a**) withdrawal of a part and
(**b**) production of the part from the preceding process.

JIT is a 'pull' system (i.e. the parts are pulled through the manufacturing process as needed). The cards each contain the necessary information to identify the part for withdrawal and for manufacture. The small batches produced are often put in a store. One card is the authorisation to produce one unit of the part: the unit can relate to one item, one pallet load or some other quantity which has been defined as one unit.

The withdrawal card authorises **withdrawal** of the part and returns with it. The production card initiates from the store upon withdrawal of the part and proceeds to the earlier process for **manufacture** of that part. The manufacture card accompanies that batch when finished, **into stock.**

(b) Line balancing

It is fundamental in JIT that no excess inventory is produced. Because of this overriding requirement, line balancing of different pieces of equipment is important. 'Line balancing' means that production is arranged so that undue bottlenecks are avoided and no high volume equipment is allowed to produce more than that required by the manufacturing card. To achieve this, **intermittent production** is often used by equipment which has a higher output than that required: each piece of equipment will operate throughout the shift in proportion to its capacity and requirements. Another method is the **slower operation** of the high capacity piece of equipment.

(c) Batch manufacture

The re-order point system can be used when triggered by a card, to initiate the next batch for manufacture as replacement for a batch of the same size just withdrawn. However, the batch size is not related to estimated longer-term needs, but is merely a **replacement batch** as noted above: good forecasting is therefore required for this method to work effectively. By its very nature, JIT involves many small batches for manufacture, and it is therefore essential that no production be undertaken without a manufacture card, nor for that matter should any withdrawals occur without a withdrawal card. For similar reasons, **standardisation of jobs** is also advantageous.

(d) Defective items

A preceding manufacturing process must produce that quantity which was withdrawn by the subsequent process. If defective units are discovered, they must not be sent on to the subsequent process. If that process discovers defective items itself, then it should stop its own process and send back those items to the preceding process. In many JIT installations, a device such as a red light is switched on for all to see when defectives are discovered. To traditional western manufacturing custom and practice, this is virtually unheard of, and is a traumatic process if implemented. This is one of the reasons why a change to JIT is more than a change in technique. It is a change to a **new philosophy of manufacture**, and as such demands backing from top management downwards.

(e) Production planning

Production planning consists, for example, of having a yearly target of production, together with a rolling three-monthly plan where the third month out is a suggested figure, the second month out is a 'let's go' figure, and next month's figure is finalised. Finalisation will include product and model variations and associated quantities. From the finalised next month's production quantity, daily production schedules can be determined. The sequence of the models during production will also be determined. The overall goal of JIT will be to effect cost reduction, and therefore profit improvement, by reducing inventory levels, particularly of finished product. The system of production is job or batch oriented, the influencing factor being the request for parts from the subsequent process.

(f) Changes in demand

It is important to be able to react to demand, although as mentioned earlier, the manufacturing card is a response to usage further down the line.

- If the change in demand is longer term (i.e. the yearly plan) and the machines have been previously loaded well below their capacity, there may well be sufficient capacity to be able to respond.
- Extra operatives can also be hired temporarily, but this will involve a learning curve. When demand drops, further surplus capacity will occur, but extra inventory should not be built owing to the cost involved. Temporary operatives will be freed, and perhaps parts bought in can be made in house.
- Other activities such as training, set-up analysis, maintenance of equipment and jigs and fixtures may also be possible.
- More rapid adaptation to short-term changes in demand will be required and this is done virtually automatically by the number of cards which are initiated by the subsequent process.

6.8 JIT Implementation

Before there is any attempt to change the current manufacturing system, it is important for the company to measure its **current performance** on as wide a front as possible, using a number of agreed criteria.

Such criteria should include at least eleven areas:

(a) **Value of inventory held**, classified into: raw material, work in progress and finished goods. These parameters can also be given as percentage of sales, all valued at cost.

(b) The number of times inventory is **turned over** per year (e.g. annual sales turnover is £2.5 million and the average inventory held in all classifications is £500,000). Inventory turnover is therefore $2.5/0.5 = 5$ times per year. This is a very useful parameter to be able to compare with other companies in the same business, as the actual size of the values does not need to be disclosed.

(c) Levels of **scrap and rework**, separately identified, measured as absolute money values, and as a percentage of sales.

(d) The key parameters of **vendor performance**, measured by on time deliveries, quantities including partials, price, quality, and lead times.

(e) The key parameters of **service to the customer** measured at least by ageing the sales orders, number of on-time deliveries, quantity and value of orders delivered on time compared with quantity and value of total orders.

(f) The proportion of **actual work content** measured by formal work study techniques, compared with the overall time those jobs are in the system.

(g) **Labour cost** and **total cost per unit of output**.

(h) Accuracy of all **key reports** currently generated.

(i) **Distance travelled** by a representative or key product during its manufacture.

(j) How long material has to **wait** at key work centres before it starts being processed.

(k) An analysis of what percentage of the current labour force can do what percentage of the **different jobs** required. Prior to a JIT installation, it is quite likely that only 10–15% of the labour force can do about 70–80% of the different jobs required.

Such an audit is an essential feature of a planned change of manufacturing system, and is best done by a small but representative team of people from the main areas of the company. This team should have the power to co-opt help where it is required.

Activity

Re-read the case study on Karta-Load Products (pp. 138–40), and decide what ought to be done if they want to change to (a) MRP and (b) JIT.

6.9 Optimised Production Technology (OPT)

OPT is a proprietary system developed in the mid-1980s by Eli Goldratt, an Israeli physicist. A key feature of his philosophy is that maximising a plant's

output does not necessarily maximise its **profitability**. Goldratt sees the goal of a manufacturing company as making money. It should achieve this by increasing net profits, return on investment and cash flow all at the same time. Such a company will therefore increase throughput and decrease inventories and operational expenses. Goldratt's system operates by using a **manufacturing simulation package** and a set of **shop floor operating rules**. There are reports of major successes as well as of rather more disappointing results.

(a) Line balancing

Goldratt contends that operating his system enables a company to increase its output while at the same time lowering its inventory and operating costs. Work must be co-ordinated by management and workers through the plant, while bearing in mind that it is **bottlenecks** which constrain manufacturing output. This is the usual rationale for the great care with which lines are balanced, when work flows sequentially through a series of operations. Any out of balance situation results in production being limited by the bottleneck operation, with work being piled up ahead of that operation, and people and equipment working non-stop after that operation.

(b) Bottleneck identification

Managers use Goldratt's software to identify bottlenecks **in advance**, so that they can then schedule accordingly. He preaches that people and equipment working at full throttle do not necessarily mean maximum output at minimum cost. If this means that key pieces of capital equipment are not always working at maximum capacity, it can be difficult to persuade managers that this is a reasonable thing to do. A supporting argument for this line of reasoning is that while it may be cheaper to run large batches of work through a piece of expensive equipment, if they are subsequently held up and cannot be used it will be even more expensive to hold them as processed parts than it will be to leave the equipment working at less than maximum. It is therefore important to balance **flow** through the entire plant rather than **capacity**.

(c) Constraint analysis

Other key rules of OPT operation are that the level of utilisation of a non-bottleneck work centre is actually determined by a constraint other than its own potential. Time lost at a bottleneck is time lost for the whole system, whereas time saved at a non-bottleneck is a mirage. This second point is very similar to the situation after a method study where the space now proposed is less than that currently required. If no use for the space to be released can be found, the saving is illusory. Schedules have to be established by looking at all of the constraints **simultaneously**. Lead times are the result of the schedule and therefore cannot be predetermined. (This last rule conflicts with the usual methodology of MRP, where the pre-knowledge of lead times is essential for using the technique.)

6.10 **World Class Manufacturing (WCM)**

'World Class Manufacturing' is the title of a book by Richard Schonberger. It is intended to indicate the breadth of changes currently taking place in industrial organisations in their effort to satisfy the customer on a regularly and economically. It implies **continual improvement** ('kaizen' in Japanese) and includes changes to the approach to:

(a) Customer requirements – these must be met regularly, completely and economically.
(b) JIT – a highly responsive system utilising minimal stocks and working closely with carefully chosen suppliers.
(c) Management – motivated, trained and committed to the achievement of all objectives.
(d) Performance measurement – the never-ending quest for increasing productivity throughout the organisation.
(e) Quality – its achievement throughout the company by everyone in everything they do.

(a) **Quality**

The emphasis is on the total elimination of all waste, the prevention of poor quality and the solving of problems causing them. **Zero defects**, a term popular 25 years ago, is the prime aim of all concerned with quality. To achieve this, the **quality ethos** must pervade the entire company so that improving quality becomes a way of life, and not just something left to the Inspection department. Indeed, the emphasis should be far removed from appraisal and moved to **prevention**. In Chapter 2 we referred to this way of thinking as Total Quality Management.

(b) **JIT**

The intention of JIT is to eliminate everything that **does not add value** to the product. Such activities include the elimination or reduction of elements in the process such as transportation, inspection, queuing, storage, scrap and rework.

(c) Management

The effect of the changes in manufacturing techniques means that there is now a greater need for employees who are well trained and motivated to understand clearly what is required, and to respond accordingly. Unless there is a feeling of mutual trust and a common aim, these key changes will fall far short of what is expected. When employees are well trained and motivated, they will accept more willingly a greater role in the striving for improvement in quality, growth and profitability: **team work** takes on a greater importance than the traditional individual and more isolated role of the employee, particularly the direct employee.

(d) Customer requirements

Much greater flexibility towards customer requirements is also of prime importance to the WCM company. Such companies must liaise closely with their **key customers**, so that their requirements can be begun to be translated into practice as soon as they have been agreed, thus reducing some elements of overall lead time. Rapid reaction to changes in design and development as well as to production all help to make a strong bond between customer and manufacturer.

(e) Performance measurement

Finally, great importance is placed upon quantifying **measures of performance**, and monitoring them with a view constantly to improving them. It is this constant striving to improve which is the driving force towards world class achievement. The performance indicators will certainly include those referred to in JIT above, but must also include non-financial indicators such as change-over times, queue times and down times.

Chapter Review Questions

1 What is meant by 'dependent demand' and 'independent demand'?
2 What is the difference between pull and push demand-led manufacture?
3 Is EOQ relevant to dependent demand manufacture? If not, why not?
4 'MRP2 is also an effective tool for non-dependent manufacture situations': True or False?
5 What does the explosion process do in MRP?
6 What elements are involved in the 'explosion process'?
7 What is a bill of materials and a 'where used' listing?
8 Identify the advantages and disadvantages of a custom-made computer package.
9 What does 'JIT' refer to in 'JIT'? What are the implications?
10 Identify at least four benefits you would expect from a successful JIT implementation.

11 How are suppliers affected when a company changes to a JIT system?
12 What is a 'Kanban' and what does it do?
13 How does JIT respond to changes in product demand?
14 Describe five criteria for measuring manufacturing performance.
15 'OPT tries to maximise output so as to minimise unit costs': True or False?
16 'Time saved at a non-bottleneck process is still worthwhile': True or False?

7 Managing the Costs

Money is the most liquid of resources, and like a liquid it can slip away very easily. It is often said that if the money is available, any other resource can be obtained: this may be a simplification, but it shows how important money is. Money is used for many purposes, including capital and cost expenditure.

It is important to be clear about the key concepts of cost management, so that the best possible use can be made of financial data: in this context, we need to know how costs are **analysed** so that comparisons can be made and interpreted on the basis of valid data.

Learning Objectives

By the end of the chapter you should:

1 know how to draw and use a **break-even chart**
2 be able to identify marginal costs
3 be able to analyse problems using the concept of contribution
4 know how to use **discounted cash flow (DCF)** techniques for evaluating different projects
5 be able to use different methods for **depreciating** capital assets
6 know the basic methods of costing.

7.1 The Break-Even Chart

(a) The concept of 'break even'

The concept of 'break even' is useful to management because it indicates the level of activity in a company where **total revenue equals total costs**. At a level above this, total revenue is greater than total costs, and a **profit** is made. Conversely, below this level of activity total revenue is less than total costs and a **loss** is incurred. The level of activity can be measured in any suitable manner (e.g. units of output).

159

It is also important to note that it is more useful to talk about a **break-even region**, rather than a break-even point, because as all costs can only be estimates and are never known precisely changes in the cost or revenue estimates will change the calculated break-even value; the term 'point' also gives a misleading impression of accuracy.

Case Study: Percy's Pizza Parlour (3P) – Break-Even Analysis

3P is a three-man business which is situated in the local high street, where it has been for the last three years. Its success seems to stem from Percy being able to deliver pizzas which are sufficiently different from the franchised versions to attract those who appreciate something approaching the genuine Italian article. Percy is the cook and cashier. There is a waitress, and someone who delivers pizzas in the local postal area in response to phone-in orders.

Percy's **fixed** costs are £30,000 per year and include rent and rates, lighting and heating, and wages. These are called 'fixed costs' because they are incurred **regardless of the level of activity** of the business, at least in the short to medium term. In the long term, all costs are variable. If his business expands greatly, or slumps badly, then even these so-called fixed costs will vary. In the event of a slump, Percy may decide to have a waitress only during the busy periods.

Percy's variable costs are those costs which **vary with the level of activity** of his business. These are mainly the raw materials from which he makes his pizzas, and his own labour cost for actually making them. Costs for the paper plates, plastic cutlery and condiments are also included. There are costs incurred for washing up and cleaning, and servicing the restroom facilities, and these are assumed to be **indirect costs** because it is rather difficult to match them closely to the production of pizzas. Percy estimates that his typical pizza sells for £5.50 and that that includes a beverage of some kind. The variable cost of that pizza is about £2.50.

Figure 7.1 is a graph of money (on the vertical axis), plotted against number of pizzas sold per four-week month (on the horizontal axis). This period was chosen because it seemed reasonable to Percy as a representative period which would include some of the quiet times as well as some of the busier ones, since he wanted to make any calculations as realistic as possible. The graph is built up by calculating the total costs and total revenue for a range of output of pizzas – in this case, from 0 to 2100 in steps of 300. The fixed costs incurred in a four-week period are £30,000/13 = £2,308.

Percy knew from his records about how many pizzas he served each month, and the activity level (horizontal axis) goes from zero to 1000. Zero is not a very realistic figure because if he sold no pizzas he would go out of business. However, it provides a starting point. From the graph, you can see that the crossover point where total costs equal total revenue is between 750 and 800 pizzas per month. Percy reckons he is selling nearer 700 pizzas and although this shows him making a theoretical loss, he thinks he has been covering himself because of the fairly substantial mark-up on wine.

(b) Calculating the break-even quantity

The break-even chart has shown that the break-even level of Percy's activity is about 750 to 800 pizzas per month. There is a way to calculate

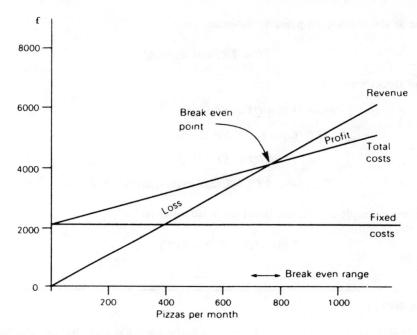

Fig 7.1   Break-even chart for pizzas

the break-even quantity without having to draw the graph, which can be convenient if the figures are particularly large, or you want to experiment with different values for those figures.

As the basic break-even chart is made up only of straight lines, the equation which can be used is for a straight line:

$$y = a + bx$$

where a is a constant
and b is the slope

Let fixed costs $= FC = a$
variable cost/unit $= VC = b$
total revenue $= TR$
selling price/unit $= SP$
break even quantity $= BQ$
quantity sold $= Q$

Total costs (TC) = FC + (VC × Q)

and at the break-even point by definition:

$$TC = TR; \text{ and } BQ = Q.$$

and therefore:

$$FC + (VC \times Q) = SP \times Q$$

$$(FC/Q) + VC = SP$$

$$FC/Q = SP - VC$$

$$FC/(SP - VC) = \text{Break-even quantity } BQ$$

In our example above, the break-even quantity is:

$$2308/(5.5 - 2.5) = 769 \text{ pizzas}$$

Activity

So that you can check that you know how to use the break-even formula, try the following:

(a) What is the break-even quantity if fixed costs are:
   (i) £2,000 **(ii)** >£2,600 **(iii)** £2,900
   and the selling and variable costs stay the same?
(b) For each of the different fixed costs in **(a)** above, what is the break-even quantity if the difference between the selling price and variable cost is:
   (i) £2.0 **(ii)** £2.5 **(iii)** £3.5

In a 28-day period, Percy is open the equivalent of 25 days, so to break even with the current cost and revenue data, he needs to sell $769/25 = 31$ pizzas per day. At present, he is not quite reaching that figure. However, by answering the questions such as those posed above and finding ways to achieve the required results, he can try to improve his profitability.

Merely putting up his prices may not be a realistic option. He commands only a small premium for being different from the big pizza chains, and he is still in a competitive business. He must try, for example, to reduce his fixed and variable costs in ways that do not have an adverse effect on his sales of pizzas.

7.2 Marginal Costs

(a) Marginal and fixed costs

We have mentioned marginal costs already in our analysis of 3P, and have seen that marginal costs are those that vary with the level of activity: when the level of activity **increases**, so do **marginal costs**; when activity **reduces**, the marginal costs also **reduce**. It is important to distinguish this category of cost from fixed costs: fixed costs are those costs which do not vary to any substantial degree, whatever the level of activity, within reason. In the long term all costs are variable, but we are considering the short to medium term.

(b) Marginal cost and operating decisions

Marginal costs can often be used to help determine the effect of different courses of action: this is because there will be differences in costs according to those different actions. We will consider the **purpose** for which the cost is being used to help us make a decision.

Case Study: Percy's Pizza Parlour (3P) – Percy's Delivery Van

The following data relates to Percy's light van:

	Pence/mile	
Petrol and oil	8.0	25 mpg £2/gallon
Maintenance	5.0	10,000 miles/year
Replacement tyres	0.5	£150/3 years

	£ per year	
Insurance	500	
Road tax	100	
Motoring association	50	
Depreciation	2,000	£8,000/4 years

Situation 1

What costs should be considered if Percy wants to decide whether or not to use the van for a particular journey? As he already has the van, and it is all ready for use, then the only cost to consider is the **variable cost** in the very short term. In this case, it is the cost of petrol and oil, 8 pence per mile. This is not to say that he can run the van for a total of only 8 pence/mile, but for the very next journey considered on its own the marginal costs are the only costs to consider.

Situation 2

What costs should be considered if the van is likely to be laid up for the next year, as Percy is going to Italy on business? He will certainly save the **running costs**, and in this case he will not have to pay the insurance or road tax. He may or may not decide to keep on with his motoring association membership.

Situation 3

What costs ought Percy to consider if he is wondering whether or not to get rid of the van and use taxis? In this case, the most realistic picture of the true cost of running a van is given by including **all costs**, and working them out on a per mile basis. If he uses taxis he may even wish to include an extra cost for the longer time most trips will **take**. If he can put a cost on an hour of his time, and has an estimate of how much longer some typical journeys will then take, that additional cost should be added on to the fare cost of the non-van journeys.

7.3 Contribution

The formula for calculating the break-even quantity was given by:

$$\textbf{Break-even quantity} = \frac{FC}{(SP - VC)}$$

where *SP* is the unit selling price, and *VC* is the unit variable cost. It is the difference between the selling price and the variable cost which contributes to **recovering the overheads** represented by the fixed costs *FC*.

This simple concept is of great importance when making decisions about different products, because although one product may make a smaller profit than another, it is still making a contribution to fixed cost recovery, and this contribution, if lost, would have to be made in some other way. The next case study will help illustrate how such an analysis can be made.

Case Study: Universal Caterers

Universal Caterers make and supply all non-food accessories to commercial caterers like 3P. They can supply condiment sets, cutlery, glassware, plates, cups and saucers, frying pans and saucepans, cooking utensils and ovens and fryers of various kinds.

Three of their most popular items are: **(a)** a cutlery set, **(b)** a condiment set, and **(c)** a three-piece frying pan set.

The cost data associated with these products is as follows:

	Product A £	Product B £	Product C £
Direct labour	1.00	0.25	3.00
Direct materials	2.00	1.00	14.00
Overheads are 150% on direct materials	3.00	1.50	21.00
Selling price	9.00	2.50	45.00
Number sold/year	15,000	30,000	5,000

Overheads are expressed by Universal Caterers as a percentage of material costs, because they see direct material costs as reflecting the main cost of that product. The accounts people hope that by allocating their total overheads in this manner, they will be fully recovered:

	£	£	£
Total cost/item	6.00	2.75	38.00
Profit/item	3.00	(0.25)	7.00

It has already been suggested that the condiment set Product B be dropped, because as it is making a small loss per unit the company will save 30,000 × £0.25 = £7,500 per year. The company also knows that 60% of its overheads are fixed:

	£	£	£
Variable portion			
of overheads (40%)	1.20	0.60	8.40
Total variable costs	4.20	1.85	25.40
Contribution =			
Selling price − Variable cost	4.80	0.65	19.60

Although Product B is making a small loss, it can be seen from the contribution line above that if it is discontinued, there will be a shortfall of 30,000 × £0.65 = £19,500 to be made up as non-recovered variable overheads from the other two products. Therefore on the basis of contribution to overheads, Product B ought not to be dropped.

Activity

If Product B were actually dropped and the £19,500 of variable overheads were to be equally apportioned between Products A and C, how many of each would then have to be sold to make the same profit per unit as before Product B was dropped? (Hint: find the total overheads associated with A and C, assign B's old share between A and C, find the required quantities of A and C.)

It should be noted that we are considering only the quantitative aspects of this problem. Non-quantitative aspects – such as what will the effect be on their overall product range; will those who buy condiment sets from them drop their purchase of other products if they drop their condiment set; what are their competition selling in a similar situation; and do they think that condiment-set purchases lead customers to buy related products from them? – are very important, and have to be answered, but this cannot be done in an entirely quantitative context.

(b) Recovery of overheads

On the basis of the information given above, we can calculate the actual amount of overheads which have to be recovered via Universal Caterers' three products. We know the volume of each product sold per year, and we know the overhead per unit. Thus overheads in total are as follows:

	Product A	*Product B*	*Product C*
Overhead/Unit	£3.00	£1.50	£21.00
× Volume	×15,000	×30,000	×5,000
= Overheads	= £45,000	= £45,000	= £105,000
of which 40% is variable	£18,000	£18,000	£42,000

We can now calculate the percentage of each product's total variable overheads which are contributed by each product's contribution:

	Product A	*Product B*	*Product C*
Contribution	£4.80	£0.65	£19.60
× Volume	×15,000	×30,000	×5,000
= Total contribution	=£72,000	=£19,500	=£98,000
% recovery =			
Total contribution	£72,000	£19,500	£98,000
Total variable overheads	£18,000	£18,000	£42,000
	400%	108%	233%

7.4 Discounted Cash Flow

(a) The value of money

There are occasions when it is necessary to try to evaluate the **financial worth** of different business proposals. When such proposals have a life of more than a year or so, a factor needs to be taken into account which in shorter-lived proposals is not quite so important. This factor is the **value of money** which is likely to be received at regular or irregular intervals over a number of years. The reasoning behind this is that if you had £1,000 given to you now, you could invest it at an annual rate of about 12%, earning you £120 at the end of the year. This amount could be added to the £1,000, the principal, and the total of £1,120 could then be left to earn 12% in the next year, which would then amount to £1,254.40, and so on. This is the **interest rate.**

It follows that if instead of receiving the £1,000 now, you had to wait until the end of a whole year for it, you would have lost the 12% interest you could have earned. Your £1,000 then is only worth the equivalent of being given:

$$£1,000/1.12 = £892.86 \text{ right now}$$

You can check that this is so by now assuming that you immediately invest the £892.86 at 12% per annum. At the end of the first year you will then have:

$$£892.86 \times 1.12 = £1,000$$

This concept is known as the **time value of money**. If you invest the original £892.86 for two years at 12% per annum, you will have:

$$£892.86 \times (1.12 \times 1.12) = £1,120$$

(b) **The payback period**

These ideas show that in such situations it is not sufficient or realistic merely to divide the initial outlay by the annual return, and calculate the so-called **payback period**. For example, a proposal requires an immediate outlay of £1,000, and over the next few years will provide £500 per year return. On the simple basis of payback, the payback period is two years as it will take two years for the proposal to break even. After that, the remaining cash inflows will be all 'profit'.

7.5 3Ps Investment Dilemma

Percy always has an eye for a sound investment, whatever the source, and a business associate of his has suggested three proposals to him as a likely new investment. Percy is particularly interested, because if it succeeds, he will be able to use the profits from this to help expand his business.

	Proposal 1 £	*Proposal 2* £	*Proposal 3* £
Invest	10,000	10,000	10,000
Return			
Year 1	3,000	4,000	6,000
Year 2	3,000	4,000	4,000
Year 3	4,000	4,000	4,000
Year 4	4,000	4,000	3,000
Year 5	6,000	4,000	3,000

At first glance, there does not seem to be very much between any of the three proposals, as in each case an investment of £10,000 is required, and all three return £20,000 over a five-year period.

Analysis 1
The very simplest conclusion might therefore be that there is no difference between projects, and some other **non-financial factors** must be considered in order to make a decision.

Analysis 2
If £20,000 is returned over five years, for an investment of £10,000, then the annual percentage rate of return, is:

$$((£20,000 - £10,000)/£10,000)) \times 100 = 100\%$$

$$100\%/5 = 20\% \text{ per year return}$$

However, such an analysis takes no account of the varying amounts of return, nor can percentages be calculated in that manner. It is, however, a quick and easy method.

Analysis 3
Using the payback period concept, Percy considers how long he has to wait until the cash income equals the initial investment:

Proposal

1	£10,000 takes 3 years to be returned
2	£10,000 takes 2.5 years to be returned
3	£10,000 takes 2 years to be returned

On this basis, Proposal 3 is preferable.

Analysis 4: Net Present Value (NPV)
The concept of *net present value* (NPV) discounts the cash flows arising from a proposal at a predetermined standard rate of interest. This gives the **present value** which is then compared to the amount being invested. To be realistically profitable, the NPV must be **greater** than the sum invested. The rate considered is usually the cost of capital. In the analysis below, 15% per annum is used as the discount rate.

The discount rate factor for any annual percentage rate, for any number of years, can be obtained from suitable tables, or calculated for a given percentage rate for each of the years required in a specific proposal. We are using 15% per annum.

At the end of Year 1, the discount factor is $1/1.15^1 = 0.87$
At the end of Year 2, the discount factor is $1/1.15^2 = 0.76$
At the end of Year 3, the discount factor is $1/1.15^3 = 0.66$
At the end of Year 4, the discount factor is $1/1.15^4 = 0.57$
At the end of Year 5, the discount factor is $1/1.15^5 = 0.50$

	Proposal 1 £	*Proposal 2* £	*Proposal 3* £
Invest	10,000	10,000	10,000
Return			
Year 1	3,000 × 0.87	4,000 × 0.87	6,000 × 0.87
Year 2	3,000 × 0.76	4,000 × 0.76	4,000 × 0.76
Year 3	4,000 × 0.66	4,000 × 0.66	4,000 × 0.66
Year 4	4,000 × 0.57	4,000 × 0.57	3,000 × 0.57
Year 5	6,000 × 0.50	4,000 × 0.50	3,000 × 0.50

	Proposal 1 £	*Proposal 2* £	*Proposal 3* £
Invest	10,000	10,000	10,000
Return			
Year 1	2,610	3,480	5,220
Year 2	2,280	3,040	3,040
Year 3	2,640	2,640	2,640
Year 4	2,280	2,280	1,710
Year 5	3,000	2,000	1,500
Total Return	12,810	13,440	14,110

On the basis of this analysis, Proposal 3 is more attractive as it provides a discounted £4,110 cash return, which is about 5% more than the Proposal 2 returns.

Activity

For the investment opportunities above, recalculate the returns using (a) 10%, and (b) 20% discount factors.

Repeat the entire set of calculations with the different discount rates if returns as stated materialise only for Years 1, 2 and 3.

If a terminal bonus is promised in Year 5 for each option, what difference does that make to the three proposals if the bonus is £5,000?

Analysis 5: Internal Rate of Return (IRR)

Such proposals may also be evaluated using the Internal Rate of Return (IRR) concept. This is the rate of interest which will discount future cash flows to a present amount which is equal to the **initial sum to be invested**. It is found by trial and error and uses discount factors for the appropriate number of years at different rates of interest. As mentioned earlier, such factors can be obtained from tables; a sample extract is shown in Figure 7.2. This procedure is done for each proposal, and the proposal showing the **highest IRR** will be the favoured proposal, other things being equal.

7.6 Depreciating Capital Assets

(a) The concept of 'depreciation'

The pizza oven that Percy uses is a substantial affair which cost £5,000 when he bought it new. He knows from past experience that it has a

Fig 7.2 Table of discount factors

PER CENT/YEAR

YEAR	6	8	10	12	14	16
1	0.943	0.930	0.909	0.843	0.877	0.862
2	0.890	0.860	0.826	0.797	0.769	0.743
3	0.840	0.794	0.751	0.712	0.675	0.641
4	0.792	0.735	0.683	0.636	0.592	0.553
5	0.747	0.681	0.621	0.567	0.519	0.476
6	0.705	0.630	0.564	0.507	0.456	0.410

useful life of about five years, at the end of which he will be lucky to get about £500 for it as virtual scrap. He has not given a lot of thought to its replacement as yet, but wants to know how he can reasonably allow for its loss in value as time passes. The process by which a capital asset loses its value, is known as **depreciation**, and applies to all such major purchases.

(b) Depreciation methods

Depreciation may be expensed as a non-cash item, but the amount that is depreciated per year differs according to the **method of depreciation** used.

(1) Straight line depreciation
Using this method, the depreciation is the **same amount per year:**

The annual depreciated amount

$$= \frac{\text{Cost} - \text{Scrap value}}{\text{Useful life}}$$

$$= \frac{£5000 - £500}{5\,\text{yrs}} = £900/\text{year}$$

End of year	Cost £	Depreciation £	Book value £	Provision £
0	5,000			
1		900	4,100	900
2		900	3,200	1,800
3		900	2,300	2,700
4		900	1,400	3,600
5		900	500	4,500

This method of depreciating capital assets is simple. If it represents what actually happens to the asset (i.e. in this case does it really lose its value uniformly?), then it can reasonably be said to be a good model.

(2) Cost per unit method
Using this method involves estimating the number of units that will be **processed by the asset** under consideration, during its lifetime, and then pro-rating that figure to the period concerned let us say annually in this example.

The net value of the oven is, as before, £4,500. The number of pizzas processed over the 5-year life of the oven is estimated to be 46,000. The depreciation cost per pizza is:

£4,500/46,000 = 9.8 pence per pizza

and this on an annual basis as in **(1)** above, would be:

$$(46,000/5) \times (9.8/100) = £901.60$$

which is not very much different from the first answer in **(1)**.

There is no need to assume a single average production figure over the 5-year period as we have done here. If there is good reason to suppose that production will be substantially different from year to year, then those individual figures can be used to calculate a **yearly depreciation figure** which will then not be the same for each year.

If pizza production is 8000, 9000, 10,000, 11,000, and 12,000 in years 1 to 5, then the depreciation cost per year will be in proportion to that production. Total production is 50,000.

In Year	£		£
1	lit will be $(8,000/50,000) \times 4,500$ =		720
2	$(9,000/50,000) \times 4,500$ =		810
3	$(10,000/50,000) \times 4,500$ =		900
4	$(11,000/50,000) \times 4,500$ =		990
5	$(12,000/50,000) \times 4,500$ =		1,080
	Total depreciated value		£4,500

(3) **Sum of years digits**

This is a method of depreciating an asset which is useful if you have good reason to believe that your asset loses more of its value **early in its life**, and less as time goes by. This method may not reflect reality for the pizza oven, although we will calculate the depreciation each year for comparison purposes. This method may, however, reflect what happens to the value of Percy's **van** as time passes.

The oven has a life of 5 years. Therefore the sum of the years digits is $1 + 2 + 3 + 4 + 5 = 15$.

End of year	Cost	Depreciation	Book value	Provision
	£	£	£	£
0	5000			
1		$(5/15) \times 4,500$ = £1,500	3,000	1,500
2		$(4/15) \times 4,500$ = £1,200	1,800	2,700
3		$(3/15) \times 4,500$ = £900	900	3,600
4		$(2/15) \times 4,500$ £600	300	4,200
5		$(1/15) \times 4,500$ = £300	0	4,500

(4) **Reducing balance method**

This is a method similar in principle to **(3)** above, because it weights **early depreciation** more heavily. It has the advantage that it is easy to continue the depreciation calculation even if at some point new assets are added. This is a fixed percentage amount method, so that it is not possible to calculate a reducing balance rate if there is zero residual value. Because of this, it is often necessary to add a fixed amount to the depreciation calculated (e.g. at the end of each year, one might add £500 in the case of the oven).

The formula is:

$$\textbf{Depreciating Rate} = 1 - \sqrt[n]{\frac{\textbf{Residual value}}{\textbf{Cost}}}$$

In our example therefore:

$$= 1 - \sqrt[5]{(500/5{,}000)}$$

$$= 0.369, \text{ i.e. } 36.9\% \text{ per year}$$

End of year	Cost	Depreciation	Book value	Provision
	£	£	£	£
0	5,000			
1		0.369 × 5,000 = £1,845	3,155	1,845
2		0.369 × 3,155 £1,164	1,991	3,009
3		0.369 × 1,991 = £735	1,256	3,744
4		0.369 × 1,256 = £463	793	4,207
5		0.369 × 793 £293	500	4,500

Activity

Straight line depreciation: Recalculate the provision if the residual value of the oven is **(a)** zero, and **(b)** £1,000.

Cost per unit method: Recalculate the depreciation cost per pizza if the oven has a 3-year life and 40,000 pizzas are made.

Sum of digits method: Recalculate the depreciation of the oven if it has a life of **(a)** 3 years, **(b)** 6 years; and a net value of **(a)** £5,000, and **(b)** £4,000.

Reducing balance method: Recalculate the depreciation for an oven life of **(a)** 3 years, and **(b)** 6 years; and a residual value of **(a)** zero, and **(b)** £1,000.

7.7 Job Costing

Knowing how to determine the **realistic cost of a job** is very important for all companies which make a product or provide a service. While pricing strategy does not depend on cost alone, cost is still an important factor. There are various ways of costing jobs, not all of them applicable to the 3P company, but nevertheless of sufficient importance to warrant discussion here.

(a) Contract costing

If 3P were to be asked to tender for a pizza party that the local football club were holding, it would be sensible for Percy to cost that quite separately from his other activities, because he may wish to alter his costs and prices for such a large single order (e.g. for 250 pizzas, with coffee, wine and beer). Such a large order is about one-third of his month's business; by keeping it separate, and later comparing **actual** with **estimated** costs, he can then see clearly what profit he made and just how accurate his estimates were, particularly if he made reductions for this contract.

(b) Batch costing

In many manufacturing organisations, the bulk of the work is done in **batches** (see Chapter 8). It is therefore convenient to calculate the cost of a batch. The batch size may vary, but the costs will take into account the direct and indirect costs and the resultant **cost per unit** will vary according to the size of the batch, but not in direct proportion.

(c) Process costing

This is commonly applied in industries such as petroleum refining and chemical production. Here, the raw material is capable of being turned into many different finished products. In some cases, the **output** of one stage in the initial process becomes the **input** for another stage and a different process. It is often not at all easy to distinguish the separate products during manufacture: what is actually controlled in these situations is the input materials, and monitoring the output is done at the various stages.

(d) Operations costing

Service industries are now more numerous than manufacturing industries, and they also need to control their costs. Costs are therefore calculated on a **per unit** basis, such as per passenger, per ton-mile, per mile, per passenger-mile, per transaction or per enquiry.

7.8 Absorbing Overheads

It is necessary to assign the indirect or fixed costs incurred in running the business to the various products or services, so that a realistic cost estimate can be made, and proper conclusions drawn at a later date. These fixed costs do not vary with the quantity of units produced, certainly not in the short term. The fixed costs have to be completely **absorbed** by the number of units produced – so that if fewer units are produced each unit has to accommodate more of the fixed costs, and so the unit cost will increase. We have also seen that by eliminating a low profit item the burden of overheads is increased among the remaining items. There are several different ways to do this.

(a) **A percentage on direct materials**

This is a simple method and is applicable where material cost is probably greater than labour cost, and the amount of material cost in the company's various products is broadly similar. The 'on' cost as it is called is expressed as a percentage of the material cost of the item under consideration, e.g. an on cost of 250% on an item with material content cost of £25.00, will mean adding £62.50 to the unit cost as a contribution to overheads.

(b) **A percentage on direct labour**

This is similar to **(a)** above, except that the on cost percentage is applied to the **direct labour portion** of the cost. This is suitable where there is little variation in the labour content and also where it tends to be the dominant cost factor.

(c) **Percentage on prime costs**

'Prime costs' are the **total of direct labour and material**, and are therefore already a substantial portion of the total cost, even before the on cost percentage is added. Once again, the method of calculation is simple, which is helpful.

(d) **Direct labour or direct machine hour rate**

Where either of these factors predominate, they are suitable as a basis for overhead absorption. An estimate is made of the total labour hours required for a given period (say, a year) for each major work centre. The estimated overheads for that work centre are then divided by the total number of direct hours, and an **hourly on cost monetary rate** is obtained. As an estimate for a new job which required, say, 30 hours of direct labour, the overhead hourly rate would be multiplied by 30, and then added to the direct cost of those 30 hours. A similar approach is taken if considering the machine hour rate.

7.9 Standard costing

(a) The purpose of standard costing

The purpose of standard costing is to be able to compare **actual** costs with the **standard** cost, to determine the **variances**, to analyse the reasons for the discrepancies, and to take corrective action to make an improvement next time.

Standard costs can therefore be set for materials, and for the cost of each operation required to make an item, and so for the finished product.

(b) A manufacturing example

For a given volume of production, the standard hours content = 20,000. The budgeted overheads for the year are:

	£
Indirect labour	90,000
Consumables	15,000
Rent and Rates	30,000
Depreciation	25,000
Heat/light/power	35,000
General maintenance	10,000
	205,000

The standard overhead rate/hour is therefore £205,000/20,000 = £10.25/hour.

For Product Y, the standard direct costs are:

	£
Direct materials	65.00
Direct Labour (12 hours)	45.00
	110.00

The standard overheads for Product Y are therefore 12 hours × £10.25 = £123.00.

	£
Direct cost	110.00
Allocated overheads	123.00
Standard cost	233.00

It is important that standard costs are **regularly reviewed**: as they form an important tool for cost control and subsequent corrective action, they must not be allowed to become out of date. **Variances** must be calculated as soon as is practicable after the actual costs have been determined. Standard costs are most effectively used for longer-term decision-making, and if used for short-term pricing decisions, they must be used with care.

Chapter Review Questions

1 What are the components of a break-even chart?
2 Why is a break-even chart of value to management?
3 What are fixed costs?
4 What are variable costs?
5 What are overheads?
6 What is contribution?
7 'DCF involves the time value of money': True or False?
8 'Net Present Value discounts cash flows at a predetermined rate': True or False?
9 Name three ways to depreciate capital assets.
10 Where is batch costing appropriate?
11 'Selling price is total costs plus a profit allowance': True or False?
12 What is meant by standard cost and variance from standard cost?

8 Managing the Processes

Organising how jobs are done is often considered to relate only to manufacturing. But while this has been true traditionally, the principles we will look at below can be applied to jobs in the service and commercial environment as well.

Learning Objectives

By the end of this chapter you should:

1 know the difference between organising work as **jobbing**, **in batches** or by **flow production** methods
2 be able to assign these broad classifications to work not in manufacturing
3 know the principles upon which **group technology** is based
4 appreciate the fundamentals of **computer integrated manufacture** and **computer aided design**.

8.1 Job Organisation

(a) By one person

Consider any job which is processed from start to finish by the same person. This is how the work has been organised because it may be economically worthwhile and practical to do so, or because the work was always done like that. If, for example, you have to send 100 invitations, it is quite feasible to have just one person write out the invitation; put it in the envelope, seal, address and stamp it; and finally mail all 100 invitations. That is not the only way; but it is a practical possibility.

(b) By batch

Similarly, work is often processed so that one operation is carried out on a batch of items before the next one is started. When dirty washing is taken to the high street laundry, the washing is batched. The first batch is washed, then spun in a separate machine, then dried in another machine, and finally folded and packed into a bag. Here, not only is the work done in batches but the separate operations must be done **sequentially.**

(c) By flow

Not all work has to be done in batches. A commercial dish washing machine is quite likely to work on a conveyor belt, and as the dirty crockery is loaded, it is then subsequently washed and dried in a smooth non-stop series of operations. We call this flow production.

There is no one ideal way of organising work which serves all purposes, so usually one or more ways will be considered and one selected because it seems to be most practical, convenient and economic. Each has its advantages and disadvantages, to which we will refer later. Quite often by looking closely at a process, it is possible to see that it involves being done in two ways, sometimes more.

8.2 Jobbing

'Jobbing' refers to organising the work so that all the operations required to make an item or product are performed **by the same person**, who completes one item before starting on the next. This is probably the earliest method of organising production, as it simply means that provided a person can be found with the requisite skills for all the tasks involved, then that is sufficient. Such skills will include the use of appropriate equipment, as well as manual and artistic skills.

(a) Repetitive nature

Where jobbing production exists, and several repetitions of the same product are required, it is very likely that each of those repetitions will not be identical. However, in the case of a sculpture or painting, for example, the fact that each repetition is slightly different from the others of the same design tends to enhance the value rather than diminish it. There may also be several people each producing the same product from start to finish. This again means some degree of non-uniformity and it then becomes necessary to ensure that key features of the product are indeed present on every repetition.

(b) Equipment

Where equipment is needed, there is unlikely to be enough for one piece per person, except for the basic tools of the trade which are usually the personal property of each craftsperson. In this case there is a need for rudimentary scheduling of such key equipment (e.g. a furnace in a pottery plant), and consequently there is a possibility of **waiting time** by those who need the same piece of equipment at the same time.

(c) Costing

Costing products produced by jobbing is often done on an **hourly rate for labour**, plus **materials** and **overheads**, and a selling price is worked out from that basis. Such prices are often higher than for similar products produced in large quantities, but many people are prepared to pay a premium when the workmanship and materials are of the highest order.

(d) Customised production

Because a jobbing shop requires people who are skilled in a wide range of operations, quantities tend to be relatively small and are often made to a customer's particular specification. Upon receipt of an order, it is therefore necessary to ensure that the customer's requirements are precisely known. It is also necessary for the craftsperson to determine what the best sequence of operations is. However, this may not be the same sequence chosen by someone else, and in a large job-shop operation there is likely to be a manager who assumes the role of operations and job sequencing as well as costing, so as to bring an element of uniformity into the set up, and to leave the craftsperson to do what he or she does best (i.e. make the product).

8.3 Batch Production

If you were to look at a batch production shop after viewing a job shop, you might not notice much difference. Both might have similar layouts and types of equipment, provided they were producing the same types of work. There is, however, a key and fundamental difference between job and batch production. In jobbing, as a product is worked on by one person from start to finish, there is very little delay in adding work content, other than that mentioned above.

(a) Work organisation

In batch production, however, the work required to make a product is very carefully defined and organised. Upon receipt of an order, the product, if new, is broken down by manufacturing engineers into main assemblies and subassemblies, right down to the definition of every **separate part**. For every such part and higher assembly a series of operations is defined which is required to make that part or assembly. These operations, and the sequence required, is specified in an **operations sheet**, together with the machines they should be processed on, what drawings and tools are necessary, and how long each step in the process should take.

(b) Batch operation

Instead of working on one product at a time, sufficient material is made available so that each operation on each part is performed on a pre-specified quantity called a **batch** (e.g. a batch quantity may be 25 units, and therefore the first operation will be performed on sufficient raw material to make 25 units). It will be seen that except for the item being worked upon at the time, the other 24 are idle. Therefore adding work content in batch production advances **in stages:** when operation 1 has been performed on all 25 units, the batch is moved to the site of the next operation, where operation 2 is performed on the batch, again one unit at a time.

Example

If we wanted to make a bolt:

- Operation 1 might be – using hexagonal mild steel bar of dimension 155 mm across flats, cut a 50 mm length on a mechanical saw.
- Operation 2 – trim one end and machine 40 mm length to 7 mm diameter.
- Operation 3 – make thread of specified type 40 mm long.
- Operation 4 – Trim face of bolt at other end to give overall length of 48 mm.
- Operation 5 – remove all rough edges.

Inspection would be carried out at predetermined stages. The first operation would be carried out on each of the 25 bolts, before moving on to operation 2, etc.

(c) Work modification

You can see that much detailed information is required for producing a batch of work. The sequence of operations, once determined, stays the same for subsequent batches of similar work until it can be shown that different machines or different materials or sequences will produce the same work quicker or at lower cost but at the same level of quality. Changes are often made, but because of the detailed nature of batch production keeping track of those changes and ensuring that subsequent batches are produced to the **latest specification** is a major task, requiring carefully documented procedures and trained and motivated work personnel.

The widespread availability of computers has made it possible to transmit information instantaneously about such changes to all those concerned. This does require, however, a very carefully designed database and a rigorous system which monitors all changes and which can guard against (for example) unauthorised alterations, or the possibility of mixing stock with old and new modifications.

(d) Batch status

Batch production is probably the most common way of organising production, and even when flow production is used, it can often be recognised as consisting of very large batches. Much effort is taken to make appropriate size batches, but as we have already seen there is no one answer to this question. In practice, there can be hundreds of batches waiting or being processed, and this makes effective management very difficult. Every batch has a different **status** (i.e. due date, works order number to which all costs are charged, etc.). Because of this, until relatively recently, much paperwork was always involved in keeping track of every batch. There was also a tendency to have a high level of work in progress, both as a result of the tremendous variety of work and in order to allow some flexibility if some batches could not be started due to lack of parts or machine breakdown.

Production control today can, however, utilise computer-based **data collection points** which are located throughout a factory, requiring a person simply to log in when they start a batch and log off when they finish. Other important information such as part number, works number and work centre are also keyed in. In the event of not being able to work productively on a batch because of waiting for work, for example, codes are used to enable that information to be entered. Management can then on a regular basis analyse **time lost**, and where and what costs were incurred for a variety of situations. Work in process can be monitored frequently by using **bar codes**, and such monitoring helps to keep the level to the very lowest possible.

(e) Set-up costs

One of the most important costs in batch work is the change-over or set-up cost involved. Large batch quantities used to be necessary to make the set-up cost economic, inasmuch as its cost could then be spread over the large number of units in the batch. Today there is tremendous pressure to **reduce the set-up cost** to minutes instead of hours. The Japanese have been very successful, calling their object the **'single minute exchange of die'** (a die being a tool for a press). In many cases the set ups are performed **off line**, so that at the end of one batch the change over time is minimal. With the advent of manufacturing cells and with specialised machinery and based on group technology principles (see below), it has become virtually unnecessary to make more than is needed at one time, simply because the set-up and change-over time has become so small.

(f) **Resource utilisation**

Because of the general complexity of batch scheduling, much effort is expended on trying to ensure that people and key equipment are fully utilised, being able to insert new jobs into the system with minimum interruption, meeting deadlines, and improving work methods, particularly on jobs likely to be repeated. The overall aim must be to operate at the lowest cost consistent with minimum down time and with maintaining quality levels and customer service.

It would be misleading however, to think that only manufacturing was applicable to batch processing. In almost every field of endeavour, much work is processed in batches.

Activity

(a) How is data processed on a mainframe computer?
(b) How are the lunches and sandwiches made in a college cafeteria?
(c) How are hamburgers and French fries made in a fast-food takeaway?
(d) How are patients processed in a doctor's surgery?
(e) How are local tax demands processed prior to being sent out to individuals?
(f) How are car repairs done in a garage?
(g) How is passengers' luggage handled at an airport?
(h) How is your dinner prepared when it is only for two or three people?
(i) How does a wedding caterer prepare dinners for 200 people?
(j) How are TVs, cars, radios and washing machines assembled?

Remember that you are concerned with how the work is being organised for 'production', not with the precise type of equipment used.

8.4 Flow Production

'Flow production' is the name given to the manufacturing or assembly process where the work content is added in a **virtually continuous sequence**. The best known example of this is the car, washing machine or personal computer assembly line, where the operators on the line move only within a small distance, but the item itself is assembled on a moving belt. This means there is little (if any) **idle time** between one operation and the next. Although there are no batches as such, it can nevertheless be seen that even on car assembly lines, very large batches of different car models come down the same line. It is, however, the way the work is processed that distinguishes flow from batch.

(a) **Fluctuations in demand**

The overall capacity of the production or assembly line has to be determined, but there is subsequently no specific problem relating to individual machine loadings. What is important is that the planning team are continuously aware of likely fluctuations in demand, so that the overall **capacity** of the line closely matches the **demand**. This may be done by adjusting manning levels, and length of working day; another strategy is to build in advance of confirmed demand, but this is a drastic measure, as we have already seen how expensive it is to hold stocks.

(b) Economics of flow production

Such flow lines do not make economic sense unless there is a **substantial and continuing demand** for the product. To set up a flow line for car assembly calls for investments of hundreds of millions of pounds. Six elements are therefore vital:

(a) Keep the line running: this means that **planned maintenance** is necessary, because the result of an emergency stop is normally catastrophic, with effects felt both ahead and behind where the stop has occurred.
(b) Keep minimal inventory: this is particularly important as very large amounts of stock are processed very quickly, and should a backlog occur the space and cost requirements soar rapidly.
(c) Ensure that every job is carefully examined: to ensure that it is done in the most effective way; industrial engineers will use appropriate work study methods to ensure that this is so.
(d) Ensure that design changes are carefully controlled and minimal: so that there is very little disruption to the line for long periods.
(e) Ensure that all material arrives just in time precisely as needed: this requires close co-operation with suppliers, and a well-organised logistics operation.
(f) Ensure that appropriate levels of quality are specified and adhered to: work content is being added all the time, and it is expensive and time-wasting to work on an item which subsequently is found to be below the required quality level or outside specification.

(c) Flow production and people

It is a characteristic of the traditional flow line that the operators are relatively unskilled: by this we mean that they tend to work on a very narrow range of work all the time. They are skilled at only a very small range of work. This has the advantage that it is easy for management to **recruit** and **train** such personnel; it also means that such work is boringly repetitive, and as such does not inspire operators to produce their best all the time.

When Volvo started to think about reorganisation in the 1970s, it seemed to be technology that was causing a problem. They felt that they could not reorganise the work to suit people unless they changed the technology that linked people to the line. In an innovative move, they did away with the assembly line and replaced it with **carriers** which were controlled by the workers themselves. This was indeed a fundamental change because, traditionally, whatever else a production or assembly line is, it is never under the control of the workers. (Having said that, there is a strong tendency for workers operating under a Kanban/JIT system who find some defective work to be allowed to stop the line.)

The Volvo approach was to allow the **work to stay still** while the operators worked on it. This is the reverse of the traditional line situation. It was this thinking that led to the development of the industrial carrier, and the concept was applied at the Kalmar car plant and the Skovde engine plant: the movement of the carriers is determined according to the workers' requirements.

The social life of production line workers is minimal while at work. They tend to work alone in a never-ending chase to keep up with the line, coupled with work which is very highly repetitive and of short duration. This generally means low motivation, low morale and high absenteeism. The solution was the formation of **work groups** who acted together as they determined, and who had a key role in how the job was done. A group was responsible for a very substantial part of the whole job, and each individual could rotate among different jobs in that group.

8.5 Group Technology

(a) Rationale of group technology

It is not unusual for equipment to be grouped so that **like machinery** is together. In this layout system, all lathes will be together, all grinding machines, all presses, and so on. This means that work follows a relatively tortuous route, as there is no inherent connection between the work being done and the machines being used.

Group technology seeks to provide an answer to this situation by grouping different pieces of equipment together which are capable of making a wide variety of items but with similar characteristics (e.g. they may all tend to be made from round material between 10 and 100 mm in diameter). The benefits expected from such a change will be due to a smoother **flow** of the work, easier and **simplified work control.**

This logic of grouping applies to the components from which products are made; the products themselves may bear little relation to each other.

(b) Component categorisation

Much of the early work on group technology appeared in eastern Europe in the late 1950s and early 1960s. Key proponents were Mitrafanov in Russia and Opitz in Germany. Other work was carried out in western Europe and the UK; this included methods of coding and classifying different components on the basis of the **closeness of their shapes** to each other. This closeness then helped determine the scope of the cell in terms of its **manufacturing versatility**. This type of organisation is particularly useful for batch processing of work. When it is combined with robotic and numerical controlled equipment, where the set-up and change-over times have been greatly reduced, the result is a very effective method for producing small quantities and wide variety.

In the conventional layout, many components may be produced on equipment more complex, larger or capable of more precision than is actually required. This is because, normally, large or very close tolerance work will have to be produced and therefore such equipment must be available when required. If, however, machine tools can be more closely matched to the requirements of groups of similar components, then better **utilisation of equipment** will result, with corresponding cost benefits.

Key factors which influence component categorisation will include size, shape, material, tightest tolerance and finish. It is not realistic to expect that every component will be able to fit into a particular category, but it should be possible for about 90% or more of all components to be so classified. The remainder will require more individual treatment for processing, but this added complexity will be devoted to those components that need it (i.e. non-run-of-the-mill items).

(c) **Component coding systems**

Coding systems, such as used by Opitz or Brisch, need to be reasonably simple, versatile and capable of subsequent **expansion** as new components need to be added. However, the work of classifying thousands of components is unavoidably complex, time-consuming and expensive.

Such coding systems may be tailor-made or proprietary. If they are the latter, then development costs will be limited to small alterations and the cost will be lower than a tailor-made system which precisely matches the company's needs; tailor-made development is also a long and somewhat uncertain process. Such codes generally consist of a multi-digit number which itself uniquely identifies at least the shape, material, finish, length and whether or not standard, which becomes the component's **drawing code**.

(d) **Production control and progressing**

When coding and grouping have been completed, it should then be possible to identify a **composite component** which, while it is not in itself any specific component, represents closely the group of components to which it refers. A group of machines is then organised together with their operators, so that it can make the composite component. When specific components in that group are required, relatively small alterations are made to the set-up to enable that component to be produced.

As a result, production control is simplified, because it will be possible to schedule work into the **cell**, rather than separately into each piece of equipment that goes to make up the cell. Progressing will also be limited to contact with the **cell supervisor** who now 'owns' everything within the cell – including the problems! The cell supervisor will also be responsible overall for quality and maintenance as well as for production.

(e) **Operative grouping**

As well as components being in a group, so too are the operatives in a cell. To this extent, they generally undertake a wider variety of work than hitherto. This may therefore mean for management different recruitment practices, problems of retraining, and sometimes pay. Many cells do not use any incentive scheme to enhance pay above the basic rate, but if one is thought desirable it should relate the output of the cell to the workers as a whole, and not as individuals. They would then each receive a bonus at the same percentage level which would be pro-rated to their own pay scale and number of hours worked.

8.6 **Computer Integrated Manufacture (CIM)**

The simplest manufacturing system can be represented by an **input**, a **black box** process, and an **output**. By 'black box' is meant an operation the precise mechanics of which is unknown. In this way the principle is simplified, and one need not become entangled with a particular process which itself is not confined in any way to manufacturing. While this is a simple model, it can represent in our case an input of labour and materials, and the conversion of them to an output of goods or services. Figure 8.1 shows this pictorially. It does not show how **control** can be exerted, although this is absolutely necessary for management purposes.

More realistically, the conversion process is not instantaneous, but occurs over a period of time, during which it is affected by variation in the process

---

Fig 8.1   The basic input–output system

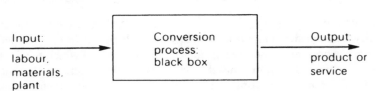

itself such as **equipment** and **quality problems,** and by outside factors such as **demand** for the service, **supply** of materials and **scarcity of labour** in specific areas. Sometimes there are changes in **specification** of what is required very late into the process. **Cash flow** problems can also provide unexpected inputs.

(a) What is a 'system'?

The overall system often consists of a number of subsystems, each designed to carry out not only its own function, but also to contribute to the achievement of the overall objective. There may be a hierarchy of such subsystems. By a 'system', we mean a number of elements carefully put together in such a way that they achieve their specific objective in the manner intended. It is a characteristic of systems that interfering to any great extent with any of the subsystems results in the degradation of the overall system. (This is often the case when the intention was to 'improve' a part of a system.)

A common example of a system with which most of us are familiar is a car. The car itself is the overall transportation system for an individual, but as far as the government is concerned it is only a part of the nation's transport system. Embodied in the car are several subsystems (e.g. the electrical, the cooling, the carburation, the braking, and the engine systems). It follows therefore that incautious interference with any of these subsystems can lead to serious unintended problems with the car's overall performance, and this is a feature recognised by car buffs.

Indeed, it is noticeable that when a car producer announces an increase in the current engine size of a particular model there are also changes (often not publicised) in the size of brakes, clutch, alternator, cooling and springing. Because of this interaction, there is a clear caution for those who try to improve the operation of a department without considering the greater operation of the **adjacent departments,** or even the entire organisation. There are implications here for work study/management services (Chapters 9, 10, 11) activities as contrasted with systems analysis, where everything is examined. If you are dealing with a system, it should not be unexpected to find that apparent improvements in one area produce unwanted effects in others. If this occurs, then it is highly likely you are indeed working within a system.

Figure 8.2 shows a rather more realistic system of material and information flow.

(b) The CIM system

If all the systems required to operate a manufacturing process are computerised so that the information on inputs, process and outputs is all automatically available to all subsystems, then the result is a **computer integrated manufacturing system** (CIMS). It is not necessary for the process

Fig 8.2   Flows of material and information

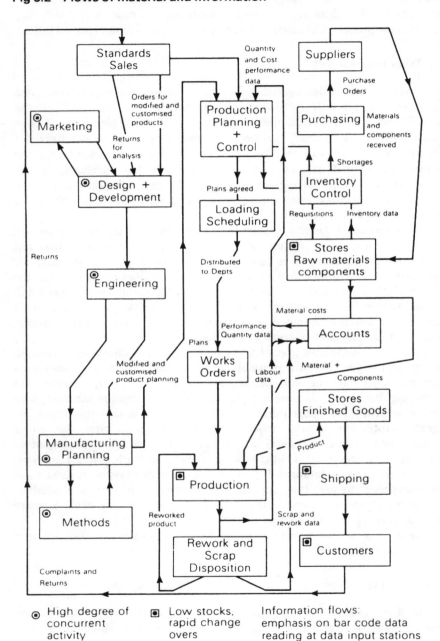

High degree of concurrent activity

Low stocks, rapid change overs

Information flows: emphasis on bar code data reading at data input stations

operations themselves to be automated or robotised: CIM really refers to the **communication and control system.**

The areas of order processing, materials control, manufacturing systems, production control, distribution, order and financial control all need to be linked so that the information management require for control can be **obtained, interpreted, acted upon** and **updated**, at any time required. Those who have implemented CIM expect benefits to include lower unit costs, faster response time, more control over resources, better equipment utilisation, and less scrap and rework.

(c) **Installing the CIM system**

Installing a CIM system is a long-term project, one which evolves as a result of careful strategic planning rather than as a result of revolutionary optimism. It may well use current technology, and current systems must be carefully examined, fundamentally questioned, and only then redesigned to allow for the requirements of the medium to long-term future.

The key word is 'integrated', so that trying to link dissimilar subsystems is unlikely to work as well as an integrated overall system consisting of carefully thought-out subsystems, all the result of proper systems analysis.

As implementing CIM is itself a major project (see Chapter 12), it requires the **team approach** coupled with formal project management techniques. It should be remembered that the implementation of CIM is a strategic issue affecting the long-term future of a company, and is bound to affect its employees in terms of job redefinition, job or personnel transference, job training, job skills, and job numbers. Workers in companies so affected are very likely to have to acquire new skills.

Because of this, the senior managers and unions must be involved in the key issue of whether CIM is really needed, desirable, what is expected from it, what has to be done, what the implications are in terms of people, equipment and capital, who is going to implement it and how is it going to be done. By its very nature, successful CIM means **flexibility**, and there should be no real reason why many of the operating decisions, hitherto made only by management, cannot now be shared with the better trained and motivated workforce.

(d) **CIM in the UK**

In 1989 a major report by A.T. Kearney on Western Europe, Japan and the USA reported that the UK was spending about £1.9 billion a year on CIM, which is about 20% of all capital expenditure. They reported that UK companies did not get the results they expected, despite a medium-sized company expenditure of about £4 million. The key reason was felt to be that CIM had not formed an integral part of an overall improvement strategy, following a thorough review of existing manufacture practice.

Instead, it was **technology-led**, and therefore integration occurred only at the **technical level** and not at the overall business or organisational level. The best UK company achieved only 65% of the theoretical maximum. Important modules such as MRP11 and computer aided design also failed to yield expected results.

8.7 **Computer Aided Design (CAD)**

Traditionally, there has always been a tremendous amount of paperwork both in the **design** and in the **control** of a product. In the design stage there used always to be very large numbers of changes, each of which used to generate stacks of paperwork in the guise of change control, specification control and pre-production control: it was largely an important but necessary evil.

In recent years there has been a marked change in this area. In the aerospace industries there has been an increasing tendency, often with the military as prime mover, to develop **non-paper methods** for design development and production. The ultimate expression of paperless production is the production of the B2 Stealth bomber, which was built without a mock-up by Northrop Corporation. About 97% of the bomber's parts fitted perfectly first time, and changes were drastically reduced. Production instructions were produced by the computer as well, and with the help of other 'intelligent' software, and computer aided layout and fabrication techniques, design and manufacture time was reduced by about 90%.

Manufacturing now appears in the USA to be the most receptive area for intelligent systems which, when combined with other specialised software ensure that tremendously complex products can be designed and produced with increasingly short lead times, more accurately and with very little paper: quality is improved as well as productivity. These new developments are helping more and more manufacturers to work smarter, not harder: something known for a long time to Management Services people!

Chapter Review Questions

1 If a portrait painter normally completely finishes one painting before starting on the next, how is his production organised?
2 Fast-food restaurants that prepare and cook 10 hamburgers at a time use what form of production?
3 Where work content is added virtually all the time and in small amounts, how is production organised?
4 'Flow production techniques often mean work has been deskilled': True or False?
5 What kind of maintenance system would you suggest for flow production?

6 What is the key difference in Volvo's Kalmar car assembly plant, compared with a more traditional assembly line?

7 'Group technology involves finding people who can work closely together': True or False?

8 What are the key characteristics of a system?

9 'Computer Integrated Manufacture refers to the ability to use computers for production purposes': True or False?

10 'Computer Aided Design helps to eliminate excessive paperwork during the design phase of a product': True or False?

9 Managing Performance: 1 – Getting the Methods Right

Chapters 9–11 deal with ways of determining and controlling the **effectiveness** with which work is done. As we have said before, we cannot disregard how well the conversion process occurs: every organisation needs to be productive, and to this end over a period of about 75 years different means have been devised to help achieve this. Much of the development work took place at the beginning of the 20th century and after, and a lot of what was done then is still valid and in use today.

In Chapter 9 we will examine ways of **recording** current work methods and **analysing** them, with the purpose of subsequently **improving** them. In Chapter 10 we look at why we may want to measure work content, and ways of doing it. Finally in Chapter 11 we look at how various types of **incentive scheme** can help improve productivity.

Learning Objectives

By the end of this chapter you should:

1 know something about the pioneers of **work improvement methods**
2 know what the formal steps of **method study** are, and how to use them
3 be able to **analyse** the Fidelity Fan Co, with reference to improving its layout.

9.1 Performance

(a) Productivity and Performance

It is useful to avoid the term 'efficiency' in the context of company performance measurement. Physically, efficiency has a maximum value of 100%, which cannot be reached, as no piece of equipment can ever be perfectly efficient: for example, an open fire in a domestic grate is about 5% efficient, a steam engine is about 20% efficient and an electric motor, about 80%.

When we refer to 'productivity' or 'performance', we are talking about **output per unit input**, and we can quite easily have a value greater than unity. If, for example, a doctor used to be able to see 40 patients in four hours at the surgery, and through subsequent improvements in the administrative process can now see 44 patients in 3.5 hours, we can analyse the situation as follows:

Prior performance was 10 patients per hour, and currently it is 12.6 per hour. This is an improvement of $(12.6 - 10) \times 100/10$ which equals a 26% improvement over the previous performance, i.e. by a factor of 1.26. The same logic can be applied to comparisons against standard performance (see Chapter 10).

The corresponding level of **quality of service** to the patient must in no way be affected by such a change.

(b) Measures of performance

The prime measure of performance is **useful output divided by total input**. It is this parameter (also referred to as **productivity**) which needs to be **monitored** regularly and **improved**, and it must be monitored at every level of a company's activities. (It is worth noting that the term 'productivity' does not appear in the British Standard 3138: 1992, the glossary of terms in work study.) When applied at the higher company level, it is often considered in monetary terms – for instance, as value added per employee. It is often also applied to labour, but should be applied to other aspects of a company's activities as well.

(c) Productivity in practice: British Coal

In 1983 British Coal employed about 220,000 people. It now employs about 90,000. However, annual output has remained about the same at about 100 million tons. Value added, mentioned earlier, is a more general measure of performance (e.g. value added per employee). When productivity has to be improved, it can be done by increasing the top term of the ratio of useful output divided by total input, by reducing the size of the bottom term, or by reducing some of both. In this example, output was initially 454 tons per person per year. Now it is 1111 tons per person per year. Output has increased by $(1111 - 454)/454$ or 1.45 times (i.e. 145%). This is about a 7% increase in productivity a year, assuming such changes took place smoothly over the five-year period.

(d) Productivity in practice: the Ford Fiesta

Another example of productivity applied as a money value is the estimated 1989 labour cost to assemble a Ford Fiesta at Dagenham (England), Valencia (Spain) and at Genk (Belgium). The labour costs were respectively $1431, $780 and $1007. Wage rises awarded in the UK are consistently higher than those in Japan, West Germany and the USA, and are greater than the current increase in productivity. Our unit wage costs also tend to rise more than productivity rises. In 1989, the OECD produced a report which showed that when British performance was measured on a per hour, rather than a per head basis, Britain's performance was very favourable when compared with that of Japan and West Germany. Manufacturing productivity in the 1980s increased by about 5% per year, somewhat better than any other leading industrial nation.

(e) **Output per hour**

International companies continually look at where they can achieve the lowest unit labour and overall costs, which is why such companies can no longer be considered commercially loyal to any one country indefinitely.

World motor industry labour costs (Deutsch Marks per hour) 1994
(Source: *Financial Times*/German Motor Industry Federation; Toyota, Ford, Nissan, Rover)

Country	DM/Hour	Country	DM/Hour
West Germany	57.06	Sweden	29.27
Japan	45.47	Belgium	27.93
USA	39.55	Italy	27.40
Netherlands	32.22	Spain	26.82
France	29.49	UK	26.72

It is not so much the hourly rate itself which is important, but what a company obtains in terms of **output per hour**. A low hourly rate can be relatively expensive when compared with a highly productive high hourly rate. While labour costs are not the only source of costs, when all the major car companies in our example have to make similar huge investments in plant and model development, what they are subsequently able to obtain in output per labour hour is one of the key variables. This means that overall productivity is a function of the amount and sophistication of equipment at the disposal of the employee as well as their level of education, training, motivation and work organisation.

Average hourly cost in dollars for textile workers
(Source: Extract from *The Economist*, July 1994, and Towers Perrin London; Werner International NY, American Textile Manufacturing Institute)

Country	Total salary $/hour	Country	Total salary $/hour
Japan	14.12	Britain	8.23
West Germany	13.12	USA	8.74
France	9.73	Mexico	1.68
Hong Kong	3.33	India	0.41

Our earlier comment that what resources are available to workers will affect their productivity, still holds true for the textile data above, but nevertheless, the more expensive hourly rated countries will be very hard pushed indeed to beat the final cost per unit output of the cheapest rated countries.

The examples above were of industrial companies. But companies in service, commerce and public sectors need to be just as quality and performance orientated, for just the same reasons. Organisations like airports, hotels, banks and insurance companies, utilities such electricity, gas and water, and schools, colleges, hospitals and local authorities, theatres and sports and leisure complexes, all need to be as productive as possible so as to give maximum the customer maximum value for money.

Activity

For the organisations above, suggest measures of output, and ratios which would indicate their overall performance levels.

9.2 Techniques of Performance Measurement

The whole range of techniques devoted to the improvement of doing human work is known as **work study**, a term coined many years ago by Russell Currie. Currie was head of work study in ICI, and the term is British.

- The two main categories of work study include **method study** and **work measurement**. Such techniques are included in the term 'industrial engineering' abroad, where it includes many other aspects of problem solving such as operations research, logistics, materials handling, JIT, quality, inventory control, etc.
- Many departments doing this kind of work are currently referred to as Management Services; they are staff departments, and as such have no executive authority, but work in an **advisory capacity** until given authority by the appropriate decision-makers.
- Quite a lot of what we are going to look at might be considered as common sense; none of the techniques is difficult to learn or apply.
- The most difficult thing is to avoid **human problems** in the application of such techniques. The reason for this is that by its very nature, work study looks at the **way people work**, and therefore it asks questions about things which up to now have always been considered a worker's own prerogative.
- Work study's strengths lie in the fact that it is organised common sense, coupled with the ruthless questioning approach which takes nothing for granted.

- We have a natural resistance to change: the author came across the following list of objections to proposals for change: the authorship is unknown. The key task is how to overcome objections such as these:
  - **(a)** Our work is **different**
  - **(b)** It won't work in a **large firm**
  - **(c)** It won't work in a **small firm**
  - **(d)** We've done it **this way** for years, with no problems
  - **(e)** We've **never done it before**
  - **(f)** We've **often tried** to do it like that
  - **(g)** We know another firm who tried and **failed**
  - **(h)** **No need to change;** it's working fine now
  - **(i)** You'll never get it **accepted** here.

9.3 **The Pioneers of Performance Measurement**

(a) **Perronet and Owen**

One of the earliest people concerned with performance was a Frenchman, **Jean Perronet**, who made time studies of pin-making in the middle of the 18th century. Britain's Richard Owen, in the early 19th century, also expressed the importance of paying close attention to human work in the same way attention was paid to ensure machinery was always carefully looked after.

(b) **Taylor**

Most of the key development work took place towards the end of the 19th century and in the early 20th century in America. Frederick Winslow Taylor carried out his experiments in shovelling coal at the Bethlehem Steel works. He experimented to discover what size and shape of shovel was most suited for use with different material, and eventually determined that about 21 pounds per shovel load was the most effective weight to be carried over a working day. Taylor arranged for work to be planned in advance, for men to work as individuals, and for them to be paid a bonus. He also developed **time study**, and examined jobs by breaking them into small elements of work. He is acknowledged as the person who instigated the term 'scientific management'.

(c) **Gantt**

Towards the end of the 19th century, the American, Henry Gantt developed the planning tool known by his name, the **Gantt chart**. This is a chart which uses a horizontal time scale where jobs can be drawn to scale and subsequently monitored for progress according to plan. Gantt also developed incentive schemes and planning systems.

(d) **Gilbreth**

Frank Gilbreth, at the turn of the 19th century, was a key pioneer along with his wife Lillian, a psychologist, in the analysis of the **methods used to do work**. He had started as a bricklayer, and took a great interest in the subject and noticed that bricklayers used different sets of movements depending on whether they were learning, showing others, or getting on with the job by themselves. By minute and careful analysis he ascertained the precise movements used, and reduced and reorganised them, so that the result was a smoother and less time-consuming process. Gilbreth developed **symbols for elemental movements**, and these symbols are called 'Therbligs' (which is Gilbreth's name spelled backwards).

Gilbreth's key principles were:

1 lighten the workload where possible
2 introduce formal rest periods
3 space out the work across the shift.

(e) **Bedaux**

In the first decades of the 20th century, Charles Bedaux developed the idea of assessing the performance of those doing work who were being time studied. Up till then, only actual times had been recorded, but Bedaux wanted to have a **common base** that all actual times could then be related to. He also introduced allowances for **rest** into his time standards.

Case Study: Fidelity Fan Co.

The Fidelity Fan Co. produce high quality fans of many different sizes and applications, ranging from small domestic models to very large industrial versions for industrial and commercial applications.

This necessitates the production of large numbers of castings, which vary in weight from 1 or 2 kilos to about a maximum of 25 kilos. Production runs to several hundred per week.

Management are reasonably satisfied with the layout and operation of their small foundry, but for several reasons, the key one being cost, are less satisfied with the situation in the Fettling Shop. ('Fettling' means cleaning up castings for their subsequent use.) They have now decided to investigate layout and handling methods in this department to see if improvements can be made to increase output and decrease costs.

(a) Fettling shop layout

The present layout of the fettling shop is shown in Figure 9.1, fettling being essentially knocking off the rough edges of the castings produced during the process. Barrowloads of castings are delivered by labourers from the foundry to the fettling shop. They pile their loads on the floor at one end of the shop. Every so often the fettling foreman sends one of his men to the pile to find out what has

It is not possible to alter the shapes or sizes of the work places.

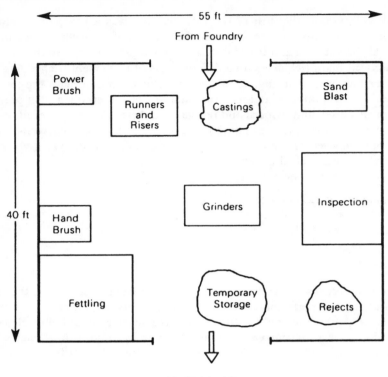

Fig 9.1   Fidelity Fan Co.: fettling shop, current layout

---

been delivered, so that he can select work for his men on the basis of priorities advised to him by the chargehand of the finished castings store. The finished castings are issued from here to the machine shop to meet the production programme requirements.

(b) Work organisation

A group of three labourers working in the fettling shop, who service the five operators, are responsible for delivering batches of castings to the first operation and passing them on to the subsequent operations as necessary. The castings are stacked on the floor for each operator at his work place, and quickly dropped back to the floor by the men as they complete their part of the job.

(c) Operations in the fettling shop

The various operations in the fettling shop are:

1 Knock off the runners and risers. These are the unwanted
pieces of metal on the actual casting, formed during the
casting process.   1.0
2 Brush by hand to remove any sand   5.0
3 Chip casting to remove fins by fettling (more unwanted metal)   2.0
4 Grind castings to remove sharp edges   1.0
5 Sandblast casting to give a smooth and even appearance overall   3.0
6 Inspect finished items   —
7 Pass OK for finished castings store, or reject for   —
rework, or discard

Operations 6 and 7 are for information only. Those operations do not have
standard times (see Chapter 10)

The existing power-driven brushing equipment is not often used by the men as
it generates a good deal of unpleasant dust. Virtually all the castings are brushed
by hand (operation (2)), even though machine brushing takes only 40% of the
manual time.

(d) Priority working

If, as often happens, the finished-goods storekeeper decides that a particular
batch of castings should have priority, work in the fettling shop is not allowed to
cause delay. Incomplete batches of work are moved aside while priority orders
are worked on. Care is taken to ensure that partly finished work, when laid aside
like this, is stored where it cannot be mixed up with rejected castings.

The rejected castings are collected by the labourers, and added to the 'rejects'
pile, before being returned to the foundry. In addition, the completed castings
stores are never allowed to become cluttered with finished work. Once a
storekeeper has all the castings he wants, he advises the fettling shop foreman,
who uses the temporary storage space for finished work on his shop floor until
such time as it can be moved to the stores.

(e) Equipment layout

The Works Manager has repeatedly been asked to look into conditions in the
fettling shop, but says that nothing can be done until the three grinders, which
are installed on a slightly higher part of the fettling shop floor, can be moved to
the same level as the other equipment. This is difficult since they must be bolted
down on to a concrete base for stability.

(f) Rejection rates

Over a period of time it has been found that about 80% of the work passing
through the fettling shop is satisfactory, some 5% is rejected by final inspection
and the remaining 15% by the operators themselves.

(g) Reducing handling and improving flow

Management are fairly convinced that the nature of the fettling operations and
their general sequence cannot be readily altered without detracting from quality:
however, it appears that changes in the layout of the shop could be made to
reduce the amount of handling and to improve the flow of the material.

(h) Labour and throughput data

Fidelity Fan's usual working week is 50 hours, of which 10 are on overtime rates at time and one-third. Labourers earn a basic £120 per 40 hours, and the operators earn £150 per 40 hours. About half the throughput of castings weigh 4 kilos or less, and about three-quarters of the castings weigh 10 kilos or less.

How can we set about analysing the situation, and advising management of the result?

9.4 Organising for Better Performance

(a) The Work Study or Management Services function

Work Study or Management Services, as we have seen, is a staff function, and so its staff have no executive authority to make decisions – i.e. they cannot tell people what to do: they **advise** and **recommend**. They then **implement** and **follow up**, once their recommendations have been authorised by the appropriate departmental manager. Such staff may work in departments also called Organisation and Methods or Industrial Engineering. They do not have to be experts in the work which they are studying, but they do have to be expert in the **human and technical skills** of work study, and have an **enquiring and open mind**. As we shall see, the techniques are relatively straightforward, but working with people – particularly when that work is quite likely to involve changes to well-established routine – is an art rather than a science.

The department may report to the Production Manager or the Works Manager. It will provide a service for the organisation; as such, its costs will be apportioned across the other departments, so there is every reason for it to be used as often as possible. It will cover a wide range of services of the types mentioned earlier. Some of these may be **projects**, such as recommending a new layout for an impending move. Other activities may be the regular **improvements in methods**, and maintenance of work measurement **standards** and **incentive schemes**. It may both plan and monitor projects.

(b) Improving methods

Before any other action such as work measurement or incentive systems can be introduced, it is fundamentally important to get the **methods right**. By 'right', we mean that methods should be the most effective under the given constraints of **time** and **money**. It is reasonable to argue that any situation could be improved out of all recognition if there were unlimited time and money available, but there never is. Additionally, the proposals must relate to the **size** of the problem: small problems generally warrant small-scale solutions, and vice versa. It is also important to remember that there is much to be gained merely from **methods improvements** alone: it is not automatically necessary to follow on with work measurement or incentives.

(i) Method study
Method study, as its name implies, seeks to improve **ways of doing work**, particularly **human** work. It relies heavily on the work of the Gilbreths, who developed a formalised sequence for working through a problem to arrive at a logically produced set of one or more proposals. The Methods are predominately **chart orientated**, and the purpose of such a logical sequence is to try to ensure that no careless assumptions are made, either relating to the present method, or when developing a better one.

A convenient definition of method study is 'the systematic recording and critical examination of existing ways of working, with a view to improving them'. This will apply, for example, to: improvement of processes and procedures; improvement of layout and design; improving the work environment; improving the use of materials, machines and people.

(ii) Organisation and methods
Where method study is done in an office or clerical environment, it is sometimes referred to as **organisation and methods**. This is largely historical and was done to avoid tainting the office with anything that might be done on the shop floor.

(iii) Ergonomics
When improvements to the workplace and people are involved, we often utilise the techniques of ergonomics, where we attempt to **fit the job to the worker**, rather than the other way round. Ergonomics is concerned that dials and instruments are easy to read, give unambiguous information and are conveniently placed; seats must be designed so that they are comfortable and at the right height for the operator in relation to the workplace; work benches and desks and illumination should be designed for safe and comfortable use.

(c) The six key steps of method study

We can identify six key steps in method study which, having stood the test of time, produce good results in a formal manner, minimising the risk of producing an unsatisfactory recommendation:

1 Select the work to be studied
There are several reasons for studying work, but they must be acceptable to both management and unions: it is not acceptable to examine a particular

job because Management Services staff are themselves a little short of work. Valid reasons for selection are:

- **High process costs**: costs may be higher than in similar plants in other divisions, or such that margins are too low, or higher than what can be achieved by buying in that part of the process.
- A job may be a **bottleneck** in a sequence of operations, thus slowing down the entire process, accompanied by a reduction of output.
- An area of work may involve a fairly **tortuous route** through the plant, with associated time loss and complexity.
- **Productivity** may be low because of poor working methods, unsuitable tools and equipment and inappropriate materials.
- There may be **excessive handling** or **poor working conditions**, contributing to high fatigue levels or unsafe working practices.
- A particular job may be **indicated for study** at the request of the operator or supervision.
- **Quality** may be low or erratic, or the job itself may be a **new one**.

2 Record the present method

Recording is done using various types of **charts**. The reason for this is that a pictorial view of what is currently being done is much more effective in conveying information than a normal report. It is also convenient when an improved method is suggested – the similar format for the proposal will contrast effectively with current practice shown in the same format.

Charts record the method by identifying five classifications:

- **Operations:** these are activities which produce or achieve something (e.g. 'cut to length', 'order material', 'serve customer', 'bandage wound' or 'enter data'). At this stage in the investigation we record *everything* without making value judgements as to whether any particular operation is necessary. Some operations may not be *necessary*, but right now we assume nothing.
- **Transportations:** where material or people are being moved, we record the **distance** and any other important parameter, such as weight involved, how moved, nature of movement and purpose.
- **Storage:** we record when something is **stored, held** or **kept** on an indefinite basis, as when a finished item is placed into a warehouse, or a patient's file is returned to its filing cabinet.
- **Delay:** a delay is a temporary or sometimes unintentional **holdup** in the sequence of operations, examples of a delay we record are a document waiting for a signature, a batch of work in a queue, a customer standing in line, a person waiting for their work to be checked.
- **Inspection:** we record where something is **checked** for its appropriate features according to the specification. Most commonly, this will be for quality and/or quantity. Examples such as verifying a signature against a

sample signature, weighing potatoes, looking for nicks or scratches on a polished surface, checking for oil or water leaks or checking that the prescription for a patient has been accurately dispensed.

(i) ASME symbols

To save time, symbols have been established over a period of many years; these resulted in the American Society of Mechanical Engineers (ASME) producing the five symbols shown in Figure 9.2. These are used when charting, and are generally accompanied by one or two words of description; the result being an informative picture of what is happening.

These symbols may be **combined** if an operation and an inspection are **done together**. This is convenient, and provided proposed methods are recorded in a similar way, no difficulty is incurred.

Fig 9.2   ASME flow chart symbols

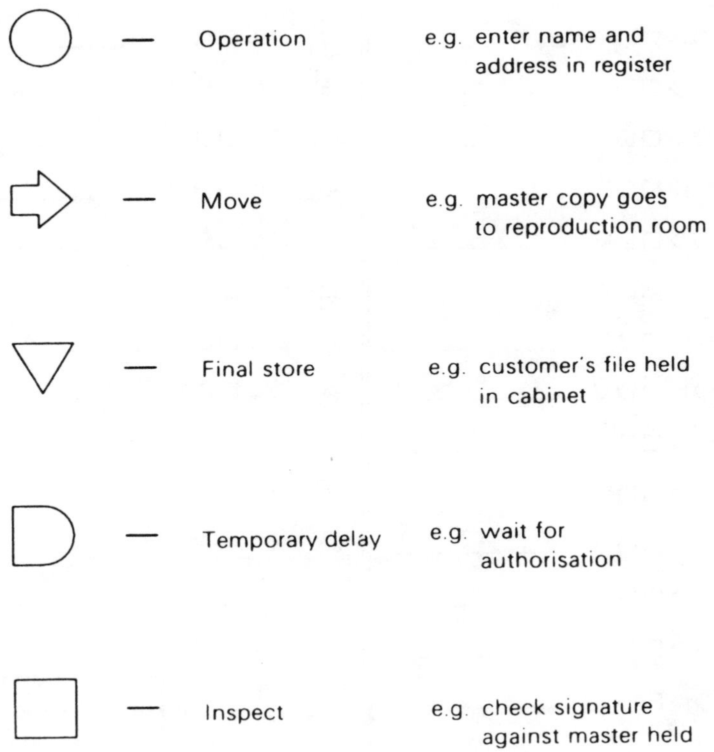

○	Operation	e.g. enter name and address in register
▷	Move	e.g. master copy goes to reproduction room
▽	Final store	e.g. customer's file held in cabinet
D	Temporary delay	e.g. wait for authorisation
□	Inspect	e.g. check signature against master held

Fig 9.3   Process chart: preprinted format

page of

Type Person/Material   Method. Present / Proposed   Dept _____

Subject Charted _____ By _____ Date _____

Chart Begins _____ Chart Ends _____

1 ○⇨□D▽ _____	21 ○⇨□D▽ _____
2 ○⇨□D▽ _____	22 ○⇨□D▽ _____
3 ○⇨□D▽ _____	23 ○⇨□D▽ _____
4 ○⇨□D▽ _____	24 ○⇨□D▽ _____
5 ○⇨□D▽ _____	25 ○⇨□D▽ _____
6 ○⇨□D▽ _____	26 ○⇨□D▽ _____
7 ○⇨□D▽ _____	27 ○⇨□D▽ _____
8 ○⇨□D▽ _____	28 ○⇨□D▽ _____
9 ○⇨□D▽ _____	29 ○⇨□D▽ _____
10 ○⇨□D▽ _____	30 ○⇨□D▽ _____
11 ○⇨□D▽ _____	31 ○⇨□D▽ _____
12 ○⇨□D▽ _____	32 ○⇨□D▽ _____
13 ○⇨□D▽ _____	33 ○⇨□D▽ _____
14 ○⇨□D▽ _____	34 ○⇨□D▽ _____
15 ○⇨□D▽ _____	35 ○⇨□D▽ _____
16 ○⇨□D▽ _____	36 ○⇨□D▽ _____
17 ○⇨□D▽ _____	
18 ○⇨□D▽ _____	
19 ○⇨□D▽ _____	
20 ○⇨□D▽ _____	

SUMMARY

○		
⇨		
□		
D		
▽		

(ii) Process charts

There are two main types of process chart:

1 A **flow process chart** records all operations, inspections, storages, delays and transports as they occur in the job being examined; materials and operator charts are both used:
   - **Materials type:** where what is happening to the **material** is recorded
   - **Operator type:** where what the **operator** does is recorded.

2 An **outline process chart** records only the operations and inspections, and sometimes where other material is introduced into the main sequence of events.

Both these chart types may be drawn on pre-printed forms of the format shown in Figure 9.3 or laid onto a plan of the department or building concerned (see Figures 9.4(a) and (b)). Figure 9.4a shows the flow chart on the plan, and Figure 9.4b shows the flow chart in its usual format.

(iii) Multiple activity chart

Where activities or operations are done in a sequence which is governed by one or more members of a team, it is necessary to record the **relationships** involved in the sequence as well as the sequence itself. For this purpose, a multiple activity chart is ideal (see Figure 9.5). Examples of such work are a dentist and nurse working together on a patient, a surgeon working with an anaesthetist and assistants during an operation, a road repair gang, a team working on the final assembly of a car, or a team in the pits changing the wheels on a racing car and refuelling it, often in as little as 7 seconds.

Case Study: The Warehouse Elevator

The warehouse in a large department store operates on two levels. The incoming and outgoing goods are serviced by two operators and a goods elevator. Their work sequence is repetitive and is described below.

Level 1 operator's work cycle

Remove the first full trolley from the elevator – 15 seconds, then remove the second full trolley –15 seconds. Take the trolley to despatch, empty it and return to the elevator – 25 seconds. Repeat for the second trolley – 25 seconds. Put the first empty trolley on to the elevator – 10 seconds. Repeat for the second empty trolley – 10 seconds.
   Elevator takes 5 seconds travel time from level 1 to level 2.

Level 2 operator's work cycle

Take the first empty trolley from the elevator – 10 seconds. Repeat for the second empty trolley – 10 seconds. Put an already filled trolley on to the elevator – 15 seconds. Fill one trolley with goods – 20 seconds. Put trolley just filled on to the elevator – 15 seconds. (The third of the three trolleys in this set up is filled during the work cycle of the Level 1 operator.)

Elevator takes 5 seconds travel time from level 2 to level 1.

A trolley costs £450 each (non-capital expenditure). Labour rate is £3 per hour per operator, The elevator must not carry people and can carry only a maximum of two trolleys at a time. There is no money available for major capital expenditure.

Fig 9.4   Flow process chart
(a)   Laid on the plan

Each symbol is numbered sequentially from 1, the summary shows that there are 4 transports and 10 operations

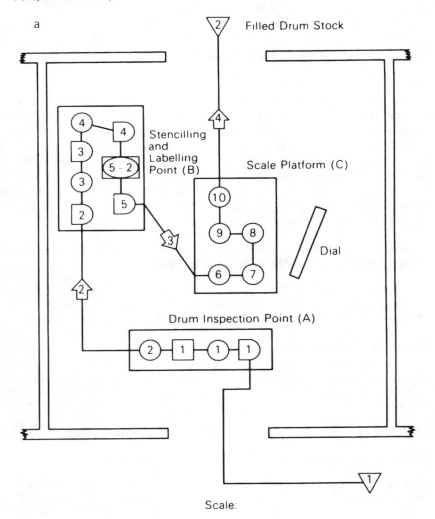

Scale:

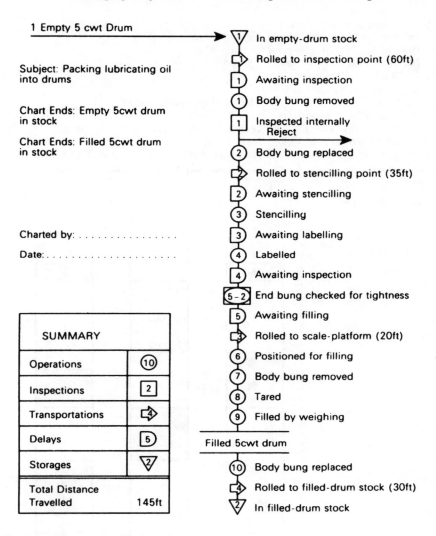

1 Empty 5 cwt Drum

Subject: Packing lubricating oil
into drums

Chart Ends: Empty 5cwt drum
in stock

Chart Ends: Filled 5cwt drum
in stock

Charted by: . . . .

Date: . . . .

SUMMARY	
Operations	10
Inspections	2
Transportations	4
Delays	5
Storages	2
Total Distance Travelled	145ft

In empty-drum stock
Rolled to inspection point (60ft)
Awaiting inspection
Body bung removed
Inspected internally
Reject
Body bung replaced
Rolled to stencilling point (35ft)
Awaiting stencilling
Stencilling
Awaiting labelling
Labelled
Awaiting inspection
End bung checked for tightness
Awaiting filling
Rolled to scale-platform (20ft)
Positioned for filling
Body bung removed
Tared
Filled by weighing
Filled 5cwt drum
Body bung replaced
Rolled to filled-drum stock (30ft)
In filled-drum stock

Fig 9.4   Flow process chart
(b)   Usual format

Activity

Making and stating any assumptions you think necessary, carry out the activities
listed below:

1 Show the present sequence of operations using a multiple activity chart.
2 What is the length of the repetitive work cycle?*
3 Critically examine the present set up and devise a new and more efficient
   sequence.

4 For **1** and **3** above, determine:
  (a) the number of trolleys processed (throughput) per hour*
  (b) the percentage idle time for each operator
  (c) labour cost per trolley processed.
5 For **3** above, determine:
  (a) proposed cycle time
  (b) total number of trolleys to be used in your proposal
  (c) cost of your proposals
  (d) how many weeks it will take to pay off any costs of your proposal, at the proposed level of trolley throughput.
6 What are the implications of your proposals and what do you suggest?

W = work   I = idle

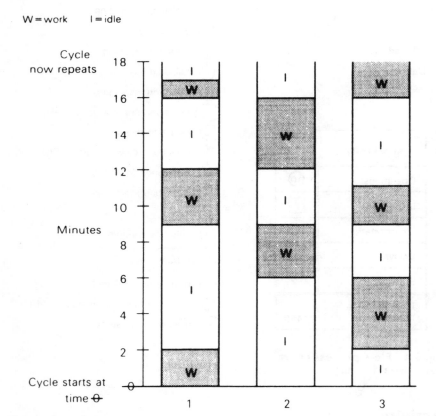

Fig 9.5   Multiple activity chart
A chart of a 3-person team: present method

(iv) String diagram
When flow is primarily **movement only,** a string diagram (see Figure 9.6) is an effective way to present the level of activity involved. On a plan of the

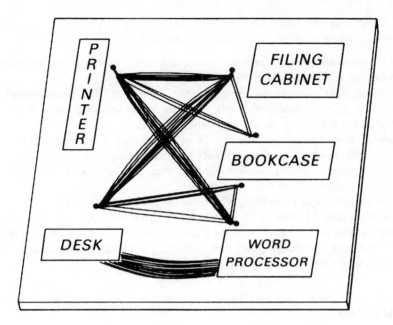

Layout to scale, wind string in proportion to the number of times the route is travelled

Fig 9.6   A string diagram
Layout to scale; wind string in proportion to the number of times the route is travelled

---

area involved, pins are stuck in at each important **start** and **destination** point. Movement activity is recorded over a representative period, and for each journey a length of string joins the two points concerned. The result is that a representative period's activity (say, a day) is clearly shown on the chart, because those points between which there is a lot of travel will have a lot of string, and little-used points will have only a little string. The device is simple, cheap and has great visual impact.

(v) Three-dimensional models
Three-dimensional solid models may be used for extra realism and flexibility. Where the problem is large and important, and a lot of money is involved, this is a good medium to present current and proposed ideas. Two or three-dimensional computer software packages are available, and these can also be used, followed by appropriate translation to a paper copy. Two-dimensional software is very cheap and does not require much computer power.

(vi) Other recording methods
Other recording methods which can be used are:

- **Video recording** using ambient light conditions, where about six hours' recording can be achieved from a standard tape.
- **Ambient light photography** using either high speed for examination of short-cycle, high-repetition work, or time lapse for long-cycle, not very repetitious work (e.g. work on a building site).
- **Elemental movement symbols** known as therbligs, for short-cycle work. It is possible to chart **hand movements** in great detail with their use.

  Recording is a time-consuming task and will be repaid primarily on highly-repetitive, high-volume work.
- **Chronocyclegraph recording**, where small light bulbs are attached to an operator, and by means of an electronic unit the lights are turned on quickly and off slowly at regular short intervals. The result is that when the operator is photographed, the intricate movement of hands, arms and legs can be clearly highlighted.

Activities

(a) Record, using suitable means, what happens to any coursework you do from when you are first given it until you finally receive the marks for it.
(b) From a sheet of A4 paper, draw and cut out with scissors the shape to make a paper cube. Use transparent adhesive tape to seal the ends. Mark each face as if it were a die. Draw a flowchart of the method used, and note exactly all details of construction.
(c) From a single sheet of A4 paper, fold and make a paper dart. Note all details of how it was made, and what you need to know to make identical replicas.
(d) Using old sheets of A4 paper and a ring binder, prepare its contents as follows:

   1 single sheet hole punched
   3 sheets stapled and hole punched
   2 sets of 5 sheets stapled and hole punched
   1 set of 4 sheets stapled and hole punched

   On each sheet write 'page x of y', except the front single sheet. Record the complete process.

---

3 Critical examination
(i) Purpose of the examination
After the current method has been recorded, the most important step of critical examination comes next. Its purpose is to ensure that a **sound reason exists** for **every activity** in the entire sequence.

- This is done by asking the key questions below, and then asking 'Why'?
- An answer must be found for **each question.**

- It is important that no **assumptions** are made, and that answers are sought by the work study officer personally, and obtained from those most likely to know at first hand.
- It is also good practice to **double check** key facts and answers by asking another person if at all possible.
- In an investigation of any size, there is no substitute for painstaking investigation, question and answer. It is somewhat like careful detective work.
- It is a key premise that the good work study officer tries to eliminate, simplify, rearrange or combine operations wherever possible, the logic being that if an operation can actually be eliminated then it is removed from the entire investigative procedure.
- It is necessary to state that under no circumstances must **quality** or **safety** or **health** be compromised.

(ii) The questioning sequence
- The Purpose.
  * **What** is being done?
  * **Why** is it done?
  * **What else might** be done?
  * **What else should** be done?
- The Place
  * **Where** is it being done?
  * **Why** is it done **there?**
  * **Where else** might it be done?
  * **Where should** it be done?
- The Sequence
  * **When** is it done?
  * **Why** is it done **then?**
  * **When else could** it be done?
  * **When should** it be done?
- The People
  * **Who** is doing it?
  * **Why** do **they** do it?
  * **Who else might** do it?
  * **Who else should** do it?
- The Method
  * **How** is it done?
  * **Why** is it done **that way?**
  * **How else could** it be done?
  * **How should** it be done?

As you can see, the critical questioning itself is straightforward; what is more difficult is to ensure you are receiving **accurate answers** based on **fact** and not **opinion.**

4 Develop new methods

It can be very useful to have a 'brainstorming' session, where ideas can be generated without initially being concerned about **cost** or **practicability**. Having then generated a number of ideas, these are then investigated for feasibility and cost, until one or more appear practical, having regard to cost and associated benefits. As mentioned earlier, it is very helpful to try to eliminate, simplify or combine activities when thinking up new methods.

There is no automatic sequence for arriving at fresh proposals, but the logical approach helps greatly. Wherever possible, try to eliminate **delays** and **handling;** this is because whenever we eliminate a delay, time is saved at no extra cost, and whenever we avoid unnecessary handling, we avoid adding to the cost without adding to the value.

5 Presenting proposals

Because Management Services are a staff function, the people conducting these assignments do not have the authority to **implement** a specific solution before those in authority, or those who commissioned the original study, have given their approval. For this reason, it is necessary for the investigators involved to make a **presentation to management**, which will indicate the current situation and associated problems, together with one or more proposed **solutions**, and their anticipated **benefits** and **costs** and **timescale** for achievement. Once management have given their approval (or asked for, and received, further information) the next step can be taken.

6 Install and maintain

Installing and maintaining are as important as the steps already taken, because it is here that the **intended benefits** will occur. For this reason this stage must be handled carefully and sensitively with particular regard to people's feelings; trade union representatives must be kept fully in the picture.

(i) Achieving co-operation

It is in the install and maintain stage that people's natural **resistance to change** will be met. This can be overcome by careful and honest explanation of what is happening, although if people have been kept informed prior to this (as they should have been) then it will be somewhat easier. Without co-operation it will not be possible to achieve all the benefits announced. For these reasons, installation should also be done with the co-operation of the supervision staff concerned – they will have to live with the changes after you, the investigator, have long since moved to another task! Where extensive changes are required, **formal retraining** may be necessary, and subsequently **reinforced**, to ensure that people do not regress to their old work methods.

(ii) Follow up

Follow up is also vital, because management, operatives and trade unions, will all want to see that the benefits the new methods promised have indeed been **delivered**. It will not be unusual for some retraining to be required some time after the new methods have been installed, simply because there are often unforeseen problems which have to be overcome after installation of the new method was thought to have been complete.

Activity

Figure 9.1 shows the present layout of Fidelity Fan Co.'s fettling shop. Analyse this layout and draw your own flow chart. Analyse and develop a proposed layout and show the new flow through the department. For each chart, prepare a summary of symbols used and distances travelled.

Activity

Draw a flow chart of the procedure described below, together with a summary of symbols.

Cost control in reprographics

Originators will hand their work in to Jill (repro supervisor) accompanied by the completed request forms (original and duplicate). When the work has been done, it win be returned with the duplicate via internal mail to the originator. Upon receipt of their work, the originator will check it and if correct, will send the duplicate to Elizabeth (short courses director). Jill will accumulate the originals and pass them to Elizabeth once a week. The short courses section will pair off all forms and check them for correct completion with regard to quantity and cost data. Where duplicates have been received with no corresponding original, or vice versa, the section will try to resolve it with reprographics and/or the originator.

The originals are then passed via internal mail to data processing on the main site. Data processing processes these every two weeks as they are not on the high priority list. The printout and summary of the reprographics section, by individual, by section, by department and by division in quantities and costs. are sent to Jill and each section, department and division head who uses the results for management control purposes.

Activity

Draw a flow process chart of the procedure below, together with a summary of flow chart symbols.

Sales Manager's secretary

Go to In tray
Pick up next incoming envelope. Return to own desk
Open envelope and read contents. Put contents in 'For attention of ' tray. Save envelope

Wait for dictation, take dictation, read it back and correct if required
Return to own desk, prepare to type, and type reply
Check letter and place in 'For attention of -' tray
Continue with other work
After letter signed, type envelope, check, place letter in envelope. Go to mail drop point, post letter and return
Pin copy of reply to original letter, and place all in folder. Go to record cabinets, file folder in customer record cabinet and return to own desk.

Activity

Evaluate a kitchen, domestic or commercial, with regard to:

(a) height, number and size of cupboards and shelves
(b) amount and height of working surfaces
(c) lighting and heating conditions considering the type of work
(d) layout of equipment, in conjunction with storage and working surfaces, together with incoming and outgoing material
(e) produce a flow chart, on a plan, of the sequence for:
   i making a pot of tea for 4, and 8 slices of toast and marmalade, consuming them, washing up and storing the crockery
   ii making a lunchtime selection of 50 each of 6 different rolls and sandwiches to be displayed in a cool cabinet for sale; make an urn of tea and an urn of coffee
(f) produce recommendations for improvements.

Activity

Prepare a suitable flow chart of the procedures outlined below for processing Sales Orders, critically examine them, suggest improvements together with any implications, and prepare a flowchart showing the proposed procedures.

Orders are received into the Sales Office via telephone, fax and letter. If telephoned in, orders are noted and held in a pending file until the written order is received. If faxed in or via letter, orders are separated into new and old customers at the end of each day. Orders from new customers are held over, pending credit check by a credit agency. If they are considered a poor risk, a letter of regret is typed in the Sales Office and sent to the customer; sometimes the requirement is made for payment in full prior to delivery. Known customers who have unpaid invoices past their pay by date are similarly treated. For approved customers, the Sales Office types up a 5 part Sales Order (top and four copies).

The sales order top is held in the Sales Office and filed by customer name. The 1st and 2nd copy goes to the stockroom. The 3rd copy goes to dispatch to await the goods via the stockroom. The 4th copy goes to Accounts. The storeperson batches the orders received since the last order pick and later picks the items during two sessions per day. The quantities filled are entered on each copy and indicates any items which are short. The 1st copy is pinned to the goods and is sent to dispatch. The 2nd copy goes to Accounts. For shortage situations, two more copies are made for use later and held in the stockroom until needed.

At Dispatch, a shipping note is prepared (top plus a copy). The top is pinned to the sales order copy and goods which are all then dispatched to the customer. The shipping note copy is pinned to the previously received sales order copy and both are sent to Accounts. When Accounts match the sales order copy sent to them from the stockroom with the sales order from the Sales Office, and the shipping note/sales order copy sent to them from Dispatch, they prepare the invoice. Two copies are made and one is stamped 'invoice sent. The invoice original is sent to the customer. The stamped copy of the sales order and the dispatch note are sent to the Sales Office, where they are all filed in the customers' records which are held alphabetically. Accounts keeps the 2nd copy of the invoice together with copies 2 and 4 of the sales order for future reference.

Chapter Review Questions

1 What is 'productivity' and how is it measured? How are changes in productivity calculated?
2 What must be done prior to any work study investigation?
3 What is method study sometimes called when conducted in an office?
4 What are the five key classifications recorded when making a flow chart?
5 What does an outline process chart record?
6 What are the two main flow chart types?
7 How could you conveniently record a week's work on a building site, without having an observer continuously present?
8 What is the purpose of a critical examination?
9 Why is the install and maintain phase so important to a successful method study?
10 How can you try to ensure success in the install and maintain phase?

10 Managing Performance: 2 – Measuring Work Content

In Chapter 9 we saw how we could obtain improvements in the way work is done, and often this is sufficient; there may be no need for subsequent work measurement or incentive schemes. But there are occasions when it is important to know how long jobs *should* take, and in Chapter 10 we examine the need for this, and how it can be done. The key word is 'should'. When we need to measure work content, obtaining an average of current or past actual times is not sufficient – we would not know if those averages are too **high** or too **low**; we could not tell what work was included, or how well it was done (there may be unnecessary idle time included). In these situations, **formal work measurement methods** produce reliable results.

Learning Objectives

By the end of this chapter you should:

1 know the most common **uses** for work measurement
2 know different ways to **measure** work
3 know what goes to make up a **standard time**
4 know how to undertake an **activity sampling study**.

10.1 Uses for Work Measurement

Work measurement techniques enable us to produce the **standard time** for a job. Standard time is a measure of **work:** if we know how long a job should take, we can estimate when it should be finished once processing has started. (We look at this in more detail in Chapter 12.)

(a) Labour cost and operator performance

When we know how long a job should take, we can estimate the **labour cost:** this is obtained by multiplying the standard time by the hourly rate. This information is used to build the **total standard cost** for a product. Comparisons can be made later between the standard cost and the actual cost; the difference is a **variance** which can be analysed into different components, such as labour, material and overhead variances.

The standard times for an existing and a proposed **method**, can be compared. Other things being equal, we would prefer the method with the shorter standard time, provided quality and safety were not jeopardised. When we know how long a job should take, we can also estimate the **performance** of the operator or a group of operators. This is essential for determining how efficiently the work is being done, and any difference between standard and actual can be investigated and corrective action taken.

(b) Labour rate and incentive schemes

Similarly, if we have trainees, the standard time can be used as a basis for introducing a properly graduated scale based on the learning curve, which closely represents the loss due to the trainees not being fully skilled: being a qualified person is one of the prerequisites for being able to achieve a standard performance.

As standard times are a measure of work, they can be used for work-study-based **incentive schemes** (see Chapter 11). These schemes pay a bonus to a person or a group related to their performance over and above their basic rate.

10.2 Standard Time

The concept of 'standard time' is fundamental to understanding work measurement. Standard time is not clock time but a measure of work. It therefore includes every activity necessary to do the job, plus personal allowances and allowances for rest, relaxation and contingencies. When making a time study, allowance has also to be made for the actual rate of working compared with a defined level of working known as **standard performance**.

(a) Qualified and motivated worker

Standard time is the time a qualified worker who is motivated to do the job, who adheres to the specified methods and who takes the appropriate amount of rest and relaxation will be able to meet when working over a day or shift. By 'meet' we mean that for a job with a standard time of 1 hour per unit, such an operator will have produced 8 units in an 8-hour shift, on average.

A person is '**qualified**' if they have been properly trained to do the job, and are used to doing it. A person who usually does the filing in an office but who is standing in for an absentee typist, is not a qualified person. A time study observer would not be prepared to study a typing job done by a temporary untrained replacement. We would not expect that person to meet a properly set standard time, but to record a performance well below standard, the difference being due to their lack of expertise.

The term **'motivated to do the job'** means that the performance of the operator will be that specified as being standard. Standard performance is the performance designated as 100 on the British Standard 0 to 100 rating scale. This occurs when a qualified and motivated operator carries out a task according to the methods already specified. Precisely what is 'motivating' the operator is not specified: what motivates one person may not motivate another. Sufficient motivation may therefore be supplied by conscientious interest in the job, a vital need to finish the job by a specified deadline, being threatened or being paid by results.

(b) Other allowances included in standard time

Because the work standard is likely to be used for some or all of the purposes outlined above, it must include all the **ancillary tasks** necessary to the main job. For example, in printing batches of documents ancillary work will include fetching new supplies of paper and ink, setting-up and cleaning down and wrapping and moving batches of finished work to the stores.

Similarly, a work standard which cannot be met over a working day or shift is not useful. Appropriate amounts of **rest** and **personal** time must be included in the standard. The final result must be a standard time which will be eminently useful for any or all of the purposes specified earlier, and one that the operator can meet without undue fatigue after a working day or shift.

10.3 Techniques of Work Measurement

There are five principal ways of measuring work:

(a) Time study
(b) Synthetics
(c) Predetermined motion time standards
(d) Estimating
(e) Activity sampling.

We shall examine each in turn, beginning with time study, which is probably the most widely used method of determining a standard time.

(a) Time study

(i) Observed and standard performance
This is the name given to the technique of work measurement where a trained observer records a **representative number of repetitions** of the job in hand, and from the details noted calculates its standard time. The job is broken down into small elements of work about 0.25 to 0.50 of a minute

each in duration. The observer uses a stop-watch to record the length of each element, and while doing so assesses the performance of the operator compared with the concept of standard performance that the observer has been trained to recognise.

The technique of time study requires an observer trained in the use of a stop-watch and who is able to compare observed performance with that of standard performance. Standard performance is called 100, or 100%. Observers are trained to recognise different levels of actual performance by training films and simple tasks. Such films, made by companies like ICI, are acknowledged to differentiate between performances from about 70 to 120%. Examples are oil drum loading and unloading, painting, and making up cardboard boxes from flat. It is not necessary for observers to be skilled themselves in the job they observe, but many observers tend to specialise in a group of work (e.g. office, assembly, machine shop or finishing jobs).

By diligent practice observers become adept at recognising varying performances in steps of about 5 percentage points. A performance of 75 is one in which the operator is not consciously wasting time, but the work is performed without the crispness and skill of the motivated person. A 75 performance is often used as the point at which incentive schemes begin to pay bonus. A performance of 125 is a **super skilled** performance, where the work is performed with speed and dexterity, often by a person with a natural aptitude for that job. The work methods are performed smoothly and very consistently, and the quality of the work produced is also consistently high.

Comparing actual performance with standard performance, is called **rating**, and compensates for the skill, speed and effort of the operator compared with the standard performance. Standard performance may be compared with walking unencumbered along a corridor, at 4 miles an hour. It may also be thought of as a brisk, businesslike and competent performance. Someone who works at standard performance makes the job look easy, appears unhurried, anticipates problems and works in a smooth and consistent manner.

(ii) Job elements

When an observer studies a job, it is broken down into short convenient lengths called **elements**. An element is a short period of similar work which makes it easy to recognise and to rate. It also makes it easier to apply appropriate rest allowances (see below), and apply different rest allowances to different parts of the job (e.g. heavy manual work requires bigger rest allowances than paperwork administration). If an operator is unloading potatoes from a lorry and wheeling them into a store, suitable elements might be **(a)** obtain a trolley from store, **(b)** unload one sack on to a trolley, **(c)** wheel to the food store, **(d)** unload the full sack, **(e)** return to lorry from store, **(f)** return trolley, and **(g)** do appropriate paperwork.

The observer must record sufficient repetitions of the entire job to be assured that a representative sample has been seen. Where possible, more than one operator should be observed doing that job. When the cumulative average of the actual times settles down when plotted on a graph, sufficient repetitions have probably been seen.

(iii) Rating performance

Let us now see how rating is done in practice. An observer has recorded a sufficient number of repetitions of an element of a job to be representative. At each repetition the actual performance was observed and rated along with the actual time of each repetition. The average rating was 90, and the average actual time was 0.40 minutes. This means that the observer was looking at a performance a little below standard.

- We multiply the average actual rating by the average actual time to calculate the **basic time**. In this case we have $(90 \times 0.4)/100 = 0.36$ basic minutes. 'Basic time' is the time for an element or a job after allowance has been made for the rate of working. As this operator was performing below standard, he is taking longer than someone working at standard performance.

  Suppose another operator had been working on the same job. He took an average of 0.35 minutes and was rated at 100. The corresponding calculation is: $(100 \times 0.35)/100$ equals 0.35 basic minutes. Similarly, if a third person averaged 0.30 minutes and had an average performance of 120, this equals 0.36 basic minutes. Rating is a levelling procedure designed around standard performance.

- This procedure is repeated for every element of work until a complete list of job elements has been obtained with corresponding basic times. Let us assume that it has been calculated that the basic time for unloading a sack is **1.5 basic minutes**, excluding elements **(a)** and **(f)**.

- If an element of work is not repeated in every cycle of the job, that element is divided by the frequency of occurrence (e.g. get and replace hand trolley from the store takes, say, 2.0 basic minutes, but is done only once for every lorryload of potatoes, i.e. 50 sacks). Here we divide 2.0 basic minutes by $50 = \textbf{0.04 basic minutes per sack}$. It is necessary to decide in advance what the **unit of output** is going to be. If every lorry were always the same size, then the unit of output might have been a lorryload. If lorries of different sizes are used then it makes more sense to make a unit of output the 'sack'.

- A **contingency** is a relatively rare occurrence, for which a small allowance ought to be made (e.g. a sack may split and all the potatoes have to be picked up and loaded into a spare sack). If this were estimated to occur once in 50 sacks, and when it did, it took 5 basic minutes, the time allowance would be $5.0/50 = 0.1$ basic minutes. But the idea of a **contingency allowance** is to save the trouble of estimating the time and frequency and nature of these rare occurrences. So we often add a fixed allowance of not more than 5% to the original basic time.

- We can now add the 1.5 basic minutes to the 0.04 basic minutes to get a total basic time of 1.54 basic minutes per sack unloaded. But 'basic time' means what it suggests: it is the time for the job having allowed only for the rate of working, but excluding any allowances for rest, relaxation, etc.

   These allowances must be included if the standard time is to be realistic. To do this, allowances have been developed over a number of years which fairly represent the extra time necessary to allow the operator to recover from fatigue. Such a table is shown in Figure 10.1.
- The principal **allowances** necessary are:

   (a) personal allowance for washing hands, etc.
   (b) rest and relaxation allowance,
   (c) contingency allowance, and
   (d) an allowance specifically related to the job (e.g. donning and removing special protective clothing).

All these allowances are each calculated as a percentage of the original total basic time, and are then added to the original basic time to find the standard time.

Let us select an appropriate percentage for each allowance. For the personal allowance we select 2.5% from section E (Figure 10.1). For a manual task like unloading, we select a rest allowance of 20% from section A5. We will allow 5% for contingencies. If appropriate, other allowances could be added, but for illustration purposes, our three selections are adequate. There are no special clothing allowances for this task.

The total percentage to be added is $2.5 + 20 + 5 = 27.5\%$. This is added to the 1.54 basic minutes to give a standard time, per sack, of **1.96 standard minutes, or 30.5 sacks per hour** at standard performance, while using the specified methods and taking appropriate rest. Clearly, using the specified methods is important: for example, the standard time above may have been arrived at by using a simple hand trolley, and unloading one sack at a time. The standard would not be valid for a significant change in method such as using a fork lift truck, or even a trolley platform which could hold 5 sacks for pushing to the store.

For a time study, a decimal minute stop-watch is conventionally used. This is perfectly adequate but cannot help in the subsequent analysis of the data. There are a selection of electronic stop-watches and allied software, which by precoding elements once identified help to simplify the recording of the elemental times, the rating and the analysis for calculating the basic and standard times.

(b) Synthetics

These make use of standard times already obtained by time study as described above. To 'synthesise' something means to build it up from small pieces. We have already mentioned that when time studies are taken, the job

Fig 10.1 Guide to relaxation allowances

(1) These tables are intended as a guide in assessing the relaxation allowances for individual elements.

(2) Although allowances are usually additive for individual elements, assessments for elements incurring high allowances may require reduction when followed by elements incurring less.

(3) The appropriate allowance for any factor present in an element should not be given until the influence of other factors upon it has been considered.

(4) Only in A, E and H has a separate allowance been indicated for women. Discretion should be used when assessing allowances for women under other factors.

(5) When special protective clothing such as gloves, footwear, suits or goggles has been worn, additional fatigue may arise. Care should therefore be taken in making allowances under factors A, C, D, F and G.

FACTORS	TYPICAL EXAMPLES	Equivalent to handling	ALLOWANCES Men per cent	Women per cent	REMARKS
A. Energy Output (affecting muscular recovery)					
1. Negligible.	Light bench-work—seated.	No Load	0 – 6	0 – 6	When selecting the appropriate allowance for an element, the influence of the energy output in adjacent elements should be considered.
2. Very light.	Light bench-work—standing.	0 – 5 lb.	6 – 7½	6 – 7½	
3. Light.	Light shovelling.	5 – 20 lb.	7½ – 12	7½ – 16	
4. Medium.	Hacksawing or filing.	20 – 40 lb.	12 – 19	16 – 30	
5. Heavy.	Swinging heavy hammer 7-28 lb.	40 – 60 lb.	19 – 30	–	
6. Very heavy.	Loading weights.	60 – 112 lb.	30 – 50	–	
7. Exceptional.	Loading heavy sacks.	above 112 lb.	requires special consideration	–	
B. Posture			per cent		
1. Sit.	Normal sedentary work.		0 – 1		When selecting the appropriate allowance for an element, the influence of the posture in adjacent elements should be considered.
2. Stand (both feet).	Whenever body is erect and support on feet only.		1 – 2½		
3. Stand (one foot).	Standing on one leg (using a foot control).		2½ – 4		
4. Lying down.	On side, face or back.		2½ – 4		
5. Crouch.	When body is bent, but supported on feet or knees.		4 – 10		

cont.

FACTORS	TYPICAL EXAMPLES	ALLOWANCES		REMARKS
C Motions				When selecting the appropriate allowance for an element, the influence of the restricted motions in adjacent elements should be considered
1. Normal	Free swing of hammer.	0		
2. Limited	Limited swing of hammer.	0 – 5		
3. Awkward	Carrying heavy load in one hand	0 – 5		
4. Confined (limbs only).	Working with arms above head	5 – 10		
5. Confined (whole body)	Working at thin coal seam	10 – 15		
		Lighting Good	Lighting Poor/Variable	
		per cent	per cent	
D Visual Fatigue				All colour contrasts wherever occurring must be considered in addition to light intensity
1. Intermittent eye-attention.	Reading meters or gauges.	0	1	
2. Nearly continuous eye-attention.	Precision machine work.	2	2	
3. Continuous eye-attention—varying focus	Inspecting moving or stationary cloth for faults	2	5	
4. Continuous eye-attention—fixed focus	Inspecting minute and/or moving objects.	4	8	
E. Personal Needs		Men per cent 2½	Women per cent 4	

F	Thermal Conditions	Temperature	Humidity Normal	Humidity Excessive	
			per cent	per cent	The selection of the ranges given must be related to the type of work done which may offset the temperature effects. and to the type of ventilation
	1 Freezing	below 30°F	over 10	over 12	
	2 Low.	32°- 55°F	10–0	12 – 5	
	3 Normal	55°– 75°F	0–	5	
	4 High	75°–100°F	0–40	5 – 100	
	5 Excessive	above 100°F	over 40	over 100	
G	Atmospheric Conditions			per cent	Additional allowance will be necessary for special conditions of altitude and climate.
	1 Good	Well-ventilated rooms or fresh air		0	
	2 Fair	Badly ventilated air, presence of non-toxic but fetid odours or non-injurious fumes.		0 – 5	
	3 Poor	Presence of toxic dusts or heavy concentration of non-toxic dusts involving use of breathing filters		5 – 10	
	4 Bad	Presence of toxic fumes or dusts involving use of respirator.		10 – 20	
H	Other Influences of Environment			per cent	
	1 Clean, healthy, dry and bright surroundings, low noise-level. Influences without effect on work			0	
	2 Where work cycle is continuously repetitive and between 5 and 10 seconds.			0 – 1	
	3 Where work cycle is continuously repetitive and less than 5 seconds.			1 – 3	
	4 Where there is a complete absence of company Day–Men. Day–Women. Night–Men.			1 / 2	
	5 Excessive noise. e.g. riveting (allowance related to continuity of noise).			0 – 5	
	6 Where effect of such disturbing influence might be detrimental to quality of output			0 – 5	
	7 Vibration of floors or machines. e.g. pneumatic drilling (allowance related to continuity of vibration).			5 – 10	
	8 Extreme condition. e.g. dirt. noise. etc.			5 – 15	

being studied is broken down into elements, one reason for this being that the elements can be categorised and used as the database for other jobs subsequently requiring standard times. When a new job arrives, it is broken down into elements, and the database searched for common elements which have already been studied. A prerequisite for this is that the new job must be of a **similar kind** to the previous jobs studied.

This means that synthetics can be used only for other similar jobs: they are not universal for completely different kinds of work. As an example, synthetics developed for use in meal preparation could not be used to build up standard times for painting; assembly synthetics cannot be used to build up times for welding jobs. Similarly, office synthetics (and, indeed, office predetermined time standards) cannot be used to build up standard times for maintenance work.

Using synthetics has the advantage of saving time on **standard setting**, because not all of a new job has to be time studied. Using synthetics means greater consistency in the standards themselves, because the same elemental time will be used wherever that particular element occurs: it is not restudied, with the attendant risk of a slightly different standard for the same element of work. Synthetics also helps to reduce the number of queries from unions or operators because of this greater consistency.

(c) Predetermined motion time standards

These are times for very short elemental movements such as **get, put, pickup, let go**, or **position**. These elemental movements are fundamental building blocks and so can be used to create standard times for almost any purpose within a very wide range of activities. These standards have been developed over the years by companies like British Rail for their Clerical Work Data, Maynard, MTM and Work Factor.

(i) MTM data
The Methods Time Measurement (MTM) Association Ltd in the UK have for many years made widely available via qualified instructors key data which it has developed. These range from the original MTM1, the most detailed set of predetermined time standards to MTM-X and MOMET in the 1980s.

- **MTM-X** is suitable for independent application, after training by a registered training body, and is effective for methods analysis and measurement of work cycles of half a minute or more. MTM-X is suitable wherever the comprehensive MTM education by specialist technicians is not required. The use of such systems enables optimum methods to be determined by careful analysis prior to production, and avoids use of the stopwatch.
- Figure 10.2 shows movement categories and elemental times; competent MTM application requires training by a registered training body which uses licensed MTM instructors.

	GE	GD	PE	PD		
N	8	17	5	19		
F	16	25	14	28		
X	13	20	9	22		

	R	HW	A	E	S	BD	AB
	6	5	14	7	18	29	32

Fig 10.2   Movement categories and elemental time for MTMX

The letters are the abbreviated code for different movements. The numbers are their elemental times in 100,000ths of an hour. One 100,000th of an hour is called a time measurement unit (tmu). One tmu is equivalent to 0.036 seconds. The level of performance is equivalent to 83 on the BS rating scale of 0 to 100.

(ii) Movement categories
Nine movement categories are defined:

Code	Definition
GE, GD	get
PE, PD	put
R	regrasp
HW	handle weight
A	apply pressure
E	eye action
S	take a step
BD	bend down
AB	arise from bend

(iii) Element description
Every element also has a carefully defined description (e.g. the action of 'get' is the action of reaching to an object and grasping it). It starts with reaching to an object, includes reaching to and gaining control over the object, and it ends when the object is grasped so as to permit its movement, or to permit the performance of the next motion.

- **GE** means an easy get and **GD** means a difficult get. When the distance is less than 16 centimetres, get is coded **N** for near. Above 15 centimetres it is coded **F** for far. If the distance is variable, it is coded **X** for variable.
- Other elements are equally carefully defined, and require similar care when being used. When two or more motions are performed simultaneously, all can be accomplished in the time for the motion with the greatest time (i.e. the limiting motion).

(iv) **MOMET**

For office work, the MTM Office Methods Evaluation Technique (MOMET) provides a range of office predetermined standards including handling general objects, paper, paper fasteners, filing-cabinet work, typing and general mail. Reading and writing are also covered.

- The movements have mnemonic names and the time values are again expressed in tmus; they were derived from MTM Core Data Analysis. Distance factors are included, covering distances less and greater than 15 centimetres.
- The example below is taken from the MOMET manual, and describes the synthesis of a time for 'Filing a letter in a filing cabinet'. The letter codes are the mnemonic descriptions referred to earlier.

Element description	Code	tmus
stand	**B-STDC**	43
pick up a letter	**GP-SP1H**	19
walk 1 step to filing cabinet	**B-WKAO**	114
open filing cabinet	**S-OPFC**	80
get file	**S-REMF**	125
open file	**S OPCV**	71
place letter in file	**S PINF**	72
close file	**S CLCV**	67
replace file in cabinet	**S INSF**	88
close cabinet	**S CLFC**	50
walk 1 step back to desk	**B WKAO**	114
sit down	**B SITC**	35
		858

858 tmus equals $((858/100{,}000) \times 3600) = 30.9$ seconds. This is the basic time, to which therefore must be added (at least) allowances for personal time, rest and contingencies, so as to produce a standard time. If in this example we use a total of 15% for all the allowances, the standard time will equal 35.5 standard seconds per occasion. Predetermined Administrative Data System (PADS) is an updated version of MOMET, which now incorporates keystroke data, not available when MOMET was devised.

(d) **Estimating**

Estimating is a useful method of setting standards for a job when there are unlikely to be more than a very few repetitions, or where no two jobs are likely to be the same. This kind of situation occurs quite frequently in repair or maintenance work. Estimating is not as accurate as time study, but this is often not as important when each job is different from the previous one. The main advantage is that a standard time can be set **prior to the start of the job**, and this is a big help in costing and scheduling. A work study officer does not normally set the standard when estimating is required; usually it is a person who has had a lot of experience in doing the particular kind of work being studied.

Experience is used to visualise what steps are required to do the repair, for example. The times for these are then estimated and some allowances are added, and the result is called the **standard time for the job**. The actual time is noted when the job is actually done, and in that way the estimator builds up an increasing body of knowledge about that kind of work. The relative simplicity of estimating, coupled with its speed, makes it ideal for low volume or very varied work. However, an estimator who is very good at estimating how long it will take to make air conditioning ducting, for example, will not be able to estimate how long different car repairs will take. Estimating is strictly related to the **particular body of knowledge** each estimator has.

(e) Activity sampling

This is a statistical technique using a large number of **random instantaneous observations** which can convey a valid indication of the percentage of time that different work categories occupy during a given time period (e.g. a week). This technique was developed by L. Tippett in the 1930s. He worked for the Cotton Board in the North of England, and was concerned with the amount of down time on looms. Activity sampling is based on statistical principles.

(i) Uses of activity sampling
Each observation records what is happening **at that particular moment**. From the total number of observations in each work category, the percentage that each category takes of the whole study period is calculated, together with statistical limits for each answer. These percentages can then be converted into the actual amount of time each category takes out of the working day or week.

This technique can be used in many different areas of business, wherever management needs more information upon which to base decisions. It can be very easily used where the work of a group of people or machines needs to be analysed. The technique itself does not solve problems, but does provide management with extra information to specified limits of accuracy. It is sometimes called by other names such as ratio delay, random observation method, work sampling or snap reading.

It is usefully employed in warehouses, loading bays, stores, offices, machine shops and assembly areas. It is helpful in calculating the utilisation of machines, to establish idle or absentee time and to help decide whether a larger or more detailed investigation would be justified.

(ii) Error in findings
Because activity sampling has a statistical basis, we can determine the error associated with our findings, and a level of confidence in the results; we

never need do more work than is necessary to provide results of the required accuracy. Where the estimated percentage occurrence of the activity is large, we might be able to tolerate a larger error. These decisions directly affect the number of observations required. Intuitively, the more accuracy is required, the more observations are needed, and vice versa. Later we shall see how to calculate precisely the required number of observations for a given activity, and an acceptable size of error.

(iii) Taking an activity sample study

This technique uses the binomial distribution, its mean and standard deviation (see Chapter 14). For most studies, it is assumed that there are an infinite number of instantaneous observation 'occasions' from which to choose the necessary number of observations. If this is the case, then the basic formula shown below is perfectly accurate. Where the required number of observations is a large in relation to the total number of observation opportunities, however, the basic formula needs to be modified.

While the technique itself is fairly straightforward, it is nevertheless most important to approach its use in a formal manner, so minimising any problems which might be encountered.

1 There must be full and adequate **consultation** for those who are likely to be affected by a proposed investigation. It is quite likely that assurances will have to be given regarding layoffs and job disruption before the study can go ahead.

2 Whoever is going to do the study should make themselves familiar with the **working environment**, so that plans made will be as practical as possible regarding when the study will be taken, who will be involved, and where the study areas are in relation to the observer's office.

3 Take a **pilot study** to estimate the approximate percentage occurrence of the main category of interest. Such a pilot study might last a day or two, and consist of taking about 25 observations at random. Absences from the work place might be a category causing concern. From 25 observations, the result might show 14 – work, 4 – idle, 5 – absences and 2 – on the telephone. If the study were to investigate the level of absences, then that would be the key category and the rough estimate is $(5 \times 100)/25 = 20\%$. This forms the basis for a more exact calculation of the number of observations to make, and what error can be tolerated.

4 Decide on the error that can be tolerated. This is usually considered as so many percentage points either side of the activity level under consideration, here 20%. There is no formula, but if the occurrence itself is about 20%, then it would be reasonable to tolerate about ±2 percentage points either side of the final answer. Suppose the final absentee level is found to be 22%. The answer would be accurate at a given level of confidence to ±2 percentage points (i.e. from 20% to 24%).

5 Calculate the **required number of observations** using the nomograph in Figure 10.3. We will assume that a 95% confidence level is sufficient. This means that if many similar studies were carried out, 19 out of 20 results would fall within the range shown above and 1 out of 20 results would exceed the upper or lower limit. Place a straight edge on the left hand column at the 20% occurrence point, and connect the straight edge to the required accuracy of 2 percentage points on the accuracy required middle line. Using the same straight edge and without moving it, the number of observations required are read off from the right hand vertical

Fig 10.3   Activity sampling nomograph (95% level of confidence)

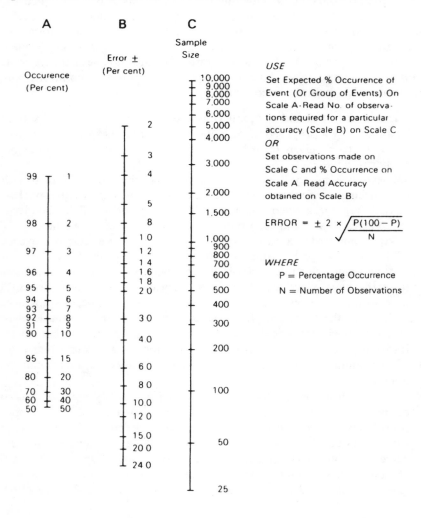

USE

Set Expected % Occurrence of Event (Or Group of Events) On Scale A - Read No. of observations required for a particular accuracy (Scale B) on Scale C

OR

Set observations made on Scale C and % Occurrence on Scale A Read Accuracy obtained on Scale B.

$$ERROR = \pm 2 \times \sqrt{\frac{P(100-P)}{N}}$$

WHERE

P = Percentage Occurrence

N = Number of Observations

line, which is about 1600 on the 95% confidence side. Note that if you think this is far too many observations to take, then see what happens if you would be willing to accept an error of 3 points. You should get an answer of 700 off the right-hand vertical line.

6 You can now plan the full study, and decide over what realistic **period of time** the study should be taken. Bearing in mind you have 700 observations to take, there is a practical limit as to how many observations are possible in a day. Note that even if you did not have to make a lot of observations, you would still not make the study very short, because the results must reflect reality, and you want to ensure the study covers sufficient time for this to occur. It would be necessary to talk to the supervisor involved. You will also plan the **route** you will take. You will prepare a checklist of the main activity headings, so that when you see them it will be easy to place a tick in the appropriate column. You must also generate 700 random times of day for the period of the study. This can be done on a computer, and you will arrange it so that no times fall during the lunch break or before or after working hours.

7 Take the actual study, and summarise the **percentage occurrences** for each activity. Let us suppose these are as follows, based on 700 readings:

	%
Work	60
Idle	10
Absent	24
Phone	6

8 The error associated with a true result for absences of 24%, can be found by using the same nomograph as before. In this case, put a straight edge on the left-hand column where percentage activity 24, and also on the right-hand column where the number of readings 700. The actual error is read on the straight edge from the middle vertical line without moving the straight edge. The answer is 3.2%. If you think you can be satisfied with this error, which is a bit more than the 3% specified earlier, then the study is finished. If you must have the error no greater than 3% then from the nomograph 810 observations are needed. As you have taken 700 observations already, another 110 are taken, which should give the required accuracy. You never do more work than is necessary to achieve the required results, and for all practical purposes, the 95% confidence level is used.

9 Now you have the final result, you must translate it into **hours per week**. For example, if absenteeism is 24% 3% (i.e. 3 percentage points), then on a 40-hour nominal working week, absenteeism ranges from 21% to 27% with a 95% confidence level. This means that in many repetitions of this study, 95% of the results will lie within the 3% range and only one will lie outside that range.

In a 40-hour week, therefore, we are confident that absenteeism ranges between 21% of 40 hours = 8.4 hours, and 27% of 40 hours = 10.8 hours.

10 The nomograph is based on a simple statistical formula, which is then manipulated to find the number of readings, and the associated error of the result:

$$\text{Number of readings} = \frac{K^2 \times P \times (100 - P)}{L^2}$$

$$\text{Percentage error } (L) \text{ of activity estimate} = \pm \left[K \times \sqrt{\frac{(P \times (100 - P))}{N}} \right]$$

where $K = 2$ for 95% confidence level

$K = 3$ for 99.9% confidence level

and $P =$ the percentage of time occupied by the activity you are mainly interested in.

(iv) Advantages of activity sampling

- It can be used when stop-watch observation is not allowed because of company or trade union policy.
- It can handle simultaneous activities, something which cannot be done when using time study.
- Interruptions do not disrupt, disturb or invalidate the study; such disturbances would, however, adversely affect any time studies being taken.
- It is often cheaper to activity sample than to time study: full-time attendance at the scene of the activity is not always required, and once the planning and calculations have been done, the more routine work of recording which activities are occurring can be done by less highly paid clerical labour.

(v) Disadvantages of activity sampling

- Activity sampling does not provide the detailed information of a time study.
- The rate of working is not always incorporated into the observations, although this can sometimes be done.
- Because of the preplanning required, activity sampling could be expensive on a very short study.
- Because of the statistical basis of Activity Sampling, its methodology and consequently the results can be more difficult to 'sell' than when using conventional time study.

Care has to be taken if the number of observations becomes a **large proportion of the observations possible**. In this case, allowance has to be made for sampling from a finite population to correct the bias which would otherwise result.

Activity

1 For the cube-making Activity in Chapter 9, clearly define the methods, equipment and size of cube. Take a time study to ascertain the work content in standard minutes. You can use a time study sheet similar to that shown in Figure 10.4.

2 For the paper-dart-making Activity in Chapter 9, establish the design, methods, and equipment, and determine the standard time for making a dart.

3 Take time studies for making different size cubes. Plot the resultant standard times; does there seem to be a trend which you can use to predict the standard time for another size of cube?

Plot each element's basic time for different sizes; is there a trend you can use for predicting basic times for that element of a different size cube?

4 Produce a standard time for typing a letter.

What do you have to specify to produce a useful standard time?

Can you produce some synthetic values?

5 Take an activity sample study of one of the offices in your college or at work. What must you do before beginning the study?

6 Walk along a level corridor and match your speed to 4 miles per hour. Do you feel this is a brisk speed? This is often used to illustrate 100 performance. Now walk at a speed at which you might go window shopping. How fast is this? Produce a basic time in seconds per step.

7 Using a standard pack of cards, deal them into four piles, each pile to be at the corner of a 30 cm side square marked on the table. Determine the standard time for this operation.

8 For the Fidelity Fan Co. in Chapter 9, calculate the quantity of castings produced at present. Suggest new arrangements which you think will improve the potential for increased production. For your present and proposed quantities, calculate the labour cost per unit. If your improvements cost money, assume some costs, and take these from your potential savings. How long will it take to recoup your expenditure? (*Hint*: note that the jobs must be done sequentially and that if there is a bottleneck it will limit the throughput of work. Try therefore to minimise bottlenecks. Remember that not all work produced is good.)

9 (a) Estimate the standard time to change a wheel on a car. Each person in the group should make their own estimate and initially keep it to themselves.

(b) Using Time Study calculate the standard time for changing the wheel. What are the factors which can affect the time for this task? How are you going to allow for them? **Can any of them be eliminated**? Don't forget to consider rest and personal allowances. What other allowances may be relevant?

10 Synthetic Times – Glazing Windows

The data below refer to glazing wooden framed windows using 4 mm glass, putty, glazing nails, putty knife, brush and hammer.

Operation description

The glazing is performed by a male operative standing in front of a bench with all necessary materials to hand.

Element description

1 Pick up a handful of putty and lay out a bed of putty in frame.

2 Pick up a sheet of glass of appropriate size and position in frame on putty.

3 Pick up hammer and nails. Drive in eight nails to secure glass. Put aside hammer.

Fig 10.4   Time study sheet
a   First page
b   Summary sheet

STUDY SHEET

ELEMENT DESCRIPTION	Assessment	Actual Mins	Basic Mins	ELEMENT DESCRIPTION	Assessment	Actual Mins	Basic Mins
Date	Dept		Section			Study No	
Operator	No	Product			Times	Hrs	Mins
Operation					Finish		
					Start		
Conditions					Elapsed		
Machine	Speed Characteristics				Observed		
					Diff %		
TOTALS				TOTALS			

STUDY SUMMARY SHEET

Operation _____ Operative _____ Study No _____

Product _____ Observer _____ Qty _____ Date _____

No	ELEMENT	Quantity	Act Mins	Ass	Basic Mins	Freq	Unit	B Mins / Unit

CONTINGENCIES	Actual Mins	Total Basic Mins. Produced	
		Other Non-Productive Time	Actual Mins
TOTAL			

Nett Studied Time _____ mins
Deduct Non prod Time _____
Actual Productive Time _____

Average Assessment = _____
Performance on Productive Work _____
= _____

TOTAL _____
% Contingency =
$\dfrac{\text{Total Cont}}{\text{Prod Time}} \times 100 =$
_____ × 100 = _____ %

4 Procure handful of putty and apply to frame over glass.
5 Pick up putty knife and brush. Finish off putty to correct shape fillet, with putty knife. Smooth down with brush. Put aside putty knife and brush.
6 Turn frame over. Clean off surplus putty from inner side. Pick up glazed window and place aside.

Data
In the table below are the basic times in 100ths of a minute for each element for a number of different sized sheets of glass.

Size of glass sheet cms	Ele 1	Ele 2	Ele 3	Ele 4	Ele 5	Ele 6
30 × 60	75	20	38	85	160	50
45 × 60	90	18	32	90	190	55
60 × 75	108	19	35	112	230	71
75 × 120	153	21	33	150	330	80
90 × 120	165	22	38	155	355	89
30 × 165	150	19	36	148	340	79
105 × 165	195	21	34	201	466	115
120 × 165	215	20	35	205	486	115

Required
(a) Determine the basic times for the constant elements.
(b) For the non constant elements, plot graphs to establish the relation between basic times and the variable.
(c) From your results, determine the standard times for two sizes of glass:
   (i) 38 cm × 113 cm
   (ii) 68 cm × 158 cm
Use the following allowances:
   Personal   2.5%   Total rest (factors A and B)   12.5%
   Contingency 4%

11 Time Study – Riveting Wheels and Spindles
Ivor is Acme Tool's Time Study Officer. Acme is a company which makes and assembles a wide range of small components for other companies in the light/precision engineering sector of the manufacturing industry.
   Ivor has just returned to his desk from the assembly department, where he has time studied a riveting assembly operation, performed by Fay, who is experienced in this kind of work. Fay works sitting down.
   The riveting assembly operation involves placing a small, toothed wheel on a spindle, putting them in a holder on a small press and then operating the press to rivet the two items together. The assembly is then placed aside and the process repeated for all items in the batch.
   The details of Ivor's study consisting of 11 repetitive cycles are:

Element 1   Take out riveted assembly from the press holder. Place it in tray on the bench. Pick up a spindle and place it one way up in the press holder. Pick up a toothed wheel and place it one way up over the spindle in the holder.

Seconds	5	5	6	5	10	5	6	5	7	6	8
Ratings	100	100	90	90	80	100	100	100	80	95	90

Element 2   Lower safety guard and hold with both hands. Operate press with foot pedal to rivet wheel to spindle. Release safety guard.

Seconds	3	2	3	2	2	3	3	2	5	3	6
Rating	100	100	100	100	100	100	100	120	80	100	70

Element 3   Load separately 2 small trays on bench with wheels and spindles prior to assembly, from 2 larger containders on floor containing large number of wheels in one container and spindles in the other. Each small tray holds 25 wheels or 25 spindles.

Seconds   15   Rating   90

Element 4   Clear the riveting tool and/or holder, using a small brush every so often, so as to remove any loose bits of metal. Wipe the tool clean with oily rag. Frequency of occurrence is about every 50 cycles.

Seconds   10   Rating   110

Element 5   Obtain a fresh supply of spindles and wheels in the large containers, also returning completed work of riveted assemblies in small trays. Get more small empty trays as required. 250 sets is a representative quantity.

Minutes   5.0   Rating   75

Required
1 Calculate the basic time for each element.
2 Calculate the total basic time for the whole task.
3 Assume 12.5% personal and rest allowances. Calculate the standard time for the whole task.
4 How many assemblies would be produced per hour at standard performance? How many would be produced per hour by a learner at a 70 performance?
5 Were the number of repetitions sufficient? Why or why not?
6 What might be considered as contingencies in a task like this?
7 There are 2 people in this work centre who work a nominal 40-hour week. Their typical performance is 85%. Could they complete a 23,000 unit batch in 2 weeks? Why or why not?

Case Study: Kleen-a-Glow Co. – Workload at Present

The busy Sales office of Kleen-a-Glow, a contract cleaning and general maintenance company, has five typists each working 34 hours per week of 5 days per week on typing and related activities. (For the remaining 6 hours they are engaged on work unrelated to typing and this work is outside the scope of this evaluation.) Their workload has been assessed by a pilot study, and some minor methods improvements have been implemented.

Their main jobs are audio typing letters, duplicating circulars, etc.

An activity sampling exercise has already been carried out. During a representative two-week period, it was found that three of the typists were occupied on:

	% of their time
audio typing	60
other productive work	30
rest/relaxation	10

These three typists were in full-time attendance during this representative period, but they did not work any overtime. They produced 1200 letters.

Activity

Choose an appropriate production unit for their work and calculate a standard time for it. You can assume that their performance was 70 on the BS rating scale of 0 to 100. The person who did the activity sample also rated their performance.

Case Study: Kleen-a-Glow – Output of a Subsequent Week

During a subsequent working week, their supervisor reports their output as follows:

- 1400 letters were audio typed
- 500 copies of a circular were duplicated from an existing original
- 300 copies of a 'special offer' were duplicated from an existing original
- One typist did filing for 8 hours
- There was no unoccupied time
- One typist was away for 3 hours on the Thursday; she had permission to see a doctor.

The standard time for circulars has been calculated as:

Set up and clean down	10.0 standard minutes per occasion
Duplicate	5.0 standard minutes per 100 leaflets

Activity

1 Calculate the performance of the typing group for the week above.
2 How can such figures be used to provide management information for control purposes?

Chapter Review Questions

1 What is 'standard time'?
2 'If a job has a standard time of 15 minutes, any operator should be able to produce 32 units in 8 hours without stopping': True or False?
3 What is 'basic time' and how is it derived from a time study?
4 Briefly describe what is meant by 'standard performance'.
5 What is a 'contingency' and how is it included in a standard?
6 What is the difference between synthetics and predetermined motion time standards?
7 Who is best suited to estimate a standard?
8 In an activity sampling study, if you want to halve the error how many more readings are necessary?
9 'Time studies require a skilled observer, whereas activity sampling observations may not': True or False?
10 List three uses for standard times, and how management would use them.

11 Managing Performance: 3 – Incentive Schemes

In Chapters 9 and 10 we saw how to establish **(a)** correct methods for a job, and **(b)** how long that job should take. In Chapter 11 we look at ways to raise working performance above its current level, and how to pay people more. Some of these methods are at departmental level and direct labour orientated; other incentive schemes are more suitable for indirect labour or company-wide schemes, and as such they will necessarily be based on different parameters.

Learning Objectives

By the end of this chapter you should:

1 know what **piecework** is, and how different schemes work
2 know the benefits expected from **work-study-based incentive schemes**
3 know how two such incentive schemes **operate**
4 be able to use the results from an incentive scheme to chart and monitor **performance levels**
5 know the principle upon which **time-saved incentive schemes** operate.

11.1 What are 'Incentives'?

A **bonus** is a payment made over and above a person's basic wage, and is closely related to their performance. It is primarily, but not always, based on work measurement techniques. Such bonuses (incentives) are for those who work directly on a product or service, and whose performance can therefore influence directly the amount of work done. We are not referring, for example, to incentives for salespeople who may get a weekend in Majorca for exceeding their preset target. We will also describe schemes which pay directly on a payment per piece basis, as well as those where bonus payment is made for time saved.

11.2 **Motivation**

It should be clearly understood that when talking about incentives, we are referring to **monetary** incentives, and that we are aware that not everyone is motivated by money: there are many forms of motivation. A person may be motivated by interest and pride in the job they do. They may be motivated because they regard the work they do as their hobby. If a person needs to meet a deadline, that may be a motivational factor. Other people respond to threats, such as the fear of the sack, or of being transferred to a less desirable working location. Many more are motivated by praise and encouragement and being highly thought of by their peers. It is also true that people may well be motivated by different factors at different times: someone who is newly hired may be highly motivated by praise from the boss, rather than being well thought of by the peer group of whom at this time the new employee may know relatively little.

11.3 **Indirect Operators**

Indirect operators are those people whose work is not directly linked to the final product or service, but who may affect the performance of those whose work is so linked. Incentives for such people may be based on the results of direct incentive schemes. In the Fidelity Fan Co., the labourers who service the direct operators are indirect workers. It might be reasonable if they were paid on an incentive scheme which was itself related to the performance of the direct workers whom they served. Such a scheme should not produce bonuses which are too variable, as indirect operators cannot directly influence the final result. Incentives for employees other than direct workers, or for employees where the term 'direct' is not applicable, may be based on a more global measure of productivity (e.g. on value added). Such employees in the company could be paid on a scheme in which a proportion of value added per quarter was shared among staff.

11.4 **Piecework**

This is a traditional form of payment. It has long been associated with workers in the garment and shoe industries, some agricultural workers, and homeworkers. A person on piecework earns an amount based on the number of pieces completed or produced. If no pieces are produced, no money at all is paid, and the more that is produced, the more a person is paid. The amount paid per piece is not based on ability or work content, but upon what the payer thinks he or she can get away with. It will also reflect what the market can stand in terms of similar work available and the availability of suitable labour. It is often presented on a 'take it or leave it' basis.

The real incentive of piecework is that you have to produce to be paid. So in the example of a person working at home, the rate for stuffing envelopes with advertising literature for subsequent distribution may be 1 penny per envelope. The reward is not related to additional effort in any way, and piecework is often poorly paid. It is sometimes considered to be sweated labour.

(a) Strict piecework scheme

Figure 11.1 shows the pay curve for a **strict piecework scheme**, which pays £0.1 per unit produced. No payment is paid for zero output.

(b) Guaranteed minimum pay

It is possible to have a piecework scheme which includes a **guaranteed minimum pay**. While this is more attractive from the worker's view, it has the disadvantage of producing units with a variable unit cost. Figure 11.2 shows pay of a minimum of £20 per week and £.05 per unit. If only one unit were to be produced, the unit cost would be £20.05. If 10 units were to be produced, the unit cost would be £2.05 each; for 100 units the unit cost would be £0.25; for 1000 units, the unit cost would be £0.07.

(c) Differential piecework

There are **differential piecework** schemes where different rates are paid for different levels of output. These schemes lose the inherent simplicity of a

---

Fig 11.1   A piecework scheme

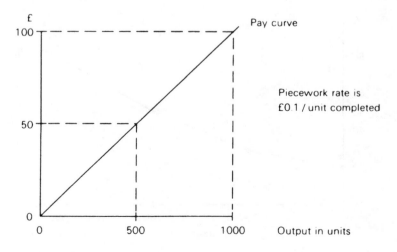

£

100 ┈ ┈ ┈ ┈ ┈ ┈ ┈ ┈ ┈   Pay curve

Piecework rate is
£0.1 / unit completed

50 ┈ ┈ ┈ ┈ ┈

0

0   500   1000   Output in units

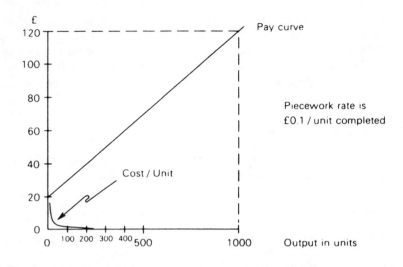

Fig 11.2   Piecework + guaranteed minimum of £20

straight piecework scheme, and are complex to administer and understand. They also give rise to variable unit costs. Figure 11.3 shows the total pay received for different levels of output. The scheme pays £20 per week and £0.1/unit up to 99 units, £0.15/unit up to 199 units and £0.20/ unit thereafter.

Fig 11.3   Differential piecework

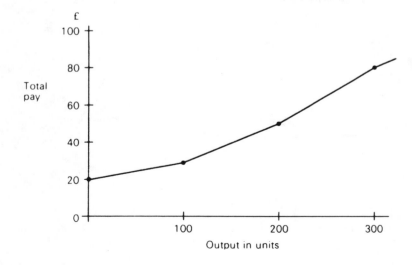

Activity

For each of the schemes described above calculate the unit costs for the following levels of output: 10, 50. 90, 150 and 500 units produced.

11.5 **Individual vs Group Schemes**

Incentive schemes in general fall into two categories. These are schemes based on the effort of **individuals**, and schemes based on the effort of **groups**. If possible, individual incentive schemes are preferable, because they tend to provide the greatest degree of incentive for a given level of reward: this is primarily because most people like to control their own wage level. As incentive schemes reward extra effort with extra pay, an individual incentive will motivate them the most.

However, there are many situations where people work in groups. In the example of the Fidelity Fan Co. in Chapter 9, the operators who process the fan castings could most appropriately be considered as a group, particularly as they all handle the same product; it would be invidious to have them paid on individual incentive schemes. One of the effects of a group incentive in this case would be to help make a group work together as a team. The reward would be based on the **overall performance** of the group, and each person would be rewarded at the same rate (i.e. at the group performance level) and would be paid for the time that they were working on measured work in the group.

11.6 **Characteristics of a Good Incentive Scheme**

What should a good incentive scheme do, both for employees and employer?

(i) **Unit cost savings**
It should make worthwhile savings in terms of unit costs, so that the company has a more competitive edge. Wages may be greater than they were before, but when related to output the **cost per unit** should be lower. There should therefore be tangible savings to the company after the cost of administering the scheme is taken into account. Even though labour costs do not always make up a large proportion of the total cost, it is important to ensure that value for money is produced. Even when companies have achieved a high level of non-direct labour processing, through investment in automation and CAD/CAM, labour costs remain the chief area where improvements can be made, albeit at the margin.

(ii) Economy of operation
The scheme must he **economic to operate** (i.e. its costs of operation must not substantially erode the gross benefits resulting from the operation of the scheme itself). A complicated scheme, or one which is too complicated for the situation to which it is being applied, is likely to be expensive to operate.

(iii) Easily understood
The scheme must be easy to understand by those whose pay will affected by it. If it is difficult for an employee to calculate his wages including bonus, such a scheme is unlikely to win approval. By its nature, an incentive scheme results in a variable total wage packet; because of this, it is desirable for each employee to know how much the wage packet is likely to be even before it is received, and to have a good idea of why it is **different from the last time**. In a good scheme, people become very proficient at working out their wages prior to receiving them!

(iv) Inbuilt safely standards
Any scheme must not jeopardise the health or safety of an employee by virtue of an attempt to achieve the standard times in the scheme. This clearly means that all standards must include appropriate time to use **safety equipment**, or to put on and take off **safety clothing**, together with time for suitable **cleansing.**

(v) Equitable to all
Any incentive scheme must be equitable to all: no groups of workers should be **excluded** by virtue of age or experience. This places a burden on employers to devise suitable schemes with equitable allowances to cover such possibilities.

(vi) Effectiveness improvement
Incentive schemes should encourage improvement in the rate of working and effectiveness of employees. This does not mean that they should have to run rather than walk, but because of methods improvements and realistic achievable standards, there will be **less wasted time** during the working day. This is often the primary factor in improving labour productivity.

(vii) Adherence to standards
Because the methods have been clearly established, such standards should encourage **adherence** to them when employees are working on incentive schemes.

(viii) Common goal

Finally, when a group incentive scheme is in operation, it should have the effect of improving **team work** and **group morale**, by providing a common goal. It is not unusual for individuals who are working as members of a group scheme, and who are not pulling their weight, to be expelled from the group by the group itself.

11.7 Incentives for Weekly Wage Systems

Three key principles must be observed here:

1 **The work must be measurable** and **directly attributable** to a group or an individual. If this is not the case, then any such incentive would be inequitable.
2 The **pace** of the work must be primarily controlled by the **workers involved**. This means that if there is a large proportion of machine controlled work, while allowances can often be made for it the incentives are unlikely to be related to the performance of those workers. The incentive power of the scheme is therefore likely to be somewhat diminished, or payments that are finally agreed will not be very closely related to performance.
3 It is management's responsibility to ensure that there is a reasonably steady **flow of work** available, and that there are minimal unplanned **changes to work methods.**

11.8 Sequence of Incentive Development

Incentives must be developed in eight clear steps:

1 In consultation with management and union representatives, decide in which **department** or **section** to start. Such decisions will be influenced by the need to achieve results as soon as possible, and to ensure that the first application is a success in terms of benefits to both the employer and the employee.
2 Identify the **objectives** for the exercise. These may include improving the rate of working, raising pay, reducing bottlenecks by improving work flow, and achieving a more uniform level of quality by virtue of carefully defined working methods and realistic standards.
3 Select appropriate **units of output** which are representative of the majority of work in the department. Where individual work is involved this is often straightforward; where group work occurs this can be more difficult. In the case of a wine and spirits distributor, the unit finally chosen was 'a crate equivalent', where this was in reality 12 bottles, 24 half bottles, 48 quarter bottles, or any combination thereof.

4 Determine the amount of **payment** for the appropriate period, together with any limits on high and low earnings. These must be based on how much the company believes it can afford for a given improvement in output. Very often, the company will accept greater output and pay operatives appropriately for the increase in performance achieved. The operator must be **responsible** for the quality of his or her own work, and it must be clearly stated that payment is for **good work** only, and rectification due to the operator's fault must be done at the operator's own expense.

5 Prepare **sample documents** to support the proposals and consult the unions and workforce on a regular basis. It is vital to ensure that management explains clearly what it expects to achieve by successful implementation of the proposed scheme, and also what **benefits** employees can expect from different levels of performance.

6 Select the appropriate method of **work measurement** and measure all (or a very high proportion of) the regularly occurring work through the department.

7 Prepare a reference period **set of results** using a representative period agreed by management and unions so that all can see what is currently being paid, and what would be paid if the proposed scheme were to be implemented. These results can then be examined by both employees and unions, and discussed until final agreement is reached. A reference period may be from one to four weeks in the recent past.

8 Once final agreement is reached, **implement** the scheme, and **monitor** results for as long as it takes for all to see that the proposed improvements in pay and performance have actually been achieved and are being maintained at (or close to) those levels.

11.9 **Work-Study-Based Incentive Schemes**

(a) **Straight proportional**

In this scheme, the **pay curve** (i.e. how much will be paid for a particular level of performance) is horizontal for performances from 0 to 75 performance (on the 0 to 100 BSI rating scale) at the basic rate per hour pay level. It then moves upwards through the intersection of 100 performance and basic rate plus one-third. Finally at some agreed but reasonably arbitrary level of performance, the pay curve continues horizontally at that level (i.e. parallel to the x axis).

Total payment will therefore consist of (basic hourly rate × hours worked) + incentive payment. This incentive payment is calculated by multiplying the extra amount per hour due to performing at a standard above the nominal (generally 75% performance) by the hours spent on measured work.

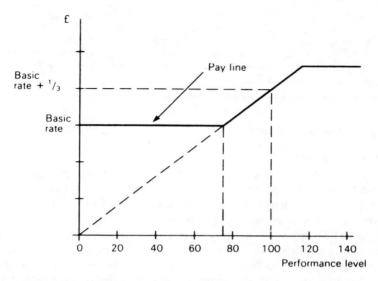

Fig 11.4   A straight proportional incentive scheme

Example 1

Suppose the person in the fettling shop of Fidelity Fan Co. who does the sand blasting produces the following data for the end of the week being considered:

hours at work = 38
hours absent = 2
hours on measured work = 32
hours on unmeasured work = 6
quantity produced = 500
good pieces (pcs) standard time = 3.0
standard minutes (sms) each hourly rate = £2.50 per hour.

Analysis

No pay is given for the 2 hours' absence. Basic pay is £2.50 × 38 hours = £95.00. As we are considering a proportional scheme, which starts bonus payments above a 75 performance, and which pays one-third of basic rate for a performance of 100, we can calculate that each performance point above 75 on the pay curve is worth (£2.5/3)/(100 − 75) = 83.3 pence/25 = 3.33 pence per point.

The performance achieved is ((500 pcs × 3.0 sms)/60) = 25 standard hours × 100/32 hours taken = 78%. Therefore the incentive payment is (78 − 75) = 3 points × 3.33 pence × 32 hours on measured work = £3.20.

The total wage for the week is £95 + £3.20 = £98.20. The bonus payment is not very large, primarily due to the modest performance just above the bonus starting level. It is therefore management's responsibility to investigate possible causes for this and take corrective action. They will not necessarily all be the responsibility of the operator. Notice that 6 hours was unavailable for bonus earnings because that work was not measured. A number of reasons may exist (e.g. management too busy to measure all of the current work, or the operator moved to new work which was not measured). If this situation persists, management may be forced to pay unmeasured work at a performance level of 80%, This is undesirable because management is not getting value for money: proper standards must be set as soon as possible.

(b) A geared incentive scheme

(i) What is 'gearing'?

'Gearing' is the term used when the pay curve is not strictly proportional to performance (i.e. when more or less than one-third bonus is paid for a one-third increase in performance). In such cases the projection of the sloping pay curve does not pass through the origin of the pay/performance graph (see Figure 11.5). However, we may wish to have an incentive scheme which begins to pay a bonus above a 60 performance rather than the more usual 75 performance: this may be because we wish to encourage low performers to become better. The sloping pay curve will still pass through the intersection of 100 performance and basic hourly rate plus one-third. Such a scheme will mean that the slope is less than if it were proportional, and this scheme will pay less bonus for performances above 100. It will still level off at some predetermined point, remaining horizontal thereafter.

As the pay curve is not now proportional, the appropriate hourly rate including bonus must either be read directly off an appropriate pay graph, or calculated as below.

Fig 11.5   A geared incentive scheme

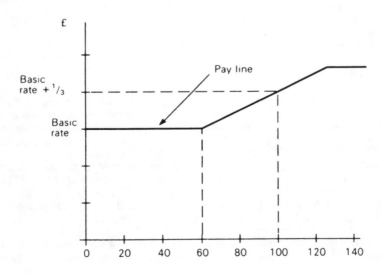

Example 2

Assume that a geared scheme begins to pay bonus for performances above 70. The basic hourly rate is £3.50. The maximum performance payable is 125. Basic time plus one-third is paid for a performance of 100.

(a) What is the gearing factor of this scheme?
(b) If a performance of 80 is obtained, what is the hourly rate including bonus?
(c) If a performance of 100 is obtained, what is the hourly inclusive rate?
(d) What is the hourly inclusive rate for a performance of 110?

Method

(a) The gearing factor of an incentive scheme is the slope of the pay/performance line. The slope is calculated by dividing the increase in pay by the equivalent increase in performance. In a proportional scheme, pay increases by 1.33 for a performance increase of 1.33 (i.e. from 75 to 100). The gearing factor is therefore $1.33/(100/75) = 1.00$ (i.e. a slope of 45 degrees which means that the projection of the pay curve would pass through the origin).

For our geared scheme, the gearing factor will be $1.33/(100/70) = 0.93$. This is a slightly flatter slope than for the proportional scheme, as we might expect.

(b) We can calculate the money per performance point gradient as: $(£3.50/3)/(100 - 70) = £0.0389$ per point. Therefore for a performance of 80, we expect an hourly rate of $£3.50 + [(80 - 70) \times £0.0389] = £3.89$ per hour.

(c) For a 100 performance, the inclusive hourly rate is $£3.50 + [(100 - 70) \times £0.0389] = £4.66$. Note that for this performance, this is the same as would be paid under a proportional scheme.

(d) For a performance of 110, the inclusive hourly rate is $£3.50 + [(110-70) \times £0.0389] = £5.06$.

Activity

What are the differences **(a)** in bonus payments alone and **(b)** in inclusive hourly rate for the performances quoted above, for a scheme which starts paying bonus at 70, one which starts paying bonus at 75, and one which starts paying bonus at 80?
Calculate the gearing factor for each scheme.
Draw each scheme on the same graph and verify your calculations.

(ii) Calculating the bonus for a geared scheme

The formulae for calculating the bonus for a geared scheme is the general method for calculating the bonus payable for any scheme of this type, regardless of the level at which payments start. The pay curve must, however, pass through the points where the **hourly rate + incentive rate intersects with a 100 performance**. The formulae apply only to the sloping portion of the pay curve: until performance reaches the performance level at which bonus payments start, only the basic hourly rate is payable. When the performance reaches the level where no further increase is payable, the formulae need be applied only once at that point, as this will apply to all higher performance levels.

The cut-off point at the high performance end is a matter for negotiation, but may be typically about a 125 performance, the rationale for this being that if standard performance is 100, and generally a standard deviation of 10 points is reasonable, then fewer than 2.5% of all operators will ever legitimately reach performances above 125. If such performances are recorded, they stand a good chance of being the result of errors, incorrect booking, incorrectly set standard times, non-adherence to specified methods (particularly safety) or because of attempts to 'beat the system'.

Activity

To see clearly how both schemes work at another performance level, calculate the bonus for each scheme if 35 standard hours were to be achieved in the same time period as before (i.e. 32 actual hours). Under a strictly proportional scheme, the bonus earned is £36.27. Under the geared scheme which starts paying at a 50 performance level, the bonus earned is £31.47, which (as expected) is lower than that paid under the proportional scheme because the performance in this example is above the 100 performance point. What is the bonus payable if a geared scheme starts paying bonus at a 60 performance? (See Example 1, p. 247.)

As well as being able to calculate bonuses as described above, the all-purpose formula shown below can be used to calculate the hourly rate factor including bonus for any scheme described, whether less than proportional, strictly proportional or greater than proportional.

Note that the monetary hourly rate including bonus must lie between the basic monetary hourly rate and the maximum monetary hourly rate allowed by the scheme.

Hourly Rate £ inc. Bonus = Basic Hourly Rate £

× Hourly Rate Factor (HRF)

HRF = [1 + ((achieved performance − scheme start performance)/E)]

where **E** can be found from the following table:

Scheme start performance	50	55	60	65	70	75	80	85	90	95
E	150	135	120	105	90	75	60	45	30	15

Suppose that an incentive scheme is proportional. It starts at 75 performance, and you would therefore expect to achieve 33.33% bonus for a 100 performance. E equals 75 and achieved performance equals 100. The hourly rate factor (hrf) $= [1 + ((100 - 75)/75)] = 1.33$ as expected. For an 85 performance, the hrf $= [1 + ((85 - 75)/75)] = 1.13$.

Using Example 2 above of a geared scheme, we have the following data. Scheme starts at 70 performance so E = 90. Basic monetary hourly rate = £3.50. What will the hourly monetary rate be for **(a)** achieving an 80 performance and **(b)** achieving a 110 performance?

(a) Hourly monetary rate including bonus = £3.50 × [1 + ((80 − 70)/90)] = £3.50 × 1.111 = £3.89 as before.

(b) Hourly monetary rate including bonus = £3.50 × [1 + ((110 − 70)/90)] = £3.50 × 1.444 = £5.06 as before.

Activity

Draw a graph of the formula above so that it can be used without any further calculations for say three different schemes. Let the Y axis be the proportion of the hourly rate from 1.0 to say 2.0 suitably divided. Let the X axis be the BS Scale of performance from 50 to 140 suitably divided. The three schemes start at 50, 75 and 90 performance respectively, with an earnings ceiling on the proportion of basic hourly rate of 1.55, 1.75 and 1.85 respectively.

Activity

Domelap Ltd

Domelap is a company which makes and assembles a variety of small electric appliances, often as a subcontractor for larger companies. Very little of its work goes out under its own label. The company works a 40-hour week. Last week, three people assembled and packed two versions of a domestic toaster.and their output was as follows:

Alf and Betty usually operate as a team of two, working sequentially on toaster assembly; Alf assembles the first part of the toaster and Betty finishes the assembly. Charlie works by himself and only handles the 'wrap, pack and label' part of the job for all models. He also gets the wrapping and packing material etc. (see below). Their basic hourly rate is £2.76. Alf worked 25 hours on toasters, Betty worked 30 hours on toasters and Charlie worked 30 hours on packaging preparation, etc.

Alf worked 11 hours on unmeasured work and 4 hours on approved union matters. Betty spent 10 hours on unmeasured work; Charlie spent 8 hours on measured packing work, came in 2 hours late on Tuesday – 'car wouldn't start' – and the remaining time on unmeasured work.

There are two types of toasters, a 2-slice and a 4-slice version.

	Standard minutes	
Model	Assembly	Wrap, pack and label
2 slice	20.00 sms each	3.00 sms each
4 slice	24.00 sms each	4.00 sms each

They assembled 90 '2 slice' and 50 '4 slice' versions of a toaster which is sold on to a well-known department chain store. All hourly paid people work on an incentive scheme. Their scheme starts at a 70 performance and is limited to a 125 performance maximum.

Required Part 1

(a) What is the team performance by Alf and Betty on their measured work?, and of Charlie on his measured wrap, pack, and label work?
(b) What are the overall performances?
(c) What did they each earn as bonus?
(d) What is their overall wage?
(e) What is their bonus as a percentage of their total wage?
(f) How many more 4-slice toasters does the Alf/Betty team need to assemble and pack to achieve a 105 performance on measured work in the same time?
(g) What would they then earn as bonus?
(h) What would their bonus earnings be under 65 and 75 performance start schemes – for **(c)** above; for **(f)** above?

Part 2

Charlie does the wrapping, packing and labelling work which is measured. He also gets the cartons, inners and wrapping material from stores, makes the cartons up to the 'lids open' stage, and positions supplies near his bench. He also moves the wrapped/packed toasters to the shipping department as necessary. Last week he spent 30 hours on such work for 250 carton sets preparation, all of which is unmeasured.

Standard minutes	Assemble 1st stage	Assemble 2nd stage	Wrap, pack and label	Total standard minutes
	Alf	Betty	Charlie	
2 slice model	7.0	10.0	3.0	20.0
4 slice model	12.0	9.0	4.0	25.0

(1) Why are the total standard times for the 2 and 4 slice models above, different from the total standard times relating to their performance for the week?
(2) What are the implications of this:
    (a) for the operators
    (b) for management?
(3) How might absenteeism affect the assembly team?
(4) What effect might the current set-up have on Charlie's work?
(5) What is the current assembly line efficiency? How might you improve it?
(6) What would be involved in such an improvement?

(iii) **Where work is variable**

Another use for the geared scheme is where the work content is variable, thus leading to a **variable performance result** by the operators, but where this variability is not due to the operators themselves. An example of this situation is where a repair shop operates an incentive scheme, and it is difficult to measure the work content accurately. This may be because of the difficulty of ascertaining the work to be done in advance of the repair, or because the low quantities of any one job do not allow the operators to achieve a performance near their natural one. Some repairs may seem to be straightforward, and the standard time will reflect this. When the job comes to be done, more work is legitimately required and has to be done. This, however, results in a low performance because the output is less than the appropriate input, as measured by the standard time.

The performance at which bonus payment starts is a matter for negotiation between unions and management. Management will not want to encourage bonus payments at too low a level; unions will want to try to ensure that as many operators as possible can earn some bonus. As there must be some benefit to both parties, it follows that a balance must be struck in the different payoffs to each party.

11.10 Management Control of Incentive Schemes

(a) Unanticipated variances

It is important that management gets the most information out of the schemes it operates, and this is best done when variances can be analysed prior to action. Because all work-study-based standards are based on specified methods equipment and material, it is important to know when **deviations** occur. This is conveniently done by having a series of **codes**, and using them to identify when the specified deviation has occurred. An operator will therefore record the start and finish time for these specified occurrences and when working under these situations, may warrant extra payment, particularly if this affects their ability to earn bonus.

When an operator is unable to work on jobs to which a standard time has been applied, they normally receive only the basic hourly rate. It is a matter for negotiation whether or not any payment over and above the norm is made. However, unmeasured work puts the pressure quite rightly on to management to ensure all new jobs are measured as soon as possible.

There are several common situations which require the operator to signify that he or she is working with non-standard methods or material, or indeed is actually waiting for work. The most important point is that management must know what causes unanticipated variances, and then do something about them.

(b) Using booking codes

A booking code is essential for the following situations:

- Working on non-standard materials
- Using non-standard jigs, fixtures or other tooling
- Where an extra operation has been specified
- Where a modification or other conversion is necessary
- Working on a prototype not similar to the normal product
- Where the operator is a learner and not yet fully productive
- Working on smaller quantities than usual
- Doing repair work rather than regular production work
- Where the parts being worked on are faulty.

(c) **Using waiting time codes**

If an operator is actually waiting and not productively employed, then specific codes must be available. Situations such as the following may occur:

- Idle due to emergency breakdown
- Waiting while maintenance is carried out
- No tools are available
- No material is available
- No work is available
- Awaiting an Inspector for initial set-up, although wherever possible the operator must be responsible and qualified for this purpose
- No supervisor to give instructions.

11.11 **Analysis of Results of Incentive Schemes**

As well as wishing to pay employees more if their output increases, the analysis of data resulting from the scheme provides management with additional information which can assist them in monitoring performance of individuals and work centres.

Example 3

Suppose that all the measured work achieved by an operator during 30 hours spent on measured work was 26 standard hours. This figure was obtained by adding the standard times of all measured work done. The remaining time of 10 hours was spent on productive work, which, however, was not measured.

The operator's performance on measured work is therefore $26 \times 100/30 = 87\%$. The overall performance which includes the time spent on unmeasured work is $26 \times 100/40 = 65\%$. These are two most important results, and should be plotted on a regular basis for analysis and subsequent action.

How can these results be interpreted? We expect the operator's performance on measured work to be somewhere about the 100% mark for a person who is qualified, motivated and applying themselves to the job in hand. If it consistently falls well short of this level, then it is management's responsibility to **investigate** possible causes and take **remedial** action. Notice that the figure of 65% is much lower than that of 87%. This is because time was spent on work for which no standards had been set. This means that management is getting less productivity during those 10 hours, and the operator has been limited in the amount that can be earned through no fault of his own. The difference between these two figures represents **inefficiencies** that must be rectified. In practice, there will be other reasons why an operator was not working on measured work, perhaps through waiting for work, etc. as indicated above.

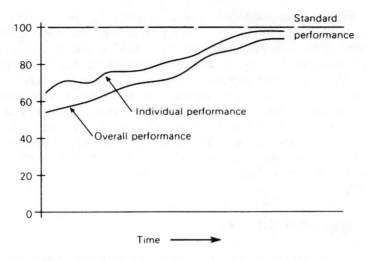

Fig 11.6 Performance monitoring

Activity

Figure 11.6 shows a graph of both these indices, when plotted on a regular basis (say, once per week). What interpretation can you place on the graph?

Also note that these graphs can be plotted for groups or teams of operators, and similar interpretations can be made.

11.12 Incentive Schemes for Supervisors

If it is thought desirable to include supervisory personnel in an incentive scheme, this can sometimes be done by basing their bonus payments on the **overall performance of the group** for which they are **responsible**. The logic for this is that by making their bonus dependent on the overall performance index, they will be motivated to close the gap between overall performance and performance on measured work, thus improving the productivity of the group. If they can also help ensure that the performance on measured work stays close to (or even exceeds) 100%, they will have raised the ceiling for their own bonus.

11.13 Measured Daywork

When a company has been operating a work-study-based incentive scheme successfully, they may find that the level of performance of their direct employees has considerably improved. They may then begin to feel that the cost of operating the scheme begins to form a significant proportion of the benefits gained, as the potential for improvement is somewhat reduced. Because of this, some firms have begun to operate what is called measured daywork: instead of measuring every job in detail, amounts of work are agreed that form **broad categories of performance**, and provided that output falls into those bands, pay will be at a fixed enhanced level and continue like that. The advantage is that the company does not have a scheme of great complexity to run, and the employees are not subject to such close control, nor do their wages fluctuate as much as under a conventional scheme.

11.14 Time-Saved Schemes

Two traditional incentive schemes were developed earlier this century, based on the time-saved principle. These, while being of historic interest, are also useful for showing how a scheme can be implemented when there is a real possibility of fluctuating work content and low quantities which make accurate standard setting more difficult – or at least less economic.

These schemes are known after their developers; the first is the **Halsey** scheme, and the second is the **Rowan** scheme. They are initially somewhat hard to understand: in each case the total wage is made up of basic wage plus bonus, but we will consider for each scheme only the appropriate calculations for the bonus. It is in the calculation of the bonus that the two schemes differ from each other:

Halsey: Bonus = half time saved × hourly rate
Rowan: Bonus = ((time taken/time allowed) × time saved) × hourly rate

Note that each scheme pays the same bonus when time taken = half the time allowed.

(a) Advantages

Halsey: 1 Insures against high earnings.
2 Safeguards against the effect of incorrect, poorly set or fluctuating work standards.

Rowan: 1 Labour cost cannot exceed a maximum value.
2 May be set to give strong incentive at lower levels of productivity. This may be important where work content fluctuates through no fault of the operator.
3 Can be used where tasks cannot easily be standardised.

(b) Disadvantages

Halsey: 1 Work-study-based standards not used.
2 Scheme does not provide a strong incentive.
3 Not too easy for operators to understand.
4 The sharing of the benefits with management may not be very popular.

Rowan: Similar to the above, although the formula is a little more complex.

Example 4

Assume that a maintenance job in Fidelity Fan Co.'s fettling shop was estimated to take 20 hours, and was scheduled to take place over a weekend, starting 6 pm on Friday. What is the difference between the two schemes when the job takes a variety of actual times ranging from 2 hours up to as much as 20 hours? Remember that had we been considering accurately set standards, there would have been no question of beating a standard by such a large amount: you will recall that work-study-based standards are there to be **met**, not beaten. However, both these schemes are designed to accommodate this kind of uncertainty.

Time allowed is 20 hours.

Fig 11.7 Halsey and Rowan bonus schemes

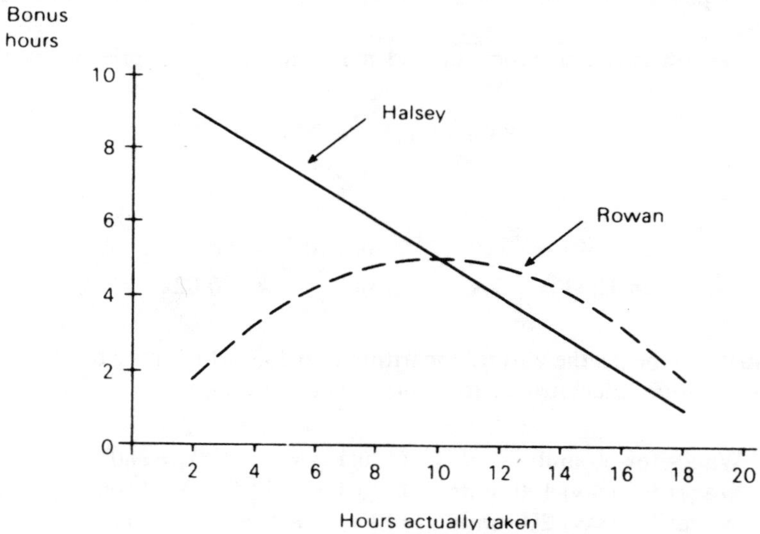

	Halsey		Rowan	
				Time taken ×
		Half time	Time taken/	time saved/
Time taken	Time saved	saved	Time allowed	Time allowed
2	18	9	0.1	1.8
4	16	8	0.2	3.2
6	14	7	0.3	4.2
8	12	6	0.4	4.8
10	10	5	0.5	5.0
12	8	4	0.6	4.8
14	6	3	0.7	4.2
16	4	2	0.8	3.2
18	2	1	0.9	1.8
20	0	0	1.0	0.0

Neither scheme pays a bonus if no time is saved. The graph in Figure 11.7 shows the amount of bonus paid by each scheme for the range of actual times taken.

11.15 Exponential Incentive Schemes

Where the work content is highly variable and it is hardly practical to measure the work content for standard setting purposes, an **exponential pay curve** provides an unusual scheme where gross pay will not become unrealistically high.

Suppose the basic wage for the week is £80 for an expected production level of 50 units. Management decides that the maximum wage they are willing to pay is £120 (i.e. 50% bonus) no matter how many units are produced.

The relation between basic pay and maximum pay is expressed by the formula:

$$£80 = £120(1 - e^{-50k})$$

To find k:

$$-40 = -120e^{-50k} \quad \text{so} \quad 0.333 = e^{-50k}$$
$$\ln 0.333 = -50k \quad \text{so} \quad k = 0.022$$

where $\ln 0.333$ means the natural logarithm of 0.333, which may be obtained using a scientific calculator or from mathematical tables.

Wages for 50 units: $£120(1 - e^{-0.022 \times 50}) = £80$
Wages for (say) 100 units: $£120(1 - e^{-0.022 \times 100}) = £106.7$
Wages for (say) 200 units: $£120(1 - e^{-0.022 \times 200}) = £118.5$

Under no circumstances of runaway production, will wages exceed the predetermined level.

11.16 Value-Added Schemes

Schemes based on value added are suitable as longer-term incentive schemes, and are particularly useful for those employees whose work is less easily related closely to output. Schemes based on value-added may be paid (say) once or twice per year.

'Value-added' is the difference between revenue and the cost of goods and services bought in. If that difference does not even cover the wages and salaries, then there is no surplus to be distributed. A highly value-added company may therefore develop a scheme which pays a proportion of the value-added to its employees, provided that the ratio of value-added to the wage bill exceeds a given ratio of (say) 1.5.

Figure 11.8 shows how such a scheme works in principle. The basic wage bill for the company for (say) six months is £100,000. The scheme is such that there is no possibility of bonus until the added value ratio exceeds 1.00. The amount available for bonus then gradually increases to a maximum amount when the added-value ratio is 1.5 or greater.

Fig 11.8   Added value incentive scheme

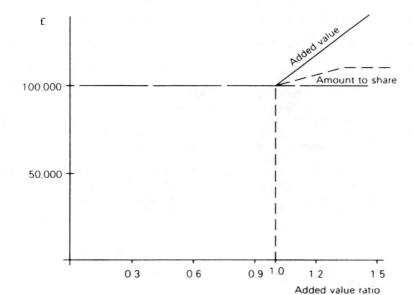

Activity

1 Management agree to pay £100 per week if 5 prototypes are assembled which are part of a preproduction run of 50. Because of the uncertainty of the process and product, they do not want to pay more than £135 regardless of how many are subsequently assembled in a week. How much will be earned if **(a)** 10 are assembled, **(b)** 15 are assembled, **(c)** 3 are assembled, and **(d)** how many need to be assembled to earn £120 per week?

2 Mary works a nominal 40-hour week at £3 per hour basic rate. Bonus is paid using a work-study-based incentive scheme and bonus payments start at 65 performance. Last week she produced 20 units with a standard time of 1.0 hours each, 30 units at 0.2 standard hours each, 10 units at 0.5 standard hours each and 40 units at 0.1 standard hours each. She worked 30 hours on this measured work. She also worked 10 hours on productive but unmeasured work which is paid for at a performance equivalent to 80, by management and union agreement.

What is her bonus earned for last week?

What is her total wage?

If she had been able to work her full 40 hours on measured work and achieved the same performance for the 40 hours as she did for the 30 hours, what would be her new bonus and new total wage?

3 Devise a suitable incentive scheme for both direct and indirect operators in Fidelity Fan Co.

Chapter Review Questions

1 What is the main difference between piecework bonus schemes and work-study-based incentive schemes?

2 In the context of introducing an incentive scheme, what is the purpose of the reference period?

3 What are the differences between a proportional and a geared incentive scheme?

4 What will be the effect of unmeasured work on the bonus earnings of a person on an incentive scheme?

5 Why is there a ceiling on the performance level at the upper end of most incentive schemes?

6 What two key parameters should be plotted regularly for control purposes from the results of an incentive scheme once in operation?

7 Why must waiting time and other non-standard working conditions be booked separately from the time spent on productive work?

8 What is the main characteristic of an exponential-based incentive scheme?

9 What is meant by 'value added'?

10 What is the lowest ratio at which a value-added scheme could reasonably be expected to pay a bonus to be shared among the employees?

12 Managing Time

It is hardly possible to manage (other than just **reacting** to events), without working to a **timetable** of some kind. It is unrealistic to suggest that all of a manager's work can be scheduled: a degree of uncertainty and 'fire-fighting' will exist. Nevertheless, always, it is important that the main tasks which need to be done are planned in advance so that it is known which jobs have priority, when they should start and finish, and what relationship (if any) exists between them. Managers will then be able to answer questions about progress, likely completion and problems to date. The information can also contribute towards monitoring individual and group **performance.**

In Chapter 12, different kinds of **scheduling** (making a timetable) will be examined. Different situations require different treatment, but in all cases, scheduling is a planning exercise, and as such needs ideally to be done well in advance of the beginning of the work itself. This does not mean that if properly done there will be no problems: but there will be a better chance of **on time completion**, and better anticipation of potential **problems** before they occur. We will consider scheduling methods for work which arrives in batches and has to follow a fixed sequence of operations for its completion; for projects like moving offices or setting-up in business or putting a new product on to the market; and for batches of work which can be considered a particularly important order for a company.

Learning Objectives

By the end of this chapter you should:

1 know what **sequential scheduling** is, and how to produce such a schedule
2 know how to **balance a line**, so as to avoid undue inefficiency
3 know what is involved in planning a project, and be able to produce a plan which shows **critical activities**, a **bar chart** and a **resource histogram**
4 be able to produce a detailed plan for an important order, to meet a customer's delivery requirements.

12.1 **Gantt Charts**

Henry Gantt (1861–1919) was a contemporary of F.W. Taylor, and worked with him at the Midvale Steelworks. He was influenced by Taylor's work, and laid the foundation for much of what is now included under the umbrella of industrial engineering. He was particularly interested in costing, extending Taylor's work on incentives, and in **scheduling**. It is scheduling for which Gantt is best remembered, through his development of the chart used for planning and timetabling which is named after him. The Gantt chart consists essentially of a graph with a suitably sealed horizontal time scale. It does not have a vertical time scale.

(a) **Function of a Gantt chart**

The chart provides an easy visual picture of the **separate tasks** required to complete a job, showing the start and finish of each task. The layout of the chart also shows the **relationship** between the start and finish of each task. The chart can be easily updated by indicating the proportion of completion at the time of review. This review should be done on a regular basis, proving a ready means of corrective action.

(b) **Updating a Gantt chart**

Figure 12.1 shows a Gantt chart for work necessary to modernise the reception area of a college. It is quite clear from the chart what tasks have to be done, and when each task should start and finish. You can also see that installation of the false ceiling can be started before the first fixing of the electrics.

Figure 12.2 shows the same chart updated as of 29 June. The dotted line under each job shows the proportion of work **completed** for each job. Demolition and new building work is ahead of schedule, and glazing has already been started. Had this been a bigger job, the updated chart could have been redrawn, and perhaps some of the future tasks brought forward.

Activity

The work passing through a department is as follows:

Product	Working time in days	Starting date (see note)	People needed
A	10	1/1	6
B	7	2/4	5
C	10	4/1	2
D	5	5/1	6
E	16	5/4	8
F	7	2/1	5
G	3	7/1	2
H	4	8/1	6

Fig 12.1 Gantt chart: work programme, front reception, Hertford campus

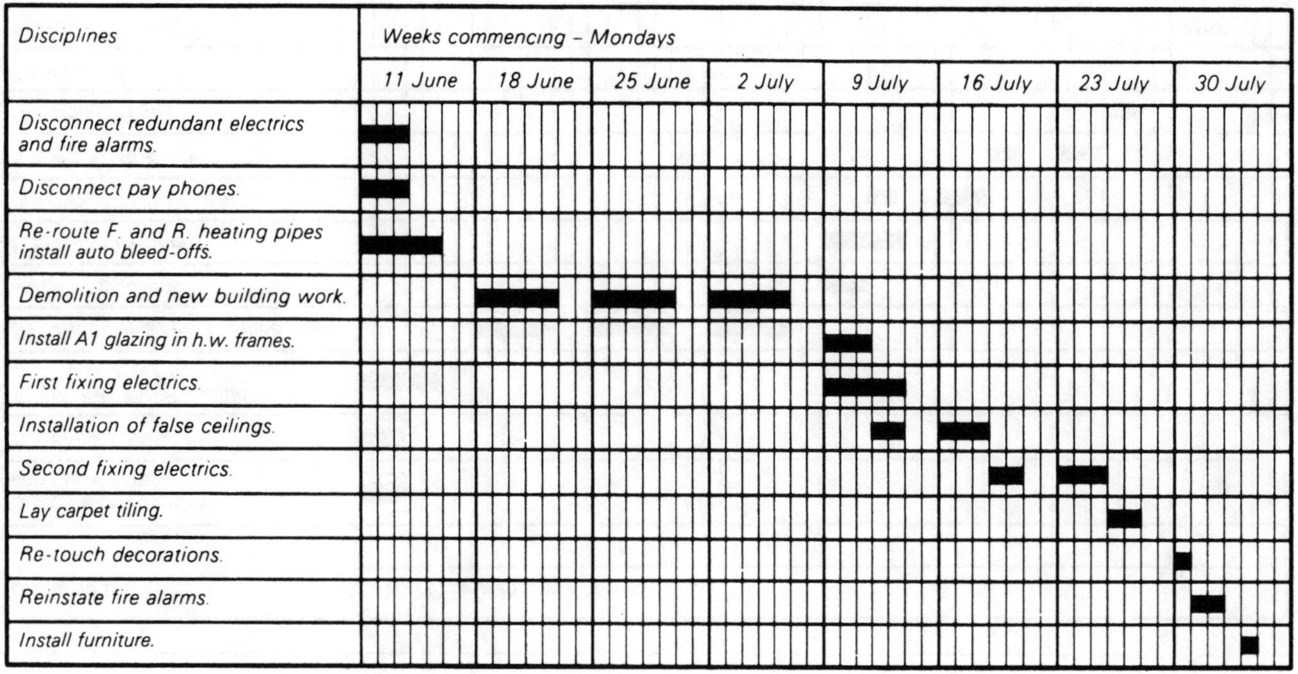

Disciplines	Weeks commencing – Mondays							
	11 June	18 June	25 June	2 July	9 July	16 July	23 July	30 July
Disconnect redundant electrics and fire alarms.	■							
Disconnect pay phones.	■							
Re-route F. and R. heating pipes install auto bleed-offs.	■							
Demolition and new building work.		■	■	■				
Install A1 glazing in h.w. frames.					■			
First fixing electrics.					■			
Installation of false ceilings.					■			
Second fixing electrics.						■		
Lay carpet tiling.							■	
Re-touch decorations.							■	
Reinstate fire alarms.								■
Install furniture.								■

Fig 12.2 Gantt chart in Figure 12.1: updated as of 29 June

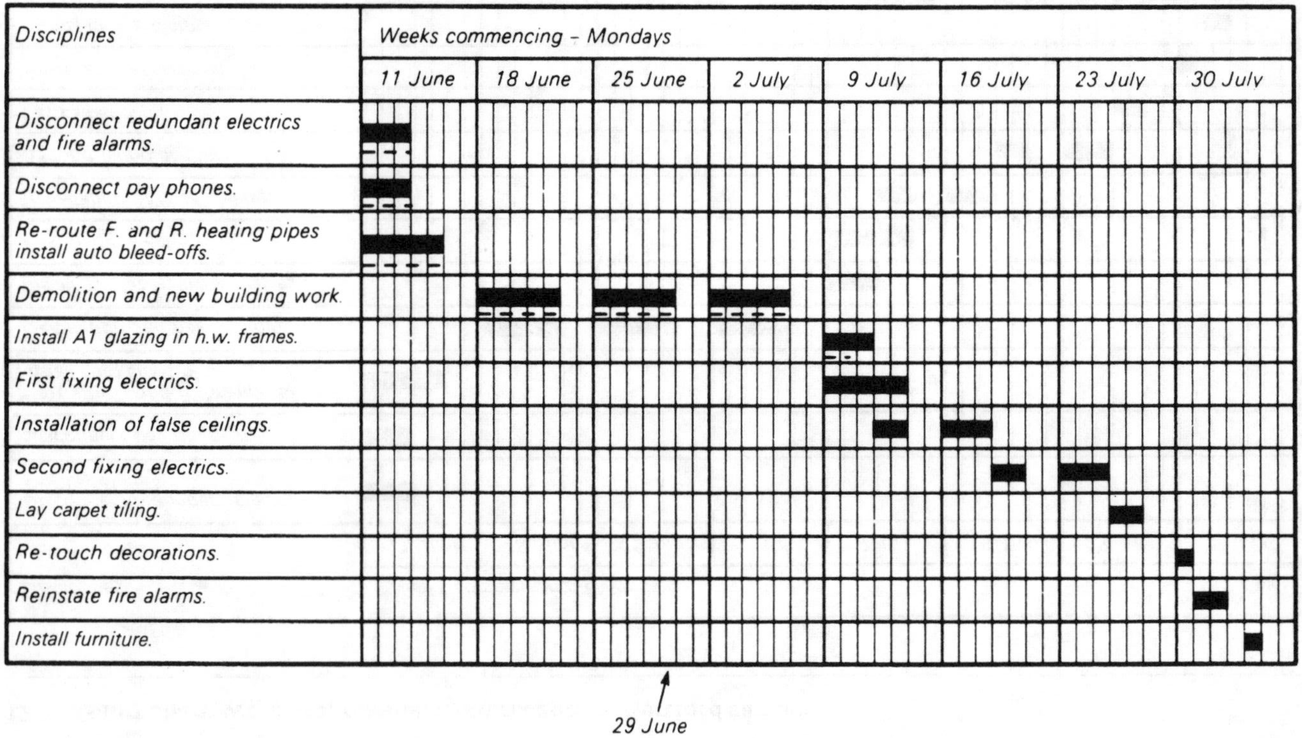

Disciplines	Weeks commencing – Mondays							
	11 June	18 June	25 June	2 July	9 July	16 July	23 July	30 July
Disconnect redundant electrics and fire alarms.	■							
Disconnect pay phones.	■							
Re-route F. and R. heating pipes install auto bleed-offs.	■							
Demolition and new building work.		■	■	■				
Install A1 glazing in h.w. frames.					■			
First fixing electrics.					■			
Installation of false ceilings.						■		
Second fixing electrics.						■		
Lay carpet tiling.							■	
Re-touch decorations.								■
Reinstate fire alarms.								■
Install furniture.								■

29 June

Note: In the date column, the format is as follows: e.g. 2/1 represents week number 2/beginning of the 1st day of the week. 5/4 represents week number 5/beginning of the 4th day of the week.

Required
1 Plot the workload in the department on to a Gantt chart.
2 Draw the labour histogram for **1** on a separate chart, to the same scale.
3 There are 11 people available in the department. Rearrange the schedule in **1** to try to reduce the overload as much as possible. Do not extend the schedule beyond week 8 or split a job. Show this on two separate charts as for **1** and **2**.
4 On a new Gantt chart, show the following situation on 5/1 for the original data in **1** when:
   A and D are complete. B is 50% complete. C is 75% complete. E is 25% complete. F is not yet started. (On this chart, weeks 1 to 4 will be blank. Maintain original finishing dates for jobs which are not yet late.)
5 Draw new histogram for this situation.

12.2 Sequential Scheduling: Batches

As we have seen, bar charts are particularly useful for the practical display of work whose progress needs to be monitored and displayed. Work which is processed in batches is as we know a common form of processing, and bar charts form a useful display and control mode. There are, however, problems inherent with the scheduling of work in batches. But first, let us look at why we need to schedule work at all.

(a) Why schedule work?

We cannot manage effectively unless we know when jobs can be expected to start and finish, and this requires a **schedule**. We also need to know which jobs should be done in the **time period** being considered. Quite often this will be a week, with closer daily control being exerted by first line supervision. It could be any other somewhat longer period (say, two weeks or one month), but this will depend on the kind of work being done.

The work being processed is needed to allow other jobs to meet a predetermined deadline further down the line, and if good control is not exercised on the jobs at the beginning of the entire process, then the **knock-on effect** of late jobs can be quite severe. If a department has an **expensive resource** (whether people or equipment), it makes good economic sense to try to make the most effective use of that resource, and careful timetabling helps here.

Effective scheduling will also help to keep **idle time** as low as possible, although as we shall see, there is unavoidable idle time in parts of any schedule involving a sequence of batches.

(b) Requirements for making a schedule

(i) Length of job

We need to know **how long** each job should take. This information may be obtained by work study techniques such as work measurement or synthetics. If for some reason it is not possible or desirable to use these more formal techniques, then **diarising** the work done and recording actual times is sometimes acceptable. It should be noted that where times are based on diaries, they are very likely to include some of the inefficiencies that formal work-study techniques would remove. Such times will also merely reflect the actual pace of performance, rather than being set against a 'should perform at "standard"' (i.e. at BS 100).

(ii) Number of jobs and resources available

The number of jobs **already in the pipeline** and the number of **new** jobs to be scheduled are also components of what is needed to build a schedule. The resources which will be available in the time period under consideration need to be known. How long is the schedule period itself? What is the current rate of absenteeism and efficiency for the department or section in question? A useful schedule cannot be produced if no account is taken of the actual proportion of time that people are available for work, or the effect of working at a performance of less than 100.

The effect of the last two factors can be seen if we take some illustrative figures. Suppose there are 275 standard hours of (human) work to be done. If people work at 100 performance, then we could expect one person working a 40-hour week to take 6.9 weeks, or about 7 people to take one week.

Suppose, however, that the efficiency of the section is 85% and the effective available hours per week are 37 out of 40. The other 3 hours per week are lost by holidays, sickness, meetings, training and unavoidable waiting time. Then the time we can more realistically expect the work to take will be 275 standard hours/85%, which = 323.5 hours, now to be divided by 37 (effective available hours per week) = 8.7 people required to do the work in one week, compared with our earlier estimate of 6.9.

Fig 12.3   Standard minute values for each operation for each batch

| | Batch number | | | |
Operation	1	2	3	4
Type: *A*	22	25	31	34
Duplicate: *B*	15	19	10	16
Collate: *C*	27	28	13	26

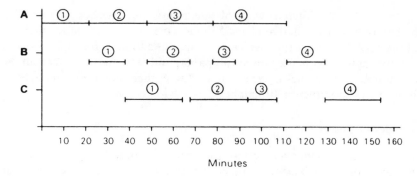

Fig 12.4   Scheduling batches in the sequence 1–2–3–4

(iii) Problems of batch scheduling

We noted earlier that there was an inherent problem with scheduling batches effectively. At least two problems are involved. First, there will always be unavoidable **idle time** between batches for operations following operation 1. This is because for any given batch operation 2 cannot start until operation 1 has finished. Operation 1, however, can be performed on the second batch as soon as that operation on the first batch has been finished.

Secondly, it is not apparent in which sequence the batches should be scheduled, assuming that all the batches are lined up waiting to go through the same sequential series of operations. This is best illustrated by looking at Figure 12.3.

The values in Figure 12.3 are the standard minutes for each batch for each operation. It is important to notice that the sequence of operations is **fixed**, regardless of the batch. Typing comes before duplicating which comes before collating, hence the name 'sequential'.

Figure 12.4 shows the bar chart for the four batches when scheduled in the sequence of batch 1, 2, 3 then 4. It can be seen that there is no idle time for batches being typed, but that there are idle time gaps between batches when they are being duplicated or collated. The sequence for scheduling the batches in order of 1, 2, 3 and 4, is, as we shall see later, purely arbitrary. The **overall elapsed time** of this schedule, from the start of typing the first batch to the end of collating the last batch, is 154 minutes.

12.3 Sequencing the Problem

Our batches could have been scheduled in a different sequence, e.g. 4, 3, 2 then 1. This may have resulted in a different overall elapsed time from the initial sequence. If it were shorter, we would have been pleased as time would have been saved, but the opposite could have occurred. There are

$4 \times 3 \times 2 \times 1 = 24$ different ways of scheduling four batches, any or all of which may produce different elapsed times. One or more of these sequences will produce the lowest time which we would like to find. But it is laborious to go through 24 sequences on graph paper, and extremely time-consuming if the number of batches is greater than 4 (e.g. there are approximately 3.6 million ways to sequence 10 batches).

(a) Rules of thumb

For this reason, managers often use 'rules of thumb', to simplify the sequencing problem. This saves their own time, and while a low elapsed time schedule may not be achieved, the result is a quickly obtained **fixed sequence for the batches**, which can be worked to.

1 Schedule on a **first come first served** basis. This is simple, widely used and accepted. It has an acceptable logic as far as customers are concerned, and can easily be implemented by using a date or time stamp to establish the sequence.
2 Schedule the batches in **ascending order of work content**, so that at any one time there are several batches with which to juggle if necessary.
3 Schedule the batches in **descending order of work content**, so that at any one time the biggest jobs are in process.
4 Schedule the batches in **descending order of monetary value**, so that cash flow prospects are as good as possible in a given time period.
5 Schedule batches by the **work content remaining to completion**, in descending (or ascending) order of that content.

Managers may also:

(a) schedule up to say 80% of capacity, to allow some flexibility later on for 'hot' jobs
(b) schedule only the **key or bottleneck resource**, other resources having some spare capacity
(c) schedule only the **major batches** (say, by value or work content) and leave the little jobs as fillers.

Activity

Make a list of situations in everyday life where a priority rule of some type has been applied. Could some other rule have worked as well, or better?

(b) Johnson's rule

S. Johnson was a USA Naval mathematician who, in 1954, produced a simple algorithm for obtaining the minimum throughput time for the

Batch No.	1	2	3	4	5	6	7	8	9	10
Operation **A**	40	20	80	35	60	65	30	15	60	55
Operation **B**	60	10	60	40	50	70	40	25	50	60

Fig 12.5   Operation time in standard minutes

schedule of any number of batches of jobs, each of which has to pass in the same sequence through two operations. It is worth examining because of its simplicity, and also because it has formed the basis for extensions of his algorithm. Some success has been achieved in producing optimal results for 3 or more operations.

Figure 12.5 shows the standard time for each of 2 operations required for each of 10 batches of work which must pass through each operation in sequence (i.e. operation **A** first followed by operation **B**).

The algorithm operates as follows:

- A new sequence of batches is formed by following certain rules. The sequence obtained is optimal, which means in this example that the sequence gives the minimum overall throughput time. The optimal result may not necessarily be unique.
- The new list is formed by placing the chosen batch initially either at the left-hand end of the list (i.e. the beginning); or at the right-hand end (i.e. the end of the list).
- Subsequent batches chosen are placed to the right or to the left respectively (i.e. working in towards the middle of the new list according to the rules below):

1 Scan the entire list of standard times and identify the shortest standard time, in our example, operation **B** batch **2**.
2 If this is a first operation, place the batch at the left-hand side of a new list of batches. Strike that batch off the original list.

BUT

3 If this is a second operation, place the batch at the right-hand side of a new list of batches. Strike that batch off the original list.
4 Repeat steps **1**, **2** and **3** for each remaining batch, placing each subsequent batch number to the right hand side of the batch already in the new list, if the shortest time was in operation **A**; or to the left of the batch already in the new list, if the shortest time was in operation **B**. In effect, the new list is formed by working in from the outside of the new list.

The sequence obtained step by step is as follows:

```
Batch                                    2
Batch    8                               2
Batch    8   7                           2
Batch    8   7   4                       2
Batch    8   7   4   1                   2
Batch    8   7   4   1              5    2
```

Note:
Batch 5 or batch 9 could have been chosen, it does not matter which. It merely means the sequence when determined will not be unique:

```
Batch    8   7   4   1            9   5   2
Batch    8   7   4   1   10       9   5   2
Batch    8   7   4   1   10    3  9   5   2
Batch    8   7   4   1   10  6  3  9   5   2
```

Activity

1 Check that you can see how the sequence above was developed, and on a piece of graph paper draw out the bar chart and identify the overall **throughput** time (i.e. from the start of operation **A** first batch, through to the end of operation **B** for the last batch).

2 Also on the same graph, draw the other optimal sequence and verify it is the same as the one shown.

3 Choose at least two other sequences (e.g. in ascending and then descending batch number order, and draw them also). Verify that they are both longer than either of the optimal sequences found by Johnson's rule.

12.4 **Line Balancing**

(a) **Work centre capacity**

In sequential scheduling, we tackled the problem involved in sequencing many different batches of work through a fixed sequence of operations. For any given operation, the batch time was simply a **function of the size of the batch**. But we did not consider how the length of each operation (i.e. the time per unit) affected the capacity of the entire system. Where one operation takes much longer than the others, it becomes a **bottleneck**, and the potential throughput capacity of the line is limited by that particular operation. So now we will consider what effect operation times have on the ability of work to flow smoothly (or otherwise) through that system. This kind of problem is called **line balancing**, and is in no way related to the line of balance technique considered towards the end of this chapter.

Line balancing therefore refers to the problem of trying to ensure that the capacity of each of a number of sequential work centres is as nearly as possible similar to each of the others. When this is true, we call this an 'efficient, well-balanced line', where little time will be lost through work centres of widely differing capacities. Each work centre may consist of one or more operations.

We do not necessarily mean that the capacity of every work centre in the sequence exactly matches the market demand, but rather that in a line of work centres the capacity of each is closely matched to the others. (As we have seen in Chapter 6, Goldratt insists that flow through the plant should be balanced to demand from the market [i.e. bottleneck flow should equal demand].)

Case Study: The Launderette

Imagine a very small local launderette which at present has one each of a washing machine, a spinner, and a hot air dryer. The sequence of operations for doing your own washing is as follows:

		Minutes
1	Unload dry washing and place in washer	1
2	Clothes go through wash cycle	24
3	Unload from washer and load to spinner	2
4	High-speed spin	4
5	Unload from spinner and load to dryer	2
6	Hot air dry	10
7	Unload from dryer and pack clean washing	3

Let us assume the unloading and loading times cannot be improved, and neither can the machine cycle times.

Question 1
What is the throughput capacity of the entire system assuming one of each machine is available, and that a load passes through all of the operations in sequence?
Answer
The throughput capacity of this system is governed by the operation taking the **longest time** (i.e. washing). In 1 hour we could process $60/24 = 2.5$ loads on average, or 20 loads in an 8-hour day.

Question 2
How efficient is the present set-up?
Answer
In the present work sequence, there is a total of **46 minutes** of work content, but the system operates as if there were 7 (work stations) × 24 (minutes) = 168 minutes. The present set-up is therefore: $(46 \times 100)/168 = 27\%$ efficient.

Question 3
How many lost time minutes are there in a complete cycle?
Answer
These are the **total** system minutes – the actual system minutes (i.e. $[(7 \times 24) - 46] = 122$ lost minutes).

Question 4
What is the percentage of lost time?

Answer

This is the ratio of **lost time** minutes divided by **total system** minutes, and expressed as a percentage:

$$[((7 \times 24) - 46)/(7 \times 24)] = 73\% \text{ lost time}$$

Question 5

How can we begin to alter the set-up to make it more efficient?

Answer

If greater efficiency is achieved, throughput capacity will be increased. We can increase it by reducing the effect of the bottleneck operation, in this case the **washer**.

If we install another washer, the effective cycle time for washing becomes 24/2 = 12 minutes. Note that this operation is still the bottleneck in the system.

Activity

Answer Questions **1** to **4** for the situation when there are now 2 washers in the set-up.

Now, suppose the requirements are that the launderette must have a throughput potential of 12 loads per hour. What possibilities exist to achieve this?

If this is to be the case, the longest operation must not exceed 5 minutes (i.e. 60 minutes/longest cycle minutes = 12). If we were to install a total of 5 washers, the effective cycle time for washing would now be 24/5 = 4.8 minutes. However, our drying operation has a cycle time of 10 minutes and would still not allow us to achieve 12 loads per hour. We therefore need to install another dryer. The effective drying cycle time is now 10/2 5 minutes. (Note that this operation is **now the bottleneck**.)

Activity

1 Draw in diagrammatic form the new proposed set-up.
2 Answer Questions **1** to **4** for this set-up.
3 If a total of only 4 washers (not 5) can be afforded, and it is discovered that only 70% of people use the dryers, answer Questions **1** to **4** under the new circumstances.

(b) Precedence diagrams

When trying to balance a line, it is useful to draw a **precedence diagram** (see Figure 12.6). This consists of nodes and arrows. The **nodes** indicate the **operations** (tasks) and the **arrows** identify the **sequence** of those operations

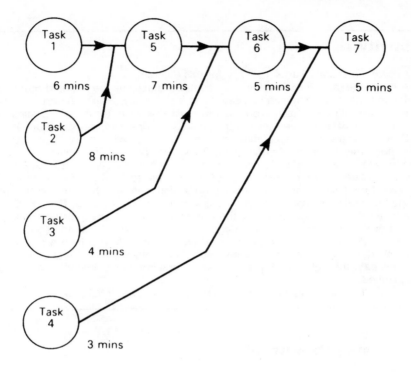

Fig 12.6 Line balancing: precedence diagram

(i.e. which ones have to be done before others). The **operation time** is marked on each node. A common requirement is then to arrange the operations into a number of **work centres** which enable a **specified** production rate to be achieved. This production rate will determine the cycle time (e.g. if we need 50 per hour, the cycle time will be $60/50 = 1.2$ minutes).

If the production rate requires a cycle time less than some of the operation times, those operations may have to be duplicated. If there is considerable expense in doing this or there is only one of a specialised piece of equipment, then duplication may not be feasible. At the same time, each work centre should have as nearly as possible the **same work content** as any other work centre in the sequence. The number of work centres is also kept as few as possible.

The precedence diagram in Figure 12.6 shows 7 tasks and which tasks have to be done before others (e.g. task 5 cannot be done before tasks 1 and 2 have been done. Task 7 cannot be done before tasks 6 and 4 have been done).

Activity

1 Answer Questions **1** to **4** (p. 271) for this diagram.

2 Arrange the tasks into suitable work centres, to achieve the required output of 10 units per hour. You can replicate tasks if necessary. (*Hint*: The cycle time is 60/10 = 6 minutes. Each work station must therefore not exceed 6 minutes' work content. Each work centre may consist of one or more operations.)

3 Draw a Gantt chart to a suitable time scale, which shows how work progresses through the sequence of tasks. (*Hint*: Task 1 conveniently fits the cycle time of 6 minutes exactly and so forms the first work centre. You will try to make other work centres' work content as close as possible to 6 minutes by combining tasks if necessary, and/or by replicating a work centre.) On your Gantt chart, the first horizontal sequence will consist of items, say **A, B, C, D, E, F, G, H,** etc. being passed consecutively through task 1 without any gaps between the end of the first item **A,** and the beginning of the next item **B,** and so on. The next work centre however, cannot start work on item **A** until item **A** task 1 has finished. When you have completed your Gantt chart, check the rate at which items pass through task 7. It should show one completed every 6 minutes, as specified.

4 Answer the Part 2 questions in the Domelap Co. case in Chapter 11.

12.5 **Project Management**

A '**project**' is usually defined as a one-off job which consists of a number of tasks. All of these tasks have to be completed before the project is completed, but their **sequence** has to be defined clearly; some tasks may start at the same time as other tasks. Some tasks may not be able to start until one or more previous tasks are completed. Because projects are so common, they generally repay the time and effort spent planning their execution. Examples of projects are building a dam or a bridge, moving an office to another site, setting up in business for yourself, building your own canoe, preparing for an exhibition, launching a new product or building an extension to an existing building.

(a) **Critical path analysis**

The most common name for project management techniques is **critical path analysis** (or CPA); other names in current use are Networking or Pert. Pert is really the abbreviation for 'Project Evaluation and Review Technique', and differs principally from CPA in that it uses **probabilities** for estimating likelihood of on time completion of a project. This is quite widely used, but it can be difficult to estimate realistic probabilities. The underlying distribution used in the calculations may also be questioned as to its realism.

It is important to realise that CPA does not necessarily need a computer. If you have a small project, then planning, analysing and following up manually, will be quite sufficient. If you have more than (say) 10 or 20 tasks, or the project looks as if it is going to be a long one, then a desk top computer with suitable software will be able to help, and cope easily with a project consisting of many hundreds of tasks.

There are many proprietary software packages; the largest packages allow for analysis of several thousand tasks and have great flexibility in their presentation.

(b) **CPA as a planning aid**

Critical path analysis itself does not solve problems. But because it is a planning aid, it alerts management to potential problems and therefore assists in the timely intervention by management to try to **alleviate their effect.**

Critical path analysis identifies those tasks which run sequentially through a project, producing the **overall longest route** and therefore the duration of the project. If any of the tasks on the critical path overrun, and no corrective action is taken, the project itself will overrun. Hence the on time completion of all critical tasks will produce on time completion of the project. Not every task in a project is critical and so it follows that some tasks will have more time available for their completion than they actually need.

(c) **Benefits of critical path analysis**

(i) **The project team**
For planning to be most effective, it needs to be done well in advance of the work itself, and CPA requires a certain amount of preparation to be done formally. This formal preparation means that a **project team** has to decide what tasks are necessary, the sequence in which the various tasks have to be carried out, and how long they ought to take. Careful thought must be given to the entire project, reducing the chances of incorrect or unnecessary work being included. The team approach also means that the management of the project can be shared between people who have been involved in the final plan.

The team need not be very big, but should consist of the people who will have **key involvement** in the project. This helps to ensure that when plans are made, they will reflect the thinking of those directly involved in the work. There need only be one person who is familiar with the technique of CPA, and he or she can act as the co-ordinator.

(ii) **The logical diagram**
From discussion within the planning team about how the project should be done, a logical diagram of the type shown in Figure 12.7 is produced. It is called a 'logical diagram' because it shows how all the tasks are **interrelated**.

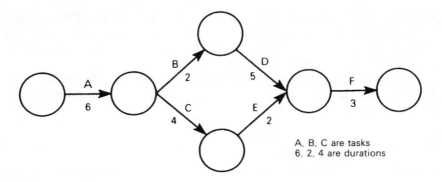

Fig 12.7   A mini project

As it is not very useful as a scheduling diagram, we convert it to a Gantt chart of the kind described above. Charts like these are eminently suitable for hanging on a wall and being used on a regular basis for **action**, **monitoring** and **feedback**. A chart derived from the logical diagram will clearly show the critical tasks as well as the non-critical tasks, as different management emphasis is placed on critical tasks, compared with non-critical ones, so making most effective use of management time.

(iii) Resource profiles

As well as scheduling, it is very useful to be able to see the resource profile of the project for each category of resource. Quite often, this refers to different categories of **labour** (e.g. plumbers, painters, carpenters or electricians). A resource profile which shows a lot of coming and going during the project is wasteful of management time and effort. By using the non-critical tasks, we can often slide them back or forth within their time constraints, and manipulate the overall profile of the entire project.

(iv) Monitoring and updating

When we have produced the Gantt chart (bar chart), we can use it for the very important purpose of monitoring and updating the original plan. Because Gantt charts are drawn to a convenient time scale, they can also be used to show the **current status** of each task when it is regularly reviewed. This can be done quite simply by underlining a task which is 50% completed with a red line whose length is half the task's length. Such updating is quick and easy, and should be done regularly.

Because all the charts used for updating stem from the original logical diagram, they provide an easy means for communicating between anyone who has a responsibility for one or more tasks. Remember that the people who work on such tasks do not need to be given the entire schedule for the whole project: they will be more concerned with their **own portion**. Only the project co-ordinator needs the whole picture, so that the implications for late running can be seen, suitable actions determined, and the plans revised and reissued. Subcontractors can also be issued with their own portion of the logical diagram, and hence develop their own bar charts.

Case Study: Midtown Solicitors – Moving Offices

Midtown Solicitors have been doing quite well over the last few years, and now that business has reached a higher and sustainable level they have recently acquired a new modern office block across the other side of town. As they have been in their present premises for some years the move will cause considerable upheaval in what has been, up to now, a very regular routine. The move is of considerable importance, because they are anxious to minimise any disruption to their routine, and above all they must be sure their paperwork is well looked after and is secure while in transit. One of their younger solicitors has had some experience of planning by projects, and he volunteered to monitor the move using project planning techniques. Summarised below are the findings from his initial survey of what the move will involve. The people who will carry out the various tasks also gave him the information regarding how long each task should take, and how many people might be involved.

Tasks		Duration days	Resources (people)	Category required
A	Take possession of new premises	5	0	–
B	Sort documents to keep	15	3	general
C	Pack documents	10	5	general
D	Pack office machines and requisites	20	2	general
E	Order removal van	5	0	–
F	Decorate ground floor offices	20	3	decorator
G	Lay lst floor carpets	10	2	carpenter
H	Lay ground floor carpets	10	2	carpenter
J	Check, list, label all packages and furniture	5	4	general
K	Load all, deliver to new site and unpack	15	4	general

12.6   Basic Activity on Arrow Notation

(i) Nodes and arrows

Figure 12.8 shows the basic logic components when using Activity on Arrow notation (or AA). In AA, a **circle** is used to identify the start and finish of an

Fig 12.8   A circle is a node; an arrow is a task

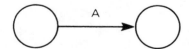

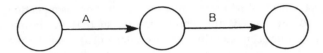

Fig 12.9   Two tasks in series

activity, and is called a **node**. The node has no duration, but merely separates one task from the next. The arrow represents the **task itself**, but is not drawn to scale. It is however, drawn from left to right (i.e. the tail of the arrow is on the left and the head of the arrow is on the right). This means that as the project is drawn it spreads from its beginning at the left-hand side to its end at the right-hand side of the paper. (There is another notation used which has its own logic and advantages, called Activity on Node, or AoN.)

(ii) Tasks in series and in parallel
Figure 12.9 shows the logic diagram when drawn for two tasks, **A** and **B**. Task **B** cannot start until task **A** is finished, that is, task **B** depends on task **A**. These two tasks are in series, meaning they follow on one from the other.

Figure 12.10 shows two tasks which can both start at the same time as each other. This does not imply anything about when they can **finish**. These two tasks are said to be **in parallel.**

We can now see that Figure 12.7 (p. 276) showed a small six-task logic network, consisting of some tasks in parallel and the others in series. All networks, however complex, are made up of similar components. The numbers underneath the arrows are the **duration** of each task – in days, weeks or months, whichever is more suitable depending on the project in question. The durations are obtained from past history or from people who are best able to estimate a reasonable time for the task. The estimates should

Fig 12.10   Two tasks in parallel

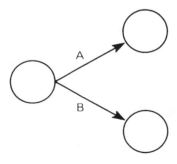

not represent the very quickest time possible, nor should there be undue pressure at this stage to obtain tight times.

It sometimes happens that, despite our best intentions, the logic diagram does not truly represent what it is meant to portray in **real life**. This is because the notation itself may cause confusion, or because the notation cannot precisely represent reality.

(iii) **Dummy activities**

Figure 12.11a shows two tasks in parallel, and indeed this is what may need to happen in reality. But confusion may be caused when a computer package is used, because to the computer the two tasks have the same start and finish nodes as each other. In a computer package, each task is identified and analysed by its start and finish node number, despite how each task is described. So when the program reaches this point, it will stop and show an error requiring correction.

Figure 12.11b shows the use of an **additional arrow** which is drawn as a dotted or dashed line. It consumes no resources and takes no time. It is there to remove an otherwise ambiguous statement. It can be analysed along with any other tasks, and a dotted arrow is called a **dummy**.

(iv) **Dependent tasks**

Figure 12.12a shows four tasks, and tasks C and D each depend on tasks A and B being finished before they can start. However, perhaps during a project meeting it becomes clear that task C depends on both A and B, but task D depends only on task B. How can the true situation be represented on the logic diagram?

Fig 12.11   Dummy arrows
a   Both tasks have same identity
b   Dummy avoids duplicating task identity

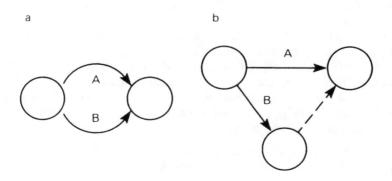

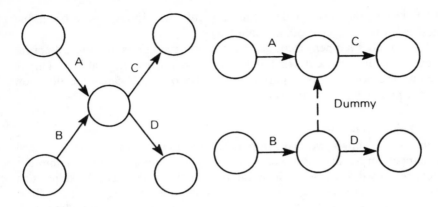

Fig 12.12   Using dummies to correct logic
a   Logic as drawn initially does not conform to real situation – i.e. that D actually
    depends only on B
b   Dummy used to correct initial drawing. which now conforms to real situation

Figure 12.12b shows how this can be done. By adding a dummy as indicated, and following the direction of the arrows in each situation, you can see that the **separate dependencies** are correctly shown.

12.7 Network Analysis

(a) Points to be identified

Now that you can put a network together based on the requirements of the real project, the next thing is to **analyse** it so that you can identify:

1 how long the project **will take**, if everything runs to time and you can live with the calculated project duration
2 which are the **critical tasks** (i.e. those which if they overrun their estimated allotted time, and corrective action is not taken, will cause the project itself to overrun): these are the critical tasks, and run in series through the network forming the critical path
3 the amount of **spare time** or **float** each of the non-critical tasks have; float, of which there are three kinds, is the amount of time within which a non-critical task can slide either backward or forward **without affecting other tasks**: subsequently you may well need to produce a bar chart from the network, and a resource histogram.

Figure 12.13 summarises a small network already drawn, together with the manpower required for each week a task takes.

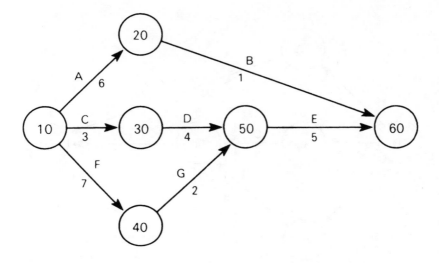

Fig 12.13 Summary of a small network: basic logic diagram

Task	Weeks	People
A	6	4
B	1	2
C	3	3
D	4	1
E	5	1
F	7	3
G	2	2

Note: The number of people needed for each task is shown in brackets against each task. in Figure 12.16, p. 285.

(b) Numbering the nodes

The numbers in the nodes are arbitrary, and are for computer identification. They must, however, be such that for each task the number of the tail node is lower than the number of the head node. It is convenient to number the nodes in tens so that insertion and numbering of new nodes for any reason is easy. Node numbers must not form a circular path through any part of the network, and every task arrow must go in a **forward** direction through the network, and not be left dangling going nowhere. The numbers under the task arrows are the **task durations** in weeks.

(c) Overall project duration

To find the overall project duration, we perform a **forward pass** going from **left to right** through the network. We give the first node an earliest start time

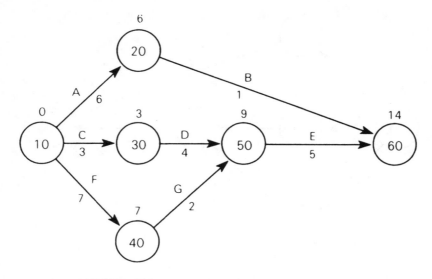

Fig 12.14   A forward pass

of 0 and place it on the top of the appropriate node, in this case node 10. If task **A** can start as early as time 0 and its duration is 6 weeks, the earliest task **B** can start is time $0+6=6$ (i.e. at the end of week 6). Similarly, both **C** and **F** can start as early as time 0, so **D** can start at the end of week 3, and **G** can start at the end of week 7.

   D can start at (the end of) week 3, and **G** can start at week 7, but as E cannot start by definition until both **D** and **G** have finished, **E** can start at week 9, i.e. the longer of $(3+4=7)$ or $(7+2=9)$. Similarly, the project duration, i.e. the end of **B** and **E**, is the longer of $(6+1$ week for **B** $=7)$ or $(9+5$ weeks for **E** $=14)$ (i.e. the project duration is **14 weeks**). We put the earliest start time for each task on top of the tail node for that task (see Figure 12.14).

(d) Critical tasks and critical path

To find the **critical tasks** and therefore the **critical path**, we perform a **backward pass** from **right to left**. We begin by putting the same time under the final node 60 as we found when we performed the forward pass. Here we calculated an earliest start time for node 60 as 14. The latest finish time for node 60 (the end of the project) must also be 14. Now if the latest **E** can finish is 14, and **B** takes 1 week and **E** takes 5 weeks, then the latest **A** can finish is $14-1=13$, and the latest **D** and **G** can finish is $14-5=9$. 13 and 9 are the latest finish times for **A**, and **D** and **G**, and are put underneath nodes 20 and 50 respectively.

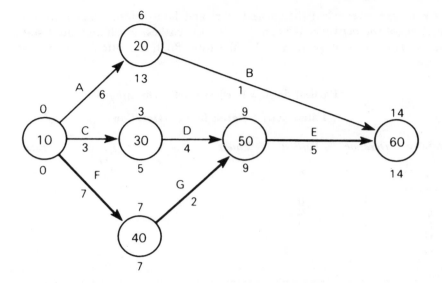

Fig 12.15   A backward pass
The critical path is 10–40–50–60

Similarly, the latest **C** can finish is week 9 – **D**'s duration of 4 = 5, and this goes under node 30.

The latest **F** can finish is week 9 – **G**'s duration of 2 = 7, and this is put under node 40.

The latest node 10 can 'finish' (i.e. the start of the project) must be the same as its earliest start time, which was 0. To get back to 0 from our backward pass, we take the lowest value of the times for week 13 – **A**'s duration of 6 weeks = 7, or 5 – **C**'s duration of 3 weeks = 2, or 7 – **F**'s duration of 7 weeks = 0. We therefore can get back correctly to 0.

Remember that when we did our forward pass, we took the **longest** of any earliest start times for all tasks whose heads converged on a single node (e.g. activities **D** and **G** converge headwise onto node 50). That is why on our backward pass, we take the **shortest** of any latest finish times for all tasks whose tails converge on to a single node (e.g. activities **A**, **C** and **F** converge tailwise onto node 10). Figure 12.15 shows the earliest start and latest finish times. The critical tasks are shown with a heavy line. They are the tasks which have **no float**.

(e) Total float

Total float for each task is calculated from the relationship:

Latest finish time – Earliest start time – Duration

We have established the earliest start and latest finish times from our analysis of the network. We can also find the earliest finish and latest start times. These four parameters, plus the total float, are often tabulated as follows:

Earliest finish = Earliest start + Duration

Latest start = Latest finish − Duration

Activity	Duration	Earliest start	Latest start	Earliest finish	Latest finish	Total float
A	6	0	7	6	13	7
B	1	6			14	
C	3	0			5	
D	4	3			9	
E	5	9			14	
F	7	0			7	
G	2	7	7	9	9	0

Activity

Complete the table above. What do you notice about the start and finish times for critical tasks?

12.8 Producing a Bar Chart

The network we have analysed provides us with a lot of useful information, but as we have mentioned before it is not very convenient to hang on a wall for use by the managers concerned. This is because the network is not usually drawn to a **time scale**, and because the notation itself needs some explanation for those who have not used it before.

(a) Changing the network into a bar chart

The bar chart format is, however, simpler, more familiar and is drawn to a time scale. How do we change our network into a bar chart?

- First of all, on some graph paper, draw a **horizontal time scale** to suit the overall length of the project + a little extra (in our case say, 20 weeks). The bar chart has no vertical scale.
- Next, it is often useful to draw on the same horizontal line all the **critical tasks**. This makes it easier for them to be **monitored**, and this important group of tasks can be the responsibility of one person. You will therefore notice in Figure 12.16, the first horizontal line consists of critical activities **F, G** and **E**, which give us by definition the project length of 14 weeks.

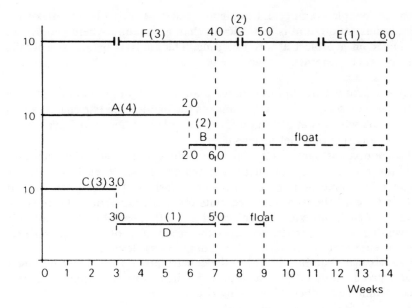

Fig 12.16   Bar chart of activities

(b) Smoothing the profile of the resource histogram

All other tasks are drawn initially as far to the left as possible. It is also convenient to draw each task in other subsets on a separate horizontal line. We therefore draw task **A** with a duration of 6 weeks, followed by a dotted line showing its total float of 7 weeks. Task **B** with its duration of 1 week is followed by a dotted line showing the same total float value of 7 weeks. The float values are the same for **A** and **B**, because the two tasks are on the same path. Also notice that the small numbers at the end of each task are the **node numbers**. These node numbers constrain the movement of tasks which are logically connected to them. Hence if we slide task **B** 3 weeks to the right, it pulls task **A** along with it, because their common node is node 20.

A similar procedure is used to draw task **C** and task **D**. It is by sliding the tasks along inside their float, that we can sometimes smooth the profile of the resource histogram, much as in the following example.

12.9 Producing the Resource Histogram

As well as the information above, it is very useful to know how the number of each resource group is likely to vary over the life of the project.

Too many people coming and going for short periods of time make for hard administration, and is less efficient than a situation where people can stay longer on a project at any one time. The analysis below is generally done for each separate resource, e.g. plumbers, labourers, carpenters, electricians, etc.

A convenient way to do this is to use another piece of graph paper, with a horizontal time scale which is the same as the one for the bar charts, and a vertical scale which is appropriate for the number of 'men' we have on the project at any one time; let us guess 12.

The resource histogram is drawn in the following manner. For each time period (in this case week) of the project beginning with week 1, we add the number of resource units required for each task, vertically down the bar chart, and record the total resource units for that time period. Then we do the same for each subsequent time period. It is often useful to draw not only the overall resource profile, but also the resource profile for the **critical tasks**, because there is no leeway for sliding, as by definition they have no float. Other tasks can be slid within the constraints of their float and a new resource profile drawn. When a smooth profile is obtained, that is the final project profile and, other things being equal, calendar start and finish times can be put to each of the week numbers.

Fig 12.17   A labour histogram

We try to smooth the overall profile by sliding those activities which have float: e.g. A, B, C, D

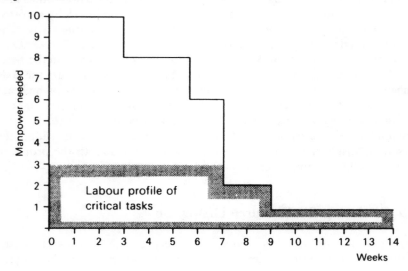

Consider week 1, tasks **F**, **A** and **C** are active and therefore require a total of $3+4+3$ people $=10$. This is the same for weeks 2 and 3 also. In week 4, task **C** has finished, and task **D** has begun, giving a total number of people of $F3+A4+D1=8$. This profile remains the same for weeks 5 and 6 also. In week 7, Task **A** has finished and task **B** begins. Total people for week 7 is $F3+B2+D1=6$ people. Weeks 8 to 9, and weeks 10 to 14, require $G2=2$ people and E1 people respectively.

Having established the resource profile, we can now try to smooth the profile to suit some given criterion. For example, if you have a maximum of 5 people available, and they can do any job on the project, can you smooth the profile to produce a maximum of 5 people required at any one time? The smoothing is done by using the **available float.**

If the project cannot be fitted into the overall time scale allowed by management, then it must be contracted in some way. Quite often this is done by finding the premium cost that is required to shrink a given critical task from its current estimated length to a new shorter length. This generally means costs associated with extra labour, extra equipment and overtime and subcontracting. The total extra cost required to shorten a project is then found, and compared with the penalty for it remaining at its current length. A management decision then has to be made as to what should be done.

Activity

1 Figure 12.18 shows the logical model (network) drawn from the information given about Midtown Solicitors' move. It is the author's interpretation of the facts, and in practice, it would have to be discussed with the project team and the logic agreed before further analysis was done.

    (a) What assumptions have been implicitly or explicitly made when drawing this network?

    (b) If you do not agree with them, draw your own version.

    (c) Why is a dummy used in the network? Is it essential?

    (d) Analyse the network to determine the project length, critical path, total float for all non-critical tasks, and the earliest and latest start and finish times.

    (e) Draw the bar chart derived from the network (a) all tasks as far to left-hand side as possible, and (b) all tasks as far to the right hand side as possible.

    (f) For each of the two versions, draw a resource histogram, noting the different profiles so obtained.

    (g) Using float, and assuming all people can do any task, develop the smoothest resource profile that you can.

2 You are responsible for a project requiring the tasks shown below. Time is short and there is a fixed £600 penalty payable if your company takes longer than the time you specify. Your boss tells you there are 10 weeks available for the project. The key tasks are represented by a letter. Durations of tasks **D**, **E** and **F** can each be reduced by 1, 2 and 3 weeks respectively at a cost for each activity of £200 per week. No other task durations can be reduced.

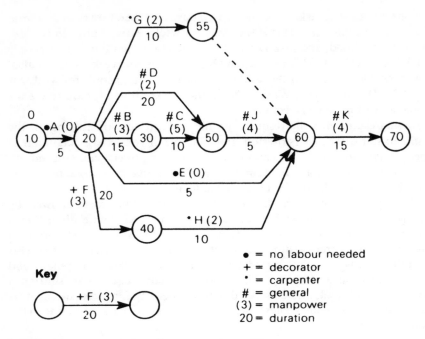

Key

```
        +F (3)
   ◯ ──────────▶ ◯
          20
```

● = no labour needed
+ = decorator
' = carpenter
= general
(3) = manpower
20 = duration

Fig 12.18   Midtown Solicitors. moving offices

Task	Duration	Immediate predecessor
A	3	
B	1	
C	2	
D	2	A
E	5	B
F	4	B
G	4	D, E, F
H	2	F, C
I	2	G, H

Analyse the data and draw the logical diagram. Identify the critical path. Draw the associated bar chart **(a)** in the extreme left position, and **(b)** in the extreme right position. What are the monetary implications of trying to avoid the penalty clause?

3 A company has received a contract to manufacture a special instrument and its wooden stand, for which it will use wood, plastic and steel. One section produces drawings for the wood and plastic parts, while another produces drawings for the steel parts. On completion of the drawings for the wood and plastic parts, the manufacture of the wooden stand and the machining of the plastic parts can proceed together. The wood is first cut to length, then machined, then assembled, and finally painted.

On completion of the drawings for the steel parts, two subassemblies can be started together. The parts for subassembly 1 are machined and then assembled along with the machined plastic parts. It is then tested. Meanwhile, the parts for subassembly 2 are machined, then assembled. The two sub-assemblies are then fixed together and finally painted.

The duration of, and labour requirements for each task in this project are as below.

Task		Duration in days	Labour (people/day)
A	prepare drawings for wooden and plastic parts	2	2
B	prepare drawings for steel parts	3	2
C	cut wood to length for stand	1	2
D	machine plastic parts	2	3
E	machine steel parts for subassembly 1	3	1
F	machine parts for subassembly 2	4	1
G	machine wooden parts for stand	1	2
H	assemble wooden stand	4	1
I	assemble subassembly 1	4	2
J	assemble subassembly 2	3	1
K	paint wooden stand	4	2
L	test subassembly 1	2	3
M	fix subassemblies 1 and 2 together	4	2

From the above data,

(a) draw the project network, find the project duration and identify the critical path

(b) draw a resource histogram assuming each task will be completed as early as possible. Re-draw it on a 'latest completion' basis

(c) smooth the resource histogram so that the project can be accomplished on time using a maximum of four people

(d) produce a tabulation of key data for each task similar to the tabulation following Figure 12.15 earlier.

4 As a small group of students of say about four people; assume you are going to set yourselves up in business. Decide on what kind of business and identify the key tasks necessary for this venture. One of your group should also act as project co-ordinator and be charged with developing the logic diagram based on the tasks you have identified. Once there is a consensus of opinion regarding the completeness of the logic diagram as drawn, assign durations to tasks by guesstimate and identify the critical path(s). By varying the estimates see how the duration and critical path will vary.

5 Draw the logic diagram based on the table below, identify the critical path and provide a tabulation of data for each task.

Draw the resource grid assuming the total labour force available is 8 people. How long will the project take if the daily working hours of the labour force cannot be increased?

Task	Dependency	Duration in days	Labour needs
A	–	12	2
B	–	18	6
C	–	20	4
D	A	15	3
E	A, B	10	2
F	A, B	15	5
G	C	10	2
H	F	5	4
J	D, E, H	10	4

6 A project has the following tasks and dependencies, durations and cost slopes. Draw the logic diagram, calculate the earliest and latest start and finish times, together with the total float available for each task. Identify the critical path.

If A and J cannot be shortened, and no other task can be shortened by more than 2 days, what is the cheapest way to reduce the overall time by four days?

Task	Preceded by	Duration in days	Cost slope £/day
A	–	6	–
B	A	5	100
C	A	4	100
D	B	6	200
E	C	5	200
F	C	4	100
G	F	4	100
H	D, E	8	600
J	G, H	3	–

12.10 Line of Balance (LOB)

There are many occasions in business when extra management control is required owing to the importance of an order which has to be processed through a plant. It is not convenient or very practical to treat them as projects, because very often the order is processed as a number of batches. But because of their importance, some extra degree of control is required. If they were regular orders they could be processed using the company's existing production control procedures: in the case of important orders this is not sufficient.

(a) An 'important' order

What is an 'important order'? Suppose you, as Bakewell Barbecues, have designed a new barbecue grill, and the design has caught the eye of one of the big chain stores. They come and see you and after some discussion say they will place a trial order with you for a specified amount, to be delivered to an agreed schedule. They will distribute them throughout their stores and if they sell well, then they will discuss with you the possibility of a big order to cover the coming year or two. The initial trial order ought to be sufficiently important to you as a manufacturer for you to take extra effort to ensure that you meet the deadlines for this order. This is where the line of balance technique can be effectively used.

(b) The line of balance technique

Line of balance has been used for many years by the construction industry as an aid for better control of their activities. Traditionally the term 'line' in line of balance derived from the use of lines drawn graphically to show the precise status of each control point in the job. However, it is more convenient to produce a table of the precise quantities expected at each control point, as a table is not dependent on how well you can draw. A **control point** is any convenient point along the process where you need to make a **status check** regarding progress (i.e. how many should have been processed at this point, and how many actually have been processed).

If too many control points are chosen, there is too much detail required, if too few control points are chosen, you will be unable to exert sufficient control. It is therefore a matter of judgement as to how many control points are chosen, but perhaps five to ten gives a reasonable guide.

(c) Requirements for use

Four key factors are involved in using line of balance:

1 There need to be sufficient control points identified along the entire process so that **management control** can be exerted. Every identifiable stage along the process does not need to be included for the purposes of control, but sufficient points do need to be chosen. Ease of identification and importance will help to identify control points to use.
2 **Lead times** to reach these control points must also be known. Control points are similar to the nodes that separated tasks in our critical path analysis above; in line of balance, the control points are nodes which separate the stages along which the product must pass during manufacture. If lead times are not known from past history, then they must be estimated by people with some experience in that type of work.
3 An agreed **delivery schedule** must be available which specifies the various batch sizes and due dates for the entire order. As LOB is also a planning technique, ideally these dates will be sufficiently far into the future that they are realistic. If this is not so, then when the analysis is done, any bunching of batches at the beginning of the schedule must be reconciled and solved in a manner agreeable to the customer and the company.
4 Because this is a planning exercise, it is quite likely that once the order begins to travel through the process, problems will arise causing difficulties with due dates. One way of softening the impact of **slippage** is to have resources which are capable of being varied to get back on schedule (e.g. can mid-week overtime be worked, is weekend overtime possible, can we subcontract out some work, can we find alternative methodology to shorten lead times, or can we put more resources on the job?).

Case Study: Bakewell Barbecues: an Analysis

An important order has been placed with Bakewell Barbecues to supply 50 barbecue grills to be delivered in four batches. The batch sizes are 5, 10, 15 and 20 units respectively, to be delivered in that sequence. Your best estimates of lead times is that they will not vary with the batch size as the batches do not vary sufficiently to warrant separate estimates for each batch.

Five control points have been identified which allow the process to broken up into four stages. The control points and stages are shown graphically in Figure 12.19, and we will refer to Figure 12.19 in our description of the analysis.

Control point	Description
1	Initiate bought in parts
2	Initiate in house manufacture
3	Initiate assembly and test
4	Initiate shipment to customer
5	Customer receives batch

Stage	Lead time (weeks)
Purchase parts	1
Make parts	1
Assemble and test	1
Ship to customer	1

Delivery schedule
Deliver batch 1 by end of week 1
Deliver batch 2 by end of week 2
Deliver batch 3 by end of week 3
Deliver batch 4 by end of week 4

For simplicity we are not using calendar dates, but the method is the same. Lead times have been estimated at 1 week each for convenience in this example, but varying lead times can be used with precisely the same procedure.

(d) Analysis notation

The notation which has been used for this analysis is very similar to what we used when we analysed a project with activity on arrow notation above. Here, control points also separate each stage of manufacture. One big difference is that the network is **open-ended at the left-hand side**, and **closed at the right-hand side**. This is because as we are making something we put together a number of pieces along the process until we have made the entire product.

(e) Monitoring progress

Figure 12.19 does not have a vertical scale. The four batches are drawn separately for clarity. There is a horizontal time scale drawn in weeks. The scale shows 'minus' weeks which are prior to delivery of the first batch. The scale also identifies days of the week, so that it is easier to see when **status checks** are taken. Note also that the time scale does not contain a week 0 when we go from week −1 to week 1.

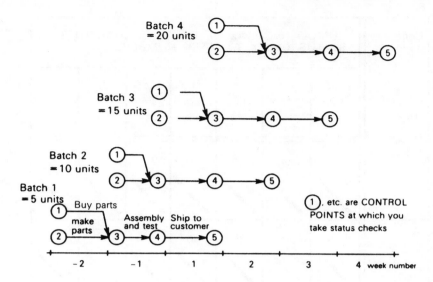

Fig 12.19 Line of balance (notation is the same as for CPA)
This important order is for a total of 50 units to be delivered in 4 batches. For each week: find LOB quantities by adding the batch quantities for the same control point in each batch, up to and including that week.

- We will monitor progress once a week, except for week −1. To help clarify when we take a check, you can see that our first check is Monday a.m. week −2, then Monday a.m. week −1, Friday p.m. week −1, Friday p.m. week 1, Friday p.m. week 2, Friday p.m. week 3, and finally Friday p.m. week 4, for a total of seven status checks over the entire process at five control points.
- What we need to do next is to begin to fill in the quantities which we would **expect to have been processed**, or **begun to be processed**, at each of the control points for each of the weeks in the entire system (i.e. from week −2 through to week 4). As this is a planning activity, we would then be in a position to check on a regular basis the **actual status** at each point, **compare** it with the planned status and take **corrective action** if necessary.
- Figure 12.20 is the table format into which we will enter our planned quantities for each control point for each week. It is these quantities which are known as the line of balance quantities.
    We will start at week −2 and determine the line of balance quantities we expect at any control point occurring in that week. To avoid any possible confusion which might arise if some of the batch quantities were the same as each other, we will cumulate all line of balance quantities as we go from week −2 to week −1 to week 1, etc. and enter these cumulated quantities into Figure 12.20.

Control point	CUMULATIVE LINE OF BALANCE QUANTITIES STATUS CHECK AT WEEK NUMBER:						
No.	−2 Mon am	−1 Mon am	−1 Fri pm	1 Fri pm	2 Fri pm	3 Fri pm	4 Fri pm
1	5	15	30	50			
2	5	15	30	50			
3		5	15	30	50		
4			5	15	30	50	
5				5	15	30	50

Fig 12.20   Entering line of balance quantities

- In Week −2, at control point 1, we expect 5 units to have been initiated for purchasing (in practice this may mean a call-off of 5 units from a blanket order). At control point 2, we expect 5 units to have been initiated for in-house manufacture. There is no other action in week −2, so these two line of balance quantities are entered into Figure 12.20 in the left-hand diagonal of the appropriate place. (The right-hand diagonal is used for entering the actual quantity when the manufacture is under way.) At week −1 on Monday morning, we can apply the same logic as for week −2, and cumulate the quantities for the reason already mentioned. At control point 1, we expect action to have been initiated for a cumulative quantity of 15. At control point 2, a cumulative quantity of 15 also, and at control point 3, a quantity of 5. These quantities are entered into Figure 12.20. Similarly at week −1 on Friday afternoon, we have 30 units cumulative at control point 1, 30 units at control point 2, 15 units at control point 3 and 5 units at control point 4.

- Similar logic produces the remainder of the entries in Figure 12.20. You should ensure you can see how the remainder of the table has been completed. The logic has remained the same as that used for week −2.

(f) Substituting calendar dates

When the entire job has been planned and agreed, calendar dates can be substituted for the week numbers, and a table issued to those concerned, so that it can be used on a regular basis for monitoring and control. At each control point at the appropriate time the **actual status** is determined and entered on to the table in the right-hand diagonal spaces. If progress is less than that planned for (or too far ahead, for that matter) then appropriate follow up and corrective action must be taken. In this way, the plan stands a good chance of being met, with most problems at least being seen some time ahead.

Activity

1 United Instruments Co. have just received an initial order for 100 of its new universal meters from Nippon Measures Ltd. Success with delivering this order may well lead to further and larger orders. You are charged with the task of successfully delivering this order. You have the following information on certain key activities.

- Obtaining each batch of components from your outside supplier takes 4 weeks
- Making each batch of subassemblies (which do not use any outside supplied components) takes 3 weeks
- Assembling the meter itself from the components and the subassemblies takes 2 weeks per batch
- Testing and calibration takes 1 week per batch
- Packing for shipping to customer takes 1 week.

Delivery Schedule to Nippon Measures Ltd

Batch No.	Quantity	Nippon Measures Ltd to receive batch by end:
1	15	April
2	25	May
3	30	June
4	20	July
5	10	August

No action has yet been initiated. It is now the first week in April. Assume 20 working days per month.

Draw the appropriate chart which will show the 5 separate batches to a time scale. Tabulate the line of balance quantities for each week of the entire programme.

Does it cause any problem that it is now the first week in April? If so, suggest some management action you could submit to your boss.

2 A company has decided to establish Line of Balance control on a new production line which is intended to produce items at the rate of 50 per day. The dependencies of the tasks are shown below, and the table shows the stock status after 40 days. Establish the lead times for the various tasks and construct a line of balance for 40 days of operation. Are there any problems disclosed by your analysis?

Tasks A, B, C, D can all start at the same time
Task G depends on C
Task E depends on A; and task F depends on both B and G
Task H depends on D
Task J depends on E, F and H
Task K depends on J

Task	Duration in days	Stock after 40 days
A – Deliver steel	18	3000
B – Deliver gears	22	2850
C – Deliver castings	20	3100
D – Deliver motors	19	2800
E – Make cases	10	2250
F – Assemble gear boxes	11	2250
G – Machine castings	5	2850
H – Subassembly	5	2200
J – Final assembly	6	2050
K – Final test	2	1900

3 Comfysit Ltd have received a trial order for 110 of their newly designed folding armchairs. If these sell well, a much larger order might result. They have decided to utilise line of balance and have just told you today (1st August) that you are responsible for the on time delivery of this order. There has been no action yet. You have the information below.

Key production stages	Lead time weeks if batch size is 25 or less	Lead time weeks if batch size is 26 or more
A – Order and receive a batch of items from your suppliers, e.g. coverings, fasteners, fittings	4	5
B – Make a batch of subassemblies, e.g. base, back, legs, sides. these do not use items in A above	3	4
C – Assemble and inspect a batch of armchairs using items in A and B above	2	3
D – Ship a batch to a customer	1	1

Batch no.	Batch quantity	Customer receives batch at end of month
1	10	August
2	30	September
3	40	October
4	20	November
5	10	December

Show graphically, the stages, batches, quantities, and delivery dates involved. What problems if any do you need to alert management to? Suggest some possible solutions.

4 A Line of Balance control has been established over a line intended to produce items at the rate of 50 per day. The dependencies of the tasks are shown below, and the table shows the stock status after 70 days. Calculate the lead times for the various tasks and construct a line of balance for 70 days of operation. Do you see any problems?

Tasks A, B, C, D can all start at the same time.
Task H depends on D.   Task G depends on C.   Task E depends on A.
Task F depends on B.   Task J depends on F.   Task K depends on E and J.
Task L depends on H, G and K.

Task	Duration in days	Stock after 70 days
A	8	4000
B	5	4600
C	4	3400
D	7	3800
E	8	3400
F	10	4250
G	5	3500
H	6	3600
J	4	3800
K	3	3800
L	2	3300

5 The data below relates to the first order for 300 of the Karta-Load wheelbarrow model PSW3. Find the line of balance quantities for the end of week 5. Complete the table in a manner similar to Figures 12.19 and 12.20. Note that seven tasks mean eight nodes as control points.

Key production stages	Immediate predecessors	Lead time in weeks per batch
A – Order and receive timber	–	4 weeks
B – Order and receive metal tubing	–	3 weeks
C – Order wire and tyres	–	2 weeks
D – Make legs and bodies	A	3 weeks
E – Make handles	B	2 weeks
F – Make wheels	C	1 week
G – Assemble and paint	D, E, F	1 week

The delivery schedule **was**:

Week	Quantity	Cumulative amount to have been delivered
1	10	10
2	20	30
3	30	60
4	30	90
5	50	140
6	50	190
7	50	240
8	30	270
9	20	290
10	10	300 (end of order)

Chapter Review Questions

1 What is a bar chart?

2 What is meant by sequential scheduling?

3 Name three simple rules of thumb for sequential scheduling.

4 What does Johnson's algorithm do?

5 In critical path analysis, why is a logical diagram useful?

6 Define the critical path.

7 'Managing a project with critical path technique is more usefully done as a team exercise rather than just one person in charge': True or False?

8 What is a resource histogram?

9 In what management control situation is line of balance useful?

10 What does the line of balance technique 'balance'?

13 Plant Related Decisions

Chapter 13 is concerned with different decisions in the following areas:

(a) where a plant should be **located**
(b) how the plant should be **laid out**
(c) **maintenance** of its equipment
(d) and factors concerning **material handling**.

In any particular situation, one or more of these areas may predominate owing to the specific needs of a company. Individually all these areas are important, because when all aspects of plant efficiency (the term 'plant' is used here as a generic term for the buildings, equipment and layout) have been carefully considered, the business will operate much better than one where such decisions have not been consciously considered.

Learning Objectives

By the end of this chapter you should:

1 be able to identify factors influencing plant **location**
2 recognise the advantages of an **efficient plant layout**
3 know how to **analyse flow** through a plant
4 be aware of the benefits expected from a programme of **planned maintenance**
5 know the criteria for efficient **material handling**.

13.1 Plant Location

The opportunity to influence the location of a plant is one which occurs relatively infrequently for most people. However, it is important to be aware of those factors which will influence such a decision, so that the shortcomings of an **existing location** can be recognised, and changes made should the opportunity occur. Seven key factors which will influence the location of a plant, whether brand new or part of an expansion programme.

(a) Financial factors

Brand new plants such as those built by Japanese car companies in the UK, are often referred to as **'green field site'** projects, as the designers have a relatively free hand to incorporate many of the latest features in a given area of technology. Because of the tremendous investment (which often runs into hundreds of millions of pounds) one of the determining factors will be the degree of **financial incentives** that might be received by the company from the local authorities concerned. Such benefits may take the form of grants, low-interest loans, reduced or deferred rates and/or rents, and in some cases ready-built ancillary buildings. When an economy is static or declining, the competition between authorities can be intense to woo international companies into their own area to take advantage of the job-creating potential that will occur. Private developers may also often help in the form of rent-free and/or rent-reduced periods, assistance with fitting-out costs and/or help with costs associated with ending existing leases.

(b) Main transport

How near to main transport linkages are various sites on a company's list? The nearness, frequency and key destinations will all be important. Transportation modes such as air, sea, road and rail each need to be considered separately, although for a particular operation one or more modes may predominate. A world-wide courier needs its offices located at or near a major airport and close to motorway links. A new hospital will of necessity be close to centres of population rather than near major transportation routes. A new fast-food outlet will consider it important to be in the high street of each local community.

(c) Natural resources

For some plants, the proximity of natural resources will be important. Gravel, sand and clay supplies must be nearby if they are the key source of raw material for a company since transporting raw material to the plant will be uneconomical in most cases. However, if a plant needs a continuous supply of coal and iron ore, or water for cooling, then nearness to a rail network with its own siding is a key consideration for the first two items, and nearness to a large river or the sea for the last one.

(d) The environment

Does a company's activity pose potential interference with the environment in terms of noise, air or water pollution? Does it make it more likely that there will be unacceptable concentrations of new population in, for example, a rural environment? The contours of the ground site for London's third airport at Stansted in Essex, were carefully sculptured to try to ensure that there were no unacceptable high level buildings which would otherwise jut out against a rural skyline. The site itself was very large, not only to allow for the anticipated traffic levels, but to help ensure that the building density and moving population associated with it were compatible with the overall surroundings. The transport facilities were also carefully designed to be not only efficient and adequate, but unobtrusive. The rail link was placed in its own cutting and tunnels.

(e) Labour facilities

What are the opportunities for a company to obtain locally the skills it will need to run and develop its business? Will an engineering company find the kind of skills it needs in a rural area? Is there an adequate supply of labour of various sorts (e.g. young and inexperienced, older and semi- or highly skilled)? If not, does the area have the reputation for having an adaptable workforce? This is important when an area where unemployment is high tries to attract different kinds of companies. Should the company seek to establish itself in an area where there are similar companies (e.g. science and technology parks spawn spin-off industries, as happened in the Silicon Valley of California in the 1960s–70s)?

(f) The market

How difficult will it be for a company to get its product to the customer? If its product is perishable (e.g. food or flowers) then fast and specialised transport may be required. If the company is providing a service, how near can it site itself to its potential customers (e.g. banks, estate agents, supermarkets)?

(g) Education and training

If adequate amounts of labour skills are not easily available, can a site be found which is near centres of learning, such as colleges, polytechnics and universities? (Examples of this are those companies clustered in the Massachusetts area in the USA, and in Cambridge in England.)

With so many factors involved, some of which are not easily quantified, it is helpful to establish a **scale** for each which can be used to **rate** the degree to which each factor meets the company's requirements. This means that it is essential for the company to have a clear idea of what it expects to achieve by the move, or what benefits, not obtainable at present, the new location will afford. This is a difficult exercise, as such decisions are made at board level as a strategic response to achieve the company's main objectives for the medium and long term.

Activity

Establish a rating system for the seven factors considered above, and try to decide which will be the most important to consider for **(a)** an out-of-town supermarket, **(b)** an out-of-town shopping complex, **(c)** a fast-food chain's next shop, **(d)** a new private hospital by a medical insurance company, **(e)** an airport, **(f)** a motel, **(g)** a golf course, **(h)** a sports complex, **(i)** a dome-covered holiday theme park.

13.2 **Plant Layout**

(a) **Where costs can be reduced**

The efficient layout of any plant will help reduce significantly the **costs** of the product or service being produced. These cost reductions compared with a poor layout arise from five key factors:

1 A smoother and more continuous **flow** of the material and product through the various work centres or departments. When the flow avoids **backtracking**, the distance the material travels is less, saving **time** and **money**.
2 Better use of plant area and volume when considering location of equipment and stores. Equipment may be laid out either on a **process** basis (i.e. all like machines together), or on a **product basis** (i.e. all the key equipment to complete a product, or a major subassembly of it, is grouped together, usually called a 'cell').
3 Considering the type of production **process** likely to be used (i.e. job, batch or flow). In many plants, one or more of these forms exist, but it is better to have them defined clearly prior to physical location of equipment than to make assumptions which may or may not materialise.
4 The careful prior consideration of the **architecture** of the plant itself (e.g. what loads the various floors are likely to be required to withstand, the avoidance of constricting roof supports and awkward roof angles which preclude the full use of space, the adequate supply and siting of electricity, gases, water, steam and oil used for processing and powering different stages of the process). Where, and what size, should stairs, lifts and conveyors be to cope with the associated operations involved?
5 The relation of the whole plant to the immediate **external environment**, so that (for example) there is sufficient room for loading finished goods, and unloading material from suppliers. Ensure that there is a smooth external flow of **incoming** and **outgoing** vehicles which do not impede each other, or the work itself, which may be travelling from building to building.

(b) Key flows within the plant

We can now summarise the parameters to consider. In any plant (and remember we are using the 'plant' in its generic form), the key flows are:

1 Flow of **people**
2 Flow of **material**; raw, in progress and finished
3 Flow of **information**
4 Flow of **services**.

(c) Safety considerations

In all cases, aspects of **safety** must be paramount. Consideration will include the provision for safe use of poisonous and/or flammable gases and chemicals, gases or liquids which are stored or used under pressure, the safe use of high temperatures, the full protection of all personnel who may use substances deleterious to their health, including facilities for changing clothing and washing or showering. First Aid posts and qualified personnel must also be established. Regular fire drills must be carried out, with personnel designated as key people in the event of an emergency. Regular maintenance of all equipment will also be necessary according to a predetermined schedule. This will particularly apply to the use of high pressures, voltages and hazardous chemicals.

(d) Analysing plant layout

(i) Existing constraints and interfaces
Plant layout is a major exercise if considering the workflow in an entirely new building; it will still be important when considering flow in a new part of an existing building, as there will be **constraints** and **interfaces** which cannot be changed (e.g. the kind of processes which are already carried out in different parts of the building, the existing physical characteristics of the building) – it may not, for example, be possible to use a certain type of vehicle in the new building, because it cannot enter or negotiate parts of the existing building.

(ii) Method study techniques
Layouts may be analysed and planned by using some of the techniques met in method study.

● Particularly useful are **flow charts** drawn on the plan of each building. These charts show clearly by the use of arrows how the material will **move through the plant**, and how the plant itself is laid out with respect to the **equipment** and **services**. These charts can then be used to summarise the present and proposed distances travelled.

- **To/From** charts are effective when needing to tabulate the **number of movements** between specified work centres, departments or buildings. Analysis of such tables then assists the planner to site those centres which have the largest number of trips between them closest together, There are computer programs which allow different weightings to be assigned to different work centres, so that a total score can be built up for a particular proposed layout. Because a computer is being used, it is relatively easy to experiment with different weighting values and traffic loads. The final scores for different combinations can then be evaluated, and they will assist in the final decision.

Case Study: The Post Room: Layout of a Single Department

The post room of a department store is concerned with packing customers' small orders and sending them by parcel post. The items for each parcel are picked and brought from the warehouse by a picker who then puts them on the assembly bench in the post room. The packer checks the items against a copy of the assembly note. The items are then packed, wrapped and weighed. The weight is recorded on the advice note, and the parcel put on to a rack for subsequent dispatch.

The present method

- An **assembly note** and **advice note** are sent by internal mail from the sales office to the post room supervisor; each note contains a list of the items needed for one parcel.
- A **picker** collects the required items from racks in the warehouse and takes them **by** trolley to the post room, where the goods, advice note and assembly note are deposited on an assembly bench.
- A **packer** goes to the assembly bench and checks the goods against the assembly note to make sure all the items are present and correct. He or she takes the assembly note to the supervisor's desk and collects the advice note.
- The packer returns to the assembly bench and picks up the all the items for the parcel, takes them all to the packing bench and leaves the goods on the bench.
- The packer then goes to the roll of corrugated paper, where a length is cut off to wrap the parcel.
- The packer returns to the packing bench, places the paper on it, moves to a carton rack, selects the appropriate sized carton, and returns to the bench and then makes up the carton.
- The packer wraps the items and the assembly note in the paper and packs them into the carton. The carton is then wrapped in brown paper, a label stuck on it, and it is tied up with string. The labels, which are preprinted, the paper and the string are all kept on the packer's bench.
- The packer next takes the parcel to the weighing machine, weighs it and returns with it to the bench. He or she records its weight on the advice note, takes the parcel to the rack for despatch and the advice note to the supervisor's desk.
- The whole routine is then repeated for the next parcel.

Figure 13.1 shows the present layout of the department.

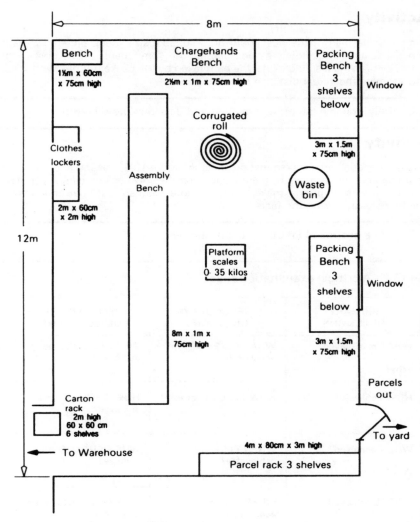

Fig 13.1 The post room: existing layout

Management have been concerned for some time that improvements could be made to the overall layout of the department, as similar operations in other branches of their stores seem to be more efficient. With ever-increasing pressure on costs, they feel now is the time to examine the post room operation closely, with a view to its improvement.

What steps need to be taken, based on the information given?

1 As the process is primarily centred around a person (i.e. the packer), a **flow process chart** should be prepared on a scaled plan of the post room, showing the route for the work cycle described.

Activity

Draw a scale plan of the post room on a suitable size sheet, preferably graph paper. Locate, as accurately as possible, all the components in the post room. Trace, by drawing a suitable line, the path taken by the packer for one work cycle and estimate the actual distance travelled.

2 Critically examine the present method and develop a **new layout**.

Activity

Using the model critical examination sheet in Figure 13.2, ask and answer, using your imagination, as many of the questions on the sheet as you can. If you have to make any assumptions. make them and note them so that your final answer will be consistent with the facts.

3 Prepare a **proposed layout** of the post room.

Fig 13.2   A critical examination sheet

PRIMARY QUESTIONS	SECONDARY QUESTIONS	SELECTED FOR DEVELOPMENT
WHAT is achieved? Why?	WHAT ELSE could be achieved?	WHAT SHOULD be achieved?
HOW achieved? Why?	HOW ELSE achievable?	HOW SHOULD it be achieved?
WHEN achieved? Why?	WHEN ELSE achievable?	WHEN SHOULD it be achieved?
WHERE achieved? Why?	WHERE ELSE achievable?	WHERE SHOULD it be achieved?
WHO achieves it? WHY THEM?	WHO ELSE?	WHO SHOULD achieve it?

Activity

From the new ideas developed during item **2** above, prepare a **new sequence of operations** for the packer. This can be done using very brief descriptions of each operation that the packer has to do.

4 Prepare a **new proposed layout** for consideration by management.

Activity

On a new plan of the department, but drawn to the same scale, locate the positions of the equipment in the post room as you now envisage them, and trace the new route the packer now takes. Estimate the new distance travelled and compare it with the present distance. What will be your annual savings in distance moved based on packing 40 parcels per day, for 5 days a week and 48 weeks per year? What time will be saved annually, if the distance saved would have been covered at a speed of 25 metres per minute? If it takes 5 minutes to pack a typical parcel, how many more parcels are potentially possible owing to the time saved?

13.3 Plant Layout: Relation between Several Departments

(a) Closeness values

When several departments or work centres need to be considered, perhaps as part of a major layout problem, it is useful to be able to consider the importance of the relationship between each department and the others. There are computer programs which can assist in this (one such program was published in *Industrial Engineering Journal* (USA) March 1983), but the principle can be applied manually in simpler cases. Figure 13.3 shows the present layout of the ground and first floors of Shine-A-Lite Co. They are a small local company primarily engaged in some fabrication and final assembly of their own range of overhead projectors.

When interdepartmental relationships are important, a table of **closeness values needs to be established from experience. Figure 13.4 shows how important certain relationships are**.

The number of categories can be reduced if you wish, and the scores can be altered to suit your own estimates of such categories.

Assume for this company that the relation matrix in Figure 13.5 below is a fair representation of relationship importances for the ground floor.

Ensure that you can see how the table is constructed. It is similar to a mileage between towns map, in that only half of the matrix is used.

Activity

1 Determine the score for the current layout of the ground floor.
2 Construct your own matrix for the current layout of the first-floor administration and determine the score.
3 Lay out both floors trying to achieve a new and higher score than the corresponding score for the current layout. Your choice for your next try will be to try to site departments 3, 4 and 5 near each other, with department 2 near to department 5 if possible. This is because Figure 13.5 indicates a category A

value for these departments. The process of having a new layout stops when you think you have made a significantly higher score than before, in the time available for planning. Bear in mind that a high score result may be incompatible with your budget. Planning permission or major structural alteration may be needed.

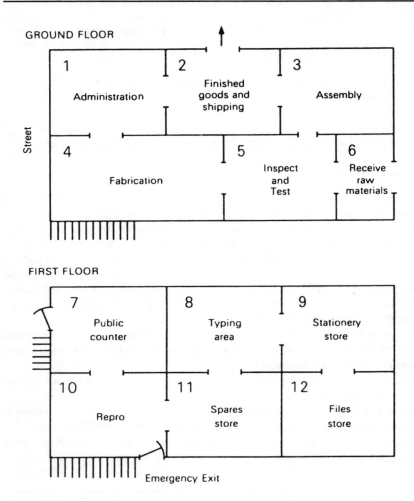

Fig 13.3   Shine-A-Lite Co.: layout of ground and first floors

(b) To/from charts

In the same way that a table can be constructed to show the relative importance between departments, a table can be constructed which shows the amount of **travelling** or the amount of **work moved** between every pair of work centres or departments. This information is obtained from a method study or O and M survey taken over a representative period of time.

The completed chart will look like that in Figure 13.5, and it can be used in a similar manner as before, because work centres placed near each other which have large amounts of travelling or work flow will be more efficient than otherwise. The same kinds of **constraints** will also apply.

Score letter	a	e	i	o	u	x
Score	8	4	2	1	0	−8
Description	vital	essential	important	OK	unnecessary	undesirable

Note: What should/must be close to each other – i.e. next to each other with access

Fig 13.4   Inter-departmental relationship scores

Ground Floor

Department	1	2	3	4	5	6
1		e	o	x	u	e
2			o	u	a	u
3				a	a	u
4					x	a
5						u

Fig 13.5   Relation matrix of important relationships for the ground floor

Activity

The office layout shown in Figure 13.6 shows the present layout and the number of journeys made between different staff and facilities, with the distances involved. Single journey distances and number of journeys are shown as: 4m/6j, with distances in metres, and journeys indicated with a j. Supervisor's travel is ignored in this exercise.

Ascertain the current distance travelled with the present layout.

Redesign this layout to reduce overall distances, to help improve communication, and to reduce costs. Aim to reduce travel by senior staff. Calculate the percentage saved in distance travelled.

The following cost factor table applies:

	Cost factor
Senior clerk	1.0
Shorthand typist	0.8
Copy typist	0.6
Junior trainee	0.4

Fig 13.6   Office layout

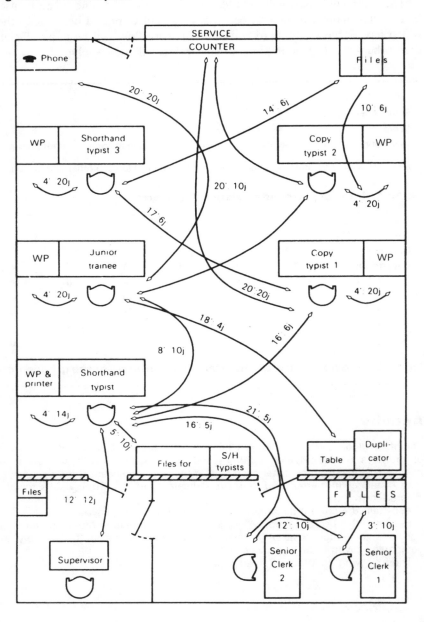

Estimate the present total 'cost' by multiplying the cost factor of the number of staff making the journey. If a journey is between two different grades, assume that the lower grade made the journey. After you have made a new layout for the office, estimate the new total cost factor, and the percentage saving made.

Case Study: The Volvo Car Plant Layout at Kalmar

The Volvo plant at Kalmar, south of Stockholm, was designed to break away from the traditional car plant layout where jobs were broken down into extremely small portions of work, and employees worked on an assembly line . This traditional way of assembling cars meant that it was easy to teach people their tasks as they were of very short duration, and the skill level very low. The motivational drive was also very low, and discontentedness and absenteeism was high.

In the Kalmar plant, established in the early 1970s, there is no assembly line (see Figures 13.7 and 13.8). Car bodies are transported on travelling carriers with underfloor guidance. Employees now work in teams. One team may assemble all the electrics, another the complete interior. The assembly module times are about 40 minutes long, and every team member can do any task in their module. The module of work is very close to being its own mini factory, with its own changing and rest areas and coffee room.

The assembly is done in a straight line in 4 to 5 work zones, each with 2 to 3 people per zone. Because of the longer work cycle, and cleaner and more modern working environment, motivation, productivity and quality is high, and absenteeism is low. The unusual layout of Kalmar appears to have stood the test of time. However, there are relatively few other major plants which operate on the same principle.

13.4 Plant Maintenance

Plant or equipment, no matter how high the quality, cannot be expected to function indefinitely without proper maintenance. Unexpected breakdowns cause loss of production, actual or potential safety hazards, personnel idle time, material bottlenecks, loss of customer goodwill and higher than usual repair costs.

(a) When to maintain plant and equipment

Maintenance is therefore required to bring the performance of a piece of equipment back up to a satisfactory level regarding performance and safety – safety not only of the equipment and its operators but also of others in the same plant. The question then arises as to **when** maintenance should be carried out. The most common time for maintenance is when there is a crisis, when the equipment has broken down or performance has been degraded so substantially that something has to be done. There is then no doubt that repairs have to be done, and therefore any costs incurred must be essential, as 'down time' must be no longer than absolutely necessary.

(b) Down time

'Down time' is a measure of the time lost on a piece of equipment because of a breakdown. Down time can be conveniently made up of 'waiting for repair' plus 'time to repair and test'.

Example

A deep fat fryer is used for 40 hours per week for 50 weeks per year, so there are 2000 hours available for it to be used. Assume it breaks down twice in that time. The first time it takes 2 days for the service person to arrive and a day for repair. The second time the service person arrives and repairs it in one day. Down time is therefore a total of $16 + 8 = 24$ hours during the year. The down time percentage is

$$24 \times 100/2000 = 1.2\%$$

The equipment is therefore available for 98.8% of the time, in this case a very high level of availability.

(c) Preventative maintenance

A better way for maintenance is to **plan it in advance**. This is called preventative' maintenance, and has been advocated for many years, although it still is not as widely prevalent as it ought to be. The advantages are many: the number of emergencies will be reduced; the costs of maintenance will be reduced; there will be fewer interruptions to regular work. When maintenance is required it is likely to mean the required spares

---

Notes to Figure 13.7

The work within a team zone is divided into 4–5 stations after each other in the direction of the production flow, so-called 'straight line assembly'. Working at each such station are two assembly workers who accompany the carrier to all the stations and carry out all the work which the team has been allotted. When the assembly workers then go back and start on a new carrier, it is usual that they change jobs with each other. This means that the working cycle for an assembly worker can comprise 16–40 minutes, depending on the number of stations and whether jobs are interchanged or not.

The system has also another possible assembly form, so-called 'dock' assembly, which is currently not being applied. Dock assembly means that the carrier automatically goes to one of the docks where all the assembly is carried out with the carrier stationary. Each such assembly station is manned by 2–3 people who can interchange their jobs.

The work content and volume per time unit are the same as with straight-line assembly. However, with dock assembly the entire working cycle is carried out at one single assembly station while straight-line assembly involves several stations.

Source: Volvo Car Corporation.

Fig 13.7   Efficient car assembly in the Kalmar plant

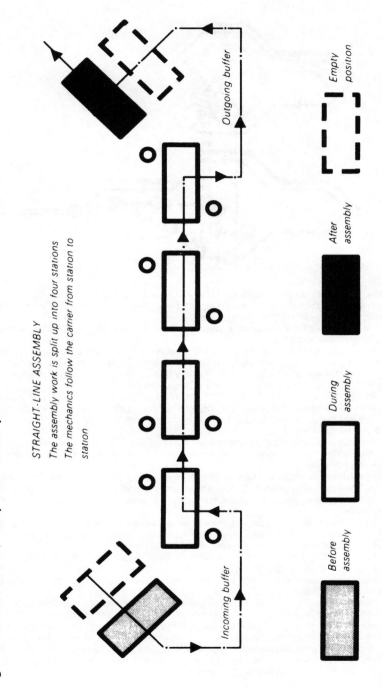

STRAIGHT-LINE ASSEMBLY

The assembly work is split up into four stations

The mechanics follow the carrier from station to station

Incoming buffer

Outgoing buffer

Before assembly

During assembly

After assembly

Empty position

Fig 13.8 The production flow in the Kalmar plant

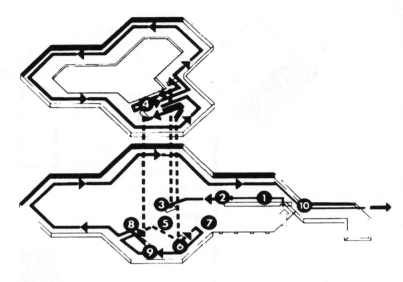

When the painted body enters the factory, it is washed and dried (1).

The body is then placed on a working platform (2) which is controlled by a computer and lifted via an elevator to the upper floor (3).

On the upper floor the body passes via a buffer zone (4) anti-clockwise through the various assembly areas.

At the same time the assembling of the chassis starts on the ground floor (5) on the high working platform (broken line). When the chassis is ready, the high working platform travels via the elevator (6) up and fetches the body. After the working platform has returned to the lower floor, chassis and body are joined together.

At (8) the car is transferred from the high to the low working platform which is transported down with the elevator (9) and continues clockwise on the lower floor.

The last thing that happens is the undercoating and rustproofing treatment (10) before the car leaves the factory.

Production is steered and materials are handled with the help of an advanced computer system where five computers co-ordinate with, among others, 50 screens and about 40 printing terminals.

The system provides possibilities for a far-reaching decentralisation and delegation of jobs. The assembly carriers automatically inform the computer of their identity and position. This considerably simplifies co-ordination of materials, assembly instructions and quality follow-up.

By the fact that the position of the carrier is reported to the computer via a monitor and the assembly instructions are written out first when a certain position is known, the carriers can follow an irregular order through the assembly process.

The assembly instructions are written out in good lime for the variant-dependent preassembly stations and provide information about the parts to be assembled. When the carrier approaches the assembly bay, the team has already built the subcomponent which is to be fitted to the body.

The Kalmar and Udevalla plants described above were finally closed in the early 1990s. A significant and groundbreaking experiment in work methods, it was ultimately found that employees using the dock assembly had difficulty knowing for sure where they were in the work cycle. It also took about 50% longer to assemble a car than when more traditional methods were used. Absenteeism also did not significantly reduce with the dock method. Volvo has returned to traditional assembly-line operation, using teams of workers rather than people working as individuals on the line.

Source: Volvo Car Corporation.

and skills will be available, as the work was expected. The quality of work produced may be higher, as the standard of equipment is high. The level of inventory held as spares is likely to be less.

(d) Overall maintenance objective

A company needs to have an **overall maintenance objective** for its maintenance operation. Such an objective may state that maintenance of plant and equipment shall be such that at all times it will be fit and safe to use for the purpose intended. To accomplish this, one or more **policy statements** are necessary. Policy statements may say, for example, that maintenance will normally be carried out to a predetermined plan, that the aim is to provide good service at lowest cost, and that inventory of spares must be kept as low as possible.

(e) Maintenance records

Various strategies are needed to accomplish these policies – for example, to have a predetermined plan, every piece of plant and equipment must be noted with regard to make, age, service history if available, maker's service requirements, special tools or lubricants. A **log sheet** needs to be designed for each piece to record this information.

Records of individual and group down times must be recorded so that service levels can be established an improved upon: **service level** can be regarded as:

$$(100 - \text{down time } \%)$$

The following need to be **obtained** or **established:**

- Plant records
- Operating conditions
- Makers' manuals
- Statutory requirements (HASAWA, COSH, etc.)
- Factors which affect deterioration
- Historical records
- Frequency and type of inspection
- Set up maintenance schedules, monitor and revise.

Once the maintenance programme has been put into operation, effort can be spent on estimating work loads, designing job cards, designating maintenance by repair or replacement, the methods to be used for maintenance and setting work standards and criteria of performance.

(f) **Measures of maintenance performance**

Measures of performance include:

$$\text{Availability} = \frac{\text{Total hours up and running} \times 100}{\text{Total hours available}}$$

$$\text{Response performance} = \frac{\text{Hours awaiting repair} \times 100}{\text{Down time hours}}$$

$$\text{Planning performance} = \frac{\text{Number of non scheduled jobs} \times 100}{\text{Total jobs done}}$$

$$\text{Labour efficiency} = \frac{\text{Standard hours achieved} \times 100}{\text{Time spent on measured work}}$$

$$\text{Cost efficiency} = \frac{\text{Total cost of repairs} \times 100}{\text{Number of repairs made}}$$

It should be noted that it is the **total** cost of maintenance that needs to be as low as possible. Figure 13.9 shows how the total costs vary for a preventive maintenance schedule. For a particular situation actual costs need to be estimated from an examination of times taken relating to waiting for repair and repair and test times. Costs of lost production and idle labour coupled with materials used and overheads rates will enable reasonable

---

Fig 13.9   Preventive maintenance

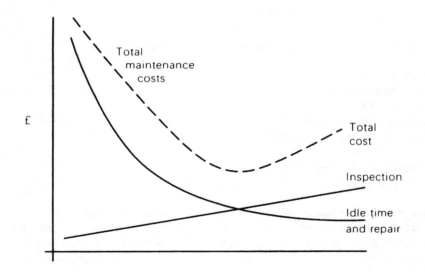

estimates to be made. Subsequent good record-keeping and analysis will mean that future information is more accurate.

(g) Replacement maintenance

Not all maintenance work is necessarily repair-only work. Some may be primarily **replacement maintenance**. Consider light bulbs, and assume that they are relatively inexpensive but that there are many in use in an organisation. Light bulbs cannot be repaired, but need to be replaced.

In a large organisation, the labour cost of changing one bulb will not be much less than to change several at that time. This is because the time to get the bulb from stores, go to the correct location, and after changing the bulb, go back to the stores, possibly with some paperwork authorising the work, is larger than the work of actually replacing one bulb. To call out a service person to change a bulb, and then find soon after that another bulb needs replacing is uneconomic. It may be better to replace **all bulbs in that area**, including ones that have not yet failed. The total cost will be a function of the set-up cost, the cost of a replacement bulb and the labour cost to replace a bulb. It will be factored by what is known about how long a bulb lasts: one does not want to replace a bulb which still has a lot of its life left.

If we never replace just one bulb at any one time, but every week replace all at the same time, it is very likely no bulbs will have failed and we will incur a certain fairly high total cost. If, however, we do the same as above but on a monthly basis, we will incur a different total cost, but we will expect some bulbs to have failed in the interim, with a loss of illumination. A third strategy could be to replace all bulbs on a quarterly basis. We could also monitor the cost of responding to a call to replace only bulbs which have burned out, replacing the appropriate number but only at the same visit. We could have a plan which meant we replaced only burned-out bulbs which we see on one of our trips on a weekly, monthly or quarterly basis.

An example of this type of maintenance will help clarify the thinking involved. It needs a careful logical approach because of the effects of probability on the various strategies possible. It will require data on the costs of different tasks involved and the past history of failed items.

In a chain of entertainment and leisure complexes, your records show that 750 lamps were replaced over a given time period. Their installation date and replacement date are also known.

Quantities	Life	Fraction of total
40 lamps lasted	1 month	.05
110 lamps lasted	2 months	.15
150 lamps lasted	3 months	.20
225 lamps lasted	4 months	.30
225 lamps lasted	5 months	.30
750 total		**1.00**

These fractions are your probabilities of occurrences. You can then calculate the average life of a lamp.

Quantities	Life in months	Total months
40	1	40
110	2	220
150	3	450
225	4	900
225	5	1125
750 total		2735/750 = **3.65 months average life**

What replacement policies exist? We could:

(a) only replace a lamp when it fails as an individual item. This costs £3 per lamp.
(b) replace all lamps every 1, 2, 3, 4 or 5 months (i.e. 5 separate policies) at a cost of £1 per lamp; and replace any that fail within the regular replacement interval, as individual replacements, as in **(a)** above. In this policy we have different combinations of £1 and £3 costs.

Policy (a)   Average life is 3.65 months. If we have 1000 lamps, say, then there are 1000/3.65 = 274 lamps to replace at £3 per lamp = **£822** total replacement cost for this policy.

Policy (b1) – Replace 1000 each month @ £1	£1000	
1000 lamps @ .05 = 50 failures @ £3	£150	**Total £1150**
		= **£1150/month**

Policy (b2) – Replace 1000 every 2 months @ £1	£1000	
Month 1 – 1000 @ .05 = 50 failures @ £3	£150	
Month 2 – 1000 @ .15 = 150 failures @ £3	£450	
50 @ .05 = 2.5 failures @ £3	£7.5	**Total £1607.5**
		= **£803.75/month**

Policy (b3) – Replace 1000 every 3 months @ £1	£1000	
Month 1 – 1000 @ .05 = 50 failures @ £3	£150	
Month 2 – 1000 @ .15 = 150 failures @ £3	£450	
50 @ .05 = 2.5 failures @ £3	£7.5	
Month 3 – 1000 @ .2 = 200 failures @ £3	£600	
150 @ .05 = 7.5 failures @ £3	£22.5	
50 @ .15 = 7.5 failures @ £3	£22.5	**Total £2252.5**
		= **£750.8/month**

Activity

Policy (b4) – Replace 1000 every 4 months @ £1   £1000
You enter the other costs involved for this policy against the failures listed below.
(Cost for this policy is **£820/month**.)

```
Month 1 – 1000 @ .05 =  50      failures @ £      = £
Month 2 – 1000 @ .15 = 150      failures @ £      = £
           50 @ .05 =   7.5     failures @ £      = £
Month 3 – 1000 @ .20 = 200      failures @ £      = £
          150 @ .05 =   7.5     failures @ £      = £
           50 @ .15 =   7.5     failures @ £      = £
Month 4 – 1000 @ .30 = 300      failures @ £      = £
          200 @ .05 =  10       failures @ £      = £
          150 @ .15 =  22.5     failures @ £      = £
           50 @  .2 =  10       failures @ £      = £      Total £_____
                                                  = £_____/month
```

Activity

Policy (b5) – Replace 1000 every 5 months @ £1 = £ 1000
You enter the failure rates and other costs involved for this policy according to
the data below. (Cost for this policy is **£890/month**.)

```
Month 1 – 1000 @        =        failures @ £      = £
Month 2 – 1000 @ .15    =        failures @ £      = £
           50 @         =        failures @ £      = £
Month 3 – 1000 @ .20    =        failures @ £      = £
          150 @         =        failures @ £      = £
           50 @ .05     =        failures @ £      = £
Month 4 – 1000 @        =        failures @ £      = £
          200 @ .05     =        failures @ £      = £
          150 @         =        failures @ £      = £
           50 @ .20     =        failures @ £      = £
Month 5 – 1000 @        =        failures @ £      = £
          300 @ .05     =        failures @ £      = £
          200 @         =        failures @ £      = £
          150 @ .20     =        failures @ £      = £
           50 @         =        failures @ £      = £      Total £_____
                                                  = £_____/month
```

The optimum policy is therefore to replace 1000 lamps all at once every
three months and replace on an 'as necessary' basis the failures that occur in
between regular replacements. It is therefore clear that a plan for
maintenance needs very careful thinking about before it is finalised, and
once put into action it should be monitored closely for **effectiveness**.

Activity

Without looking at your car handbook, make up a checklist of your own which outlines the jobs you ought to check for and do on a daily, weekly and monthly basis; and, if you can, on an every 5000 mile basis, too.

13.5 Materials Handling

(a) The basic premise

Materials handling is an activity which, while necessary, adds nothing to the value of the good or service, but can add considerably to the **cost**. As the price is likely not to based solely on total cost, any avoidable material handling costs will reduce its profitability.

(b) Key criteria

If possible, you should consider the following in the order suggested:

1 **Eliminate** as much handling as possible (i.e. does it have to be moved at all?)
2 **Simplify** the material handling requirements as much as possible.
3 **Combine** material handling with a productive operation (i.e. work on it while moving it).
4 Always try to **use the volume** of the building effectively.

(c) Unnecessary handling

We must avoid repetitious picking up and putting down of material: this will also have the important benefit of reducing potential for damage. If you have to pour out some powder weighing a specific amount, instead of pouring it and then weighing it separately, pour it out on the weighing machine. An example of **(3)** is the car assembly line where the car is moved along the conveyor while being transported.

(d) Gathering the facts on material handling

The most useful way to analyse what is happening is the critical examination method used earlier. In this way, you can find out precisely the current situation and generate some ideas as to what should happen. This should include a **to/from chart** or a **material flow chart**, to ensure that you will have collected sufficient quantitative information to help you in the next step.

• You will know by then precisely what has to be moved, where from and where to, and when and how much of it has to be moved.

- What has to be moved will influence the type of containers/holders (e.g. you may be moving edible substances, chemicals, raw or processed materials, metal, wood or plastic materials, etc.)
- Food may require refrigerated vehicles and/or stainless steel containers.
- Chemicals may require stainless containers or pressurised containers.
- Material may arrive in bulk in liquid or powder or granules. It may arrive continuously or intermittently.
- It may arrive prepackaged or need packaging.
- Upon arrival it may need to be broken down into manageable sizes, or be processed immediately.
- You will need to know how long it will take to move the material through your own process, as in some cases deterioration may occur after unpacking. Your own processes will determine in some cases what material handling aids you need if, for example, your own processes begin on the top floor of your plant, you will need conveyors and/or elevators to move your material up there.

(e) Premises and material handling

As you begin to make your decisions as to what you will use to move and handle your material, you will need to assess the suitability (or otherwise) of your existing premises for those handling aids.

- Are there any alterations to aisles, entrances and exits that need to be made?
- Are the floors strong enough, and do door joists need to be added or strengthened to take additional loads?
- Are electrical and pneumatic power supplies sufficient?
- Will you be compromising safety requirements if certain alterations are made?

(f) Materials handling equipment

Handling and using material in bulk is often the cheapest way for high volume material requirements.

- If material is handled in small quantities, then **palletisation** is convenient and widely used. A 'pallet' is a wooden tray into which the forks of a fork lift truck can fit. The material to be moved is stacked onto the pallet.
- It is sometimes possible to have the benefits of a pallet by forming the **material itself** into a rigid load by banding it or transparently sealing it, and leaving space for the truck's forks; bricks are often moved like this.
- For containers like barrels, a fork lift truck can be fitted with clamps. For moving rolls of carpet the forks can be replaced with a spindle.
- Whereas hand trucks, pallet trucks, trolleys and fork lift trucks take up floor space, conveyors can be used as overhead movers, so more

effectively using the volume of the building, and allowing maximum use of floor space for other purposes. Conveyors are very widely used and may be electrically or gravity powered.

- If the amount of material to be moved allows it, and the material is moved in small units, narrow reach high lift trucks can utilise high bay shelving, yet again utilising fully the volume of the building.

(g) Material handling costs

In all cases, however, there are costs to be considered. These costs consist of **(a)** the capital cost, **(b)** the equipment running cost, **(c)** the cost of floor space used, **(d)** the labour cost associated with using the equipment, **(e)** maintenance costs and **(f)** the depreciation costs; note that this last cost is not a cash cost but must be allowed for so as to build up a **replacement fund**.

The **capital costs** are the costs involved in **acquiring** the equipment you have chosen. The decision will be one made at a high level, often by the board, for major capital expenditure. To justify such expenditure you will have to present, clearly and persuasively, the costs and benefits of your proposal. You will need to be able to quantify the benefits in terms of time saved, reduction of damage potential, reduction or stability of labour involved in materials handling, reduction in potential for theft and reduction in costs per unit moved. You may need to show how your proposals integrate with those of your present suppliers and customers. The time scale of such savings will also be important, and some discounted savings calculations may need to be made.

For **equipment running costs**, the suppliers can sometimes provide data, but it is prudent to check these against your own experience, particularly regarding overheads.

Maintenance is important, particularly as once a comprehensive system is installed, unexpected breakdowns cause chaos, as well as cost: this is where the benefits of **planned maintenance** pay dividends.

(h) Computerised materials handling

- For some work, computerised handling systems provide an effective, if capital-intensive, solution. The Royal Mail has for many years employed a variety of complex sorting and moving devices to process millions of pieces of mail per day throughout the country.
- The use of computerised high bay stacking equipment with automated (customer) order picking and conveyor routeing systems is widely used. Random location ability in set-ups like these means that no space is wasted merely because items allocated to specific locations happen to be out of stock. This principle of fully computerised random location high density stacking is epitomised in the 18-storey-high automated car park in Seoul, Korea.

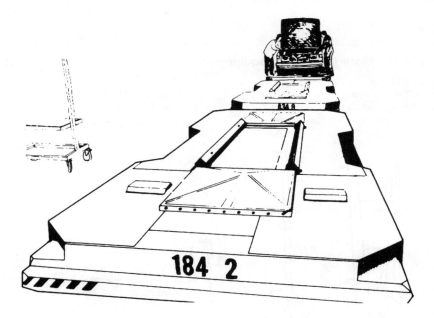

With the Kalmar plant, a new production technology was introduced into Sweden: the computer-controlled carrier (the assembly platform).

The assembly is carried out on the assembly platforms, which move themselves independently of each other. Each platform contains four batteries, an electric motor for driving the platform and a computer receiver. The platforms are controlled individually by signals from a central computer. The signals are transmitted in cables in the floor.

With the help of the batteries, the body can also be tilted 90° to facilitate work under the body.

This system with assembly platforms gives a very high flexibility and is used today in several plants within the Volvo Group.

Source: Volvo Car Corporation.

Fig 13.10   The carrier which has written history

- Many manufacturing operations use computerised job preparation derived from a predetermined schedule, and combine that with automatically delivering work to the cell which needs it. Finished work is also collected and returned to stores. Work in progress is monitored continuously. Parts are stacked in random locations in a warehouse in locations chosen by the computer.

Figure 13.10 shows the computer controlled carrier used at Volvo's Kalmar plant. Figures 13.11 to 13.13 show a selection of the more common material handling equipment.

Fig 13.11   Material handling equipment

a   Sacktruck
b   Wheeled towing handle
c   Handpallet truck
d   Counterbalanced fork truck

e   Reach truck
f   Overhead chain installation
g   Gravity wheel conveyor

Source: Department of Industry

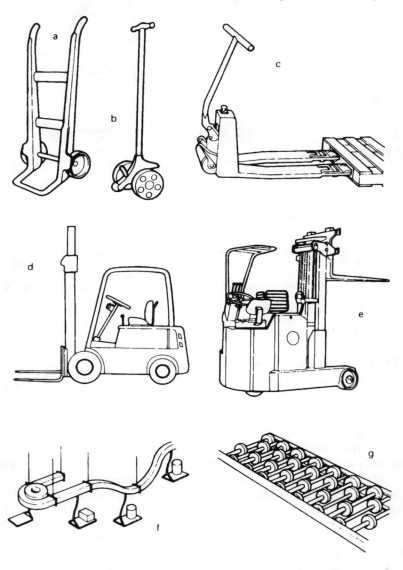

Fig 13.12 Continuous material movement

Continuous movement — Conveying equipment

TRANSPORTING					FREE ROLLING	SLIDING	PROPELLING	VIBRATING
Towing mechanism	Powered conveyors				Line			
	Continuous carrying	Linked carriers	Detachable carriers	Continuous propulsion	Unpowered	Unpowered	Powered	Powered
						Intermittent	Continuous	Continuous
Overhead towline trolley conveyors In-floor towline trolley conveyors Robot tugs	Flat belt; troughed: closed belt; slat; carrier and chain conveyors	Bucket, *en masse*, apron and pan conveyors, crossbar conveyors	Overhead trolley conveyors Overhead chain conveyors	Powered roller conveyors Pneumatic conveyors Air film conveyors	Roller, wheel and ball tracks	Chutes	Screw conveyors Spiral elevators	Vibratory feeders, screens, elevators

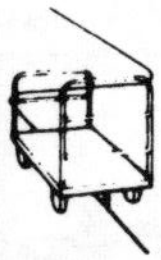

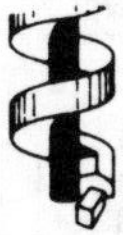

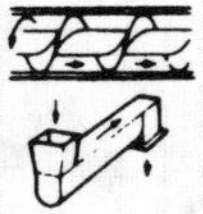

In conveyors of this type the transporting mechanism travels forward with the material conveyed

In conveyors of this type the transporting mechanism travels forward

In conveyors of this type the transporting mechanism does not itself travel forward

326

Fig 13.13   Forms in which material is moved and stored

Forms in which material is moved and stored

BULK	PIECE PARTS	PACKAGE	UNIT LOAD – SUPPORTED	UNIT LOAD – WITHOUT SUPPORT	INTER-MEDIATE BULK CONTAINER	CONTAINER
	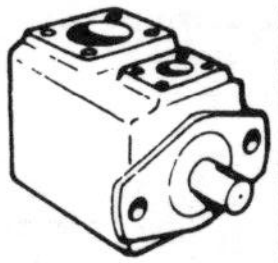		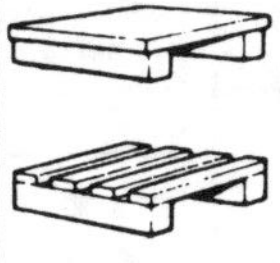			
Liquids Solids Pastes	Castings Forgings Components, etc.	Bag/Sack Drum Carton Cask Cylinder	Pallets Stillages Post pallets Box pallets	Built-in unit Shrink wrapped Stretch wrapped Strapped	Metal Plastic Other materials	End-loading Side-loading Top-loading

Activity

What kind of materials handling equipment can you find in a visit to **(a)** a department store, **(b)** a supermarket, **(c)** a garage, **(d)** the college cafeteria, **(e)** a DIY supermarket?

Chapter Review Questions

1 What is meant by the term 'green field site'?

2 Identify three key factors influencing site location.

3 'To be efficient, flow through a plant must be a straight line': True or False?

4 What are the four key flows in a plant?

5 How can you record and analyse flow in a plant?

6 What is required for a planned maintenance regime?

7 Identify three types of records needing to be established for planned maintenance.

8 Identify four measures of maintenance performance.

9 'Materials handling adds to the value but not to the cost': True or False?

10 'When considering material handling, efficient use of the plant's physical volume rather than area needs to be considered': True or False?

11 Identify three costs to consider in material handling.

12 'The more expensive and advanced the handling technology, the more efficient the result': True or False?

14 Managing Numbers: 1 – Key Distributions

Lord Kelvin said that if we can **quantify** something, we know more about it than if we have only subjective information about it. If we can then marshal the quantitative data and analyse it, we will know even more, provide ourselves with useful information and use what we have obtained for other purposes (e.g. forecasting, planning, scheduling, estimating or costing). For these reasons, we will examine the most common and useful ways to **manipulate** and **analyse** numerical data.

Learning Objectives

By the end of this chapter, you should:

1 be able to calculate the **mean** (the average) of a set of values, after choosing the most appropriate type of mean for the purpose
2 know what the relation is between the **mean**, the **median** and the **mode**
3 be able to produce a **histogram** for data in grouped form and with grouped frequencies
4 know what the **standard deviation** is, and be able to calculate and use it
5 be able to calculate the **least squares regression** line through a set of data, after first calculating the coefficient of linear correlation
6 know when and how to use the **normal, binomial, Poisson** and **hypergeometric distributions**, and the simpler relationships between them
7 be able to calculate from a labour learning curve the **expected time for the nth item produced**.

14.1 Averages

(a) The arithmetic average or mean

This is probably the most commonly used of several different types of average. An 'average' is used to obtain a single value from a set of several values, which can then replace them as a **representative indicator** of all the values from which it has been obtained. The arithmetic average is widely used, easy to calculate and understand. It may or may not correspond to one of the values in the set from which it was calculated, and it is affected by extreme values in the set. We usually use the term 'mean' for the average.

The mean is calculated from the formula:

Sum of all values in the set
Number of values in the set

For the mean to be most useful, the values from which it comes should not be too greatly different from each other.

The following values are the oil production in millions of tonnes for Africa for 1989 (these and other oil production figures are reproduced from the *BP Statistical Review of World Energy* (June 1990)):

Algeria	50.4
Angola	23.1
Egypt	44.5
Gabon	10.9
Libya	54.8
Nigeria	79.1
All others	24.5

The Arithmetic Mean is $287.3/7 = 41.0$ approximately. As can be seen, no country produced 41 million tonnes exactly, but it does seem to be a reasonably representative value.

Let us, however, repeat the calculation for the 1989 oil production figures for Asia/Australia, also in million tonnes:

Brunei	7.0
China	138.3
India	34.2
Indonesia	66.9
Japan	0.6
Malasia	28.3
Other Asia	5.0
Australasia	26.5

The arithmetic mean is $306.8/8 = 38.4$ approximately. While the numerical result is correct, it is apparent that 38.4 is hardly representative of the set. What is causing the problem is the **wide range of values**. The mean on its own is not sufficient to describe this set of values; a measure which describes their **spread** would be more useful, and we shall consider measures of spread later.

Notice also that if China's production were omitted, the new mean would be $168.5/7 = 24.0$ approximately, substantially less than the result above: the mean was heavily influenced by extreme values in the set.

Activity

Analyse the following data showing the oil production for 1989 in millions of tonnes for the Middle East, and calculate the arithmetic mean.

How could you present averages to make them more representative of the data?

What is the new average if the largest producer's output is misread as 2565 million tonnes?

Abu Dhabi	75.4
Dubai and N. Emirates	23.2
Iran	142.2
Iraq	138.6
Kuwait	79.4
Neutral Zone	20.9
Oman	29.4
Qatar	18.7
Saudi Arabia	256.5
Others	29.7

Activity

The following data is the oil production in millions of tonnes in the United Kingdom, from 1975 to 1989.

1975	1976	1977	1978	1979	1980	1981	1982
1.4	11.8	37.5	53.3	77.9	80.5	89.4	103.4

1983	1984	1985	1986	1987	1988	1989
114.9	125.9	128.2	128.6	123.3	114.4	91.9

Using a suitable calculation method for the mean, describe numerically, and very briefly descriptively, the United Kingdom's output from 1975 to 1989.

(b) The harmonic mean

The harmonic mean is used when **rates** are being considered (e.g. miles per hour or cost per unit). This is because time or number of units are not specified.

As an example, a motorist records the following average speeds on four different occasions. These averages are: 35 mph, 55 mph, 60 mph and 65 mph. What is the average speed?

The harmonic mean $= 4/(1/35 + 1/55 + 1/60 + 1/65)$
$$= 50.76 \, mph$$

Check that you agree that the arithmetic mean in this situation would be 53.75, which is inappropriate here.

Assume he drives 100 miles on each occasion. The time for each trip is therefore:

hours

$100/35 = 2.86$

$100/55 = 1.82$

$100/60 = 1.67$

$100/65 = \underline{1.54}$

7.89 hours for 400 miles $= 50.7$ mph

Now consider that the motorist bought some petrol on each of four separate occasions. The four prices per gallon were £1.90, £2.10, £2.25 and £2.40.

The true average price per gallon is given by the harmonic mean:

Average price $= 4/(1/1.90 + 1/2.10 + 1/2.25 + 1/2.40)$

$$= £2.146$$

and not the arithmetic mean $= £2.163$.

In this case there is not a lot of difference between the two means; however, one is the correct mean and the other is not. Verify them by assuming that the motorist purchased, say, £25 of petrol on each occasion.

Activity

Some campers bought eggs on each of their last five camping trips. The prices varied considerably, depending on where they were. The prices were: 70p, 85p, £1.20. £1.25 and £1.45 per dozen. What was the average price of eggs per dozen?

(c) The mode

The mode is a measure of **central tendency,** and we express it by noting the **most frequently occurring value** in a set of values. A set may have no mode, but if it does, there could be one or more. It is not affected by extreme values.

As an example, the number of hamburgers served weekly for 7 weeks in the summer by a small shop were: 425, 475, 504, 367, 342, 389 and 422. Although you can calculate the arithmetic mean, there is no mode to this set of values.

A shoe-shop's record of the sizes of its mens' shoes sold each week for the first 6 weeks of the new year were: 37 of size 8, 55 of size 9, 38 of size 10, 21 of size 11 and 3 of size 12. The modal size of shoe is size 9. Notice that even though we have ignored half sizes, the arithmetic mean is not a useful result, as the size 9.34 is meaningless. A similar situation exists with clothing sizes, which are themselves not a direct measurement of size.

(d) **The median**

The median is the item which separates the **top half** of the values from the **bottom half**. To find the median, we lay them out in **ascending order** and find the **middle value**. That value is the median. If there are an even number of values, we take the **arithmetic mean of the middle two values**, and that becomes the median value.

Activity

The number of patients seen daily by a doctor during two weeks in August were: 20, 18, 11, 23, 33, 22, 20, 27, 19, 25, 29, 31. If we lay out the number seen each day, in ascending order of magnitude, we get: 11, 18, 19, 20, 20, 22, 23, 25, 27, 29, 31, 33. The median value is therefore $(22 + 23)/2 = 22.5$ (note that the modal value is 20 appointments per day).
   Calculate the arithmetic mean number of patients seen.
   Notice that all three calculations produce different numerical results.
   In a department of six weekly-waged people, their wages are: £121, £104, £136, £129, £143 and £139. In ascending sequence of magnitude, they are: £104, £121, £129, £136, £139 and £143. The median wage is therefore $(£129 + £136)/2 = £132.50$.
   Notice that there is no modal value.
   Calculate the arithmetic mean wage correct to the nearest penny.

(e) **Relationship between the mean, median and mode**

There exists an empirical relationship between the mean, median and mode, which is:

$$\text{Mean-mode} = [(3 \times \text{mean}) - (3 \times \text{median})]$$

Graphically this is shown in Figures 14.1a and b. It is valid for single mode distributions which are only moderately asymmetrical.

(f) **The geometric mean**

The geometric mean (GM) is the correct mean to use if we want to average rates of change. It is sometimes also used for constructing index numbers.

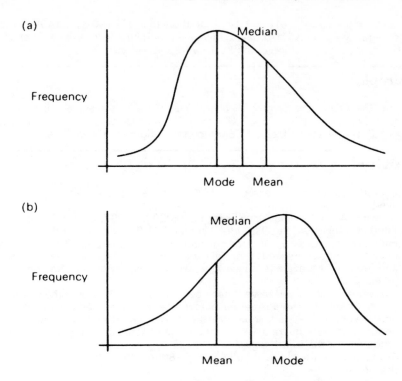

Fig 14.1 Relationship between the mean, median and mode
a Distribution skewed to the left
b Distribution skewed to the right

The geometric mean of two numbers is: $\sqrt[n]{x \cdot y}$ where x and y are the two numbers and n is how many there are; in this case there are 2. We therefore multiply the numbers together and take the nth root of the answer.

Suppose we want to find the GM of 2, 4, 6 and 8.

$$\text{GM} = \sqrt[4]{2 \cdot 4 \cdot 6 \cdot 8} = 4.427$$

(Note that the arithmetic average of the above four numbers is 5.)

Example

Suppose production has increased from a base value of 100 at the start of year 1, to 110 at the start of year 2, to 130 at the start of year 3. What is the average rate of increase over the two year period? The percentage increase for the first year is 110% and the increase for the second year is $(130 - 110)/110 = 118.18\%$.

The GM= $\sqrt[2]{1.10 \times 1.1818}$ = 1.1402 i.e. if we multiply 100 by 1.1402 and by 1.1402 again we obtain 130; our end of year 2 production level. We can therefore say our production level increased by 14% for each of two years.

Example

If productivity has increased by 8% over the last 3 years, the average increase in productivity per year is: $\sqrt[3]{1.08}$ = 1.026 i.e. 2.6% increase per year. If we calculate $1.00 \times 1.026 \times 1.026 \times 1.026 = 1.08$ which is the figure we were given.

Activity

(a) If productivity has increased by 15% over the last six years, what is the average annual productivity increase?*
(b) Sales for Acme Services have been: £200,000 for 1992; £400,000 for 1993; £600,000 for 1994, £800,000 for 1995 and £1,000,000 for 1996. The sales manager says sales are increasing 'quite nicely thank you'. The managing director is not convinced. What are the percentage increases year on year, and what is the average percentage sales increase per year for the entire period?*
(c) The value of scrap and rework has been reduced by 75% over the last three years. What is the average annual percentage reduction? If the value of scrap and rework at the start, three years ago, was £45,000 and improvements continue at the same rate, what is the value of scrap and rework likely to be at the end of the fourth year?*
(d) Productivity in the UK rose 155% from 1980 to 1991. What was the average rise per year?*

14.2 Dealing with Grouped Frequencies

(a) Range of values

When data has been summarised before it is presented for analysis, it is often in the form of a **range of values** and their associated **frequency of occurrence**, rather than presenting each value individually. This makes no difference to the calculations if it is remembered that the number of values is the **sum of the individual frequencies**. In other words, the frequencies are treated as if they are **weightings** for their associated value.

Consider the following data related to the number of life test results for an experimental heating element:

Frequency:	15	35	45	40	20	5	2
Hours:	0–10	10–20	20–30	30–40	40–50	50–60	60–70

We could calculate the mean by laying out the appropriate number of individual values, adding them together, and dividing by the number of values.

It is quicker, more convenient, and probably less error-prone if we multiply each value by its frequency of occurrence, add the results, and divide by the sum of frequencies. Because the results have already been grouped, the value for each time interval is assumed to be at the mid-point of each interval.

$$\text{Arithmetic mean} = \frac{\textbf{Sum of (mid-point hours)}}{\textbf{Sum of frequencies}}$$

$$= \frac{75 + 525 + 1125 + 1400 + 900 + 275 + 130}{15 + 35 + 45 + 40 + 20 + 5 + 2}$$

$$= 27.33 \text{ hours}$$

Activity

Find the modal life in hours. Find the estimated median life. (Remember that this involves placing all values in sequence of ascending magnitude.)

As the values are grouped, the median is the $(162/2) = 81$st value. This lies in the third group with a group frequency of 45 lamps in that category. It therefore lies $((81 - 50)/45) = 0.689$ of the way between 20–30 hours.

(b) Histograms

When dealing with numerical data, and particularly with data with which you are not familiar, it is often helpful to plot it, in order to get a **visual picture**. This is very useful when deciding if certain patterns such as cyclical or linear exist. In Figure 14.2, we have drawn a histogram of the data on lamp life test results we have just considered. It is a matter of some judgement when deciding on the **width** of the histogram columns. If the width is too narrow, there will be too many empty columns; if too wide, the shape will be hidden.

Notice that each column is centred on the **middle of the class interval**, which in this case is 10 hours. The total area under the histogram must equal the sum of each individual frequency × its average life. If the class intervals given are not all of the same width, when drawing a histogram the area under any one column must be **proportionately the same** as any other column (i.e. if a class interval is twice as wide as another, it must be drawn with a frequency of half the height).

Activity

In an analysis of lead times for a supplier, a company tabulated the following data.

Plot an appropriate histogram, and calculate the average lead time.

Find also the modal lead time and the median lead time.

What percentage of the lead times are less than 6 weeks, 12 weeks, 18 weeks and 20 weeks?

| **Frequency:** | 5 | 20 | 10 | 14 | 8 | 6 |
| **Weeks:** | 0–2 | 2–4 | 4–6 | 6–10 | 10–14 | 14–20 |

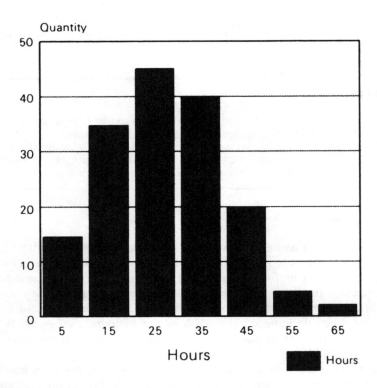

Fig 14.2 Test results: the histogram

14.3 Variation

Knowing the mean for a set of data is useful, but in most cases does not supply us with sufficient information for subsequent use. The reason is that we have not yet considered how a set of data **varies about its mean**. So far, we have just considered the mean alone. Intuitively, we can imagine that it will be harder to exercise control over values with a large variation than over those which cluster closely around the mean.

Consider the three sets of values below:

1	11	2	4	1	7	9	3	6	8	9
2	6	5	6	5	4	6	7	8	7	6
3	5	6	7	6	5	7	5	7	7	5

If we calculate the arithmetic mean for set **1** and set **2** data, the means are 6.0 for both. Is that sufficient to describe the data? If we look closely we can probably see that set **1** is rather more variable about its mean than set **2** is about its mean. We say that set **1** data has a **greater spread**, and we can also see that set **2** has a greater spread than set **3**. How can we describe this spread?

(a) Range

We could measure the **range** of each set of data. The range is the difference between the **smallest** and **largest** value in each set. In set **1** the range is $11 - 1 = 10$ units, and in set **2** the range is $8 - 4 = 4$ units. What is the range of values in set **3**?

By its nature the range is dependent only on the **extreme values** and says nothing about how the remainder of the data is distributed. It is however a quick and easy measure of spread.

(b) Mean absolute deviation

If we calculate the difference between each value and its mean, ignore the sign, add them together and divide by the number of values, we obtain an indication of the variation which considers all values. This is called the **mean absolute deviation**. The 'absolute' sum means that we ignore the negative sign when adding:

$$\text{Mean absolute deviation} = \frac{\text{Absolute sum of } (x - \text{average})}{n}$$

where x is each value taken in turn.

In the case of set **1** we have:

$11 - 6 = 5$, $2 - 6 = 4$ (omit sign), $4 - 6 = 2$ (omit sign), $1 - 6 = 5$ (omit sign), $7 - 6 = 1$, $9 - 6 = 3$, $3 - 6 = 3$ (omit sign), $6 - 6 = 0$, $8 - 6 = 2$, $9 - 6 = 3$

Sum of deviations $= 5 + 4 + 2 + 5 + 1 + 3 + 3 + 0 + 2 + 3 = 28$

Mean absolute deviation $= 28/10 = 2.8$

Activity

Calculate the mean absolute deviation of sets **2** and **3**.

14.4 **The Standard Deviation**

(a) **The basic formula**

The standard deviation is the most important measure of spread of a set of values, not only because it considers all values but because it has certain well-defined properties which allow it to be used for further important purposes (e.g. **statistical process control**). The standard deviation is the **root mean square** of a set of values. The basic formula is:

$$\text{Standard deviation} = \sqrt{\left[\frac{\sum (x - \bar{x})^2}{n}\right]}$$

where $\sum$ is 'sum of', and '$\bar{x}$' is the mean.

Other formulae exist to facilitate calculation, and for using grouped data. Most scientific calculators have a standard deviation function enabling its easy calculation.

Note:

If we do not take the square root of the above calculation, we obtain the **variance**. While the **variance** is essential for more complex statistical calculations, we shall concern ourselves only with use of the standard deviation.

Consider again our set **1** data:

We have already calculated the variation from the mean for each value:

$$(x - \bar{x}) = \quad 5 \quad 4 \quad 2 \quad 5 \quad 1 \quad 3 \quad 3 \quad 0 \quad 2 \quad 3$$

$$\frac{\sum (x - \bar{x})^2}{n} = \frac{\sum (25 + 16 + 4 + 25 + 1 + 9 + 9 + 0 + 4 + 9)}{10}$$

$$= 10.2 = \text{variance which are 'squared' units}$$

To revert to the original units, we take the square root $= 3.19 = $ standard deviation.

If the set **1** values were those of the whole population, we use the above formula, but if the values are a **sample** of the population, we divide by $(n - 1)$ not by n. This is because the sample standard deviation tends to underestimate the standard deviation for the whole population. This **correction factor** is hardly necessary if n is about 25 or above. In this case where $n = 10$, the sample standard deviation $= 3.37$ or an increase of 5.6%.

Activity

For set **2** and **3** data set, calculate the standard deviation using both formulae, and using the properties of the standard deviation below, check the percentage of values lying within given ranges.

(b) **Properties of the standard deviation**

As we mentioned earlier, the standard deviation has certain well-**defined** and useful properties. For a population of about 30 or more values, we expect the mean ± 1 standard deviation to include about 68% of all values. The mean ± 2 standard deviations will include about 95% of all values. The mean ± 3 standard deviations will include about 99.8% of all values. The data plot shown in Figure 14.3 has been calculated to enable us to find the percentage of values which should fall within a **specified** number of standard deviations around the mean: this assumes that the values are reasonably symmetrically placed about the mean. The percentages and ranges for standard deviations have been tabulated in a standardised form and will be referred to again in this chapter.

In our case of set **1** values, 95% of the values should fall within the mean = $6.0 \pm (2 \times 3.19) = 0$ to 12.38. In this case they all lie within this band. Just over two-thirds of all values should lie within $6.0 \pm (1 \times 3.19) = 2.81$ to 9.19. For the set **1** values, 7 lie in this range.

14.5 **Comparing Variability of Different Sets of Data**

It is sometimes useful to be able to compare the relative variability of two sets of data. This can be done by calculating the ratio of standard deviation to the mean. In the case of our set **1** values above, the mean is 6.0 and the standard deviation is 3.19. The coefficient of variability = 3.19/6.0 = 0.53.

Activity

Calculate the coefficient of variability for sets **2** and **3** data above. Notice that because this coefficient is a **ratio**, we can compare the **relative variability** of different items.

Example 1

The mean monthly sales of coffee are 125 packets with a standard deviation of 11. The mean monthly sales of tea are 238 packets with a standard deviation of 19. The coefficient of variability for coffee is 11/125 = 0.088. For tea, it is 19/238 = 0.08. Tea has a greater absolute variation than coffee and is less variable relative to coffee.

14.6 **Correlation and Linear Regression**

(a) **Data relationships**

In many situations it is useful to determine if a **straight line association** presents a reasonable picture of two sets of data (e.g. sales and time, or

Fig 14.3   Plots of different data
a   Excellent linear association
b   Modest linear association
c   Probably a curvilinear association
d   No linear association at all

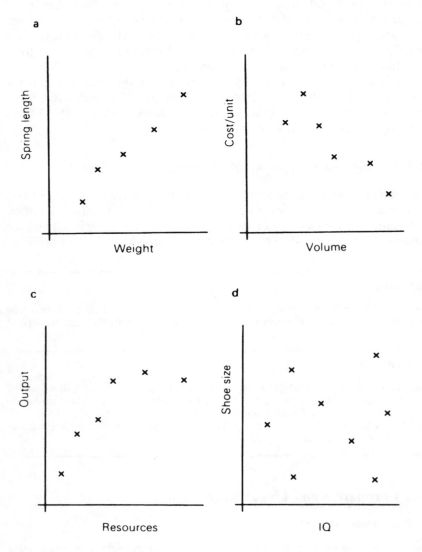

height and weight, or the length of a spring and the weight hung on it). We are not referring here to cause and effect, merely a **numerical association**. If there is such a linear association, then a straight line makes a convenient model because of its simplicity. It may be, of course, that if there is no apparent linear association, then some particular curved line model may be more suitable, but for our purposes, we will consider only straight lines.

Consider Figure 14.3.

In Figure 14.3a there is a **very close linear relationship** between the y and x values, and it would be reasonable to try to find the best straight line through them.

In Figure 14.3b there seems to be a **modest linear association** between the y and x values, although not as close as in Figure 14.4a.

In Figure 14.3c there seems to be a **curvilinear relationship** between the data, and an attempt to put a straight line through the data is not a realistic thing to do.

In Figure 14.3d there seems to be **no relationship** of any kind between the data, and certainly not a linear one.

(b) Correlation

There is an indicator which can be calculated to show the degree of linear association between two sets of data. It varies between $+1$ and -1. A positive value of 1 indicates a perfect linear association and the trend line slopes upwards from lower left to upper right. A negative value of -1 indicates a perfect linear association and the trend line sloping from upper left to lower right. A value of zero indicates no linear association at all. Values in between show varying levels of linear association.

The coefficient of linear correlation 'r' can be calculated from the expression:

$$ r = \frac{n \cdot \sum xy - \sum x \cdot \sum y}{\sqrt{[((n \cdot \sum x)^2 - (\sum x)^2) \cdot (n \cdot \sum y^2 - (\sum y)^2))]}} $$

Here, $\sum (x^2)$ means 'square each x value' and add as you go, and the . means 'multiply'.

Example 2

Consider the data below, which relates sales to advertising expenditure: we assume that y is the dependent variable (i.e. sales volume depends on advertising).

Advertising £1000	Sales volume £1000
x	y
2	50
4	70
4	83
4	97
5	100
5	110

Plot the data to get a visual picture. It seems to suggest a modest linear association.

x	y	x.y	x^2	y^2
2	50	100	4	2500
4	70	280	16	4900
4	83	332	16	6889
4	97	388	16	9409
5	100	500	25	10,000
5	110	550	25	12,100
24 $\sum x$	510 $\sum y$	2150 $\sum x \cdot y$	102 $\sum (x^2)$	45,798 $\sum (y^2)$

Number of readings $n = 6$.

$$r = \frac{(6 \times 2150) - (24 \times 510)}{\sqrt{[((6 \times 102) - (24 \times)) \times ((6 \times 45,798) - (510 \times 510))]}}$$

$r = 660/\sqrt{(36 \times 14,688)} = 0.908$ (i.e. quite a good linear association).

Statistically, an 'r' value less than about 0.75 indicates a fairly poor linear association. In this case, however, it is not unreasonable to calculate a linear regression line for this data.

(c) **Linear regression**

This is a mathematical technique which finds the **best straight line** through a set of data. It is based on the principle that the best line is one which minimises the sum of all the squared errors of each point away from the line itself. It is called the method of **least squares**.

A straight line model (see Figure 14.4) is simple, which is one of its main attractions. You can see from Figure 14.4 that the straight line cuts the y axis at a point 'a' above zero. The slope of the line, which can be up or down, is given by the tangent of the angle of slope.

Any straight line can be described fully by:

$$y = a + b \cdot x$$

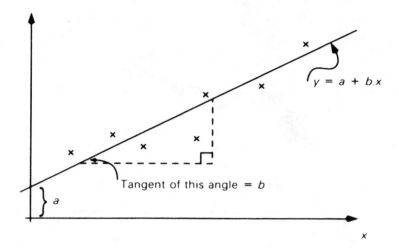

Fig 14.4   A straight line model

where *a* is the intercept, and *b* is the tangent of the angle of slope. If the algebraic sign of '*b*' is negative, the line has a downward slope. If '*a*' has a negative sign, the line cuts the '*y*' axis below zero.

In Figure 14.5 you can see the principle of least squares illustrated graphically. For any given line, and for each point on it, the vertical distance from the point to the line is squared and summed. This can be done for a variety of different lines. For the 'best' line, that sum of squared errors will be a **minimum**. The formula below enables us to calculate the value '*a*' and '*b*' for this line:

For the regression line $y = a + b \cdot x$

$$b = \frac{n \cdot \sum (x \cdot y) - (\sum x \cdot \sum y)}{n \cdot \sum (x^2) - (\sum x)^2}$$

$$a = \bar{y} - b \cdot \bar{x}$$

where $\bar{x}$ is the mean of all *x* values, and $\bar{y}$ is the mean of all *y* values.

Referring to our sales volume and advertising problem above, we can calculate:

$$b = \frac{(6 \times 2150) - (24 \times 510)}{(6 \times 102) - (24 \times 24)}$$

$$b = 18.33$$

$$a = (510/6) - (18.33 \times 24/6)$$

$$a = 11.67$$

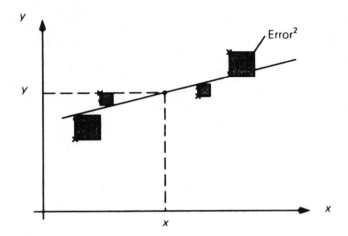

Fig 14.5   The least squares principle

Finally, superimpose this calculated regression line on to your original plot, and see how close your own line by eye was compared to this calculated line.

You should be aware that in presenting the essential tools for analysis, we are not questioning the **statistical significance** of our results (i.e. could such results have occurred by chance?) for correlation coefficients, of the '*a*' and '*b*' values in our regression line. More advanced statistical techniques are available to answer these questions satisfactorily. Where we have a reasonable number of values for analysis (say, 10 to 15 or more) then we can probably avoid such tests without running too many risks.

Activity

In the regression problems below, you are not concerned with the statistical significance of the results, just the results and their interpretation.

1 Plot the data below, calculate the coefficient of linear correlation and the regression line of the form $y = a + bx$. Ensure you are clear which is the *x* data and which is the *y* data. What load will result in a spring length of 25 cms? What will the spring length be if a load of 20 Kgs is applied?*

Load in Kgs	0	2	4	6	8	10	12	14	16	18
Spring length in cms	20	22	22	26	26	28	30	32	34	34

2 Plot the data below, calculate the correlation coefficient and the regression.

Average number of errors per 100 units produced	3.0	2.1	2.0	1.5	1.6	1.4	1.3
Minutes to produce one unit	5	5.5	6	6.5	7	7.5	8.0

How many errors might you expect if the cycle time per unit is 8.5 minutes?*
Comment on the meaning / interpretation for the approximate results (a) $y = 5$,
$x = 0$ and (b) $y = 0$, $x = 10$. What does this suggest about predicting results
from regression lines?

3 First, estimate the correlation coefficient and regression line for the data, then
plot the data and calculate the correlation coefficient and regression line, and
compare your guess with the calculation:*

x	1	2	3	4	5
y	1	2	3	4	0

How might you interpret the results?

4 The results of a three-stage advertising campaign are shown below, in terms of
the cost of the campaign, and the demand attributable to different levels of
advertising.

Advertising expenditure in £000s	0 zero adv.	5 Stage 1	10 Stage 1	15 Stage 1	20 Stage 1	25 Stage 1	35 Stage 2	45 Stage 2
Attributable demand in £000s	50	100	90	110	240	280	310	550
Advertising expenditure in £000s	55 Stage 2	65 Stage 2	75 Stage 2	90 Stage 3	105 Stage 3	120 Stage 3	135 Stage 3	150 Stage 3
Attributable demand in £000s	600	780	760	975	1000	1100	1050	1150

For each of the following stages and combinations of stages in sequence, plot
the appropriate sets of data, calculate the correlation coefficient and the
regression line:

stage 1,   stage 2,   stages 1 and 2,   stage 3,   stages 2 and 3,   all three stages.*

   For each stage and combination of stages, forecast the likely demand for an
advertising expenditure **outside** the range of data in that particular stage and
compare it with the actual demand. What does that suggest to you about
forecasting results (a) from partial data, and (b) from outside the data set
collected? Do the coefficients of *x* seem to reflect the data you plotted?
Considering the data for all three stages together, does this regression model
seem to be the most appropriate; what else could you suggest?

5 The data below shows the price and capacity for two types of hard disk
(capacity in megabytes).
   Plot the data for each type of disk. Calculate the coefficient of correlation and
the regression line for each type of disk, and for the combined data.*
   What would you expect the price to be for a 400 Mb IDE disk based (a) on IDE
regression and (b) on SCSI regression? How meaningful is the (b) answer?
   What would you expect the price to be for a 1200 Mb SCSI disk based (a) on
SCSI regression and (b) on IDE regression? How meaningful is the (b) answer?
   How meaningful is the regression line based on combined data? What does
this suggest about such analysis in general?

Hard disk capacity Mbs (type IDE)	£ cost retail	Hard disk capacity Mbs (type SCSI)	£ cost retail
42	115	426	899
89	175	676	940
130	268	811	1000
211	339	1037	1149
245	389	1415	1299
330	579	1900	1649

14.7 Distributions – Various

Distributions are mathematical models which describe the way different sets of data are related to frequency of occurrence. Their importance lies in the fact that if a suitable mathematical model can be found which closely matches the distribution of the data, that data can be **summarised by the model**, which is then used for predictive or other analytical purposes.

There are five important mathematical distributions which we shall consider:

- Normal
- Binomial
- Poisson
- Hypergeometric
- Negative exponential – Learning curve.

(a) The normal distribution

(i) Properties of the normal distribution
The normal distribution is used where the actual distribution of values around their mean is reasonably **symmetrical** (i.e. there about as many below the mean as above the mean), and where measurements of data are taken. When there are large numbers of discrete data, the normal distribution is often used for convenience. It was developed by the mathematician Gauss, and is sometimes called a Gaussian distribution. It is a **smooth bell-shaped curve**, whose approximate shape is found in many situations in real life. Because of this, we often use the normal distribution as a suitable model. Although it has a complicated formula, it has been completely tabulated in standardised form (see Figure 14.13, p. 369). It has the property of being able to tell us the theoretical percentage of all values which lie between any specified number of standard deviations.

Whenever a measurement is affected by a large number of small independent factors, none of which predominates, the distribution tends to be normal. The distribution of means of samples (a feature of statistical process control) tends to normality regardless of the shape of the parent population. An important result in this regard is:

$$\textbf{Standard error of the mean} = \frac{\textbf{Standard deviation}}{\sqrt{n}}$$

where n = number in the sample.

Example 3

Suppose the number of days lost per month in a company = 5.4 with a standard deviation = 3.5. If the sample size from which it came = 500, the standard error of the mean = $3.5/\sqrt{500}$ = 0.16. We can expect with a confidence of 95% (corresponding as before to the mean ± 2 standard deviations), that the average days lost will lie between $5.4 - (2 \times 0.16)$ and $5.4 + (2 \times 0.16)$ (i.e. between 5.08 and 5.72 days).

Notice that if our data had come from a sample of 100, the standard error of the mean would now = $3.5/\sqrt{100}$ = 0.35. Hence our limits at the same confidence level would be $5.4 - (2 \times 0.35)$ and $5.4 + (2 \times 0.35)$ (i.e. between 4.7 and 6.1 days).

Fig 14.6   The normal distribution: the bell-shaped curve

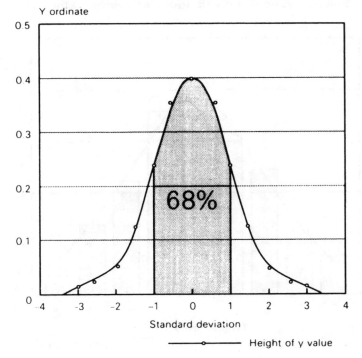

Height of y value

Figure 14.6 shows the **normal distribution**. For the normal distribution, **the mean = the mode = the median**. The curve is tabulated in standardised form, so that the mean = 0, and the standard deviation = 1. The area under the curve = 1.00 (i.e. 100%). The table itself quotes the probability of exceeding a particular value of z. To convert this probability to a percentage, we multiply by 100. This standardising of the normal curve enables it to be useful for any suitable data from any source.

To use the normal table we transform our own data to 'z' values by the transformation:

$$z = (x - \mu)/\sigma$$

where μ = population mean, and σ = standard deviation.

If we are using the normal as an approximation to the binomial (see p. 352), Figure 14.7 shows we must make a correction because the binomial deals with discrete data, and the normal with continuous data.

If $z = (x - \mu)/\sigma$, we let $x = 12$ (say), and we can ask 'what percentage is more than 12?'. We must find z by substituting in the above conversion equation: $z = (11.5 - \mu)/\sigma$.

Fig 14.7   Binomial vs normal distributions: an approximation

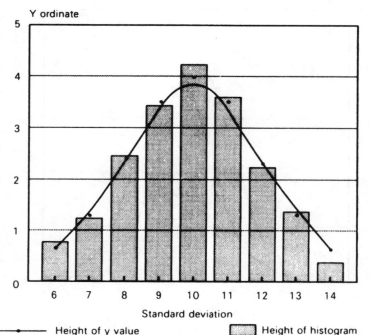

Y ordinate

Standard deviation

———•——— Height of y value   ▨ Height of histogram

(ii) **Using the normal distribution**

Example 4

Consider a telephone coil which should have a nominal mean electrical resistance of 23 ohms with a maximum allowable resistance of 26 ohms. From an extremely large number of coils the following results were obtained: mean resistance $= 24.3$ ohms and standard deviation $= 0.7$ ohms. Because of the extremely large number of coils used to obtain the values, we can assume them to represent the true values of the population.

(a) What percentage of the coil population should we expect to be **greater than** the 26.0 ohm maximum value?

$$z = (x - \bar{x})/\sigma$$
$$= (26.0 - 24.3)/0.7 = 2.43 \text{ standard deviations}$$

Looking at our standardised normal table the probability lies, by interpolation, three-fifths of the way between the probability for $z = 2.40$ and $z = 2.45$, in this case our probability $= 0.0082 - (0.6 \times (0.0082 - 0.00714)) = 0.0076$ approximately or 0.76%.

(b) Suppose the maximum allowable resistance were to be shifted from 26.0 to 26.5 ohms, what difference would that make to the percentage of rejects produced? As before we have:

$$z = (x - \bar{x})/\sigma$$

$z = (26.5 - 24.3)/0.7 = 3.14$ standard deviations; by inspection in our table we can see that the probability is going to be less than 0.00135 or about 0.135%.

(c) What percentage of all coils will have a resistance value **between** 23.0 ohms and 25.0 ohms? These values have been chosen arbitrarily, and the method for solution will be the same for any values. We first need to find the z value for each of the two resistance values quoted. $z1 = (23 - 24.3)/0.7 = -1.86$. The minus sign indicates that the value 23 ohms is below the mean. $z2 = (25 - 24.3)/0.7 = 1.00$. Our table of normal values shows probabilities from the extreme right-hand tail, in towards the left. If we have negative z values we can use the same table as the curve is symmetrical, and assume that the probabilities lie from the extreme left hand tail, in towards the right.

For our $z1 = -1.86$, the tail area $= 0.032$ approximately, by interpolation; and for our $z2 = 1.00$, the tail area $= 0.159$ approximately. But these values show the probability of all coils lying from the extreme tips of the curves, in towards the values stated. We also know that the entire area under the curve, by definition, equals 1.00 (or 100% of all items). Therefore the probability of all coils having a resistance between 23 and 25 ohms is $1.00 - (0.032 + 0.159) = 0.809$ or 80.9%.

(d) When something went wrong with the process, it was later found that the standard deviation was in fact 0.9 ohms, and the mean had shifted to 24.5 ohms.

1 What is the percentage of all coils now with a resistance **greater** than 26 ohms?

2 If the standard deviation could not be improved (i.e. reduced) what should the actual mean be set to, so as to produce no more than 1% of all coils above 26 ohms maximum?

1 As before we have:

$$z = (26 - 24.5)/0.9 = 1.67$$

The probability of this being exceeded is, by interpolation 0.048 or 4.8%.
2 We can write:

$$z = (x - \bar{x})/\sigma.$$

This time we are told z must equal 0.01 (i.e. 1%). Look in the body of the table to find a z value which has a probability equal to 0.01 of being exceeded. By interpolation, we find that z lies half way between 2.30 and 2.35 (i.e. 2.33 approximately – make sure you can see how interpolation is done here). This time we find how far down 0.01 is from 0.01072, and divide it by the difference between 0.01072 and 0.00939. We then pro-rate the proportion between 2.30 and 2.35 = 2.33 approximately.

We then write:

$$2.33 = (26 - x)$$

Therefore by rearranging the equation to find x, we have:

$$2.097 = (26 - x)/0.9,$$

hence $x = 23.90$. You can check this by writing:

$$z = (x - \bar{x})/\sigma; \quad (26 - 23.0)/0.9 = 2.33$$

and you can check back in your table that this indeed does come to about 0.01 (i.e. 1%).

Figure 14.8 shows all these calculations diagrammatically.

Activity

The Hammy Hamburger Company produces thousands of its famous '150 grammers' per week. A weight check on several thousand produced an actual mean weight of 148 grams and a standard deviation of 3 grams.

(a) What percentage of the hamburgers is **less** than the nominal weight of 150 grams?
(b) What percentage of hamburgers is **heavier** than 155 grams?
(c) The company may be prosecuted if more than 1% of its hamburgers is lighter than 145 grams. What percentage is **below** this weight?
(d) To what weight must they set their actual mean so as to avoid possible prosecution?
(e) Based on **(d)** above, how many extra kilos of meat do they use per week, assuming 25,000 hamburgers per week?

(f) To what new value do they have to improve their standard deviation bearing in mind **(c)** above, so that they can set and hold their mean weight to 150 grams?
(g) They achieve **(f)** above, and then take a sample of 100 hamburgers. The mean weight is 149 grams and the standard deviation is 2 grams. Is the machine likely or not likely to be running at an actual mean of 150 grams?

Fig 14.8   Coil population calculations: questions a, b, c and d in diagram format

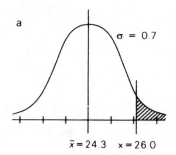

a

σ = 0.7

x̄ = 24.3   x = 26.0

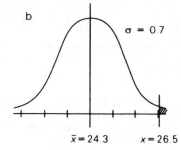

b

σ = 0.7

x̄ = 24.3   x = 26.5

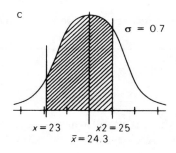

c

σ = 0.7

x = 23   x2 = 25
x̄ = 24.3

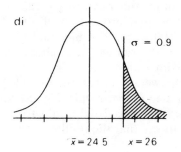

di

σ = 0.9

x̄ = 24.5   x = 26

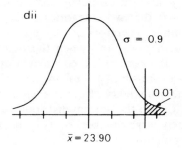

dii

σ = 0.9

0.01

x̄ = 23.90

Activity

(a) Measure the heights in centimetres of each member of your class. Calculate the mean and standard deviation.

Determine the 68%, 95% and 99.7% limits to the heights from the table, and compare by counting the actual number of class members who fall between each set of limits.

If the theory and actual results differ, why might this be?

(b) Take samples of 5 class members and calculate the mean height. Calculate the standard error of the mean, and compare the percentage of all means that lie between the standard error limits set at (say) 95%.

Note that for a class of 30 members there are: $30!/(25! \times 5!) = 142{,}506$ ways to select groups of 5 from 30. (The '!' sign means factorial, and 5! means factorial $5 = 5 \times 4 \times 3 \times 2 \times 1 = 120$.)

Activity

Get prior permission to time how long it takes to pay for snacks and/or meals at your cafeteria. Calculate the mean time and the standard deviation.

Can you explain, if necessary, why there is a small or why there is a large standard deviation?

How might you try to reduce the mean time to pay?

If the standard deviation is large compared with the mean (say, a ratio of standard deviation to mean of 0.2 or greater) how could you try to reduce the standard deviation?

Do you see a real difference between what influences the mean and what influences the standard deviation?

(b) The binomial distribution

The binomial distribution is a distribution which is useful when the events being considered can be separated into only **two** categories – for example, items being classified into 'OK' and 'not OK'.

For convenience, the proportion as a decimal in one category is often called 'p' and the proportion as a decimal in the other category is called 'q'. Note that the two categories make up the total proportion of 1.00 (i.e. everything). Therefore $q = 1 - p$ or $q\% = 100 - p\%$. The binomial is symmetrical if $p = q$, and when the number in the sample, n, is about 30 or greater, the normal is a convenient approximation to it.

The expression $(p + q)^n$ means 'to the power of n', can be expanded to give the probability of occurrence of each item in the sample. Notice this is in contrast to the normal distribution where we considered results from 'an extremely large number' so as to be able to say that the results came from the population.

For the **binomial distribution, the mean** $= n \times p$ **as a number, or the mean** $= p$ **as a proportion.**

The **standard deviation** $= \sqrt{[n \times p \times q]}$ **as a number, or** $= \sqrt{[(p \times q)/n]}$ **as a proportion.**

As an example of how to use the binomial distribution, suppose we have a sample of size $n = 4$ test results, where we expect from our experience the proportion of negative results to be usually 0.1 (i.e. $p = 0.1$ and so $q = 0.9$). In repeated samples of size $n = 4$, what would be the probability of getting 0, 1, 2, 3 or 4 negative results in our sample?

The probability of 'r' occurrences, where r is taken in turn to have a value from 0 to n, is given by:

$$\text{Probability of } (r \text{ occurrences}) = nCr \times p^r \times q^{(n-r)}.$$

The first term nCr is the number of ways you can select r things from n things (e.g. how many ways can a 3-person interview panel be selected from 7 people?) – the answer is:

$$7!/[3! \times (7-3)!] = 35 \text{ ways}$$

where 7! means $7 \times 6 \times 5 \times 4 \times 3 \times 2 \times 1 = 5040$.

The easy way to calculate the coefficients for r in turn from $r = 0$ to $r = $ the sample size n, is to use the layout invented by the mathematician Pascal:

n				nCr				
1				1		1		
2			1		2		1	
3		1		3		3		1
4	1		4		6		4		1
5	1		5		10		10		5		1
6	1		6		15		20		15		6		1

and so on. It can be seen that each term on a line is the sum of the two terms in the line above to the left and right of it. Once these values have been tabulated they do not have to be recalculated, as the coefficients are chosen for the appropriate sample size 'n'.

In our example we therefore have, the following:

Probability (0 negative test result) $= 1 \times 0.1^0 \times 0.9^{(4-0)}$ $= 0.6561$
Note:
Any value raised to the power $0 = 1$ by definition.
Probability (1 negative test result) $= 4 \times 0.1^1 \times 0.9^{(4-1)}$ $= 0.2916$
Probability (2 negative test results) $= 6 \times 0.1^2 \times 0.9^{(4-2)}$ $= 0.0486$
Probability (3 negative test results) $= 4 \times 0.1^3 \times 0.9^{(4-3)}$ $= 0.0036$
Probability (4 negative test results) $= 1 \times 0.1^4 \times 0.9^{(4-4)}$ $= 0.0001$

Total probability　　1.0000

There are several points to notice here.

- When all possibilities have been considered for a given problem, the total of all the resultant probabilities must add up to 1.00. If they do not, then errors in calculations have been made, not all possibilities have been considered or approximations have been made in the calculations.
- We can turn the probabilities into **percentages of occurrence** by multiplying them by 100.
- The distribution for a sample size $n = 4$ and $p = 0.1$ is very skew. (A distribution is skew if it is **not symmetrical**.)
- In nearly two-thirds of such samples, no negative test results occurred, yet we know that there are about 10% of test results which should show a negative result. This is an indication that if only a few small samples are taken, the results can be an unreliable indicator of the **true nature** of the population and must be treated with caution.

Activity

Draw the histogram for the above distribution to show diagrammatically the skewness of the results.
  Repeat the calculations for sample size $n = 8$ and draw the histogram.
  Repeat the calculations for $n = 4$ and $n = 8$, when the proportion of negative test results are **(a)** 0.25 and **(b)** 0.50.
  Draw the histograms for each result.

Activity

In your class, ascertain the proportion of left-handed people. For a sample of $n = 5$, calculate the probabilities of getting 0, 1, 2, 3, 4 or 5 left-handed people in the sample.

Activity

Ascertain the proportion of female students in your class and calculate the individual probabilities of getting a female student in a group of 3 (i.e. $n = 3$ students).

The binomial gives exact results for sample sizes which are not too big, but if we were to try to calculate the exact probabilities for a sample of (say) 35, it would be virtually impossible. We can make a very good approximation to the normal, when n is larger than (say) 30, by calculating the mean and standard deviation of the binomial, and using them in the normal distribution above. Below 30 we can still approximate, but we should allow for the width of the histogram as mentioned earlier, to get the best approximation.

Activity

A 10-bed hospital ward usually has an occupancy rate of 60%. What is the probability that the ward will:

(a) have half its beds empty*
(b) be 70% or more occupied*
(c) be completely full
(d) have between 3 and 6 beds occupied
(e) have fewer than 3 beds occupied?

Use the normal approximation to the binomial to calculate these results. First calculate the binomial's mean and standard deviation. Draw an 11-column histogram in rough so that you can see where you should make an allowance for the 'width' of the histogram. If you are considering (say) exactly 2 beds, find the z for 1.5 and the z for 2.5. The difference between the areas of the normal curve corresponding to the two z values will give the required probability. As $n = 10$ is not too large, also calculate the exact probabilities using a calculator which has combinations on it, to check how little or how much the answers differ between the two methods.

Activity

In a small general office, the word processors are used about 20% of the time. If in the word-processing section there are 4 of them:

(a) How often will 2 or fewer be used?
(b) How often will none be used?*
(c) How often will 3 or 4 be used?
(d) How often will half of them be used?*
(e) If one machine is sold, and the usage increases to 25%, how often will 1 or fewer machines be used?*
(f) As a manager would you therefore be willing to have only 3 rather than 4 word processors?

(c) The Poisson distribution

The Poisson distribution is named after the mathematician Poisson, who discovered it in the early 19th century. It is very useful when we want to calculate the probability of an event which occurs **at random over a period of time or distance**. It is the correct distribution to use when the 'q' in the binomial has no real meaning. It is also used widely as an approximation to the binomial when the 'p' in the binomial is very small (say, ≤ 0.1, and the 'n' in the binomial is greater than about 40, while when $n \times p$ is less than about 5). The Poisson distribution in this situation is very skewed (i.e. asymmetrical). The big advantage is that the Poisson distribution is easy to use, and has been completely graphed, so that although there are formulae available, we can virtually avoid calculation by the use of commercially available Poisson graph paper. The Poisson is used when we **count** events, not when we **measure** them.

The **standard deviation of the Poisson distribution equals the square root of the average** (i.e. we do not have to do a calculation of the kind we did for the normal distribution).

Example 5

As an example of selecting the Poisson distribution because it is the correct one to use, assume that we use a terminal which is one of many connected to a mainframe computer at the company headquarters. From time to time, the connection, known as being 'on line' is broken, which is called being 'off line', and it causes severe disruptions to our normal work. Records taken over a representative number of weeks show that on average there are 1.5 off lines per week. As far as we can tell, these off line situations occur at random over a period of time. The number of 'on line' situations has no real meaning. This is therefore a proper use for the Poisson distribution in its own right.

We know immediately that the standard deviation is:

$$\text{Standard deviation} = \sqrt{(\text{Mean})}$$

In this case, standard deviation $= \sqrt{1.5} = 1.225$

The probability of c occurrences exactly if we know the mean number of occurrences, a, is:

$$\textbf{Probability of } c \textbf{ occurrences} = [e^{(-a)} \times a^c]/c!$$

where e is 2.71828 ... which has no exact value.

We can now calculate the probability of 0, 1, 2, 3, 4 etc. off lines, and draw the corresponding histogram. We will then use Poisson graph paper to avoid the calculations, and compare the accuracy of the results.

Probability (0 off lines) $= [\{2.718^{(1.5)}\} \times 1.5^0]/0!$
                           $= [0.223 \quad\quad \times 1]/1$
                           $= 0.223$
Probability (1 off lines) $= [0.223 \quad\quad \times 1.5^1]/1!$
                           $= 0.335$
Probability (2 off lines) $= [0.223 \quad\quad \times 1.5^2]/2!$
                           $= 0.251$
Probability (3 off lines) $= [0.223 \quad\quad \times 1.5^3]/3!$
                           $= 0.125$
Probability (4 off lines) $= [0.223 \quad\quad \times 1.5^4]/4!$
                           $= 0.047$
Probability (5 off lines) $= [0.223 \quad\quad \times 1.5^5]/5!$
                           $= 0.014$
Probability (6 off lines) $= [0.223 \quad\quad \times 1.5^6]/6!$
                           $= 0.0035$

and there is no real purpose in continuing, as the probability of expecting 6 events when the mean is 1.5 is very rare at 0.0035 (or about 4 chances in 1000). However, we do expect, therefore, that all such possibilities up to and including 6 events when summed, should come very close indeed to a total probability of 1.000, as we will by then have included virtually all possibilities. The total of the calculated probabilities actually comes to 0.9985. We could continue calculating, but it would have no practical value. If we draw the histogram of the probabilities we have just calculated, it will look as in Figure 14.9.

Notice how asymmetrical the distribution is, and also that in nearly 25% of the cases there were no off lines (i.e. $p(0) = 0.223$).

Activity

Repeat the above calculations and histogram drawing for a mean number of off lines for **(a)** mean $= 1.0$ **(b)** mean $= 3$ **(c)** mean $= 10$. What do you notice about the shape of the histograms as the mean becomes greater?

Now look at the Poisson graph paper in Figure 14.10.

Fig 14.9   Being 'off line': probability vs occasions

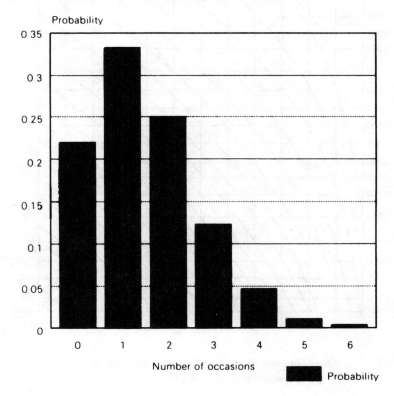

Do not be put off by the large number of lines. A little practice will show how easy the chart is to use, and how it avoids the calculations we have just done.

The horizontal axis shows the **mean number of occurrences** = '*a*'. The vertical axis shows the probability of *c* **or more** occurrences. Note the use of

---

Fig 14.10   Poisson graph paper

The theoretical information given in these curves is sufficiently accurate for those cases where the proportion defective is small – say, less than 10%; higher proportions require different values

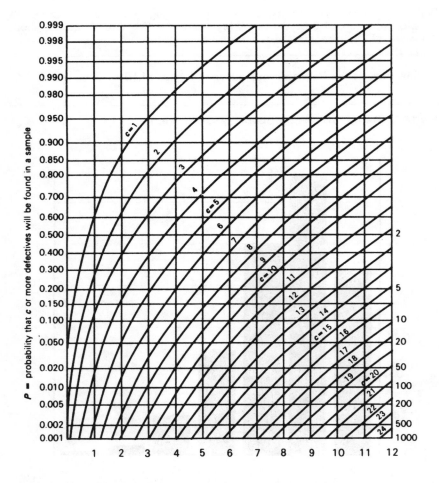

Average number of defectives expected in the sample = *a*

(proportional to the number in bulk)

'or more'. The graph paper has cumulated the results that we calculated separately. Each curved line across the paper shows $c = 1$, $c = 2$, $c = 3$, etc. occurrences. To see how we use the paper, remember that our mean is 1.5. What is the probability of $c = 1$ or more occurrences? Find on the horizontal axis where mean $= 1.5$ and go vertically up that line until you meet the first curved c line which represents '$c = 1$'. Now read horizontally across until you reach the vertical probability axis and read off the probability in this case, $p(1$ or more$) = 0.78$. If the probability of 1 or more is 0.78, the probability of 0 exactly must be $1.00 - 0.78 = 0.22$. We obtained 0.223 as our more exact result by calculation.

Activity

What is the probability of 2 or more occurrences if we expect 1.5 as our mean? Repeat the procedure and you should find $p(2$ or more$) = 0.44$. The probability of exactly 1 occurrence is $p(2$ or more$) - p(1$ or more$)$, which is $0.78 - 0.44 = 0.34$. By calculation we found $p(1) = 0.335$.

What is the probability of 3 or more occurrences? In like manner we find from the graph $p(3$ or more$) = 0.2$. The probability of 1 occurrence exactly is $p(3$ or more$) - p(2$ or more$) = 0.44 - 0.2 = 0.24$. By calculation, we found $p(2) = 0.251$.

Continue in a similar manner until you have found each of the cumulative probabilities for $c = 4$, 5, 6, and 7 or more. Then find the specific probabilities for $p(3, 4, 5,$ and 6 occurrences). Then compare the values from the graph with those from calculation. You should not find much difference between the two sets.

Activity

(a) The average number of indentations deeper than 3 cm per sample 50 metre length of pavement is 2.5. What is the probability of zero indentations?

(b) The average number of surface nicks or scratches larger than pin-head size on silverware is 0.6. If a piece has more than one such mark, it is repolished. What proportion of silverware needs this repolishing process?

(c) The number of people using the library who say they have lost/forgotten their library card, is 8 in a typical week. When only 4 people did this, library staff commented that 'memories are improving'. Would you agree?*

(d) In Stylers, the high-class hairdressers, the average number who get scratched by the scissors in a typical month's business is 0.2. If 3 people got scratched in this manner last month, are things getting worse or staying about the same as usual?*

(e) The number of flashes per 15-minute period of a thunderstorm is, on average, 3. What is the probability of getting exactly 1 flash?

(f) The mean number of goals scored per match last season by Rovers United was 1.3. In their first two matches this season they scored 3 and 4 goals respectively. Does this mean that things have changed for the better?

(g) The number of telephone kiosks out of order in any one-week period in the town centre is 5. What is the probability that on two successive occasions there will be 4 or more out of order?*

(h) The average number of pulled threads on a sample piece of yarn is typically 0.8. On how many occasions out of 100 can we expect no pulled threads, while the process remains as it is?

(i) About 10% of light bulbs are burnt out each week in a ballroom lit by ten chandeliers of ten bulbs each. How frequently can we expect to find 4 bulbs exactly burnt out? If we use the Poisson as the approximate model, what is the correct distribution to use?

(j) If we have a sample of four test results, and we expect, on average, 10% of such tests to show negative results, use the Poisson distribution to calculate the probabilities for 0 to 4 negative test results and compare them with the true results in the binomial example above.
Was it a good idea?
Why or Why not?

(k) During a cricket test match series, England scored 200 runs off 500 balls. What is the probability of scoring 0,1 2, 3, or more runs from a ball?

(l) Approximately 2 people per year in the USA are killed by vending machines falling on them, after they have assaulted the machines because of non-delivery of goods. What is the probability that no people will be killed? What is the probability that more than 2 people will be killed?

(m) From time to time, a contractor requires special pieces of earth-moving equipment. He may obtain them via long-term hire arrangement for £100 per day hire cost and £200 per day operating cost. Alternatively he can hire only when needed and at no notice for an all in cost of £500 per day. Average demand approximates a Poisson distribution with a mean of 2 pieces. How many pieces if any, should he hire via long-term arrangement? *Hint* – consider different numbers of long-term hire pieces, and factor them with 'no notice' numbers and appropriate costs and probabilities.*

(d) **The hypergeometric distribution**

The hypergeometric distribution provides us with an accurate means of calculating the exact probability of occurrence of sampling results, when sampling is conducted **without replacement**. 'Without replacement' means that as we discover a 'defective', it is not replaced by a 'good' one from another source which is then put back into the batch. Without replacement has no practical effect on our calculated results if the sample is small compared with the batch, and the proportion of detectives is also small. Hitherto, our sampling (see Chapter 2) assumed that the relatively small number of items we sampled was still many times larger than the number of 'defectives' in the sample which was, we hoped, representative of the batch. You will have noted in our discussion of the Poisson distribution, that there is no mention of either the sample size n, or the batch size N. In the binomial distribution, there is no mention of the batch size N, only of the sample size n. Now in the hypergeometric distribution, because of the small batch and sample sizes, we cannot ignore either, hence we must include both the sample size n and the batch size N in our calculations.

The distribution therefore provides exact results for all situations, but because its calculations are rather tedious without a scientific calculator, we generally use the hypergeometric distribution for small batch sizes, where the sample is a large proportion of the batch, and where the proportion of 'defectives' is also large compared with the batch. It can be used whenever what is being sampled consists of an 'OK' and 'not OK' situation, or whenever there are just two states or groups under consideration.

Example 6

Suppose we have a batch of size N items, and take a sample of size n items from it. There are d defectives in the batch.

We require to know the probability of c defectives, where c can be 0, 1, 2, ... n. If d is less than n, then c can lie from 0 to d. We can conveniently state three components of the problem, and bring them together to provide us with the final probability of c defectives.

- First, the number of ways we can choose a particular number c from the defectives in the batch is:

$$d \subset c \text{ ways}$$

where c, as before, means 'taking c things from d things', sequence not being important.

- Second, the number of ways we can choose the remaining items in the sample from the non-defectives in the batch is:

$$(N - d) \subset (n - c) \text{ ways}$$

- Third, the number of ways we can choose the sample size from the batch size is:

$$N \subset n \text{ ways}$$

The probability of getting specifically c defectives in a sample of size n from a batch size N, when there are d defectives in the batch is:

$$\frac{d \subset c . (N - d) \subset (n - c)}{N \subset n}$$

Example 6 illustrates the use of the formula above, in a situation where we are not referring to OK and not OK situations, but where the model is still applicable.

Example 7

There are 12 people working in a small department. The results of a competence test show that 8 people pass and 4 people fail. If Personnel choose 4 names from the list of 12, without knowing the test results, what are the probabilities of getting 0, 1, 2, 3 and 4 failures individually on the list?

$$p(0) = \frac{4 \subset 0 \times (12 - 4) \subset (4 - 0)}{12 \subset 4} = 1 \times 70/495 = 0.141$$

$$p(1) = \frac{4 \subset 1 \times 8 \subset 3}{12 \subset 4} = 4 \times 56/495 = 0.453$$

$$p(2) = \frac{4 \subset 2 \times 8 \subset 2}{12 \subset 4} = 6 \times 28/495 = 0.339$$

$$p(3) = \frac{4 \subset 3 \times 8 \subset 1}{12 \subset 4} = 4 \times 8/495 = 0.065$$

$$p(4) = \frac{4 \subset 4 \times 8 \subset 0}{12 \subset 4} = 1 \times 1/495 = 0.002$$

Total probability of all possibilities   1.000

It can be seen that in the long run the most likely result is to have one failure on the list with a probability of 0.45, or nearly one chance in two. There will be no failures on the list, with a probability of 0.141 or just over one in eight.

Activity

1 A five-person committee is to be set up from a list of 15 nominees. Six of the nominees have a poor attendance record on previous committees. If the selectors have no prior knowledge of this, what is the probability of a list with **(a)** all good attenders,* **(b)** one poor attender and **(c)** one good attender?

2 A sample of four pieces are taken from batches of 10, when the process is running at 50% defectives. What is the probability of the sample containing **(a)** zero defectives **(b)** four defectives, and **(c)** what is the most likely number of defects in the sample and how frequently will it occur?*

3 On a business trip to France, three people are to be chosen from eight fluent French speakers. Four are poor at written French. What is the chance that the three-person team has no one who can write French?

4 A sample of three units is taken from a batch of five. There tends to be, on average, 40% defectives in the batches. What is the probability of each of the possible number of defectives in the sample?

(e) **Negative exponential: the learning curve**

(i) **What is a 'learning curve'?**
The concept of the learning curve is very helpful where repetitive work is done, largely (but not necessarily) by human effort. It has been known for many years that the time per unit gradually reduces as the number of repetitions increases, if the work content is largely performed by people

rather than by machine or automatic means. This concept seems also to apply where new applications of work similar to that done previously are installed. In these situations, the work can be quite complex. An example such as the introduction of a new product on to the market could benefit from learning curve analysis to see whether improvements in the procedure show themselves in the kind of curve one might expect. The learning curve concept is strictly an **empirical result**, which uses a convenient mathematical distribution for its analysis.

(ii) **Plateaux in learning**
This reduction in unit time represents the improvements in how to perform the work since the previous repetition. Initially, the reduction in time is large, and it gradually becomes **less and less** as the number of repetitions increases until the person is skilled in that task and performs it at a level consistent with that defined in work study terminology. The learning curve is therefore useful in predicting how long a job will take if certain assumptions are made, and materialise.

In practice, there are **plateaux** where people seem not to be able to make improvements despite still learning; but some time after reaching a plateau such learning materialises as an improvement in ability and a reduction in time per unit. Figure 14.11 shows the general shape of the learning curve, without the plateaux just described.

(iii) **The negative exponential curve**
The shape of Figure 14.11a is a curve known as the **negative exponential**, which has a **constant rate of fall**. This constant rate is used in the learning curve, where it is known as the **learning curve factor**. It is often quoted as a percentage. This curve appears in many situations, and describes, for example, how the temperature of a hot liquid cools to ambient temperature (i.e. the temperature fails rapidly at first, and more gradually thereafter). The higher the initial temperature is, compared with the ambient, the faster it initially cools,

Figure 14.11a is drawn on graph paper with normal scales. The steepness of the curve depends on the learning curve factor. A factor of 80% indicates that the time per unit fails to 80% of what it was, each time the quantity 'produced' has doubled. This is not a very steep learning curve. A factor of 50%, however, indicates that upon each doubling of the quantity 'produced', the time per unit is half what it was previously. This is a very steep curve and may suggest the work is very simple and/or that the person is a very good learner.

Figure 14.11b has the vertical and horizontal axes each drawn on logarithmic scales (i.e. the distance between 1 and 10 is the same as that between 10 and 100, which is the same as that between 100 and 1000, etc.) The result is a straight line. A factor of 50% produces a steeper straight line than when the factor is 80%.

a *Arithmetic scales*
b *Log log scales*

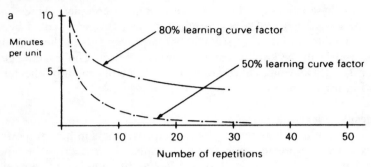

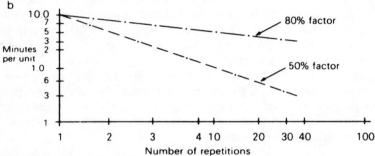

Fig 14.11   The learning curve

The learning curve equation is:

$$t(n) = t(1) \cdot n^m$$

where $t(n)$ is the time to perform the task for the nth time

$t(1)$ is the time for the task when first performed

m is a negative number.

If $t(1) = 10$ minutes = unit time for task when first performed, and $t(2) = 8$ minutes = unit time for task when performed twice, then:

$$\frac{t(2)}{t(1)} = \frac{8}{10} = 0.8 \text{ (i.e 80 learning curve) for } \frac{n(2)}{n(1)} = \frac{2}{1} = 2$$

Therefore

$$\frac{t(2)}{t(1)} = \frac{k \cdot n(2)^m}{k \cdot n(1)^m} = \frac{(n(2))^m}{(n(1))^m} = 2^m$$

$$\frac{8}{10} = 2^m$$

$$\text{so } \log 0.8 = \log 2 \cdot m$$

$$\text{and } m = -0.322$$

Our learning curve equation is now:
$$t(n) = 10n^{(-0.322)}$$
What will the predicted unit time be for the 5th, 10th, 25th and 50th cycle?

		minutes
$t(5)$	$= 10 \times 5^{(-0.322)}$	$= 5.96$
$t(10)$	$= 10 \times 10^{(-0.322)}$	$= 4.76$
$t(25)$	$= 10 \times 25^{(-0.322)}$	$= 3.55$
$t(50)$	$= 10 \times 50^{(-0.322)}$	$= 2.84$

Activity

1 Plot the 1st, 2nd, 5th, 10th, 25th and 50th cycle unit times on a graph with arithmetic scales
2 Plot the same data on graph paper with two cycles of log scales on each of the vertical and horizontal axes (log log paper). Verify that the graph is now a straight line, and estimate from the graph the unit cycle time for the 100th and 500th cycle.

It is also very useful to be able to calculate directly the total time for a specific number of units along the learning curve. For example, we might want to know the total time to produce the first 10 units, or the last 50 in a batch of 100, or the total time to produce the 20 items beginning with the 25th item.

If $n(1)$ is the beginning number of cycles, and $n(2)$ is the ending number of cycles, the cumulative time for $n(2) - n(1)$ items is approximately given by:

$$\frac{t(1)}{(1 + m)} \cdot [(n(2) + 0.5)^{(1+m)} - (n(1) - 0.5)^{(1+m)}]$$

What is the total time for the first five units, in the example above?

We can first calculate it exactly (and tediously) by using our first formula for the individual time.

		minutes
$t(1)$	$= 10 \times 1(-0.322)$	$= 10$
$t(2)$	$= 10 \times 2(-0.322)$	$= 8$
$t(3)$	$= 10 \times 3(-0.322)$	$= 7$
$t(4)$	$= 10 \times 4(-0.322)$	$= 6.4$
$t(5)$	$= 10 \times 5(-0.322)$	$= 6.0$

for a total $= 37.4$ minutes.

Using our approximate formula for total time, for $n(1) = 1$ and $n(2) = 5$, we have:

$$[10/(1 - 0.322)] \times [5.5^{0.678} - 0.5^{0.678}] = 37.7 \text{ minutes.}$$

The total time formula becomes more accurate as the number of cycles used increases.

Activity

How long will it take to 'produce' the 15th to the 19th items? Calculate the exact total time using the individual time formula and the summing. Calculate the total time using the approximate total time formula, and compare the two results. Calculate the percentage difference between the two, based on the exact result.

Activity

When a customer of a bank loses his credit card, he contacts the bank, who upon receipt of the appropriate details, takes actions to stop further use of the card. They also take other action to prevent loss through fraud. The procedure is by nature rather detailed and must be followed exactly for maximum protection for the customer, bank and shopkeepers.

The supervisor of the department concerned with this operation has recently implemented a revised procedure for greater security and efficiency. It has run for a short while in its new form. The staff operating this new routine are therefore still learning it. The supervisor knows from experience that similar procedures are fully learned, and the staff proficient, after 6 weeks.

Although timings are not available for the early cycle times of the new routine, records show that after 50 cycles the routine took 10 minutes, and after 200 cycles (which is where they are at present) the routine took 7 minutes. It is estimated that about 30 such repetitions per day of this new routine can normally be expected.

1 On log log graph paper, draw the learning curve based on the two points given. Extend the graph back to cycle 1 and read off the cycle time. Assume a 5-day-week operation and extend the graph forward to the total cycles expected in 6 weeks, and read off the cycle time. Ideally, 3 cycle log paper is required, otherwise extend your line by drawing it parallel to your existing data, but on an overlapping scale for the cycle 1 to 10, if you are using 2 cycle log paper.
2 From the graph read off the time for the 2nd cycle and calculate the percentage learning curve.*
3 Calculate exactly the learning curve from the two times given in the credit card problem, bearing in mind that when going from 50 to 200 cycles you have doubled twice. Had you doubled once only, the learning curve would have been 70%.
4 How long will the total time be for **(a)** the first 10 cycles **(b)** the last 100 cycles **(c)** from the 300th to the 400th cycle?
5 If the cycle time for the last repetition at the end of 6 weeks is the time for a competent staff person to take, what can the difference in cycle time between the first cycle and the last cycle represent and what can it be used to monitor?

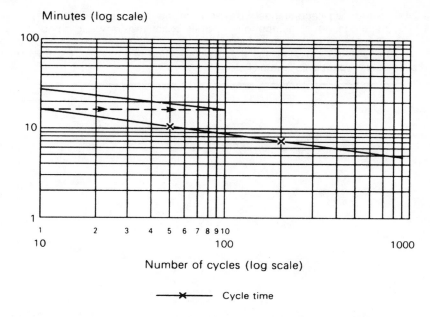

Minutes (log scale)

Number of cycles (log scale)

———✕——— Cycle time

Fig 14.12 Learning curve: lost credit card banking procedures

Chapter Review Questions

1 What are the advantages and disadvantages of the arithmetic mean?

2 In what real-life situations would the mode be more useful than the mean?

3 Identify three measures of the variation in a set of numerical data. Which is the simplest to calculate, and what is its limitation?

4 Which two parameters are most commonly used to summarise a set of numerical data?

5 'Correlation provides an indication of the strength of the cause and effect relationship between any two sets of data': True or False?

6 What does the term 'least squares' refer to, when using the technique of least squares linear regression?

7 In the line '$y = -a - bx$': **(a)** is the line linear or non-linear? **(b)** does the intercept lie above, on or below the $y = 0$ axis? **(c)** describe the slope of the fine.

8 What is the relationship between the mean, mode and median for a normal distribution?

9 How is the normal distribution's complicated formula used in practice?

10 (a) When can the binomial distribution be useful in its own right? **(b)** When can it reasonably be approximated to the normal distribution?

11 Express the mean and standard deviation of the binomial distribution as a proportion.

12 When can the Poisson distribution be useful in its own right?

13 What is the mean and standard deviation of the Poisson distribution?

14 'The hypergeometric distribution provides exact results when sampling is without replacement': True or False?

15 'A 70% learning curve means that the task time reduces to 70% for each successive repetition': True or False?

Table of Normal Distribution Values

Figure 14.13 shows the normal distribution.

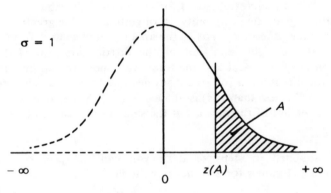

Fig. 14.13

Now look at the table of standardised values, $z(A)$, for a normal distribution of mean $= \mu = 0$ and standard deviation $\sigma = 1$.

The tabled values below are for $z(A)$.

$$\text{where } z(A) = \frac{(x - \mu)}{\sigma}$$

$z(A)$	A	$z(A)$	A	$z(A)$	A
0	0.5000	1.00	0.1587	2.00	0.0228
0.05	0.4801	1.05	0.1469	2.05	0.0202
0.10	0.4602	1.10	0.1357	2.10	0.0179
0.15	0.4404	1.15	0.1251	2.15	0.0158
0.20	0.4207	1.20	0.1151	2.20	0.0139
0.25	0.4013	1.25	0.1057	2.25	0.0122
0.30	0.3821	1.30	0.0968	2.30	0.0107
0.35	0.3632	1.35	0.0885	2.35	0.0094

369

z(A)	A	z(A)	A	z(A)	A
0.40	0.3446	1.40	0.0808	2.40	0.0082
0.45	0.3264	1.45	0.0735	2.45	0.0071
0.50	0.3085	1.50	0.0668	2.50	0.0062
0.55	0.2912	1.55	0.0606	2.55	0.0054
0.60	0.2743	1.60	0.0548	2.60	0.0047
0.65	0.2575	1.65	0.0495	2.65	0.0040
0.70	0.2420	1.70	0.0446	2.70	0.0035
0.75	0.2267	1.75	0.0406	2.75	0.0030
0.80	0.2119	1.80	0.0359	2.80	0.0026
0.85	0.1977	1.85	0.0322	2.85	0.0022
0.90	0.1841	1.90	0.0287	2.90	0.0019
0.95	0.1711	1.95	0.0256	2.95	0.0016
				3.00	0.00135

Infinity (at the right-hand side) = 4.00   0.00003

This table can therefore be used for any normal distribution.

The value z gives the probability 'A' of getting a value **greater or equal** to $z(A)$. This value 'A' corresponds to the area under the curve from + infinity ($z = 4.000$ at the right-hand end of the distribution), to $z(A)$. As the distribution is symmetrical and the total area under the entire curve $= 1.0$, only half the distribution (of area 0.50) need be tabulated. The probability of getting a value **less than** $z(A)$ is $[0.5000 - z(A)]$. A negative $z(A)$ indicates that it is to the left of the mean, but the same table can still be used.

Note:

As z is tabulated in steps of 0.05, you can interpolate to find the corresponding A values for z values not shown

Example

To find A for $z = 0.52$, note that it lies two-fifths of the way between 0.50 and 0.55.

   A will lie two-fifths of the way between 0.3085 and 0.2912.

   $A = [0.3085 - 2/5(0.3085 - 2912)] = 0.3016$.

15 Managing Numbers: 2 – Statistical Process Control

In Chapter 15 we utilise some of what we learned in Chapter 14. Statistical process control provides a powerful tool for helping to assure quality as the process is being performed. It enables us to establish trends and to make alterations only when necessary.

Learning Objectives

By the end of this chapter, you should:

1 know the **purpose** of statistical process control, and the basic **principles** behind it
2 be able to set **control limits** for sample means and ranges using conversion tables
3 be able to prepare a traditional **Shewart means and range control chart** for variables
4 be able to prepare a **Poisson based control chart** for numbers expected
5 know the difference between a **Shewart control chart** and a **cusum control chart**
6 be able to prepare a **cusum chart** with its mask.

15.1 The Concept of Statistical Process Control

(a) Control limits in real time

Statistical process control takes information gained from analysing the **current state** of a process, and uses it to decide whether or not there have been significant statistical changes to that process. By 'significant', we mean whether such changes could have been expected to occur by chance or not, given the information upon which certain parameters were based. In the traditional Shewart chart (developed in the 1920s by the American Dr Shewart), these parameters are the **control limits** set either side of the process average and which, by definition, will include about 95–99% of all such average values taken from small samples on a regular basis. These results are then plotted and monitored. When more results fall outside the statistical limits than would be expected by chance, **corrective action** is taken (e.g. to realign the process mean closer to the specification mean).

The importance of statistical process control is that it enables decisions such as what corrective action may need to be taken to be made at the time the process is **running** (i.e. in real time). This contrasts sharply with the sampling that we considered in Chapter 2, which reflects **past history**. Naturally in that case also we take corrective action if necessary, but in no sense can that be thought of as 'current', with regard to the problem being corrected.

(b) Statistical process control charts

Statistical process control uses a chart to display the **deviations** of a process from a **norm**, and includes statistically set control limits to alert us to the situation where more deviations lie outside those limits than we would expect. Ordinary charts are used for many purposes and preparing and maintaining them is relatively easy. Characteristics such as trends, jumps and dips are easily seen.

What is not so easily seen is whether or not they are leading to an **out of control** situation (i.e. does the process need adjusting?), or are they inherent fluctuations of that process. If corrective action is taken when it is not required, then no benefits will be obtained, and disturbance to the process may have unwanted side effects. If no corrective action is taken when it should have been, then the risk of producing 'defectives' is increased. (A 'defective' is an item with one or more defects; a 'defect' is a parameter – or perhaps several – which fails to meet the required standard; it may be dimensional or visual.)

As can be seen in Figure 15.1, there appears to be a trend upwards, although there are some dips and jumps along the way. It is not clear if this trend is likely to cause a problem, and whether or not to make an adjustment is uncertain.

If we set statistical limits and incorporate them on our chart, we can then detect shifts which, if allowed to go uncorrected, will cause problems. Perhaps the mean of the process has moved significantly, and is now sufficiently away from where it should be that rejects may be caused. This is because the inherent variation of the process coupled with the shift of the mean results in some of the output lying outside the drawing limits. (It should be noted that there is no inherent connection between drawing limits and statistical limits.)

Figures 15.2a and b illustrate the situation where some rejects are inevitable (Figure 15.2a), and where they are not (Figure 15.2b). In both cases, however, unnecessary rejects could be caused if the process mean was not centred over the design mean.

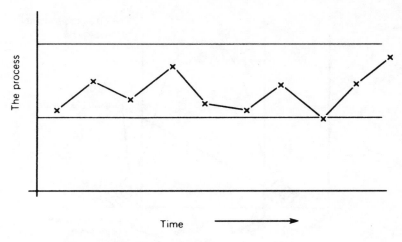

Fig 15.1   A conventional Shewart chart

(c) **Relative capability**

Even though a process may be in statistical control, its inherent variability may still mean that some of the output is outside the specification limits. This may still be the case even though the process mean coincide's with the specification mean. The ratio of **specification tolerance** to **standard deviation** indicates the **relative capability (RC)** of the process:

$$\text{Relative capability} = \frac{\textbf{Upper drawing limit} - \textbf{Lower drawing limit}}{\textbf{Standard deviation}}$$

For a given process, once the RC is calculated, we can decide whether a process is too good for the specification. Alternatively there may be scope for allowing for the drift of means if the RC is high, or for calculating the percentage of unavoidable rejects if the RC is low.

Example

The specification for a dimension calls for a tolerance of 0.006 inches, and three processes are available. Process 1 has an inherent standard deviation of 0.002 inches. Process 2 has an inherent standard deviation of 0.001 inches. Process 3 has an inherent variability of 0.0007 inches. For process 1 the RC is 0.006/0.002 = 3.

For process 2 the RC is 0.006/0.001 = 6.
For process 3 the RC is 0.006/0.0007 = 8.6

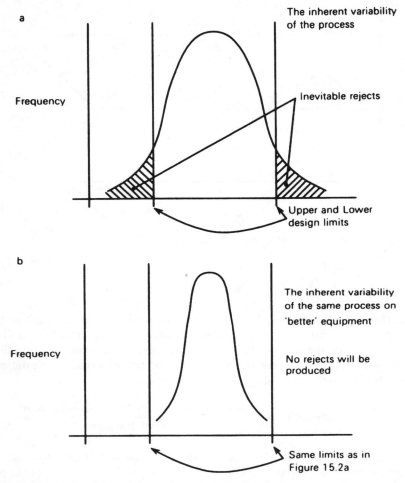

Fig 15.2   Inherent variability vs design limits
a   Initial inherent variability
b   The same process on 'better' equipment

Activity

For each RC value, calculate the percentage of unavoidable rejects if the process mean coincides with the specification mean. Repeat the calculations if the process mean is 0.002 below the specification mean. Assume a normal distribution.
  Which process has a high, medium and low RC value?

There are many kinds of statistical process charts. We will consider the basic chart **(a)** for monitoring a process where we **count** the key parameter, and **(b)** for monitoring a process where we **measure** the key parameter. In the former we will use the Poisson distribution to give us the information we need to produce the chart, and in the latter we will use the normal distribution. In both cases, however, we will utilise the standard deviation to determine the control limits.

15.2 The Poisson Based Control Chart

The Poisson based control chart is used when we want to exert control over a process where defects are **counted**, and the average number expected per unit time (or area, or length) is known. This situation means that we can use the Poisson distribution. When we know the number expected, we can then set control limits at a designated level of probability to alert us when the actual number of defects exceeds the control limits set. These limits can be set on one side of the mean only, or on either side. To set such limits we will use the Poisson chart that we discussed earlier.

Case Study: The Typing Pool

A small typing pool of five audio typists is responsible for typing the sales reports generated by a company's sales force arising from the client contacts they make. Such a report is typically about three sides of A4 in length, and contains between 1000 and 1100 words. Recently, the supervisor whose responsibility includes this pool has become concerned about spelling errors detected, and wants to monitor the current situation with a view to improving it. Initially, a close examination of large number of these reports from previous weeks revealed that a typical report contained an average of 2 misspelled words. How can control limits be set to monitor this situation?

The Poisson distribution is used in this situation because the number of defects can be counted, rather than measured along a continuous scale, and because the proportion of defects is extremely small. We know the expected number of misspellings per report is 2. Let us assume that we consider that limits set to correspond with a probability of 0.05 and 0.01 of being exceeded are reasonable. Corresponding limits of 0.95 and 0.99 cannot be set in this particular case, as you will discover below. If, however, the first two limits are exceeded with a frequency greater than that expected as subsequent work is monitored, the situation will have deteriorated.

In Figure 15.3a and b we see such a control chart.

The horizontal line at 2 misspelled words, represents the current situation. Using our Poisson chart paper, we read vertically up from the horizontal axis at the point where the average equals 2, until we are level with a point on the vertical scale where the probability equals 0.01. We read horizontally across and interpolate the value of the appropriate 'c or more' curve which equals 6.3. If we repeat this procedure for a probability of 0.05, we get a 'c or more' value of 5.0. You will notice that the lowest 'c or more' curve of $c = 1$ is beyond the range for our average $= 2$ situation for probabilities of 0.95 and 0.99.

We draw the two control lines at 5 and 6.3, and continue to record the number of misspelled words on a daily basis. The inner limit line is often called a warning line and the outer limit line an action line. From the way we have set up this chart

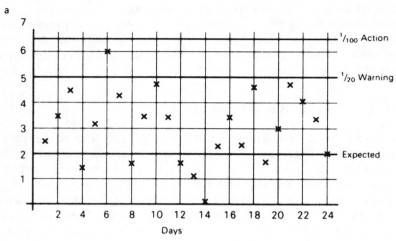

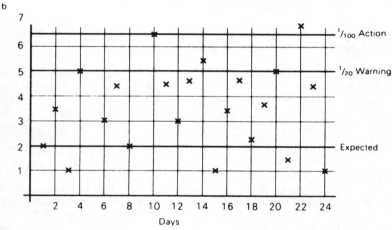

Fig 15.3   A Poisson control chart
a   In control
b   Out of control

we will not be surprised if about one in twenty points lie on or above 5 misspellings. Similarly we expect only about one in a hundred points to lie on or exceed 6.3 misspellings. If they occur more frequently, we would be alerted to a statistically significant event with a known probability of occurrence, and act accordingly.

Figure 15.3a shows the situation in control statistically, with just one point above (or it could be on) the 5 misspellings line. Such a point may occur anywhere in the sequence of plotting. Figure 15.3b shows the situation statistically changed, with three points on (or above) the 5 misspellings line and two on (or above) the 6.3 misspellings line. Also note that the range of plots in Figure 15.3b is much greater than in Figure 15.3a. which suggests a more fundamental problem, than one of mere drifting upwards. As such points can occur in any sequence when plotting, it could be said that a chart with about 25 plots on it as above, could still be in statistical control even if there were a point on the 5 line and on the 6.3 line. However, we would probably become suspicious.

Activity

Draw a control chart similar to that in Figure 15.3 for the situation of 5 misspellings expected.
  Set upper and lower control limits and interpret their meaning.
  Why are the two sets of control limits not symmetrically placed about the mean?

15.3 The Measurement Based Control Chart

The principles which we used to set up the control charts above, will still apply to a measurement based control chart; there are, however, some key differences. This control chart is used when we **measure** the process we are interested in, rather than counting it. This means that there has to be a **continuous scale** from which we can read as accurately as necessary, and the most common examples are for size, weight or distance. Instead of using the Poisson we use the normal distribution. The normal is a symmetrical distribution and we can expect the upper and lower control limits to be symmetrically placed either side of the mean.

  This situation will apply to the mean, but does not apply to the range (of means in samples), as the range is not normally distributed. We often, but not always, work from small samples rather than from individuals, because regardless of the shape of the parent population of individuals, the means of samples tend to be normally distributed. We usually set upper and lower control limits at the mean, ± 2 and 3σ. This corresponds for practical purposes to probabilities of 1 in 20, and 1 in 333 respectively, of plots falling outside those limits.

Case Study: The Perfect Perfume (PP) Company

The PP Company is one of the smaller but longer established perfumeries, and is well known for its quality range of products. One of the increasingly popular fragrances is Eau de Fleur, this is packaged in small 5 ml bottles. An extensive check on a large number of individual bottles determined that the filling process did indeed produce an average filling of 5.0 ml, with a standard deviation for individual bottles of 0.1 ml. As production was not very high volume, a control chart for individuals was to be established, and subsequent individual fills plotted from the result of 1 bottle per hour being checked. Some time later, as the success of this particular perfume increased, a change to the equipment meant that higher and more continuous production could be achieved. Control charts were now to be based on samples of 5 bottles taken at regular intervals, with both the mean fill and fill range to be monitored.

(a) Control chart for individual fills

With a mean fill volume of 5.0 ml and a standard deviation of 0.1 ml, 2 and 3σ limits can be established. We therefore have the following:

$$5.0\,\text{ml} \pm (2 \times 0.1) = 4.8\,\text{ml and } 5.2\,\text{ml } \textbf{Warning Limits}$$

$$5.0\,\text{ml} \pm (3 \times 0.1) = 4.7\,\text{ml and } 5.3\,\text{ml } \textbf{Action Limits}$$

Figure 15.4 below shows the limit lines and subsequent plots of individuals as the process continues. It appears to be in statistical control. We can detect one point on the lower Warning Limit, but out of 32 plots we can expect this. Remember we do not know **when** such points will occur. Statistically we **could** get a point outside our Action Limit now, even though we have plotted only 32 points to date. However, this would seem somewhat unlikely. The same logic for interpretation and action applies here as applied to our Poisson charts above.

Fig 15.4   Control chart for individual fill volume

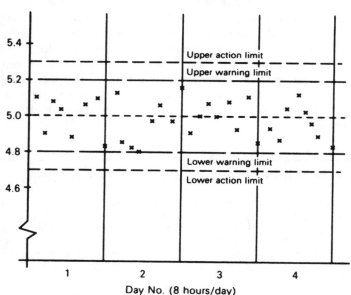

Day No. (8 hours/day)

(b) **Control chart based on samples**

A **sample** is a small number of items taken from current production. It may be taken in rapid succession (i.e. consecutively) or over a short period of time (i.e. more or less at random). If it is taken consecutively, we obtain a good picture of the process at that time. If we take it at random (say, from the last quarter hour's production), we obtain information about what happened during that period of time.

The data below is the result of taking 25 samples, each of 5 successive bottles, from the filling line, and finding **(a)** the mean fill volume of the sample, and **(b)** the range of fill volume within the sample. The mean fill volume is obtained for each sample by adding the 5 fill volumes and dividing by 5. The range of fill volume for each sample is obtained by subtracting the smallest fill from the largest fill:

- **Mean fill volume for 25 samples**

5.00	5.01	5.01	5.01	4.99
4.92	5.01	5.03	4.99	5.01
5.05	5.03	5.05	5.02	5.04
5.02	5.01	5.04	5.04	5.02
4.97	4.99	5.03	5.03	5.03

The grand mean fill volume is 5.01 ml.

- **Range of fill volume**

.37	.21	.35	.19	.14
.23	.35	.28	.19	.30
.09	.12	.28	.14	.19
.14	.16	.23	.25	.23
.16	.28	.30	.35	.09

Mean fill range is 0.225 ml.

- **Calculating the standard deviation**

Next we need to calculate the **standard deviation**. This can be done in the conventional manner using a statistical calculator, or by using the appropriate conversion factor from the table below in conjunction with the range for each sample. This is quick and easy and sufficiently accurate for our purposes.

- **Estimating the standard deviation from the range of a sample**

n = number in sample	Factor 'a' for given n	
2	0.886	
3	0.591	standard deviation,
4	0.486	$sd =$ 'a' × sample range
5	0.430	
6	0.395	
7	0.370	
8	0.351	Note also that the
9	0.337	standard error of the
10	0.325	mean = $sd/\sqrt{n}$
15	0.288	
20	0.267	
25	0.254	

We therefore select an '*a*' factor for an *n* of 5, which gives '*a*' = 0.43. For our mean fill range, we calculate the standard deviation as follows: As the mean fill range = 0.225, then standard deviation = 0.43 × 0.225 = 0.097 ml.

(c) Control chart for sample means

The overall standard deviation is 0.097 ml. The standard error of the sample means we will plot = $sd/\sqrt{n}$ = 0.097/2.24 = 0.043. We can now set 2 and 3 standard error control limits, and plot the sample means.

The ±2 standard error control limits are grand mean ±(2 × 0.043) = 5.096 and 4.924 ml.

The ±3 standard error control limits are grand mean ±(3 × 0.043) = 5.139 and 4.881 ml.

Figure 15.5 shows the sample means chart and control limits. The grand mean, based on 25 samples of 5, is also plotted. There appears to be no upward or downward trend, and the means lie comfortably within the limits. If subsequent sample means were to exhibit a **trend**, we would be alerted by the control limits as to when it became statistically significant, and make some adjustment to the filling mechanism to centre it nearer the required 5.0 ml average.

(d) Control chart for range

As well as the means control chart above, we can also prepare a control chart for the range. When the range fails outside its control limits, it signifies a more fundamental problem than merely drift. Generally, this occurs when, for example, the equipment might need some **basic maintenance**, or there is

Fig 15.5   Sample means chart

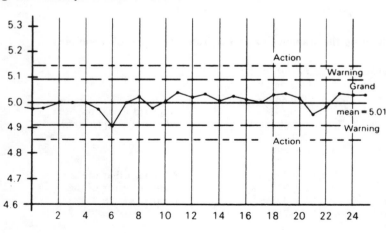

Sample No.

some vibration causing a problem, or perhaps a spindle or tool holder has become loose. The key point here is that **investigation**, rather than a quick fix, is needed for an out of control range chart.

Limits for the range control chart are not symmetrical about the mean range. The action limits for sample ranges can be obtained directly from the table below (BS 2564: 1955: (1993)). We generally plot the upper limits only, rather than the lower limits as well. However, these can be calculated if desired. In a situation where above the upper limits was a 'bad' result, below the lower limits would be a suspiciously 'good' result. That may correspond to a situation where the samples having a wide range were removed from the machine before they could be included in the results.

Calculating the upper limits for the range using the factor *b*'.

The warning limit = mean range × '*bw*'.

The action limit = mean range × '*ba*'

n = number in sample	Factor 'b' for a given n	
	'bw' Warning limit	'ba' Action limit
2	2.81	4.12
3	2.17	2.99
4	1.93	2.58
5	1.81	2.36
6	1.72	2.22

Figure 15.6 shows the range control chart.

Fig 15.6   Range control chart

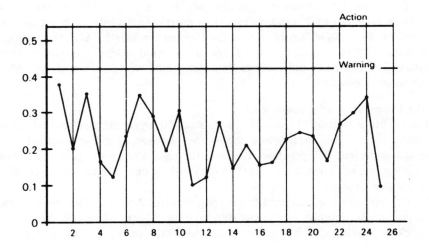

In our situation with sample size $n = 5$, we therefore have a Warning Limit = mean fill range $\times 1.81 = 0.225 \times 1.81 \times 0.407$, and an Action Limit mean fill range $\times 2.36 \times 0.225 \times 2.36 \times 0.531$.

(e) Cumulative sum control charts

These charts are a variation of the traditional limit line charts described above. Such charts ('**cusum**' for short) use a truncated v-shaped mask which is placed over each successive point as it is plotted, and action is taken if a prior point touches or goes inside the sloping edge of the v-mask. The cusum charts have the same objective as the traditional control limit chart (i.e. to detect an increase in the rate of defectives). Both charts are based on the same probability models.

(i) Changes occurring in the process
A cusum chart vividly illustrates on the chart any changes that are occurring to the process, without recourse to decision rules, and so uses existing data more effectively with less effort. A cusum chart will give a clear indication of **where** a change occurred, and the **size** of that change. The mean is shown by the slope of the plot, and as such is rather more difficult to get used to, and to interpret. Some training and familiarisation is definitely helpful if you intend to use cusum charts for the first time.

(ii) Using cusum charts
The calculations might appear rather more complex, and are not so intuitively apparent as those for a traditional chart. The relevant British Specification is BS 5703: Parts 1, 2, 3 and 4: 1992. The cusum chart is most appropriate for a process where you want to detect **small changes in the mean of a variable**. Note that cusum charts can also be used for **attributes**, and for controlling the **range**, as well as the **mean** in a variables chart.

If you want to monitor a process which is subject only to large step changes (say, about 2 standard errors or more) the traditional chart can be superior. The reason for this is that the average run length (ARL) for plots 2 standard errors or greater away from the nominal is less. This means that you will detect the change sooner than you would with a cusum chart under the same conditions.

(iii) Preparation of a cusum chart
Let us use a simplified example to illustrate the preparation and use of a cusum chart. The data below shows the changes in a hypothetical 'cut spaghetti to length' operation. It shows the results of 16 samples, the mean length x, the variation from target $(x - 8)$ and the cumulative variation from target (the cusum).

This operation is supposed to cut spaghetti to a length of 8 inches (8 is the target value). Samples of the cut spaghetti have been taken and the length checked. This has shown that the process has been cutting to a mean length of

6 inches. This was then raised to 10 inches, which was maintained for a while, whereupon the length gradually fell back to 6 inches, which it maintained.

Sample no.	x	$(x-8)$	*Cusum $(x-8)$*
1	6	−2	−2
2	6	−2	−4
3	6	−2	−6
4	6	−2	−8
5	10	2	−6
6	10	2	−4
7	10	2	−2
8	10	2	0
9	9	1	1
10	8	0	1
11	7	−1	0
12	6	−2	−2
13	8	0	−2
14	8	0	−2
15	8	0	−2
16	8	0	−2

where x is the mean length of the spaghetti units in each sample.

Fig 15.7   Plotting data on a cusum chart
a   Plot of mean lengths of spaghetti samples
b   Plot of cusum values of column **4** data

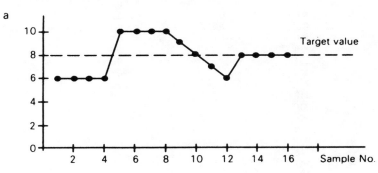

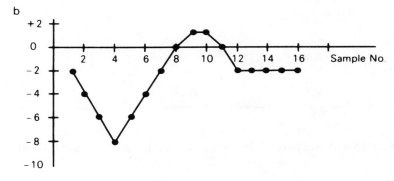

Figure 15.7a shows the plot of the means of the samples as we would normally plot them. Figure 15.7b below shows the plot of the cumulative sum of the variations from the target value of 8 inches (i.e. the right-hand values in column **4** of our data table).

By looking at each plot carefully on the cusum chart, try to make sure you can see how the cusum plot moves, compared with how the same data moves in the traditional plot in Figure 15.7a. It is not immediately apparent, and does need some practice. Notice that when the mean length in successive samples is constant, but below the target value the cusum chart plot slopes down in a straight line. Similarly when the mean length in successive samples is constant and above the target value, the cusum plot slopes upwards in a straight line.

Activity

The table below shows the results of 25 samples of the mean weight of one additive in a feed compound for cows. The measurements are in grams. Complete the remaining entries in columns **3** and **4**. The target value is 20 grams.

Sample no. (1)	$\bar{x}$ (2)	$(\bar{x}-20)$ (3)	cusum $(\bar{x}-20)$ (4)
1	19.8	−0.2	−0.2
2	19.7	−0.3	−0.5
3	20.0	0	−0.5
4	20.2	0.2	−0.3
5	19.9	−0.1	−0.4
6	19.8		−0.6
7	20.1		−0.5
8	19.8		−0.7
9	20.2		−0.5
10	19.9		−0.6
11	20.0		
12	19.9		
13	19.8		
14	20.2		
15	19.8		
16	20.2		
17	20.0		
18	20.2		
19	19.9		
20	20.1		
21	20.2		
22	20.3		
23	20.0		
24	20.5		
25	20.6		

Figure 15.8 shows part of the plot of the cusum data in column **4** of our table.

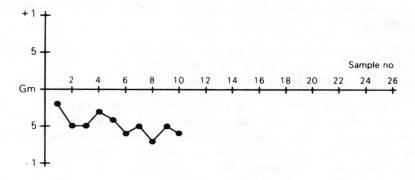

Fig 15.8   Part of cusum plot of column 4 data

Activity

Complete this cusum plot. Plot the 25 sample means on a traditional means chart. Compare them and decide which you think more vividly portrays what is happening.

Figure 15.9 shows the general details for constructing the v-mask, which is used over the cusum chart to ascertain when action is needed.

Fig 15.9   General *v*-mask dimensions

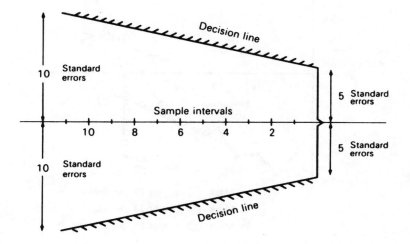

Activity

Calculate the standard deviation and the standard error of the mean, assuming the number of items in the sample is 5 and the mean range is 1.50 gms.

Now plot your cusum chart on graph paper for monitoring purposes, and make the vertical scale such that if the horizontal plotting interval is (say) 1 cm, then 1 cm on the vertical scale equals about 2 times the standard deviation. You can see that the physical dimensions of the graph play a part here, as well as the information itself. The standard error is 0.136 gm, and twice this is 0.272 gm. A convenient vertical scale would be for 1 cm. to equal 0.25 gm. This is quite close to the 2 standard error value.

Figure 15.10 shows the same data as Figure 15.9, but is now drawn to the appropriate scales suggested. By using the mask on each cusum plot in sequence, you will notice that the out of control condition detected on plot 24 of the traditional chart has also been detected on plot 24 of the cusum chart. The jump of 0.5 gm from plot 23 to plot 24 is greater than 3 standard errors. This seems to confirm the suggestion of increased sensitivity of traditional control charts when large jumps are expected. However, the visual picture of the cusum trend is quite clear in comparison with the means plot.

Fig 15.10

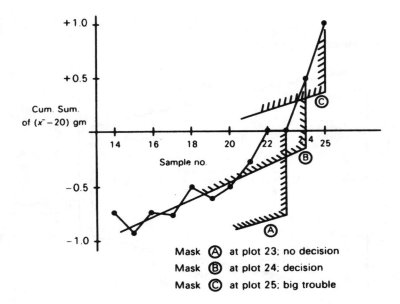

Mask Ⓐ at plot 23; no decision

Mask Ⓑ at plot 24; decision

Mask Ⓒ at plot 25; big trouble

Chapter Review Questions

1 What is meant by a 'significant change' to a process?

2 Why is statistical process control important?

3 What distribution is used as a basis for control charts where we count the results?

4 What distribution is used for a variables control chart?

5 On a Poisson control chart, if we expect 1.5 deaths per year, caused by people falling off buses, what will the 0.05 control limit be set at?

6 What is meant by 'the 0.05 control limit' in **5** above?

7 If a range chart goes out of control, what can this signify?

8 What is meant by 'the standard error-of the mean'?

9 Why is a plot of sample means preferable to a plot of individuals?

10 What is indicated by relative capability?

11 What data is plotted on a cusum chart?

16 Forecasting: Managing the Future

Much of an organisation's success depends on how accurately it can forecast the **level and timing of demand** for its goods or services. Other things being equal, which they hardly ever are, the company which gets its forecasts correct stands a good chance of doing better than a company which does not. This is because the **forecast** is one of the prime pieces of information a company needs to help ensure that it has the **people**, **cash** and **material** when its forecasts suggest they will be needed.

Learning Objectives

By the end of this chapter, you should:

1 be able to calculate **moving average forecasts** and be aware of their advantages and limitations
2 be able to produce a **straight trend line** by eye, and produce forecasts for the required periods ahead
3 know how to apply **empirical weights** to a moving average
4 be able to produce a **one period ahead** forecast using single exponential, Trigg-Tracker and Box-Jenkins techniques and know when to choose them
5 be able to produce a **time series** forecast using a multiplicative model, and know the implications of such a forecast.

16.1 Forecasting Techniques

Forecasting will therefore play a prominent role, particularly in the planning activities of a company. There are many different forecasting techniques; many of them are based upon **quantitative methods;** and we will look at the most common of these. 'Quantitative' implies that non-quantitative aspects of the current situation are not incorporated into the forecasting model.

There are two points to note here. The first is that forecasting requires looking into the **future** and divining the outcome. Reading the future is difficult to say the least, and whatever the refinement of the forecasting process it is more of an art than a science. Management decisions should therefore never be made only on the basis of numerical results.

The second point is that numerical forecasting methods are mathematical models of different situations which seem to resemble a reasonable representation of past reality. If your model is too simple, or does not include the key parameters of the situation, or past data is too sparse or unrepresentative, you are unlikely to have too much success. Forecasting like this also implies that the model of the **past** is going to be a valid model for the **future**. However, forecasting is important and necessary.

(a) Method 1: forecast equals last period's actual

One of the simplest forecasting methods is to assume that the forecast for the next period, or for each of a number of periods ahead, will be the same as the **actual figure** for the **most recent** period just ended. This is simple, requires no calculations, is quick and is easily understood. It can hardly be called a model, but nevertheless it will produce a forecast. It assumes that only the most recent period has any bearing on the matter.

Take forecasting the sales of pizzas for the month after next. If you want to make a forecast and use it for planning purposes, you have to make that forecast sufficiently ahead of time so that you have enough lead time to do the things you have to do.

Assume you are now in the middle of April. May's forecast was made in March. You need to forecast June's pizza demand now, so you look at your records for the most recent completed period which is for March. The actual number of pizzas sold then was 750. You therefore make your forecast for June to be 750. Provided that there is nothing special about June, 750 is your best figure and you can now use it as the basis for ordering supplies. Naturally, before you opened your pizza parlour in the first place you would have had to make two best guesses based on very little else than your intuition.

(b) Method 2: forecast equals average of past results

After a while, you may well begin to feel that while Method 1 is simple, it leaves something to be desired, inasmuch as there is no accounting for past history except for the single figure you have used up till now. It may well be rather more realistic to use a method which does not rely so much on one figure alone.

Consider the last six months' demand for pizzas from an earlier example:

Oct	Nov	Dec	Jan	Feb	Mar
850	700	600	800	550	750

Your forecast for June will be the **average of the figures for October to March**. By 'average', we are referring to what is more properly called the arithmetic mean. The mean is, as we now know from Chapter 14, the sum of a set of figures divided by the number of the figures used. In our case, the sum of the figures used equals 4250, and there were six figures used. The mean is therefore 4250 divided by 6, which equals 708.3. Your forecast for June is, say, 700 pizzas. This is not a lot different from the 750 obtained using Method 1, and as it happens to be less, let us hope that you will in this case not be underestimating the actual future demand!

(c) Method 3: forecast derived from a moving average

In Method 2 above, what would you do when you wanted to forecast July's demand? Would you really keep on using the figures from October to March? Of course not, because common sense would tell you those figures are rapidly becoming out of date. The way out of this problem is to use a forecast based on moving averages. These are averages calculated in the same manner as above, but when the forecast for each subsequent period is required, the **oldest** demand figure is **removed** from the list, and the **newest** demand figure takes its place.

The new average is then calculated and used as the forecast. This has the advantage of not allowing the forecast to be based on very old information. It also means that any one month's figures has only a partial effect on the final average figure obtained, in this case one-sixth, as there are six figures being used. We call this a **six-month moving average**. This is particularly useful if there are big fluctuations in demand.

Consider the data below:

Oct	Nov	Dec	Jan	Feb	Mar	Apr	May	Jun	Jul
850	700	600	800	550	750	(700	750	850	800)

The average demand per month from October to March is 4250/6 equals 708.3 as before.

When the April demand of 700 is known, it is added to the list and the October demand of 850 is removed. The new average for the most current six demand figures is now the sum of November to April's demand – 4100/6 = 683.3. Notice, as we observed earlier, that the effect on the average that we are using for our forecast, when we replace a 850 demand with the newer figure of 700, is –one-sixth of the difference (i.e. –25 units). We can check this by noting that 708.3 – 25 = 683.3, our new forecast. In other words, there is a damping effect upon the average, and this effect increases as the number of data we use in our moving average increases.

Similarly the average for December to May will be $(600 + 800 + 550 + 750 + 700 + 750)/6 = 691.7$.

The average from January to June is 4400/6 = 733.3.

The average from February to July is also $4400/6 = 733.3$ because we removed January's demand of 800 and replaced it with a new demand for July also for 800, hence the average remains unchanged.

(d) Graphing data

It will be instructive to graph the data we have been using, so that you can see the effect of the moving averages, and how they relate to the actual monthly demand data. It is always useful to look at a picture of data with which you are unfamiliar, as a picture is more effective than a set of figures in transmitting information. Look at Figure 16.1.

Notice that the graph in Figure 16.1 is drawn with a false vertical scale, which is indicated by the short diagonal lines below the value 500 on the vertical axis. This has the effect of magnifying the vertical scale. This is convenient for our purpose, but should not be used if avoidable, and if used then attention should be drawn to it.

You can see that the monthly data is quite variable, and swings up and down quite a lot. The second half of the data seems to be somewhat less variable than the first half. There appears to be a downward trend in the earlier data followed by an upward trend later on. By eye, the grand average appears to be something over 700 units, which when calculated $= 735$ units. (The grand average is the total of all units divided by the number of data used. In our case we have $7350/10 = 735$ units.)

Notice how the data is plotted. As you might expect, the monthly data is plotted at each month's position on the graph. Each six-monthly moving

---

Fig 16.1 Moving averages vs actual data

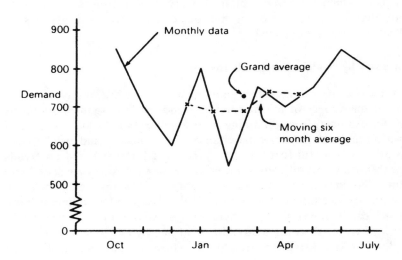

average value is plotted in the middle of its own six values, so our initial moving average of 708.3 is plotted half way between the December and January marks, and similarly for subsequent moving averages. The grand average is plotted halfway between October and July. Notice also that, as we suggested above, the moving averages do not fluctuate as much as the individual values, and so they are quite useful for the purpose described. However, if you want to use six-month averages, you have to wait for six sets of data to come in. You have to only wait three months if you want to use a three-month moving average.

(e) Using the moving average method

We can summarise six steps here:

1 You need to have **n sets of past data** before you can produce the first *n* period moving average.
2 The **larger** *n* is, the less the moving average **fluctuates,** and the older some of your information is that you are using to produce your forecast.
3 Each set of data in the *n* moving average is given **equal weight** (i.e. importance). This may not matter if circumstances externally do not change very much, but if they do, you may feel that some of the older data may be irrelevant.
4 The method is reasonably simple to use, and the forecast produced is equivalent to a horizontal line being drawn at the moving average value, and extended into the future horizontally for as many periods as required, but usually for **one period.**
5 Because of **4** above, moving averages are best used when there is **no significant trend** in the data, up or down.
6 Moving averages can produce a **cyclical pattern** where none existed in the data from which they were obtained. Care must therefore be taken to ensure that no interpretation or spurious conclusions are drawn if such cyclical patterns are detected.

(f) Forecasts by straight line trends (by eye)

Many forecasts are produced from moving averages which imply no trend, because of the danger of misinterpreting trends and consequent problems arising (for example) from obtaining more supplies than needed because of an upward trend which did not materialise. The opposite could also happen.

However, it is useful to be able to produce a forecast based on trends because this will give a different forecast value for each **successive period into the future**. To do this we will draw a straight trend line through some or all of the data, and see how different parts of the data produce different trend lines which can be interpreted in different ways. All our lines will be straight and drawn by eye. Drawing a straight trend line by eye is easy and quick, and is done by visualising the straight line which will have about the same

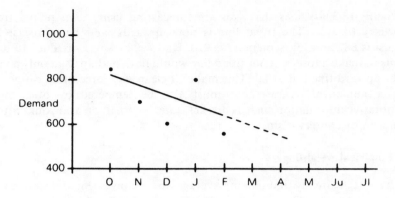

Fig 16.2   Drawing straight trend lines visually (early data)

number of data points below, as above the line. Drawing a line by eye is also useful as a preliminary step towards statistical calculation of such a line (see Chapter 15).

Figure 16.2 assumes that you have data only for October to February, and you can see that the trend line drawn is sloping downward. The line slopes down because the line as drawn seems to fit the points quite well (i.e. the trend line is neither too near nor too far away from any of the points). Our forecast for March therefore would have been 580, and for April it would have been 540, and so on. Notice that a trend line cannot pass through all data points unless they all happen to be on an absolutely straight line themselves.

Fig 16.3   Drawing straight trend lines visually (later data)

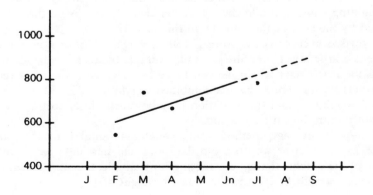

Figure 16.3 assumes that you are forecasting using data points from February to July. The trend line is now upwards, and our forecast for August is 880 and for September is 920. Had we, however, used all 10 data points to make a forecast, our trend line would have perhaps had only a very slight upward trend, if at all. This makes it clear why forecasting cannot be only a numerical exercise, but must also be tempered by other non-quantitative information such as market state, competition and your natural optimism or conservatism.

(g) Empirical weighting

We have seen already that moving averages are a convenient and simple way to make a forecast. This implies, however, that equal weight (importance) is, by definition, given to each piece of data making up the average. This is fine if you think that this corresponds with reality (i.e. that even though each piece of data is older than the previous one, each of them is just as good a predictor as the other).

Look again at the six months' data above, from October to March:

Oct	Nov	Dec	Jan	Feb	Mar
850	700	600	800	550	750

The ordinary six-month moving average for the six months was calculated to be 708.3. If you assume we are now in May, it presupposes that the worth of October's data of 850 is just as important as March's. Clearly in many cases this is not so, as in six months many factors could have caused a change in the operating environment. Therefore let us add, somewhat arbitrarily, a set of weights that indicate the value of each piece of data:

Oct	Nov	Dec	Jan	Feb	Mar	
850	700	600	800	550	750	Data
1	2	4	7	8	10	weight

To find the new average, for each month's data we multiply the sales by the weighting value and add them together. Finally we divide the total so obtained by the sum of the weights, in this case 32.

The revised average is therefore $22150/32 = 692.2$. Notice how the new average is a little lower than the previous average, because it is being **pulled towards the newer data** which happen to be lower values. The most recent three months sales' figures have a combined weighting of 25/32 or 78% of the total weighting, and this situation may be much closer to the real life importance than the earlier method.

The moving average method using weights is similar to the earlier method, except that as we drop old data and add new data we leave the position of the weights the same – so that, for example, the most recent data always has a weight of 10, and the oldest a weight of 1.

(h) Single exponential smoothing

Earlier, we saw how applying a set of weights to a set of values, enabled the **worth** of each piece of data to be taken into account. Of course, the weights chosen would be chosen by the forecaster, and if someone else were choosing weights, the precise values would vary.

The method of exponential smoothing has the effect of applying weights to **past data**, so that the values of those weights fails away exponentially as the data gets **older**. This method of forecasting is usually used to forecast one period ahead, and is then updated. It is often used as a **stock control forecast** method. Although in this method we use only the most recent piece of data, the method can be related to the moving average method by the connection:

Number of periods in the   is equivalent to $\dfrac{\textbf{2 - Smoothing constant}}{\textbf{Smoothing constant}}$
moving average method

If n = number of periods and a = smoothing constant, then $n = (2 - a)/a$ approximately.

In our example of a six-month moving average, we would now use a smoothing constant, a, of about 0.3 or a little less. If you check in the equation given you can see that 0.29 would be a reasonable equivalent value for a.

To make a forecast using the single exponential method, we use the relationship:

$$\text{New forecast} = \text{Old forecast} + a \,(\text{Error})$$

where Error = (Actual − Forecast)
Look at Figure 16.4.

Fig 16.4   Single exponential smoothing

New forecast = Old forecast + a (Forecast error)

a = 0.2

Forecast (1)	Actual (2)	Error (3)	a (Error) (4)
160.0	150	−10	−2.00
158.0	140	−18	−3.60
154.4	160	+5.6	+1.12
155.5	140	−15.5	−3.1
	120		
	130		
	120		
	125		
	115		
	120		−2.3

Column **2** shows some past actual demand data, which we are going to use in order to illustrate how the single exponential technique is used, and how the forecast responds to the actual data itself.

To initiate the forecasting process, we start with an initial guess, in this case 160, and this is put in column **1**. There is an error of $150 - 160 = -10$ units, and this is entered in column **3**. The smoothing constant of 0.2 is multiplied by this error of -10 and therefore $= -2.0$. The forecast for the next period is $160 + (-2) = 158$, and this is entered into column **2**, line 2. The process repeats itself. Follow the calculations for lines **2** and **3** to ensure that you can see how they were arrived at.

Activity

Continue with the calculations and complete the entries in Figure 16.4. Your last entry on the last line, column **4** should be -2.29.

Activity

Take the forecast data which you obtained from Figure 16.4 (column **1**) and plot them onto the graph shown in Figure 16.5.

Is it a 'good' forecast? What do we mean by 'good'? Remember that we forecast only **one period ahead** at a time in this method, unlike our previous methods.

Fig 16.5   Single exponential forecasting

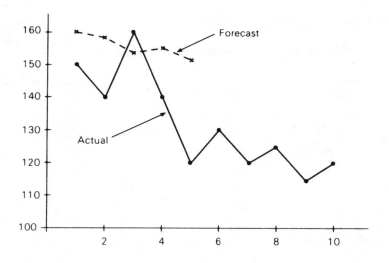

Activity

Using a smoothing constant of $a = 0.5$, and then of $a = 0.8$, plot both the new forecasts on the graph in Figure 16.5, or redraw it on a larger scale and combine all three sets of forecast data.
 Which is the best forecast smoothing constant?
 What is the effect of altering the value of the smoothing constant?
 How do you decide which one to choose?

(i) The Trigg–Tracker technique

If you have no idea of the trend, then a system of forecasting which begins to **home in on the data** will be more appropriate. This system of forecasting uses a Signal, which is generated by the expression:

$$\text{Signal} = \frac{\textbf{Cumulative error including algebraic sign}}{\textbf{Cumulative error excluding sign}}$$

This has the effect of producing a factor which compares the error to date with the gross error to date. It is used in the following way.

As before, New Forecast = Old Forecast + a (Error), where Error = Actual Demand − Forecast Demand. We start with $a = 0.2$ as our initial guess, and recalculate the signal as each actual demand comes in. When the signal drops below 1.0 we replace a with the current value of the signal. The table below shows the first few calculations. Follow through these calculations, to ensure that you understand them, and complete the table entries. If you have done it correctly, the last entry in column **7** should $= +1.6$.

Forecast (1)	Actual (2)	Error (3)	Cum. error with sign (4)	Cum. error without sign (5)	Absol. value of signal (6)	a(error) or s(error) (7)
160	150	−10	−10	10	1	−2
158	140	−18	−28	28	1	−3.6
154.4	160	+5.6	−22.4	33.6	0.67*	+3.8
158.2	140	−18.2	−40.6	51.8	0.78*	−14.3
	120					
	130					
	120					
	125					
	115					
	120					+1.6

* against absolute value of signal in column **6** denotes that value of signal has replaced *a*.

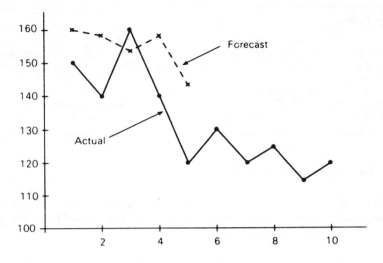

Fig 16.6   The Trigg–Tracker mechanism

Activity

Plot the forecasted values produced by the Trigg–Tracker on to Figure 16.6. How does this forecast plot compare with the forecast plot of the single exponential smoothing method above?

Activity

Repeat the calculations starting with a forecast of **1** 140 and **2** 170. Then plot the results on a suitable graph.

(i) The Box–Jenkins technique

This method of forecasting developed, by the two people named above, helps to establish a **trend**. In the same way that the Trigg–Tracker was a little more involved than single exponential smoothing, so the Box–Jenkins technique is a little more involved than the Trigg–Tracker. It is a matter of experimentation and judgement as to the advantages to be gained from each.

The forecast is obtained from the expression:

New Forecast = Old Forecast + $c1$ (Error) + $c2$ (Cumulative Error) where Error = Actual Demand − Forecast Demand as before. $c1$ is set at 0.2 and $c2$ is set at 0.1.

The table below shows the first few calculations using the same actual data as were used in the two earlier examples above. Follow through the calculations on the first four lines to make sure that you can see how they were done. Then complete the remainder of the table entries; if you did them correctly, the last entry on the last line in column **6** should be −5.2.

Forecast *(1)*	*Actual* *(2)*	*Error* *(3)*	*c1 (error)* *(4)*	*Cum. error with sign* *(5)*	*c2 (cum. error)* *(6)*
160	150	−10	−2	−10	−1
157	140	−17	−3.4	−27	−2.7
151	160	+9	+1.8	−18	−1.8
151	140	−11	−2.2	−29	−2.9
	120				
	130				
	120				
	115				
	120				−5.2

Activity

Plot the forecasted values on to Figure 16.7. Draw a new graph and put all three original sets of forecasted values on to it as well as the original actual demand values used.

Which do you prefer, and why?

Fig 16.7   The Box–Jenkins technique

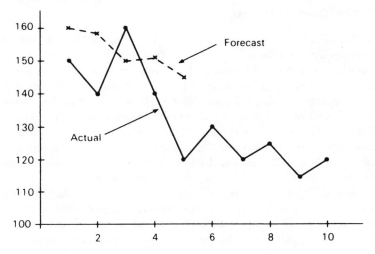

Activity

Try the Box–Jenkins method using slightly different values of c_1 and c_2 (e.g. let $c_1 = 0.1$ and $c_2 = 0.2$). What difference does this make?

Activity

Here is some data concerning UK oil production from 1979 to 1989.

Year	1979	80	81	82	83	84	85	86	87	88	89
Million tonnes	78	81	89	103	115	126	128	128	123	114	92

(a) Plot the data on a graph whose large scale y axis starts at 50 million tonnes.
(b) Repeat **(a)** above but use a small scale y axis which starts at zero, and decide which of **(a)** or **(b)** gives a truer visual picture of output variability.
(c) Produce a straight line trend through the first four points and forecast output for 1983 and 1986. How useful is this trend line as a forecasting tool?
(d) Use all three exponential methods to see which is the best one for the data. Use three different smoothing constants for the single exponential method. Initial forecast is 78 million tonnes.
(e) Use a three period moving average, move through the data, and produce a forecast on each occasion.
(f) Could any of the techniques be relied upon as a reasonable forecasting method with such data?

(j) Time series forecasting

By 'time series', we mean that the data concerned, in our case some quarterly demand data, looks as if it varies in a way that suggests that the **time of the year** has influenced it. There may or may not be a cause and effect relationship; however, because of the pattern displayed it seems reasonable to utilise a model which is capable of analysing the trend and some seasonal factor. There may or may not also be a **random factor** in the data: in reality, all data has a residual or random factor. What this means is that there is no reasonable way to determine the cause (or causes) for this effect, and so we call it 'random'. All effects really have a cause, but we often analyse out only the major effects, such as **trend** and **seasonal factor.**

Look at Figure 16.8. Figure 16.8a represents data which has neither **trend** (other than horizontal) nor **cyclical pattern**. It would be unreasonable, on the face of it, to imply that time has had a visible effect upon the data collected. It appears to continue in the same way as it started.

Fig 16.8   Identifiable features of past data

a   No trend, no cyclical pattern
b   Upward trend, no cyclical pattern
c   Upward trend, cyclical pattern
d   Upward trend, 4 cycles per 1 large cycle

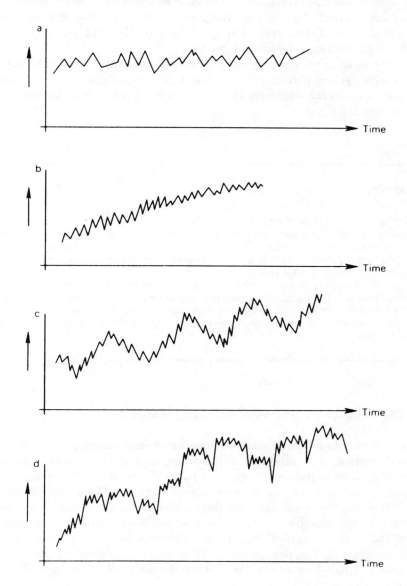

The data in Figure 16.8b exhibits an **upward trend**, suggesting growth as time passes. There is still no discernible cyclical pattern, and any variations would be ascribed to random (unknown) effects.

The plot of data in Figure 16.8c exhibits an **upward trend** as well as a **cyclical pattern**. Superimposed upon the cyclical pattern are some random effects of unknown cause. If that data were on an annual basis, we could say that perhaps the main cyclical effect was due to seasonality. But it would be important to check that such an assumption was reasonable. Because this particular form of data collection is so common, we will use it later to analyse and produce a forecasting model.

Figure 16.8d shows not only an **upward trend and a short-term cycle**, but a **longer-term cyclical pattern** also. As drawn, it appears that there are four short-term cycles for one larger cycle, and these longer-term cycles form an overall upward trend.

Activity

Check through a book of economic statistics (e.g. the Monthly Digest of UK Statistics), to see if you can find some real data which reflects some or all of the patterns shown above. There are other patterns, such as a 'spike': this might be the pattern that demand for fireworks or Remembrance Day poppies takes. Can you see why this might be so?

Bear in mind that the horizontal time scale considered will also affect the pattern observed. On an annual basis, the two examples above may well exhibit spikes for the demand. On a time scale considering only the three weeks before and the week after the events, the demand may well exhibit a growing upward trend followed by a sharply falling trend.

(k) The multiplicative time series forecasting model

This is a technique which analyses **time based data** seeming to exhibit a **cyclical pattern**, and produces a trend line and a factor which varies according to each part of the cyclical pattern. The trend line is used to project a new value for one or more periods ahead, and it is then adjusted by multiplying the trend value by the cyclical factor to produce the final forecast. In our example, we will assume we are dealing with some demand data, and that the cyclical pattern is actually a seasonal pattern for a three-year period. The data has been collected and is shown as one figure for each quarter of each year. We will use the table below to illustrate the process.

Time series forecasting multiplicative models
(regression line by eye produces trend)

Period (x) (1)	Qtr (2)	Actual 4 demand (y) (3)	qtr moving total (4)	4 qtr moving average (5)	Trend (y = 12 + x) (6)	Ratio = actual/ trend (7)
1	3/89	10			13	0.77
2	6/89	19			14	1.36
			53	13.25		
3	9/89	17			15	1.13
			58	14.50		
4	12/89	7			16	0.44
			61	15.25		
5	3/90	15			17	0.88
			68	17.00		
6	6/90	22			18	1.22
			74	18.50		
7	9/90	24			19	1.26
			77	19.25		
8	12/90	13			20	0.65
			83	20.75		
9	3/91	18			21	0.86
			82	20.50		
10	6/91	28			22	1.27
			85	21.25		
11	9/91	23			23	1.00
12	12/91	16			24	0.67
13	3/92	–			25	
14	6/92	–			26	
15	9/92	–			27	
16	12/92	–			28	

Column **1** represents the horizontal time scale and for convenience is called x. The oldest piece of data is from period 1, the next oldest from period 2, and so on. Column **2** shows the time of year each piece of data represents. Period 1 data represents March 1989, period 2 represents June 1989, and so on. This demand data may well have existed as separate 13 weekly figures, for example, but we are dealing with the **quarterly aggregate figures**. Column **3** represents the actual demand data we are going to analyse and use as our basis for predicting the future. For simplicity the data is as shown, but it could equally have been in the hundreds (i.e. period 1's demand of 10 units could have represented a demand for 1000, and so on).

Activity

How in reality, would we tell that our column **3** data is somewhat cyclical? Perhaps it really is not very apparent to you. Plot on a graph of suitable scale, the data for periods 1 to 12, and see if you agree that there seems to be a cyclical pattern. It is always useful to plot new data so that you get a feel for what the **pattern** looks like. It is a fundamental mistake to analyse data mathematically in a manner which does not match the pattern it exhibits. For example, should you do a linear regression on a set of data which exhibits very little linearity?

We need to produce a forecast of demand for periods 13 to 16. The first thing to do is to calculate a 4-period moving total as shown in column **4**, and to place each figure just as is shown in that column. If we add periods 1 to 4 our total is 53 and is positioned between periods 2 and 3 in column **4**. We then remove period 1's value of 10 and replace it with period 5's value of 15, giving us a new moving total of 58. Note where it is positioned. Check that you can see how the remaining moving total values have been obtained.

Column **5** is obtained by dividing each of column 4's values by 4, to produce a moving 4 quarter average. Each value is placed as shown next to its moving total.

We now need to produce a **trend line by eye**, as we originally did earlier on in this chapter. If you look at Figure 16.9 you will see the column **5** values plotted. Take note of the precise position of their plot on the time scale. We now draw a straight line through the points which seems to have about the same number above it as below it, and seems not to be unduly pulled towards any one point. Because we are using moving averages, by definition, they do not vary as much as the individual points.

Fig 16.9   Plot of moving averages

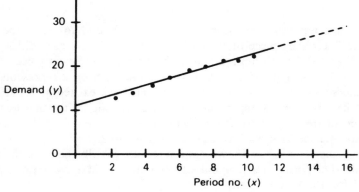

From the line so drawn, we can obtain the trend average for each of periods 13 to 16. By eye from the line we have drawn, we obtain the values as follows:

For period 13, average demand = 25, for period 14, average demand = 26, for period 14, 27 and for period 16 demand = 28.

But these new values are only **averages**. They came from an average line. They take no account of the **seasonal factor**. Column **6** shows the trend values for each period from 1 upwards.

To take into account the seasonal factors which are so apparent from the graph you drew in the Activity on p. 404, we must calculate the ratio of actual / trend for each of the points from 1 to 12. These are shown in column **7**. If you look closely, you will see that they also have a **cyclical** pattern. However, owing to random effects, the 3 March seasonal factors are not identical, nor are the others.

We therefore obtain an average value for each seasonal figure by adding the March values for each of the three years and dividing by 3. Similarly for the June, September and December seasonal factors.

The results are

For March:	$(0.77 + 0.88 + 0.86)/3 = 0.84$
For June:	$(1.36 + 1.22 + 1.27)/3 = 1.28$
For September:	$(1.13 + 1.26 + 1.00)/3 = 1.13$
For December:	$(0.44 + 0.65 + 0.67)/3 = 0.59$

The sum of these new average ratios come only to 3.84, when ideally it should equal 4.00. That it does not is owing to random factors we cannot identify. To overcome this discrepancy, we multiply each ratio by $4/3.84 = 1.04$.

Our final factors now become:

March	0.88
June	1.33
September	1.18
December	0.61 for a total of 4.00

To produce our forecasted demand for periods 13 to 16, we calculate its value from: **trend times ratio**

March 1992	$25 \times .88 = 22.0$
June 1992	$26 \times 1.33 = 34.6$
September 1992	$27 \times 1.18 = 31.9$
December 1992	$28 \times .61 = 17.1$

You should now plot these four forecast values and satisfy yourself that they produce a forecast which follows the trend line and the seasonal pattern.

Activity

In Chapter 16 we have drawn trend lines by eye, and not by calculation. Drawing them by eye is quick and easy, different people would produce different trend lines, and you may not produce the same line from a second attempt. If you are not familiar with calculating trend lines, then read about linear regression in Chapter 15, and enter your calculated values in the table shown and produce a new set of forecast demands.

The results are different. Are they different enough to make the extra effort worthwhile?

Time series forecasting multiplicative model (regression line calculation produces trend)

Period (x) (1)	Qtr (2)	Actual demand (3)	4 qtr moving total (4)	4 qtr moving average (5)	Trend (y = 12.44 + 0.8x) (6)	Ratio = Actual/ Trend (7)
1	3/89	10			13.24	0.76
2	6/89	19			14.04	1.35
			53	13.25		
3	9/89	17			14.84	1.15
			58	14.50		
4	12/89	7				
			61	15.25		
5	3/90	15				
			68	17.00		
6	6/90	22				
			74	18.50		
7	9/90	24				
			77	19.25		
8	12/90	13				
			83	20.75		
9	3/91	18				
			82	20.50		
10	6/91	28				
			85	21.25		
11	9/91	23				
12	12/91	16				
13	3/92	–				
14	6/92	–				
15	9/92	–				
16	12/92	–				

Activity

The following data represents the usage per month in litres x 10,000 of non-CFC propellant for 1993, 1994 and 1995.

	1993	1994	1995
January	5	11	17
February	8	14	20
March	6	10	18
April	7	12	19
May	9	14	21
June	6	13	20
July	9	13	19
August	11	16	23
September	8	14	22
October	11	15	20
November	13	18	24
December	11	16	21

(a) Plot the data for each year on a suitable scale.
(b) Produce a monthly forecast demand for 1996

(l) Z charts

Z charts are a particularly convenient way to record and display information, because three different forms of the same information can be shown without confusion on the same display. It is also possible to make a simple **forecast** from the display and **update** it on a regular basis.

Consider a full year's demand data based on the pizza sales example on p. 390 above:

Oct	Nov	Dec	Jan	Feb	Mar	Apr	May	Jun	Jul	Aug	Sep	
850	700	600	800	550	750	700	750	850	800	700	600	Total = 8650

Last year's annual demand for pizzas was:

Oct	Nov	Dec	Jan	Feb	Mar	Apr	May	Jun	Jul	Aug	Sep	
800	750	550	600	500	700	600	550	750	650	700	650	Total = 7800

Look at Figure 16.10.

The process of plotting the data is as follows. On a suitably sealed chart, first plot on the vertical axis the total level of demand for the previous year; in this case it is 7800. For each month of the current year, we plot three pieces of data:

(a) the demand for **that month**
(b) the **cumulative demand to date**
(c) the **moving annual total demand for the year to date**. This is obtained by taking the last annual total, subtracting the demand in the appropriate month a year ago, and adding the demand for the current month.

You can see the partly completed chart for the months up to and including March. At this time, the cumulative demand to date from September is 4250. The 12-month moving total is 8150. You can also make a forecast based on this graph. Looking at the moving annual total you can say that that your best estimate for the year ending September is the current moving annual total of 8150 units. Alternatively, you could interpret the somewhat upward trend of the moving annual total as being significant, and produce a trend line shown chained, which cuts the September vertical axis at a value of about 8150. You could also produce a trend line upwards from the cumulative monthly data line. In this case such a line extended upwards, intersects the September vertical axis at about the same value as before.

Activity

Complete the remainder of the Z chart in Figure 16.10. Can you see why it is called a 'Z chart'? What would your forecast of demand to September have been if you had made a forecast as above when data up to and including June had been plotted?

Fig 16.10   Drawing a Z chart

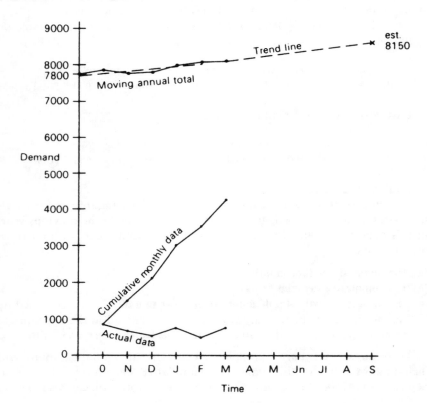

Activity

Using the set of data below, plot the resultant Z chart for the current year, making forecasts for the year at the 3, 6 and 9 month stage of plotting.

Last year

Month	1	2	3	4	5	6	7	8	9	10	11	12
Demand	7	11	9	15	19	22	18	24	22	30	28	27

Current year

Month	1	2	3	4	5	6	7	8	9	10	11	12
Demand	8	11	12	13	14	19	18	27	21	29	32	37

Chapter Review Questions

1 'Numerical forecasting techniques also include non-quantitative aspects of the business': True or False?

2 'A forecaster's model will include every feature of the business in its make-up': True or False?

3 'A forecast based on an average of past data will be better than one based only on the most recent figure': True or False?

4 'Moving averages assign equal weight to each piece of past data': True or False?

5 'Using a scale which excludes zero in its y axis will exaggerate any variation in the data plotted': True or False?

6 'Establishing a trend line by eye is unsatisfactory because no calculations are involved': True or False?

7 'By empirically weighting past data, we can assign a level of importance to each value': True or False?

8 'In single exponential smoothing, we forecast ahead one or more periods at a time': True or False?

9 If we have been using a three-period moving average, what is the equivalent smoothing constant?

10 If we are using the Trigg–Tracker mechanism, when do we stop using the smoothing constant of $a = 0.2$, and use our signal?

11 What is the key feature that the Box–Jenkins forecasting method tries to do?

12 What are the three sets of data which we can conveniently plot on a Z chart?

17 Managing Complexity

Operational Research is concerned with producing optimal results in situations where there are **conflicting objectives** and **limited resources**. This generally means lowest cost solutions or maximum profit solutions depending on the problem in hand. As operational research is based on mathematical techniques, because of their versatility they lend themselves to the numerical solution of a very wide range of business problems.

Learning Objectives

By the end of this chapter you should:

1 be able to solve graphically a **two variable linear program problem**, and know the basis for its calculation
2 be able to solve a **transportation problem** to achieve the optimum result
3 be able to solve an **assignment problem** to achieve the optimum result
4 to be able answer **'what if'** type questions relating to the optimal solutions found.

Operational Research was developed during the Second World War in order to solve a whole range of ·wartime operational problems – for example, how deep should depth charges explode so as to maximise the potential for damage to submarines? What mix of incendiary and high explosive bombs should be carried so as to optimise the damage to the enemy target? After the war it was recognised by some key industries such as coal, steel and electricity that some of these techniques could help solve business problems, and they were used with some success. Since then, the application of these techniques to solving business problems has grown enormously, so that there are many such problems which lend themselves to a numerical solution, based on operational research methods. The techniques shown below, give an idea of their power, and how solutions can be obtained that would be difficult to achieve in other ways. As I have mentioned before, management decision-making uses inputs from many sources, and it is unrealistic to say that managers would make their decisions based solely on numerical results.

Among the areas where operational research can help achieve useful results are problems such as queuing, inventory control, material cutting, container loading, decision-making, planning and scheduling, route planning, replacement, allocation, and econometric modelling.

17.1 OR methodology

Figure 17.1 shows how the key procedure for using operational research methodology is performed.

(a) Defining the problem

No technique can be effective if the **real problem** has not been isolated and correctly defined, so this step is crucial. If a supervisor says 'I need more staff to serve my customers', the real cause could be any number of reasons such as erratic demand, poorly trained staff, poor supervision, ill-defined procedures, lack of proper equipment.

(b) Making a model

Making a **physical** model of the situation is a common method of problem solving because it is simple, flexible, avoids the complete complexity of the real situation, is often cheaper than real life experimentation and can

---

Fig 17.1   Using OR methodology

Real world	*Mathematical world*
1 Define and state the problem	
2 Collect data	
3 Formulate a model:	
a Physical, or	
b Schematic, or	
	c **Mathematical**
	4 Manipulate model
	5 Evaluate and refine model
	6 Predict outcome, then
7 Verify against real data	
8 Implement	
9 Maintain	

sometimes be safer than real life when testing is required. Physical models are very commonly used. Many people have seen clay models of new cars in the prototyping stage prior to design finalisation, models of planes being tested in wind tunnels and models of liners or oil tankers being tested in water tanks.

Schematic models are best exemplified by flow charts such as those in procedure manuals and other instructions (e.g. for the rules as to who shall be eligible for unemployment benefit or a tax refund). An example of a graphical model is the economic order frequency graph which we examined in Chapter 5, which is most helpful within a modest range of results for showing the interaction of the two variable costs. Another example of a graphical model is the break-even chart. Because of their simplicity both are very useful for conveying the essential components of the simple problem.

Mathematical models are, however, the most versatile, and need not in some cases be very complex.

The statement: $y = .02v^2 - .02v + .25$ is a non linear model of the costs of operating a warehouse, where y is the operating cost and v is the value of annual throughput; all costs being expressed in £millions. It was developed from operational data for throughput volume of up to £10,000,000 per year, and is not valid for throughput above this. We can see that with no throughput it costs £250,000 per year to run, i.e. those are the fixed costs. The operating costs stay at that level for throughput of £1 million. If throughput is £2,000,000 the operating costs are £290,000. If throughput is £10,000,000 the operating costs are £2,050,000. Thus for five times the throughput it cost seven times as much. We can also see that at £2 million throughput the operating cost per throughput pound is 14.5 pence. At £10 million throughput the operating cost per throughput pound is 20.5 pence. The relationship between operating and throughput is therefore **non** linear.

The statement: $y = a + bx$ is, however, a model of a **straight line** because there are no powers of x greater or less than unity. It says enough about the line for us to calculate the value for 'y' if we know 'a' and 'b', and 'x'. The value 'a' tells us where the line cuts the y axis, and the value 'b' tells us the slope of the line: a positive b value and the line slopes upwards to the right. If b has a negative value the line slopes downwards from the right. If $a = 0$ then the line passes through the origin of the graph; we no longer have to draw it, and we certainly would not want to make a physical model from wood or card as that would be far too limiting.

In many situations we also find that mathematical modelling produces lifelike three-dimensional visual models of products when allied to computer aided design technology and shown on a computer's visual display unit. Architects can make good use of 3D computer aided design for building design and visualisation, and then use 2D visualisation to produce the plans required. This method has not entirely eliminated the use of physical models but often precedes them.

(c) **Graphical presentation**

Two factor models can be shown quite clearly as graphs. They provide a simple way to summarise a lot of data and provide an easy way to show where an optimum zone might be (in these examples – minimum cost). Figure 17.2 shows five such models.

If a linear relationship exists, some problems can be easily illustrated and solved graphically, provided the problem does not contain more than two

Fig. 17.2   Examples of simple two factor models which indicate an optimum zone

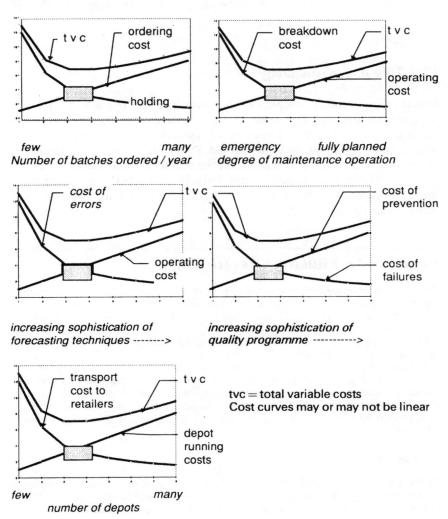

variables. A variable in a problem may be a product or an item whose output we wish to optimise so as to maximise the total profit obtainable under a given set of circumstances.

Problems also have **constraints**. A constraint is a limiting factor in the problem. If 3P Pizza parlour can make only 800 pizzas a month, the quantity 800 is a production constraint. If they cannot work more than 40 hours per week then 40 is a time constraint. Where the problems are of any realistic size either in terms of number of variables, or constraints, or both, powerful mathematical methods can be used on desk top computers to solve such problems fairly simply. The software used requires very little specialised knowledge and not only are the. results available quickly, but extra information is produced which enables a large range of 'what if' questions to be asked and answered.

17.2 Linear Programming

Linear programming, including the Transportation method and the Assignment method, are some of the mathematical techniques falling under the general heading of operational research, or operations research as it is called in Europe and the United States. It is one of a family of optimising techniques, and depends on the relationship between the various problem criteria and outcome being **linearly associated** (e.g. selling three times the quantity brings in three times the revenue; making twice as much incurs twice the cost, etc.).

Case Study: Bildemup Estate Co.

Consider the following problem; linear programming can help in many different areas, and this example contains each type of constraint (i.e. a 'less or equal to' constraint ($\leq$), an 'equal to' constraint' ($=$), and a 'greater or equal to' constraint ($\geq$).

On a 20-acre site, there is the opportunity to build a maximum of 10 semi-detached dwellings per acre or 7 detached dwellings per acre, with a maximum of 180 dwellings in all. Other planning requirements are that there must be at least 100 semis and at least 50 detached. There must be not more than 3 semis to 1 detached, and there must not be more detached than semis. Gross profit of £20,000 per semi – and £36,000 per detached are expected. How many of each type should be built to maximise gross profit, assuming any dwellings built can be sold?

Procedure

As there are only two variables, each constraint can be drawn on a graph which has 's' for semis as its y axis, and d for detached for its x axis. Each constraint is taken, considered on its own, and translated into a straight line and superimposed on to

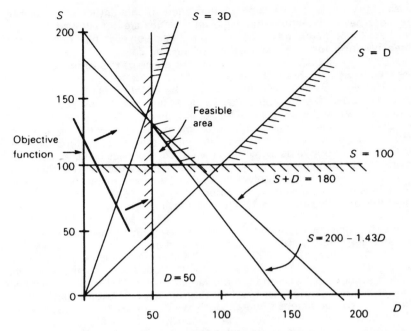

Fig 17.3   Linear programming: an estate of houses

---

the graph (see Figure 17.3). Note that when drawing the constraints, we can draw each constraint only as an equality (i.e. as a limit line) and we then cross-hatch out that part of the graph where the constraint will be **exceeded**.

- **Maximum number of dwellings constraint:** If there were no semis, then there would be 180 detached; but if there were no detached, then there would be 180 semis (i.e. $s + d \leq 180$).
- **Density constraint:** We have 20 acres available to build on. Therefore with 10 semis per acre and 7 detached per acre, we have $s/10 + d/7 = 20$, or $s + 1.43d = 200$.
- **Minimum number of semis constraint:** $s \geq 100$.
- **Minimum number of detached constraint:** $d \geq 50$.
- **Proportion constraint (semis):** There must not be more than 3 semis to 1 detached (i.e. $s \geq 3d$) or written in another way, $s - 3d \leq 0$.
- **Proportion constraint (detached):** There must not be more detached than semis, i.e. $s > d$ or written another way, we can write, $s - d \geq 0$.
- **Non-negative constraint:** Every linear programming problem has the requirement that none of the variables must be negative (i.e. there is no such thing as -2 semis or -5 detached, therefore s and d cannot be less than zero).

Note:
$\leq$ means less or equal to, and $\geq$ means greater or equal to. If you are in doubt as to how a constraint works, substitute a value for 'd' and check the value of 's', or

vice versa. If the resultant value is bigger than allowed, that portion of the graph is to be cross-hatched to show that values in that area are not allowed.

We call the equation formed by the gross profit made on each type of dwelling, the **objective function** and it is usually indicated by **Z**.

$Z = £20,000s + £36,000d$. These values **set the slope of the function**.

To see how we can draw the objective function onto our graph, let us arbitrarily (for convenience) set our returns to be equal to (say) £1,080,000. Then: £1,080,000 = 20,000s + 36,000d. To draw this line, let us assume that $s = 0$, then $d = 30$. and if we assume that $d = 0$, then $s = 54$.

If we draw this line on our graph and look at the area within which the answer must fall, we can see that we must move the objective function line parallel to itself and outwards away from the 0,0 co-ordinates as far as possible but staying inside the allowable area marked with a heavy border. The objective function can therefore move outwards until it hits an intersection of two constraint lines which are as far away as possible from the 0,0 co-ordinates. In this case, the objective function finally hits the intersection of: $s = 100$ and $s + 1.43d = 200$.

Note that the objective function will indeed move out to the intersection of $s = 100$ and $s + 1.43d = 200$, because of the slope given to the objective function by the coefficients 20,000s and 36,000d. If we divide each coefficient by 20,000, we obtain s and 1.8d. As 1.8 is a greater slope than 1.43, the objective function line swings clockwise and is more vertical than $s + 1.43d = 22$, and will therefore hit that intersection last (i.e. furthest from the 0,0 co-ordinates).

Solving these two equations simultaneously we obtain $s = 100$ by inspection, and substituting 100 for s in the second equation we obtain $100 + 1.43d = 200$ or $d = 70$ (only integer answers are realistic).

The optimal (maximum) answer is therefore to build 100 semis and 70 detached, for a total expected gross profit total of:

$(100 \times £20,000) + (70 \times £36,000) = £4,520,000$

Note that there are other permissible answer combinations within the rather small permitted (feasible) area, but these will yield a lower total gross profit. Answer combinations outside the permitted area will yield a higher gross profit, but within the constraints as set in this situation, any such combinations are unallowable.

Further analysis is possible, answering questions such as 'what is the effect of moving (relaxing) one or more of the constraints affecting the solution by one unit?' This information is very helpful in deciding if effort should be put into relaxing such constraints, and by how much.

Activity

1 In the example above, what is the effect on gross profit of having the limit on semis lowered to 99? What is the effect on gross profit of trying to buy an extra acre? What would be the effect of having both of the above situations occur?

When you know the answer to questions like these, it becomes clearer how much you can spend in order to achieve that change.

2 Maximise the objective function: $x + 1.5y$ subject to the constraints:

$2x + 3y \leqslant 6$, $x + 4y \leqslant 4$, $x, y \geqslant 0$ (maximum $= 3$).

3 Maximise $x + y$ subject to:

$5x + 10y \leqslant 50$, $x + y \geqslant 1$, $y \leqslant 4$, $x, y \geqslant 0$.   (maximum $= 10$).

4 Minimise $2x + y$ subject to:

$5x + 10y \leqslant 50$, $x + y \geqslant 1$, $y \leqslant 4$, $x, y \geqslant 0$.   (minimum $= 1$).

5 A cell in a production shop concentrates on making up to four different products. There is always enough raw material to keep the cell supplied. Product A makes a contribution of £25 to overheads, product B makes a contribution of £30, product C a contribution of £35, and Product D of £40.

The cell manager is an experienced person, but would like to know if there is another way to suggest how many of each to make so as to maximise total contribution. All that are produced can be sold. There are five key work centres, and not every product requires to go through every work centre (see the table below).

Using graphical methods, find the optimal production mix for any pair of products and the corresponding contribution. Using any proprietary software your college has, find the optimal production mix for any three products, and for all four products.

	Capacity	Hours required/product			
Work centre	in hours	A	B	C	D
Drilling	600	6	4	0	2
Threading	180	3	0	1	4
Milling	200	2	1	4	0
Turning	300	0	3	2	6
Grinding	450	0	5	1	0

6 Maximise $y - 0.75x$ subject to:

$y - x \leqslant 0$, $y - 0.5x \leqslant 1$, $y, x \geqslant 0$ (maximum 0.5)

7 Minimise $6x + 4y$ subject to:

$2x + y \geqslant 1$, $3x + 4y \geqslant 1.5$, $x, y \geqslant 0$

8 Among its leather products, a company makes two kinds of belt. Belt A is a high quality embossed two tone belt, and belt B is a plainer version. The respective profits are £2 and £1.25 per belt. Belts of type A need twice as much time as a belt of type B. and if all belts were 'B' the company could make 1000 per day. Leather supplies being somewhat uncertain, mean there is only enough to make 800 per day. Supplies of the fancy buckle on belt A are limited to 400 per day. A maximum of 700 buckles are available for belt B per day. Formulate the constraints and determine the quantities of A and B to achieve maximum profit.

9 Minimise $2x - 10y$ subject to:

$x - y \geqslant 0$, $x - 5y \geqslant -5$, $x, y \geqslant 0$

10 Maximise $-5y$ subject to:

$x + y \leqslant 2$, $-x - 5y \leqslant -10$, $x, y \geqslant 0$ (Ans. 0)

11 Minimise $x - 10y$ subject to:

$x - 0.5y \geqslant 0$, $x - 5y \geqslant -5$, $x, y \geqslant 0$ (Ans. 10.556)

12 A distributor has a warehouse in which two key products are stored, A and B. A sells for £15 each and B sells for £25 each. They make 30% and 25% profit respectively. What would be the optimum mix of products to hold to maximise total profits, subject to the following conditions? What effect if any would there be on the optimum mix, if the profit margins were to be changed around; i.e. B to A and vice versa? In both situations, what would be the effect of unit relaxation in the constraints at the optimum solution?
(a) The warehouse can hold a maximum of 3000A or 2000B.
(b) For insurance purposes, the value held in the warehouse must not exceed £60,000.
(c) To provide a reasonable service level, the distributor must hold not less than £20,000 of stock.
(d) It is not practical to hold more than three times as many B as A.
(e) The stock of A should not be allowed to fall below 20% of B.

The full linear programming technique, of which the graphical method above shows the principle, is very broad and powerful. It is not, however, quite so efficient at solving special types of linear problems which can be more simply defined. There are two simpler methods which are applicable in many situations. These are the Transportation method, and simpler still – the Assignment method.

17.3 **The Transportation Method**

Providing we can fit a problem to the simpler Transportation model, we can solve it more quickly than a full linear programming formulation might take us. This method can be applied to (a) optimising distribution problems, (b) location problems of plant, (c) set-up time minimisation and (d) allocating products or parts to specific machines. In general, these problems are characterised by having several 'sources' and several 'destinations'. There may be an overall surplus at the source and an overall deficit at the destination.

(a) **The approach**

1 Formulate the problem according to the transportation format
2 Give every possible 'journey' a unit cost
3 Find a first feasible solution, i.e. one that is possible but necessarily optimum

4 Test it for optimality
5 If it is not optimum, improve the solution
6 Repeat steps 4 and 5 until the optimum is reached

An example

In a small department, there are three machines and there are four parts which need to be processed. Each machine can process each part, although at different unit costs. Each machine can process up to ten items in a given time period. The schedule calls for:

7 of part A,   6 of part B,   7 of part C,   and 5 of part D

The contents of the table in Figure 17.4 show the processing cost per unit on each machine for each part. How many of which part should be processed on which machine to achieve the required schedule at the lowest overall cost? (mu = money units)

Figure 17.5 shows the cost tabulation together with the production needs (bottom row) and capacity limits (right-hand column).

To be a genuinely formulated transportation model, the row and column totals must sum to the same grand total. In this example they do not, so we introduce a **dummy product** to absorb our excess capacity.

We now need to find an initial feasible solution. It can be an educated guess or some automatically generated solution. Sometimes educated guesses

Fig 17.4   Cost table

	Part A	Part B	Part C	Part D
Machine 1	30 mu	20 mu	35 mu	35 mu
Machine 2	25 mu	25 mu	40 mu	50 mu
Machine 3	35 mu	25 mu	25 mu	35 mu

The cost table can be simplified by dividing by a suitable figure, in this case say 5.

	Part A	Part B	Part C	Part D
Machine 1	6 mu	4 mu	7 mu	7 mu
Machine 2	5 mu	5 mu	8 mu	10 mu
Machine 3	7 mu	5 mu	5 mu	7 mu

	A	B	C	D	Capacity
Machine 1	6	4	7	7	**10**
Machine 2	5	5	8	10	**10**
Machine 3	7	5	5	7	**10**
needs ⟶	**7**	**6**	**7**	**5**	

Fig 17.5   Cost, production needs, and capacity table

take a bit longer than guesses, but may be nearer to an optimal solution. We will find an initial feasible solution using two methods.

You must also ensure that you have exactly (**rows + columns − 1**) entries in your table. If you do not, you must enter a **very small non-specified amount = S,** into the cheapest appropriate cell. Because you can imagine it to be as small an amount as you wish, it does not affect any other quantities added to it, and if multiplied by a unit cost, the result is still zero cost.

The first is an automatic rule, i.e. it does not give a good guess solution but it is quick to apply. Because of where it starts from, it is called **'the north-west rule'**.

(b) 'North-west rule' method

Allocate as much as possible to the north-west square of the table in Figure 17.6, and work across and down the table, allocating as much as possible into each cell without violating the capacity or need constraints.

Notice we have treated the dummy quantity of 5 in the second column from the right just as if it were a real product, but it has a processing cost of zero mu per item. The total processing cost is therefore the sum of quantity

Fig 17.6   1st solution: north-west rule

	A	B	C	D	Dummy	Capacity
Machine 1	7 @ 6 mu	3 @ 4 mu				**10**
Machine 2		3 @ 5 mu	7 @ 8 mu			**10**
Machine 3				5 @ 7 mu	5 @ 0 mu	**10**
needs ⟶	7	6	7	5	5	**30** grand total

	A	**B**	**C**	**D**	**Dummy**	Capacity
Machine 1	2 @ 6 mu	6 @ 4 mu	2 @ 7 mu			**10**
Machine 2	5 @ 5 mu				5 @ 0 mu	**10**
Machine 3			5 @ 5 mu	5 @ 7 mu		**10**
needs ⟶	7	6	7	5	5	**30** grand total

Fig 17.7 1st solution: cheapest squares rule

x processing cost per unit for each cell. This $= 160$ money units. This method is quick, but is likely to need more iterations, i.e. cycles of calculation to reach the optimum.

(c) 'Cheapest squares' method

Allocate as much as possible to those squares having the cheapest unit processing cost. Start with those squares and leave the more expensive squares until last. In this example you will therefore have $3 + 5 - 1 = 7$ entries. This method may take longer than the previous method, but it is more 'sensible' and the result will require fewer iterations to reach the optimum than the previous method. Figure 17.7 shows the result.

The total cost for this initial solution is 135 mu. Now let us use this as our first feasible solution and show how to test for optimality; i.e. in the case of costs, is the overall cost the lowest achievable? In the case of profits, is the overall profit the highest achievable?

(d) Testing for optimality

Using our 'cheapest square' solution we set up a new table. This table identifies the unit costs associated with our solution and splits them up into a column 'cost' and a row 'cost'. These row and column 'costs' have the property that for each occupied cell, when added together, they sum to the real life unit cost. To develop this new table of row and column 'costs' we identify with an X each occupied cell, and assign arbitrarily, a 'cost' = zero for the first column. Figure 17.8 shows this.

Therefore:

(a) Mark the occupied squares from the initial solution (Figure 17.7) with an X in our new table.

(b) Enter a zero for the column 'cost' in column 1, i.e. Part A. (As there eight unknown values to determine, 5 column and three row 'costs', we have to assign an arbitrary value to one of them.)

	A	B	C	D	**Dummy**	Row 'cost'
Machine 1	X @ 6 mu	X @ 4 mu	X @ 7 mu			**6** 2nd entry
Machine 2	X @ 5 mu				X @ 0 mu	**5** 7th entry
Machine 3			X @ 5 mu	X @ 7 mu		**4** 5th entry
Col. 'cost'	**0** 1st entry	**−2** 3rd entry	**1** 4th entry	**3** 6th entry	**−5** 7th entry	

Fig 17.8   1st split cost table

(c) Split the real life cost per unit for an occupied cell, starting with the cost entry in the column above the arbitrary column 'cost' of zero, by the relationship $0 + 6\,mu = 6$, i.e. the row 'cost'. Enter 6 in the end of that row.

The row and column 'costs' are sometimes called split costs.

In Figure 17.8, the notes 1st entry, 2nd entry etc. denote the sequence in which the split costs were determined.

Still testing for optimality:

(d) for each of the **unoccupied** cells, enter in the same table:

Real cost − (row split cost + column split cost)

The 'costs' for **unoccupied** cells give the cost for not using that 'journey'. They are often called shadow costs. These shadow costs are shown in Figure 17.9.

The shadow costs in Figure 17.9 show the penalty ($a + ve$ shadow cost) or advantage ($a - ve$ shadow cost) for not using any particular cell.

Fig 17.9   1st shadow cost table

	A	B	C	D	Dummy	
Machine 1	X	X	X	−2 shadow	−1 shadow	6 split
Machine 2	X	+2 shadow	+2 shadow	+2 shadow	X	5 split
Machine 3	+3 shadow	+3 shadow	X	X	+1 shadow	4 split
	0 split	−2 split	1 split	3 split	−5 split	

	A	B	C	D	Dummy	
Machine 1	2 @ 6 mu	6 @ 4 mu	–	+ 2 @ 7 mu		10
Machine 2	5 @ 5 mu				5 @ 0 mu	10
Machine 3			+ 7 @ 5 mu	– 3 @ 7 mu		10
	7 reqd.	6 reqd.	7 reqd.	5 reqd.	5 reqd.	

Fig 17.10   2nd solution

For example, had we used part B on machine 2 it would have cost us an **extra** 2 mu per part allocated. Had we used part D on machine 1 we would have **saved** 2 mu per part allocated.

(e) **Improving the solution**: When improving a current solution, we therefore start by choosing a cell with the largest negative shadow cost, and re-arranging the entries to put as much as we can in that cell (currently it is an empty cell).

We adjust the other occupied cells to make the row and columns still add to the row and column totals. Here therefore we pick the -2 shadow cost cell and adjust accordingly.

Recalculate the new real total cost for the new allocation of parts to machines, and the new total cost will be lower than the previous total.

Test again for optimality, i.e. are there any cells remaining with $-ve$ shadow costs. If there are none, the solution is optimum. Figure 17.10 shows the next allocation of parts and 17.10 the shadow cost table. From Figure 17.11.

The plus and minus entries in the cells c1, d1, d3, c3 show how we removed 2 parts from c1, put them into d1. We had therefore to reduce d3 by 2 parts to keep that column total unchanged, and had to increase c3 by 2 parts to keep that row total unchanged. *Note*: The route taken in reshuffling the cell quantities must always be an unbroken path back to where you started from.

Activity

Ensure you are able to calculate the above real total cost (Ans. 131 mu).

	A	B	C	D	Dummy	
Machine 1	X	X	1 shadow	X	−1 shadow	**6 split**
Machine 2	X	2 shadow	2 shadow	6 shadow	X	**5 split**
Machine 3	3 shadow	3 shadow	X	X	1 shadow	**4 split**
	0 split	−2 split	1 split	−1 split	−5 split	

Fig 17.11   2nd split cost and shadow cost table

Notice the linearity of the problem as mentioned earlier. We put 2 extra units in an unoccupied cell with a shadow cost of −2 mu per part, and saved $2 \times 2\,mu = 4\,mu$ from the previous solution of 135 mu.

We can see in Figure 17.11 that if we put as many parts as we can into cell Dummy 1, we will save 1 mu per part moved.

Activity

1 Re-sequence the number of parts assigned to cells Figure 17.11, to produce a new table of allocation and calculate the new total costs. Produce the new split cost–shadow cost table. Is this new solution optimal? How can you tell? Ensure you start by allocating 2 parts from cell A1 into cell Dummy1. This will leave the Dummy column total too large, so you must reduce cell Dummy2 by 2 parts. This leaves the Machine 2 row total too small, so we must increase the cell A2 by 2 parts and all totals balance again.*

2 Take any cell with a $a + ve$ shadow cost and put parts into it from the optimum solution you have found. Satisfy yourself that the optimum solution does indeed increase by that +ve shadow unit cost × the number of parts you put into it. Of course, all row and column totals must not be violated.

3 There are three warehouses and four stores. The warehouses have stocks of 11, 13 and 19 respectively. The stores need 6, 10, 12 and 15 respectively. The unit costs of transportation are given below. What quantities should be sent from each warehouse to each store at what total optimal cost.*

Costs per unit	Store 1	Store 2	Store 3	Store 4
Warehouse 1	21	16	25	13
Warehouse 2	17	18	14	23
Warehouse 3	32	27	18	41

4 Solve the following transportation problem by finding the minimal cost allocation.

Costs per unit	Destination 1	Destination 2	Destination 3	Destination 4
Source 1	16	19	12	14
Source 2	22	13	19	16
Source 3	14	28	8	12
Needs	10	15	17	

5 As a result of business expansion, you now have three production plants with four distribution centres. The plant capacities, distribution demand, and the transport cost per unit are shown below. Find the optimum distribution arrangement and lowest cost. (Can you reduce total cost below 800 mu?)

Costs per unit	Centre A	Centre B	Centre C	Centre D	Available
Plant 1	10	4	10	5	100
Plant 2	6	3	6	10	50
Plant 3	8	7	4	4	50
Needs	40	30	40	60	

6 A contractor has three pools of labour located at three different sites. They can however be employed on any of four jobs contracted for next week. Travelling costs per person to each job is shown below. (Can you reduce overall costs below 1775 mu?)

Costs/unit	Category 1	Category 2	Category 3	People needed
Job 1	25	15	20	25
Job 2	20	15	22	20
Job 3	20	10	18	20
Job 4	30	12	15	40
Pool available	30	40	50	

7 Transportation costs/unit incurred in shipping goods from factories 1 and 2 to warehouses A, B and C are shown below in £. Factory 1 has a capacity of 40 units and Factory 2 a capacity of 25 units. The demands from A B and C are 20, 10 and 25.

How many units should be shipped via each route so as to minimise costs?

£ costs/unit	A	B	C
Factory 1	4	4	7
Factory 2	5	2	2

8 Monthly factory capacities are 160, 150 and 190 mu respectively. Monthly requirements are 80, 90, 110, and 160 respectively. Determine the optimum distribution to minimise shipping costs.

Costs/unit	Destination D	E	F	G
Source A	42	48	38	37
Source B	40	49	52	51
Source C	39	38	40	43

17.4 The Assignment Method

These are still linear programming problems, but are more simply solved by putting the data in tabular form.

These types of problem typically consist of say, assigning 5 people to 5 jobs; or 7 players to 7 playing positions; or 14 vehicles to 14 work bays; or 10 buses to 10 garages. In each case there must be a specific cost or 'score' for assigning each item from its source to any destination. We aim to minimise cost or time, or to maximise 'profit'.

Example

Four maintenance staff are now multiskilled, and are freely available for any task. Because of this, they can each do the repairs required on any of four vehicles in the repair bay. The supervisor has an estimate from past experience as to how long it will take each person to make a small adjustment to each vehicle. The question is: how should these people be assigned to the vehicles, so as to minimise the overall time?

We will use this example to illustrate the formal procedure for solving this type of problem.

Adjust time in minutes	Vehicle 1	Vehicle 2	Vehicle 3	Vehicle 4
Alf	8	26	17	11
Betty	13	28	4	26
Chris	38	19	18	15
Donna	19	26	24	10

Step 1

Reduce each row by its minimum element to get at least one zero per row. You can see that the minimum element in row 1 is 8; in row 2 it is 4; in row 3 it is 15 and in row 4 it is 10.

Adjust time in minutes	Vehicle 1	Vehicle 2	Vehicle 3	Vehicle 4
Alf	0	18	9	3
Betty	9	24	0	22
Chris	23	4	3	0
Donna	9	16	14	0

Step 2

Reduce each column **if necessary** by its minimum element to get at least one zero per column. Notice that only column 2 needs this treatment. What is the constant amount to reduce column 2 by?

Adjust time in minutes	Vehicle 1	Vehicle 2	Vehicle 3	Vehicle 4
Alf	0	14	9	3
Betty	9	20	0	22
Chris	23	0	3	0
Donna	9	12	14	0

Step 3

Look at the first row. If it contains 2 or more zeros go on to the next row.

   If not, select the cell with the zero and mark it, i.e. you have assigned it (in the table below an assigned cell is shown with two asterisks beside it). Disqualify any zeros in the same column as the selected zero.

   Look at the next row and so on for all rows.

Adjust time in minutes	Vehicle 1	Vehicle 2	Vehicle 3	Vehicle 4
Alf	0**	14	9	3
Betty	9	20	0**	22
Chris	23	0**	3	0 deleted
Donna	9	12	14	0**

Step 4
Repeat step 3 but do it for columns

Adjust time in minutes	Vehicle 1	Vehicle 2	Vehicle 3	Vehicle 4
Alf	0**	14	9	3
Betty	9	20	0**	22
Chris	23	0**	3	0 deleted
Donna	9	12	14	0**

The assignment of people to vehicles which minimises vehicle adjustment time is therefore:

A1   B3   C2   D4 for a total time of 41 minutes

What to do if the procedure above runs out of zeros?
You must protect the zeros you already have, and change your base:

1 Mark the **rows** with no assignments.
2 Mark the **columns** which have zeros in the **marked rows**.
3 Mark the **rows** which have assignments in the **marked columns**.
4 Repeat steps 3 and 4 if necessary.
5 Draw a line through each **marked column** and **unmarked row**.
6 Select the **minimum uncovered element** and **subtract** it from all **uncovered elements**. Add it to the element at the intersection.
7 Now attempt a completely new solution, by following the normal procedure.

Note: Sometimes you can select from several zeros. In this case these answers are optimal but not unique.

Further modifications
1 We can maximise instead of minimising.
2 Dummies may have to be incorporated, similar to those used in the Transportation Technique.
3 If necessary, you can use **H** as a cell entry to discourage it being used as an assignment. The **H** is merely interpreted/treated as **'a very high cost'** and does not have to be calculated.

These modifications make the Assignment method quite versatile.

Activity

1 Minimise the assignment data below:*

	1	2	3
A	3	5	6
B	7	3	1
C	10	2	2

2 Minimise the assignment data below:

	1	2	3
A	21	22	24
B	31	36	30
C	45	40	43

3 Minimise the assignment data in the table below:

	1	2	3	4	5
A	3	7	6	11	4
B	6	41	1	1	6
C	7	3	9	10	5
D	7	14	8	10	5
E	15	10	12	10	11

4 Assign a person to each job so as to minimise the total time. The time for each person to do each job is in the table below:*

Hours per job per person	Job 1	Job 2	Job 3
Annette	8	26	17
Betty	13	28	4
Carrie	38	19	18

5 Make a minimum time assignment for the data below:*

Hours per person per job	Job 1	Job 2	Job 3	Job 4
Eleanor	8	26	17	11
Andy	13	28	4	26
Ruti	38	19	18	15
Lizzie	19	26	24	10

6 If the normal procedure does not lead to a solution, use the second procedure to 'save your zeros' and try the normal procedure again.*

Time/person/job	Job 1	Job 2	Job 3
Fred	8	8	17
Gary	13	28	4
Howie	38	19	18

7 **Maximise** the performance ratings of the people below, given their individual ratings for each job. A rating of 0 means that person cannot do that job.
Select the largest element and replace each entry by the difference between it and the largest element. Now use the normal procedure.

Performance rating per person per job	Job 1	Job 2	Job 3	Job 4	Job 5
Ida	5	4	2	4	2
Jack	1	4	4	4	7
Kelly	2	9	2	5	1
Laura	6	5	8	6	0
Mick	2	0	6	1	9

8 Minimise the assignments in the table below. It is likely that you will have to use the 'save your zeros' procedure as well as the normal procedure.

	1	2	3	4
A	20	36	19	45
B	18	6	19	21
C	14	33	17	6
D	9	6	18	7

9 There are five incoming flights and five outgoing to/from a small airfield. The layover times are as shown below. What assignment of planes will minimise total layover time?

Layover times	Out F1	Out F2	Out F3	Out F4	Out F5
In F1	86	83	8	36	36
In F2	85	86	5	33	39
In F3	16	13	78	10	16
In F4	31	28	15	83	77
In F5	36	33	20	36	82

Chapter Review Questions

1 Name three different kinds of statistical models that we can develop.
2 What does the term 'linear' in linear programming imply?
3 What is an objective function when carrying out linear programming?
4 What affects the slope of the objective function when it is drawn?
5 What is the interpretation when an objective function and an optimal constraint are parallel?
6 'The transportation method can only be used where physical movement of material is involved': True or False?
7 How is a shadow cost interpreted?
8 What can we do if we fail to get 'row + column − 1' entries initially?
9 What do we do if we have more stock available than we want to transport?
10 What is meant by a feasible solution and what are ways to find it?
11 'A transportation problem could be formulated as a linear programming problem': True or False?
12 'If we run out of zeros when trying to solve an assignment problem, then no solution is possible': True or False?
13 'We can maximise using the assignment method as well as minimising': True or False?
14 If we do not want to make an assignment to a cell, we ...
15 If we can choose from several zeros in an assignment, it means ...

Answers to Chapter Review Questions and Selected Activities

Chapter 1

1 People, equipment, material, money and time.

2 They both convert their resources to give customers what they want, hopefully when they want it and at a price they can afford.

3 Efficient conversion of a company's resources.

4 To help ensure that what is developed is what the customer wants.

5 Because it has very little value, but costs a lot to hold.

6 Price, product, promotion, and place.

7 Operating company personnel policies, negotiations, training and statutory policies.

8 False.

9 Planning, scheduling and inventory control.

10 Number of jobs in queue and in process, department capacity, and current load, work content of jobs in queue, time span of schedule and department efficiency.

11 It will often by then be too late to take corrective action.

12 Buying power and simpler administration.

13 Evaluate delivery, quality, price, plant and people.

14 There is a set of hierarchical levels, from mission statement at the top, to plans/procedures at the lowest level. From the lowest to the highest level, each is designed to help achieve the one above it.

15 Assessing the strengths and weaknesses (internal to the company, together with the opportunities and treats (external to the company).

16 Functions within the company such as Finance, Personnel, Marketing, R and D, and Production. Each one is designed to complement the other with a view to achieving the overall targets of the company.

17 The purpose of R and D is to help give a company a competitive edge over its competitors, and to improve its longer-term profitability. R and D is an investment rather than a cost.

18 Blue sky or basic research into fundamental principles; applied research to link current knowledge more closely to future products or processes; development as an improvement process to existing products.

19 By exerting tight control over expenditure and task allocation and monitoring of results and problems. Project management techniques may help in this.

20 False. Aesthetics can only be one factor of design. It happens to be the most visible one.

21 Design management using a matrix approach to organising design projects and design teams is an effective way to manage this activity.
22 The six key stages are: objectives, conception, embodiment, detailing, pre-production and customer feedback. They should not be done solely sequentially but wherever possible, concurrently with the other stages. In diagram form we would expect to see arrows feeding back from each stage to previous stages.

Chapter 2

1 Value engineering.
2 Quality.
3 Value in esteem, use, exchange.
4 Useful value + esteem value.
5 The team approach provides the most valuable results.
6 The free expression of ideas without regard to their practicality at that time.
7 True.
8 Quality fit for its intended purpose, at an appropriate cost. Two factors, quality of design and quality of conformance.
9 Appraisal, scrap, rework, warranty and non-warranty, and prevention.
10 Prevention, e.g. training.
11 It is a cause and effect diagram.
12 False.
13 Losses caused after shipment by a product's functional variability.
14 Producer's risk is the risk of a batch of acceptable quality being rejected by a pessimistic sample. Consumer's risk is the risk of a batch of unacceptable quality being accepted by an optimistic sample.
15 True.
16 The level of defectives at which there must be a very low chance of acceptance. These levels must be continually reduced by proactive measures forming part of the Total Quality Management programme.
17 False.

Chapter 3

1 Ability to perform to stated specification under stated conditions for the required time.
2 Sudden, intermittent and catastrophic.
3 Failure rate is the number of failures per unit time.
4 Hazard is the ratio of failure in a period to survivors at the start of that period. Hazard rate is the hazard per unit time.
5 Mean time between failures is the reciprocal of failure rate.
6 The standard deviation equals the mean. The distribution has a constant rate of decrease.
7 The normal distribution.
8 Elements in series are connected end on end to each other. Elements in parallel have a common input and a common output.
9 False. Connection in parallel achieves this.
10 $6!/(3! \times 3!) = 20$ ways.
11 The system will still function when some of its elements fail.

Chapter 4

1 False. It is more concerned with the management of production.
2 Planning, implementation, recording and dissemination of information, monitoring and corrective action.
3 False. If too close to the actual event, planning is unlikely to be possible or effective.
4 True. Lower level plans contribute to higher plans objectives.
5 Getting everything ready which is necessary to do the job, so that it can start at the first work station as planned.
6 Planning layout, job card, route card, move ticket.
7 Because it is essential to follow closely the progress of jobs, and to take corrective action if necessary.
8 They stay close to the work they are monitoring, are aware of any actual or potential problems, can work well with people, and are able to initiate promptly corrective action as necessary.
9 (a) Absenteeism may be greater than planned
  (b) Equipment unexpectedly breaks down
  (c) Customer makes last-minute changes to agreed design
  (d) Errors are found in drawings
  (e) Shortage of required material.
10 It exerts control within pre-defined limits.
11 (a) Feedback is action/information fed in at the beginning of a process, but which is based on earlier results from that process
  (b) Positive and negative.
12 It can oscillate with ever-increasing frequency, and may ultimately destroy itself.
13 A variance. It may be negative or positive.
14 False. Performances will then appear better than they actually are.
15 By monitoring closely the targets set at weekly, monthly and quarterly intervals.
16 To see how current and future workloads compare with current capacity.
17 Improve methods, consider overtime, possibly subcontract, hire extra plant if possible, hire temporary labour.
18 Because the actual quantity may be less than the planned quantity and work may have to be re-done to conform to specification.
19 A learning curve is a mathematical model of how the cycle time of a largely manual operation reduces as the skill level increases. Schedules may have to take account of this if it is felt to be a significant factor.

Chapter 5

1 Inventory which is not part of a product or used in conjunction with other parts (items on supermarket shelves, products in a pharmacy, shoes in a shoe shop and parts in a maintenance stockroom are considered 'independent' inventory).
2 Primarily to ensure that the customer gets good service. In essence, yes (i.e. to ensure that they can complete their manufacturing schedule). However, with JIT, stocks are always minimal.
3 Raw material, work in progress, finished goods and inventory held by service vehicles out in the field.
4 They might run out or hold excess inventory.

5 Yes – because the following factors have a cost of their own: opportunity or interest costs, space, insurance, handling, obsolescence, spoilage, theft, auditing etc.
6 Holding cost factor (hcf) is the annual cost to hold inventory expressed as a percentage of that inventory value. Order processing cost (opc) is the administrative cost to push the order through the plant and to receive the goods into the plant when received.
7 Re-order level (ROL) and Re-order quantity (ROQ).
8 When the order processing cost equals the holding cost for a given annual demand.
9 False. You may have to divide the year into separate demand segments and do separate calculations.
10 True.
11 When receiving price discounts the price varies, so it has to be included in the calculations for each option.
12 They decrease average stock held, because stock is being used while new goods are still being received.
13 Where stock requires special storage facilities such as glass vats for corrosive chemicals or stainless steel tanks for milk.
14 It is rather more flexible than the simple ROQ/ROL system, and allows for a variable order quantity.
15 False. It is the other way around.
16 If both options are available, when demand is slack, items bought in can be made in-house, thus contributing to improved utilisation of people/equipment; and vice versa.

Chapter 5 Activity (p. 135)

To make or buy widgets: (a) £11.40 (b) £12.00.

Chapter 6

1 Dependent demand means that all component quantities are dependent on the final product itself. Independent demand is unrelated to any particular product requirement.
2 Pull demand led manufacture is illustrated by the JIT approach, where the impetus for action comes at the finished product end of the chain. MRP1 illustrates push demand led manufacture.
3 EOQ is not really relevant for dependent demand-orientated manufacture. It does not produce convenient and consistent batch sizes in that situation; nevertheless, it is still used.
4 False.
5 The explosion works back from the required date and calculates the quantities and dates for all lower level items in a product.
6 Basic quantity required, scrap level, spares, allocated items and work in progress.
7 A bill of materials lists every item required to make a product, and is in product sequence. A where used listing indicates where every single item held in stock, and is used for every different product on which it occurs.

8 Advantages – should meet your precise needs including future needs. Disadvantages – very expensive, long development time, some uncertainty involved.

9 Just in Time. It is a change in philosophy of manufacture throughout a company's lifetime.

10 Smoother production flow, lower levels of work in process, lower change over times, higher levels of quality, better adherence to schedules.

11 They can expect a very much closer relationship with the key manufacturer, a higher level of internal quality and, again, close adherence to schedules.

12 Kanban is the card which initiates action further back along the line.

13 Tends to absorb latent underloading in equipment.

14 You should have chosen from scrap and rework levels, delivery performance, supplier quality, unit costs, work-in-progress levels, labour efficiency, equipment utilisation.

15 False.

16 False.

Chapter 7

1 Fixed costs, variable costs and revenue together with different levels of output.

2 It is useful because it shows graphically the area where revenue equals total costs.

3 Fixed costs are those costs which are unrelated to levels of output, and they do not vary in the short to medium term. In the long term, all costs are variable.

4 Variable costs are those costs which vary with the level of activity or output.

5 Overheads are the costs which are incurred to run the operation regardless of the level of activity, at least in the short to medium term.

6 'Contribution' refers to the difference between revenue and variable costs, and is therefore the contribution that a product makes towards the recovery of the fixed costs.

7 True. Money now is worth more than the same amount received in the future.

8 True. It is a convenient way to estimate the return a project is likely to make.

9 Straight line, sum of digits, reducing balance.

10 When work is predominantly processed in batches, it is convenient to cost in this manner.

11 Generally false. While selling price should be greater than costs, it may still be useful to have a product whose selling price is somewhat less – or as is often the case, the selling price is related to what the market can bear.

12 Standard cost is the cost a particular item should incur. The variance is how much actual cost has varied from the standard, and may be positive or negative.

Chapter 8

1 Job production.

2 Batch production.

3 Flow production.

4 True. This has implications for job satisfaction, which sometimes manifests itself in excessive absenteeism.

5 Preventive maintenance, to avoid emergency breakdowns as far as possible.
6 At Kalmar, small teams work on the car's assembly and are responsible as a team for large amounts of work.
7 False. It is based on identifying the key characteristics of a representative composite component, and forming a cell for manufacturing appropriate components.
8 Its elements all work together to achieve a clearly specified objective.
9 False. It really refers to the communication and control system.
10 True. Many designs are kept up to date solely on the computer. Paper copies may be made.

Chapter 9

1 Useful output divided by total input. It can be measured by money (e.g. value added per employee), or as other relevant units per unit of input. Increase or decrease in productivity is the change in output per unit input from the previous period, divided by the previous period output per unit input.
2 All personnel in the affected department, including their supervisors and trade union representatives, must be put fully in the picture. Such briefings should also extend to regular updates.
3 Organisation and methods.
4 Delay, inspect, operation, store and move. These are the ASME symbols.
5 Only operations and inspections are shown. This enables a broad picture to be obtained rather quickly.
6 Person and material. It sometimes is a matter of judgement which kind of chart is most suitable for a particular situation.
7 Time lapse photography or video recording will show sufficient information, as the work does not progress very fast. The loss in detail does not matter.
8 To ensure that all possibilities have been considered and that no unwarranted assumptions have been made.
9 Unless install and maintain are implemented successfully, the benefits suggested in the proposals are unlikely to materialise.
10 Successful install and maintain phases are those where the willing co-operation of the operators and supervision concerned has been obtained. Retraining nearly always needs the active help of supervision, so that adherence to new methods can soon become the norm.

Chapter 9 – Activities (pp. 207–3)

Warehouse Elevator: Question **2**: 3 minutes per repetitive cycle. Question **4a**: 40 trolleys per hour.

Chapter 10

1 A measure of work which includes basic time, and all appropriate allowances.
2 False. 32 units will be produced only by a motivated operator taking the appropriate rest allowances.
3 Basic time = (actual time × rating factor) ÷ 100. (e.g. for a performance of 90 and an actual average time for an element of 1.5 minutes, the basic time = (1.5 × 90)/l00 = 1.35 basic minutes).

4 Brisk, businesslike and competent. Equivalent to walking unimpeded on a level surface at 4 miles per hour.

5 It is usually a non-productive occurrence which can be reasonably expected to occur infrequently in a job. A percentage allowance is often made for contingencies.

6 Synthetics are derived from time studies, and are used to develop new standards for similar work. Predetermined motion time studies are taken only for those elements in a new job where synthetic values are not available. Predetermined motion time standards are proprietary standards for very small elements such as 'get', 'position' or 'place'. Because they are so small such elements can be used to build a wide variety of work values.

7 Someone who has worked for a long time at the jobs for which estimates are required.

8 Four times as many readings will be required.

9 True. A time study observer must be trained formally in the skills required to conduct such a study.

10 Scheduling, costing and work study based incentive schemes.

Chapter 11

1 Piecework bonus schemes pay a set amount of money per piece produced and no money is received for zero production. The amount paid is not based on work-study-based criteria. Work-study-based incentive schemes relate bonus payment to performance on a graduated scale. Generally there is a level below which pay will not fall.

2 A reference period is a representative period in the past which can be used to illustrate bonus earnings on a scheme to be introduced. The reference period chosen should be agreed by both management and unions.

3 A proportional incentive scheme pays bonus in proportion to the increase in performance achieved. For example, for an increase in performance of one-third, the bonus will be one-third of basic rate. A geared incentive scheme may pay more than proportionately for performance below 100 on the BS scale, and less than proportionately for performances above 100.

4 Unmeasured work reduces the amount of bonus that can be earned. This is because it is often paid at basic rates. There will be pressure from unions and operators to minimise or eliminate unmeasured work.

5 It is unrealistic for an operator to be able to achieve consistently a performance much above 125 to 130. If this appears to be occurring, it may not represent what is actually happening. A ceiling is therefore applied to protect both management and the operators.

6 Performance while on measured work, and overall performance. The first parameter is standard hours achieved divided by hours spent on measured work, and should be expected to show a trend towards 100. The second is standard hours achieved divided by attendance hours, and therefore includes time spent not only on measured work but also on unmeasured work and waiting time. This ratio should show a trend towards the first ratio.

7 If waiting time and other non-productive time is absorbed in the total time taken for productive work, there is no indication to management of the extent or trend of such occurrences.

8 Maximum wages agreed on can never be exceeded regardless of output. Where work content and/or production potential is highly variable, there can be a use for a scheme like this.

9 Value added is revenue – the cost of goods and services bought in. Once value added has paid for the wage bill, there will be some money available for bonuses.

10 The ratio will have to be greater than 1 : 1, perhaps 1.5 : 1; so that if the actual ratio is above this figure, the difference will be shared out among the employees.

Chapter 12

1 A chart with a horizontal time scale. It shows the duration of each job which has to be done. It is then used to monitor progress.

2 Scheduling a number of jobs, each of which requires the same operations which must be performed in a fixed sequence.

3 (a) First come, first served.

(b) Schedule the little jobs first.

(c) Schedule the important jobs first.

4 It produces a schedule with the lowest overall throughput time, for any number of jobs each needing the same two operations to be done in sequence.

5 It shows which jobs need to be done before others, and which can be started at the same time as others.

6 It is the path made up of activities which have no float.

7 In practice, CPA is better done with a team than as an individual exercise.

8 A resource histogram shows the amount of a particular category needed period by period for the project's life.

9 Line of balance is useful when extra management effort is needed to ensure on time delivery for a new or important order.

10 It indicates period by period, for each key activity, the quantities needed at that time, in order to stay on schedule.

Chapter 13

1 This is a site not previously built upon, giving great scope for a fresh approach.

2 Transport availability, a pool of suitable labour, financial incentives.

3 Not necessarily True. Backtracking and convoluted routes should, however, be avoided.

4 People, material, information and services.

5 By using flow charts, to/from charts and the critical examination technique.

6 It needs a predetermined programme for maintaining all equipment and services.

7 Makers' manuals, current and anticipated operating condition and frequencies.

8 Machine availability, response time to repair, planning performance and cost per repair.

9 False. That is why we try to minimise unnecessary handling.

10 True. Utilising more of a building's volume makes more use of an expensive capital asset.

11 Capital, running and maintenance costs.

12 False. It does not necessarily follow. Choice must result from clear statement of objectives and an analysis of needs.

Chapter 14

1 The arithmetic mean is simple to calculate and easy to understand. It may not correspond to any particular value in the set, and is affected by extreme values.

2 The mode is a quick and easy indicator of central tendency. It is useful where numbers are used to indicate values, where those numbers are not themselves a direct measure. Modes are often used in clothing sizes e.g. dresses, hats shoes.

3 Three measures of variation are (a) the range, (b) the mean absolute deviation, (c) the standard deviation. The range is the simplest measure but it is affected by extreme values in the set of data, and by definition uses only two values regardless of how many the set contains.

4 The arithmetic mean and the standard deviation conveniently summarise a set of data.

5 False – it provides an indication of the degree of linear association between the data. Its sign indicates the slope. positive indicates a slope from bottom left to top right, and a negative sign, the opposite.

6 The minimum value for the sum of squared errors, taken as the perpendicular distance of each point to the regression line. The errors are squared to avoid them cancelling each other out, and so producing a sum of zero.

7 **(a)** The line is linear, **(b)** below the $y = 0$ axis, **(c)** from top left to bottom right.

8 They all have the same value, i.e. they coincide, for a Normal Distribution.

9 It is tabulated in a standardised form by using the conversion: $z = (x - \mu/\sigma)$. As the normal is symmetrical about the $z = 0$ value, only the right half is tabulated up to a value of $z = 4$.

10 **(a)** When a situation can be classified into only two mutually exclusive categories, e.g. present or absent, and when the number in the sample is not much bigger than $n = 20$. **(b)** When p is approximately equal to q and n is greater than about 20, ideally greater than 30. If p is not very equal to q, then n must be even larger, for a reasonable approximation.

11 As a proportion, the mean is p, and the standard deviation is $\sqrt{[(p.q)/n]}$.

12 It is useful for occurrences which happen at random over a period of time or distance. It is the correct distribution to use when the 'q' in the binomial has no real meaning, e.g. p may be goals scored in soccer match, but 'q' the non-goals. has no real meaning. The value n should be very large compared with the average occurrence expected.

13 The mean of a Poisson is the average occurrences expected, e.g. in a market town for a given period there was an average of 2.5 cases of arson. The standard deviation is: square root of the average.

14 True – it takes into account the changing probabilities caused by non-replacement, and uses both the sample size 'n' and the batch size 'N' in the calculations. It must be used when N is small, e.g. about 10, and n is large compared with N. The calculations are tedious when N is greater than about 15, but approximations can then reasonably be made.

15 False – the time taken falls to 70 per cent of what it was before, each time the number of repetitions doubles, i.e. the rate is constant.

Chapter 14 – Activities (p. 334)

Geometric mean: **(a)** 102.357% per year **(b)** 149.44% per year **(c)** 82.99% per year, £17976 **(d)** 4.1%.

Linear regression **pp. 344–5**:
1 load on spring: $r = .99$, $y = 19.93 + .83x$, 6.11 kgs, 36.53 cms
2 errors v. time: $r = 0.9$, $y = 5.05 - .493x$
3 x and y correlation: $r = 0$, $y = 2$
4 three-stage advertising campaign:

Stage Number	Coefficient r	Regression line $y = a + bx$
1	.92	$31.4 + 9.09x$
2	.94	$-21.5 + 11.3x$
1 and 2	.98	$11.75 + 10.69x$
3	.88	$735 + 2.67x$
2 and 3	.94	$249.5 + 6.61x$
1, 2 and 3	.97	$89.1 + 8.13x$

5 IDE and SCSI hard disk data:

$r = .988$ $\quad$ $y = 43.9 + 1.53x$ $\quad$ SCSI data: $r = .987$ $\quad$ $y = 613.1 + .52x$

combined data: $r = .957$, $y = 241.5 + .81x$
10-bed hospital **p. 355**: **(a)** 0.20 **(b)** 0.37
General office **pp. 359–60**: **(b)** 0.4096 **(d)** 0.1536 **(e)** 84.4% of the time
Library usage: **(c)** probably not agree, only about a 1 in 20 chance.
Stylers hairdressers: **(d)** probably getting worse.
Telephone kiosks: **(g)** about 0.50
Contractor hire question: **(m)** long term hire 2 pieces for £752.6 average cost
Five-person committee **p. 362**: **(1a)** 0.0839
Samples from batches: **(2c)** 2 defectives, 0.4286
Learning curve **p. 366**: **(2)** About 85%

Chapter 15

1 The change occurred more frequently than would have been expected on a statistical basis.
2 Because it avoids unnecessary adjustments to the process.
3 The Poisson distribution.
4 The normal distribution.
5 At a value of 4.3 approximately..
6 That there is a slightly greater than 1 in 20 chance of 4.0 or more people being killed, if we expect on average 1.5 per year.
7 A fundamental problem with the process itself, which will not be curable by a 'quick fix'.
8 The standard error of the mean is the standard deviation/the square root of the sample size.
9 Because regardless of the shape of the population, the means of samples tends towards normality.
10 It enables us to provide an index indicating how well a process should be able to meet the specification tolerance. An RCI greater than 8 is considered high, an RCI between 6 and 8 is considered medium, and an RCI below 6 is considered low (i.e. the process will generate a large proportion of unavoidable rejects).
11 The cumulative difference between the mean and a target.

Chapter 16

1 False.
2 False.
3 This may be True if the average is not based on data which is too old.
4 They may or may not, depending on how appropriate past data is thought to be.
5 True.
6 False. It can provide a quick and fairly accurate result.
7 True.
8 False. Just one period ahead.
9 The smoothing constant equals 0.5.
10 When it drops below 1.0.
11 It tries to establish a trend.
12 Actual by period, cumulative to date and moving period total.
CFC forecasts: trend line $y = 5.22 + .489x$
for: January 23.276×10^4 May 27.751×10^4 September 25.006×10^4
December 27.212×10^4

Chapter 17

1 Physical, graphical and mathematical.
2 For an increase or decrease in quantities, there is a proportional increase or decrease in cost, profits, or 'benefits' or 'regrets'. 'Benefits' or 'regrets' are numbers assigned to qualitative results, which themselves cannot be measured e.g. on a scale of 1–10: walking in the countryside in the rain 3 regrets; walking to work in the rain 5 regrets.
3 The objective function is what you are trying to maximise (if profits), or minimise (if costs).
4 The coefficient of each variable in the objective function.
5 There are an infinite (or very large) number of optimum solutions.
6 False.
7 It is the cost of not using that cell.
8 Enter a very small quantity as **S**, and manipulate it together with the other entries.
9 You need to set up a dummy customer.
10 A first real but not necessarily optimal solution. This can be found by using the north west rule or by the cheapest squares method.
11 True.
12 False.
13 True.
14 Assign a very high cost as **H** and treat it along with other costs.
15 There are several optimum solutions.

Answers to Transportation problems:
a1 (total costs are now 129 mu. The solution is now optimal. This is: Machine 1 6B and 2D ; Machine 2 7A ; Machine 3 7C and 3D.)
a3 (Ans: 796 mu) a4 (Ans: 517 mu).

Answers to Assignments:
a1 (Ans. A1, B3, C2) a4 (Ans. A1, B3, C2)
a5 (Ans. A1, B3, C2, D4) a6 (Ans. A1, B3, C2).

Glossary of Terms and Acronyms

Average Outgoing Quality Level (AOQL)

The long-term percentage level of defectives which can be expected to occur from the application of acceptance sampling schemes. It is the combined result of batches which have been accepted by the scheme, and those which were rejected and subsequently screened 100%.

Computer Aided Design (CAD)

The use of specialised software and powerful desk top computers with good graphic capability – both 2D and 3D, which reduce substantially the time for product design, manufacture and associated layouts. It is also effective in controlling design changes and reducing paper output.

Computer Integrated Manufacture (CIM)

A system where all the information on inputs, processes and outputs is readily available to all subsystems. The production processes themselves do not have to be automated.

Critical Path Analysis (CPA)

A planning and monitoring technique which is useful for project control. It helps ensure that management can identify and exert control on those tasks which if delayed will cause the project to run late. It also shows the tasks with less impact on project completion. It is effective for both small and large projects, and lends itself to answering many kinds of 'what if' questions.

Discounted Cash Flow (DCF)

A technique which recognises the time value of money (e.g. £100 received now is worth more than £100 received a year hence). The technique is often useful when comparing projects having different cash inflows and outflows.

Economic Order Frequency (EOF)

This is obtained by dividing the annual demand in units for an item by the Economic Order Quantity (EOQ). For example, if 2500 units are required annually, and the EOQ is 200 , then the EOF = 2500/200 = 12.5 times per year, or about one order each month.

Economic Order Quantity (EOQ)

A quantity calculated as a result of balancing order processing costs against holding costs. This quantity is often used as a guide for the re-order quantity for independent demand items. It excludes the effect of quantity discounts, and seasonality of demand.

Failure Rate (FR)

The number of items failing per unit time period. This result is obtained from items put on test and the results noted. The FR is the reciprocal of the mean time between failures (see MTBF).

Group Technology (GT)

The arrangement of manufacturing cells so that components of fundamentally similar shapes, but differing in detail, can be made within that cell. Such a cell must therefore contain all the equipment for that range of manufacture. It also requires multi-skilled personnel who are well motivated and quality aware.

Holding Cost Factor (HCF)

This is the cost of holding stock for a year, and is expressed as a percentage of the average monetary value of that stock. A reasonable value is 25% per annum, or (when expressed in the EOQ formula) 0.25. For example, at 25% holding cost per year, it costs £250,000 per annum to hold an average inventory of £1,000,000.

Just in Time (JIT)

An integrated production system, which pulls work through the plant in response to actual demand for the product. It requires commitment to quality, close vendor relations, minimum stock and flexible manufacturing with short change over and set up times, together with an ability to produce in small quantities.

Line Balancing (LB)

The task of ensuring that in a number of sequential work centres the capacity of each is as nearly the same as all the other, and that the line can produce the required output with as little idle time as possible. Bottlenecks are also undesirable.

Line of Balance (LOB)

This is a planning and monitoring tool, useful for progressing a number of important batches according to an agreed delivery schedule. The plan shows the quantities of parts for all batches, for each week of the production and delivery schedule, at each of a specified number of control points. It is not related to line balancing.

Manufacturing Resource Planning (MRP 2)

A planning process developed from materials requirements planning, which integrates all information available on stock, procurement, accounting, capacity, sales and distribution, so that the plans produced closely match the capacity and other limitations of the plant.

Materials Requirements Planning (MRP1)

A planning process which pushes batches of work through the manufacturing system, and is based on estimates of future demand and timing for the major end products, coupled with data held on lead times. It copes well with varying demand patterns.

Mean Time between Failure (MTBF)

The total time that items survived on test, divided by the number of items which failed. This is a measure of an item's reliability. Very reliable items have a large MTBF.

Net Present Value (NPV)

This refers to discounting cash inflows at a predetermined rate of interest, so that they can be compared with the amount required to be invested.

Optimised Production Technology (OPT)

A proprietary system developed by E. Goldratt, based on the premise that maximising a plant's output does not necessarily maximise its profitability.

Order Processing Cost (OPC)

All the (marginal) administrative costs of pushing a purchase order through your system, until you have subsequently received the goods into your stores. For most companies this is a large cost per order, but can be reduced substantially by electronic data interchange and electronic call off procedures.

Quality Assurance (QA)

The procedural aspects and systems requirements for doing what is necessary to ensure that a company can exert effective control over its quality.

Re-Order Level (ROL)

The level at or just below which an order is triggered, as part of a stock control system. Its calculation includes usage during lead time, plus safety stock.

Re-Order Quantity (ROQ)

The amount for which a purchase order is raised, as part of a stock control system. when triggered by the ROL being reached or just passed, This quantity may or may not be the EOQ (see above).

Statistical Process Control (SPC)

The application of statistical methods to determine if a significant change in a process has occurred, and to know this in a timely manner. Unnecessary corrective action can then be avoided.

Total Quality Management (TQM)

The overall concept of quality and the ethos which needs to pervade any organisation which purports to be concerned with giving complete customer satisfaction, on a continuing basis.

Value Analysis (VA)

A formalised questioning technique, developed by L. Miles, to help ascertain and eliminate all unnecessary costs which reduce the value of a good or service. If such analysis is conducted at the design stage, the process is called Value Engineering.

World Class Manufacturing (WCM)

A term used by R. Schonberger to denote a company's commitment to high productivity, continual improvement in their approach to quality, Just in Time methods, their employees, their management style and their suppliers, so that they are ever more able to satisfy their customers needs economically and in a timely manner.

Bibliography

Journals

The following journals often contain articles relevant to Operations Management; as well as reading current issues, many articles of interest will be found by looking at older articles:

The Economist

Fortune International
R. Henkoff, 'Service is everybody's business' (27 June 1994)

Harvard Business Review
P. Drucker, 'The information executives truly need' (January/February 1995).

R. Kamath and J. Liker, 'A second look at Japanese Product development' (November/December 1994).

J. Dyer, 'Dedicated Assets: Japan's manufacturing edge' (November/December 1994).

A. March, 'Usability: the new dimension of product design' (September/October 1994).

H. K. Bowen et al., 'Special Section: Recognising the lead in manufacturing' (September/October 1994).

E. Teisberg et al., 'Making competition in health care work' (July/August 1994).

M. Fisher et al., 'Making supply meet demand in an uncertain world' (May/June 1994).

J. P. Womack and D. T. Jones, 'From lean production to the lean enterprise' (March/April 1994).

R. Hayes and G. Pisano, 'Beyond world class: the new manufacturing strategy' (January/February 1994).

G. Hall et al., 'How to make re-engineering really work' (November/December 1993).

A. Kohn, 'Why incentive plans cannot work' (September/October 1993).

R. Norman and R Ramirez, 'From value chain to value constellation: designing interactive strategy' (July/August 1993).

J. Juran, 'Made in USA: a renaissance in quality' (July/August 1993).

D. Niven, 'When times get tough, what happens to T Q M?' (May/June 1993).

J. Fuller et al., 'Tailored Logistics – the next advantage' (May/June 1993).

P. S. Adler, 'Time and Motioned regained' (January/February 1993).

447

R. Venkatesan, 'Strategic sourcing: to make or not to make' November/December 1992).

B. Shapiro *et al.*, 'Staple yourself to an order' (July/August 1992).

G. Stalk *et al.*, 'Competing on capabilities: the new rules of corporate strategy' (March/April 1992).

S. Wheelwright and K. Clark, 'Creating project plans to focus product development' (March/April 1992).

J. Sensenbrenner, 'Quality comes to City Hall' (March/April 1991).

P. Zipkin, 'Does manufacturing need a JIT revolution?' (January/February 1991).

J. Rehfeld, 'What working for a Japanese company taught me' (November/December 1990).

F. Reichheld and W. Sasser Jr, 'Zero Defections: Quality comes to Services' (September/October 1990).

G. Taguchi and D. Clausing, 'Robust Quality' (January/February 1990).

C. Ferguson, 'Computers and the coming of the US Keiretsu' (July/August 1990).

W. Wiggenhorn, 'Motorola – when training becomes education' (July/August 1990).

C. Bartlett and S. Ghoshal, 'Matrix Management – not a structure, a frame of mind' (July/August 1990).

P. Drucker, 'The emerging theory of manufacturing' (May/June 1990).

D. Finkleman and T. Goland, 'Case of the complaining customer' (May/June 1990).

W. Taylor, 'Business of Innovation' (March/April 1990).

R. Venkatesan, 'Cummins engine flexes its factory' (March/April 1990).

J. Quinn *et al.,* 'Beyond products – services based strategy' (March/April 1990).

Industrial Engineering (Journal of the Institute of Industrial Engineers, USA). 10 separate articles on MRP2 (March 1991).

D. Bowman, 'If you don't understand JIT, how can you use it?' (February 1991).

C. Ziemke and M. Spann, 'Concurrent engineering requires total effort' (February 1991).

M. Raymond, 'The outcry to abolish work measurement systems' (December 1990).

Y. Gupta and W. Willborn, 'JIT and Quality Assurance form new manufacturing partnership' (December 1990).

J. Calvert, 'Quality customer service: a marketing weapon for high performance banking' (November 1990).

'Effective storage system enhances Jaguar's productivity' (IE case study) November 1990.

D. Rhodes, 'Critical imperative in flexible manufacturing is information' (October 1990).

L. Forbes and J. Edosomwan, 'Eastman Kodak streamlines its products distribution' (September 1990).

A. Whitman, 'Productivity implementation management needs commitment from the top' (August 1990).

J. Johnson, 'Fully automated isn't always the best solution to warehouse operations' (July 1990).

D. Sourwine, 'Improved product costing – beyond traditional financial accounting' (July 1990).

J. Usher, C. Ciesielski and R. Johanson, 'Redesigning an existing layout' (June 1990).

T. Willis and J. Shields, 'Modifying ABC inventory system for a focussed factory' (May 1990).

M. Gettings, 'Computer aided application to manufacturing quality' (March 1990).

P. Rossler and D. Sink, 'Roadmap for productivity and quality improvement' (March 1990).

A. Badiru, 'Systems approach to Total Quality Management' (March 1990).

H. Danzyger, 'Strategic manufacturing plan – your company's competitiveness depends on it' (February 1990).

P. Bernard, 'The carrying cost paradox – how to manage it' (November 1989).

D. Castle, 'The IE and Deming's 14 points' (September 1989).

M. Shinnick and W. Erwin, 'Work measurement system helps workers share responsibility at Ford' (August 1989).

G. Nadler, 'Design processes and their results' (July 1989).

A. Wilt and D. Godlin, 'Simulating staffing needs and work flow in an outpatients diagnostic centre' (May 1989).

International Business Week

Long Range Planning (Journal of the Strategic Planning Society).
Contains many articles on strategic planning and management, including the selection below.

M. Shadur, 'Total Quality: Systems survive, cultures change' (April 1995, vol. 28, no. 2).

R. McTavish, 'One more time – what Business are you in?' (April 1995, vol. 28, no. 2).

P. Matthyssens and C. v. d. Bulte, 'Getting closer and nicer: partnerships in the supply chain' (February 1994, vol. 27, no. 1).

M. Zairi, 'Competitive Manufacturing – combining T Q with advanced technology' (June 1993, vol. 26, no. 3)

T. Urakawa, 'How Bridgestone creates new business through research' (April 1993, vol. 26, no.2).

R. Gehani, 'Concurrent product development for fast track corporations' (December 1992, vol. 25, no. 6).

R. Osborne, 'Building an innovative organisation' (December 1992, vol. 25, no. 6).

T. Sekita, 'Value Added distribution of parcels in Japan' (December 1990).

W. Currie, 'Investing in CAD – ad hoc decision making' (December 1990).

M. Haroda, 'CIM at Nippon Seiko Co.' (October 1990).

P. Bolwijn and T. Kempje, 'Manufacturing in the 1990s – Productivity, Flexibility, Innovation' (August 1990).

D. Cox, 'Doubling productivity at a major brewery' (August 1990).

B. Lloyd, 'Office productivity – time for a revolution?' (February 1990).

J. Williams and R. Novak, 'Aligning CIM strategies to different markets' (February 1990).

J. Quinn, 'Brief case – strategic management of R and D' (February 1990).

T. Nishikawa, 'New product planning at Hitachi' (August 1989).

D. Rose, 'Woolworth's drive for excellence' (February 1989).

K. Ishikawa, 'Achieving Japanese productivity and quality levels at a US plant' (October 1988).

G. Potts, 'Raising productivity levels in customer services' (April 1988).

A. Pendlebury, 'Creating a manufacturing strategy to suit your business' (December 1987).

Management Accounting

Management Services (Journal of the Institute of Management Services).
'Administrative J I T' (December 1992, vol. 36 no.12).

Management Today
A. v. d. Vliet, 'Order from Chaos' (November 1994).

'Britains Best Factories – 994' (November 1994).

M. Weyer, 'Mission Improvable' (September 1994).

R. Heller, 'Putting the Total in Total Quality' (August 1994).
P. Bartram, 'Re-engineering re-visited' (July 1994).
R. Heller, 'Clean Machine' (May 1994).
J. Levi, 'Russells Broadway Hit' (May 1994).
'Transport and Distribution – 4 articles' (April 1994).
A. v. d. Vliet, 'The Brent Conversion' (March 1994).
'Britains Best Factories – 1993' (November 1993).
J. Oliver, 'Shocking to the core' (August 1993).
S. Caulkin, 'Make or Break' (May 1993).
G. Foster, 'The Innovation Imperative' (April 1993).
A. Patrick and A. Jolley, 'How to make the Office Work' (January 1993).
M. Wheatley, 'Gosppel according to Schonberger' (June 1992).
T. Lester, 'Squeezing the supply chain' (March 1992).
A. Gabb, 'Making it with M and S' (February 1992).
H. Syedain, 'An endangered species' (disappearing middle managers) (May 1991).
A. Lines, 'Hands off stock control' (May 1991).
H. Syedain, 'Rolls Royce Model' (April 1991).
M. Wheatley, 'The price is right' (JIT) (September 1990).
T. Farmer, 'Fit to manage' (July 1990).
J. Myerson, 'Ten out of ten' (design and quality) (June 1990).
D. Thiesdell, 'Shimano's dream machine' (March 1990).

Purchasing and Supply Management (Journal of the Institute of Purchasing and Supply). All the following are by Howard Barnett
'Japanese System of Sub-contracting' (December 1995).
'Getting the Measure of it' (September 1992).
'Reliably Informed' (March 1990).
'The Economics of Sampling' (August 1987).
'Process Control Charting' (May 1987).
'Acceptance Sampling, rationale and use' (July 1986).
'Quality: Its creation and control' (June 1986).
'SIMQ: simulating a single server queue system' (May 1986).
'Analysing stock using the Pareto approach' (December 1985).
'Simulating a stock control system' (September 1985).
'A model Supplier rating system' (June 1985).
'Quantifying the Make or Buy decision' (January 1985).
'Time Series forecasting on a micro' (October 1984).
'Line of Balance scheduling on a micro' (August 1984).

Quality News (Journal of the Institution of Quality Assurance).

Research and Development Management (quarterly).
M. Bruce, 'Success factors for collaborative product development' (January 1995).
M. Berry and J. Taggart, 'Managing technology and innovation, a review' (October 1994).
H. Tschirky, 'Role of technology forecasting and assessment in technology management' (April 1994).
N. Roome, 'Business strategy, R and D management, and environmental imperatives' (January 1994).
N. Peacock, 'Communications between R and D and its customers – B T Laboratories' (October 1993).
T. Rickards, 'Innovation and creativity; woods, trees and pathways' (April 1991).
M. Carlsson, 'Aspects of integration of technical functions for efficient product development' (January 1991).

A. Gupta and D. Wilemon, 'Improving D and D/Marketing relations: an R and D perspective' (October 1990).

R. van Dierdonck, 'The Manufacture/Design interface' (July 1990).

P. Fahrini and M. Spatig, 'Application oriented guide to R and D project selection and evaluation methods' (April 1990).

N. McGuinness and H. Conway, 'Managing the search for new product concepts – a strategic approach' (October 1989).

Single topic issue on the 'State of the art in R and D management', various articles April 1989.

Handbooks

These are useful for reference purposes.

Annual Abstract of UK Statistics (CSO/HMSO).

Monthly Digest of UK Statistics (CSO/HMSO).

G. Salvendy, *Handbook of Industrial Engineering* (Wiley, 1982).

R. Wild, *Handbook of International Production and Operations Management* (Cassell, 1990).

R. Kulweic (ed.), *Handbook of Materials Management*, ASME and IMMS (McGraw-Hill, 1985) 2nd edn.

D. Lock (ed.), *Handbook of Quality Management* (Gower Press, 1994).

J. Juran (ed. in chief), *Juran's Q.C. Handbook* (McGraw-Hill, 1988) 4th edn.

D. Lock (ed.), *Project Management Handbook* (Gower Press, 1987).

D. Farmer (ed.), *Purchasing Management Handbook* (Gower, 1985).

Abstracts Service

Anbar, a division of MCB University Press. Anbar abstracts are taken on a monthly basis from a variety of articles published in many different journals. The abstracts are published in five categories, of which:

Category 2 Management services and production (of most relevance for Operations Management)

British Standards Specifications

The following standards are a selection of those relevant to Operations Management

BS 2564: 1955 (1993) Control chart techniques ... special reference to dimensional tolerances

BS 3138: 1992 Glossary of terms used in work study and organisation and methods

BS 3375: 1984 (1993) Parts 1–4 Guide to Work Study, and Organisation and Methods

BS 4335: 1993 Glossary of terms used in project network techniques

BS 4778: 1993, 1991 Parts 1–2 Glossary of terms used in quality assurance

BS 5191: 1993 Glossary of terms used in production planning and control

BS 5192: 1993 Parts 1–6 Guide to Production Control

BS 5700: 1992 Process control using quality control chart methods and cusum techniques

BS 5701: 1993 Guide to number defective charts for quality control

BS 5703: 1992 Parts 1-4 Data analysis and quality control using cusum techniques

BS 5729: 1993 Part 5 Storekeeping

BS 5750: 1993 Parts 0–4 and 8,13,14 (1993) Quality systems (now EN ISO 9000)

BS 5760: 1993 Parts 0–14 Reliability of systems, equipment and components; (pt. 0 introductory guide)

BS 6000: 1993 Guide to BS 6001; sampling procedures and tables for inspection by attributes

BS 6001: 1991/94 Parts 1–4 Sampling plans by AQL, sampling plans indexed by limiting quality for isolated lots, skip lot plans,sequential plans

RS 6002: 1993 Sampling plans; inspection by variables

BS 6046: 1984/92 Parts 1–4 Guides to use of network techniques in project management

BS 6143 Guide to the economics of quality

BS 7850 Total Quality Management

BS EN ISO 9001, 2, 3: 1994 Quality System Standards (was BS 5750)

Index